Practical Web Accessibility

A Comprehensive Guide to Digital Inclusion

Second Edition

Ashley Firth

Foreword by Greg Jackson,
Founder of Octopus Energy Group

Apress®

Practical Web Accessibility: A Comprehensive Guide to Digital Inclusion,
Second Edition

Ashley Firth
London, UK

ISBN-13 (pbk): 979-8-8688-0151-8   ISBN-13 (electronic): 979-8-8688-0152-5
https://doi.org/10.1007/979-8-8688-0152-5

Managing Director, Apress Media LLC: Welmoed Spahr
Acquisitions Editor: James Robinson-Prior
Development Editor: James Markham
Editorial Assistant: Gryffin Winkler

Cover designed by Pete Miller

Illustrations designed by Amy Ottley

Distributed to the book trade worldwide by Springer Science+Business Media New York, 1 New York Plaza, Suite 4600, New York, NY 10004-1562, USA. Phone 1-800-SPRINGER, fax (201) 348-4505, e-mail orders-ny@ springer-sbm.com, or visit www.springeronline.com. Apress Media, LLC is a California LLC and the sole member (owner) is Springer Science + Business Media Finance Inc (SSBM Finance Inc). SSBM Finance Inc is a **Delaware** corporation.

For information on translations, please e-mail booktranslations@springernature.com; for reprint, paperback, or audio rights, please e-mail bookpermissions@springernature.com.

Apress titles may be purchased in bulk for academic, corporate, or promotional use. eBook versions and licenses are also available for most titles. For more information, reference our Print and eBook Bulk Sales web page at http://www.apress.com/bulk-sales.

Any source code or other supplementary material referenced by the author in this book is available to readers on GitHub. For more detailed information, please visit https://www.apress.com/gp/services/ source-code.

Paper in this product is recyclable

For my wife.

Table of Contents

About the Author

Ashley Firth is the Global Director of Engineering at award-winning energy technology company Octopus Energy, responsible for building and overseeing the online experience of its many millions of users worldwide. Starting at the company as one of its very first employees (now standing at over 5,000), Ashley has championed the need for inclusive and accessible websites from the very beginning and has spoken internationally on the subject, taking into account both customer and colleague needs when doing so.

Octopus Energy, along with being one of the best energy companies in the world for customer service, has won numerous customer and digital experience awards thanks to Ashley's approach to accessibility. In 2020 – just four years after starting up – the supplier also became the 15th tech unicorn born out of the United Kingdom. The year after, it became a quintuple unicorn.

Along with his demanding day job, Ashley is determined to make web accessibility a cornerstone of any company's handbook. He spends his spare time as a consultant to government bodies and private companies to help them improve their approach to accessibility. He is also a technical reviewer for books on the subject. He was shortlisted for the Young Energy Professional of the Year award, and is a W3C Invited Expert in the Accessibility Guidelines Working Group - helping to develop WCAG specifications to make content on the Web more accessible for people with disabilities.

All of Ashley's experience culminated in the production of *Practical Web Accessibility*. The first edition of this book reached number one on the Amazon technology charts and is used by readers and companies around the world to understand accessibility and improve their approach to it. Outside of accessibility, Ashley blogs and consults about management, which you can find at mrfirthy.me.

About the Technical Reviewer

 **Katherine Joyce** is a user experience professional, accessibility advocate, and design leader with over ten years of experience having worked across a variety of sectors, including finance and government. She creates innovative, intuitive customer experiences and is an advocate of accessible design. As Director of User Experience at Unisys, she is scaling multidisciplinary design and increasing the UX maturity of a global organization, promoting inclusive and accessible design best practices, standardizing UX and research methodology and processes, while supporting the UI modernization of products driven by user needs. She is also a Design Mentor at DesignLab, where she provides professional global mentorship across a variety of courses combined with career development and portfolio advice for individuals who wish to pursue a career in product design. She also provides content, research, and design mentorship on ADPList, is a LUMA Institute certified Human-Centered Design Practitioner, and is Nielsen Norman Group Certified in the specialism UX Management.

Acknowledgments

This part of the book was rather long in the first edition. I mentioned then that it's never guaranteed that you'll write another book (or edition), so I wanted to ensure that I got the chance to thank everyone who's helped me. For this edition, let me simply say this: the words I committed to print then are just as true now. Thank you immensely for the love and support you show me, that I try every day to return in kind.

For the second edition, I'd like to start by thanking the amazing team at Apress – James Robinson-Prior, Sowmya Thodur, Shaul Elson, Gryffin Winkler, and James Markham. Part of me had forgotten how hard it was to write a book. It'd also forgotten just how great all of you are at turning a book idea into reality and supporting authors. Thank you, sincerely.

I get to thank the brilliant Katherine Joyce again for being the technical reviewer. Thank you for coming back for the second edition and somehow bringing even more insight into it than the first. You found issues, challenged my assumptions, and helped make this book as good as it could be.

I'd like to thank Pete Miller, who followed up his cover design for the first edition with an even better cover. I stretched to two bags of Skittles as a token of my appreciation this time around. Thank you for taking the time out from drawing an Octopus to do it. Cheers, tiger.

Special thanks to the immensely talented Amy Ottley for her help in bringing the illustrations and visual examples in this book to life. They're such a massive step up from the first edition, and they'll help a lot more people understand the topic. I'd also like to thank my senior developer for our design system at Octopus Energy, Tom Sansome, for his sage advice on the pages about component libraries.

To Greg Jackson, who followed up his support of the first edition with some words of his own in the foreword of this edition. He speaks humbly of his involvement in this topic within Octopus, but he was undoubtedly one of the catalysts of its growth, as well as a constant and vocal advocate of it to anyone that's visited us. As a CEO, he uses his platform to speak loudly about an important and often ignored topic. The people within Octopus are well aware of his importance – I'm glad the rest of the world is catching on.

ACKNOWLEDGMENTS

Since writing the first edition, my team has grown rather large and is somehow based in over a dozen countries around the world. It's because of all of you that accessibility remains at the heart of everything we do globally as a company. Every one of you has taken the topic to heart, safeguarded its importance within our culture, and remained curious and caring enough to ask questions. Thank you for teaching me several things every day, supporting one another, and using your talent to do great things in this world. I'm incredibly proud of all of you.

Finally, to my wife. We didn't live together when I wrote the first edition, and so she wasn't entirely aware of the toll writing a book around a full-time job takes. She knows now! She's been boundlessly supportive, forgiving when I'd accidentally disappear into thought, and understanding of the commitment required, all while running her own business. She is my best mate, my teammate, and my soulmate. I promise I probably won't do this again.

P.S.: My fish got a shout-out last time for having to listen to my stupid ideas, and this edition is no different, but my dog had to listen far more often when we went on walks, so a special shout-out to Louie. He always reacted enthusiastically, and that's because he's a very good boy.

Foreword

Nothing makes me prouder than writing this.

I've been lucky enough to have Ashley as a colleague almost since the very beginning of our business – and his work and dedication have not only helped drive the business from startup to $20 billion of revenue but, more importantly, created deep and meaningful connections with millions of customers from every background.

When Ashley joined Octopus as our first and, for some time, only Front-End Developer, he told me very clearly that he wanted to make accessibility a top priority.

For too long, in many critical sectors, accessibility was considered to be Braille bills, text relay phone calls, and little else. Yet, only a fraction of those with a registered visual impairment can read Braille.

Meanwhile, the Internet is everywhere, and more and more people with disabilities are empowered online through computers and smartphones – devices capable of reading out web pages and emails, adding captions to videos, and catering to any number of other needs.

Indeed, when Ashley discussed his work with me, I learned so much about how to write with autistic readers in mind, or how to design for people with various kinds of color blindness – the importance of thinking about motor skills and neurodiversity.

No company is perfect – but Ashley taught us how to create user experiences that deliver all of the brand and design goals, but in the most inclusive ways possible. And without huge expenses in rework, review processes, etc. – by just making it "how we do stuff."

I was delighted when regulators, citizens' organizations, government officials, politicians, and even competitors used the first edition to help democratize services for everyone.

Thousands of developers and organizations have benefited from Ashley's work – and I sincerely hope it helped hundreds of thousands, maybe millions, of users access services and products that may otherwise have been inaccessible or too hard to use.

With this second edition, Ashley not only brings us up to date with technology changes and opportunities but also builds on the myriad learnings and pieces of feedback. All of this makes it easier than ever for anyone, of any company or discipline, to learn the topic for the first time.

To be able to make the world better for many people, without compromising for others – and at no extra cost – is a huge privilege, maybe even a moral responsibility, and I am delighted that this book enables that.

Thank you Ashley and Apress for publishing this. And, most importantly, thank you for reading it.

Greg Jackson
Founder of Octopus Energy Group

Introduction

Welcome to the book! I know there are a lot of tech books in the world, so I do appreciate you giving your time to this one, and this topic. Let's start by clearing one thing up: this is not a book aimed at just developers. It is written for anyone involved in a website being on the Internet – be that its creation, design, content, maintenance, or running the business that put it there. More generally, it's for anyone interested in understanding an area that so many people are now talking about and one that is so vital to building a Web for everyone.

The truth is, accessibility is something everyone needs to know about for us to be ultimately successful in that goal. Accessibility guidelines, which we'll get to in a moment, state that even if a web page is accessible, but is part of a wider online process or journey that isn't (e.g. like the checkout page of a shopping website), then the **whole** journey is considered inaccessible, including that page.[1] For the same reason, if one person in a team or organization is considering accessibility in their work but nobody else is, they'll make positive gains but will ultimately be swimming against a stronger tide around them.

My point is that it's everyone's responsibility, and the more people involved that are considering and engaged with this topic, the better and more likely that accessibility will become the norm in a company. This idea is at the heart of why this book isn't written for any one discipline. Instead, it's written to allow everyone to explore the topic of web accessibility, understand it and its importance, and apply what they learn to the companies, teams, and sites they're involved with.

---

[1] *Web Content Accessibility Guidelines 2.21 (WCAG)*, W3C, (05/0610/202318), <www.w3.org/TR/WCAG22/> [Accessed 15/0628/11/2023].

Practical Examples

As you'll see, there will be practical examples throughout the chapters to demonstrate the use of a feature or change to improve accessibility. These are designed for all levels of expertise and are not essential to understand the concepts we'll explore, so don't worry if you're not familiar with code. They're simply a reference for those that may want them, and a complimentary resource. For those interested, the code used in each example will be available on GitHub (GitHub is an easy-to-use site where you can share code and track changes) at `https://github.com/Apress/practical-web-accessibility` – each folder will correspond to the chapter it's used in. Alternatively, in each chapter, there will also be a link to a website that you can visit that will show that feature in action without you having to touch any code. I'll make these links short and easy to type, but you can also find links to every practical example in this book at `https://inclusive.guide/examples`.

These chapters will also sometimes include small code snippets, but feel free to skip them and keep reading if you're not a developer – I've ensured that you'll still understand the points we're covering without them. Alongside these snippets will be design principles, user and customer experience examples, relevant case studies, and some other expert opinions from people who care about accessibility as much as I do. You are of course free to take the project code here and implement it in your sites or use it as a conversation starter with people in your team. It's all here for you to use as you'd like. If you find any of the examples difficult, you can contact me directly using the details in this book.

An Explanation of the Book Format

Over the course of this book, I'd like to share with you, on a chapter-by-chapter basis, a wide range of different disabilities and access needs (an access need is anything a person requires to communicate, learn, or take part in an activity). Some you may have heard of (and even catered for) before, and some will be less well-known. Through understanding the barriers that different people encounter online, we can identify practical ways in which you can alter a website's build, design, content, and user experience to overcome these and cater to all users. After discussing specific impairments, we will move on to areas of websites and user journeys that have, or hold the potential to have, an effect on many access needs.

Here is a quick overview of what we'll be looking at.

The Accessibility Problem (Chapter 1)

We begin with a holistic examination of what web accessibility is and where it's at as a topic today. We'll explore the rise in legal cases, how one of the "fathers of the Internet" saw its purpose for accessibility, the merits of truly understanding access needs rather than just being compliant, and why now is the perfect time to understand it.

Blindness (Chapter 2)

Here we'll explore the role of screen readers that allow users to listen to a web page and how to optimize for them using a range of features. We'll then look at how to make navigating and interacting with content easier for all users by adjusting layout, structure, and functionality.

Low Vision and Color Blindness (Chapter 3)

In this chapter, we'll cover several different types of visual impairment and the impact they have on how a user interacts with your website. We'll look at how you can avoid common pitfalls that exclude those with vision issues, from navigation to color and content, before turning our attention to user preferences that you can utilize to provide catered accessibility.

Motor Impairments (Chapter 4)

Those who navigate the Web using only a keyboard, or other special apparatus, commonly encounter several major barriers. This chapter will provide an overview of some of these challenges, as well as some simple design and experience wins that can drastically improve their experience.

Deafness and Hard of Hearing (Chapter 5)

Audio and video can be a great way to provide different kinds of content on the Web, but it can also inadvertently exclude deaf users. This chapter introduces WebVTT: a technology to help with subtitles and closed captioning. We'll also look at the importance of servicing customers without a telephone and the empowering world of deaf-friendly language.

Cognitive Impairments (Chapter 6)

Cognitive disabilities impact a large percentage of the population and can take many forms. This chapter will look at making the Web more inclusive for those with impaired language, visual, and visual-spatial comprehension, as well as those with inhibited executive function, focus, and memory. We'll look at the importance of language and word choice, the positives (and pitfalls) of using iconography to convey meaning, mastering self-contained actions, and how sites like Reddit have made life easier for those with heightened sensory awareness.

Mental Health (Chapter 7)

This subject has seen a massive increase in exposure over the last few years, yet remains largely undocumented compared to most access needs. In this chapter, we will take a comprehensive look into common causes of anxiety online, known as "dark patterns," that increase site revenue and metrics but at the expense of a user's well-being, and how to quell them. We'll consider how to support users with a range of mental health impairments and why the issue of dark patterns is so important that the inventor of the Web itself is fighting against them.

Imagery (Chapter 8)

This chapter is among the biggest "quick wins" a user will be able to make using this book. Imagery is a major part of nearly every site, yet nearly always contains accessibility issues. We'll assess the pros and cons of images, videos, icon fonts, and different image types, as well as how to make these accessible for sites both old and new.

Accessible Email (Chapter 9)

A website is only part of your user's online journey with you. In this chapter, we'll look at how to ensure that your email formats, content, and styling are all accessible – even if you rely on a third-party email service to handle yours. We'll also look into a feature that makes user actions both quicker to complete and possible without even opening the email you send them.

Outsourcing Accessibility (Chapter 10)

There have been a range of tools and platforms that have risen dramatically in popularity on the Web over the last few years – changing the process of how websites are built and used. Accessibility overlays you can "bolt on" claiming to solve all of your accessibility problems with a line of code and a toolbar, the "build your own website" phenomenon of websites like Wix and Squarespace bringing large numbers of people without accessibility (or coding) knowledge to the Web, and the rise within the development community of pattern libraries like Material UI with pre-built accessible components, but a complete disengagement from their maintenance and decision-making process – for each of these, we'll dive into what you're gaining vs. what you're giving up and whether they're helpful or detrimental in the fight to make the Web more accessible.

Tools and Auditing (Chapter 11)

Building an accessible website is great, but ensuring it remains that way is paramount. We'll discuss how to make sure accessibility is considered during the development process and some key tools to test and improve your site with – both manual and automated. Accessibility is easier when added at the start of a site build, but there are far more sites where that won't be possible. We'll cover auditing an existing website through the two frameworks I wrote to help me and my teams – the **FAIR** framework and the **ACCESS** checklist.

Abbreviations

The word "accessibility" is often abbreviated to a11y, which is something I'll be doing moving forward in this book. The abbreviation is a numeronym, with "11" representing the number of letters between the letter "a" and the letter "y" in "accessibility." It's much shorter to write and read and can also read like "ally." This is a nice reminder to me that, as someone getting involved with accessibility, you're becoming an ally in supporting the effort of making the Web a better place.

I will also use the words "website" and "site", and "web page" and "page" interchangeably, as they are common abbreviations.

CHAPTER 1

The Accessibility Problem

Accessibility can be a difficult subject to approach, and it's often tough to know where to start. This is why I have decided to write this book. My aim is to help you understand accessibility and build it into your websites so that together, we can make the Internet the inclusive, empowering place it has the potential to be, for the estimated 1.3 billion people – or 16% of the global population – who experience a significant disability today.[1] Before we get there though, let's begin with a more holistic examination of what web accessibility is and where it's at as a topic today. We'll explore how it's become a problem, the merits of a "disability-driven" approach, and why now is the perfect time to understand it.

> *The Internet is for everyone – but it won't be until it can be accessed without limitation.*[2]
>
> —Vinton Cerf

Vinton Cerf is recognized as one of the "fathers of the Internet" for his work in co-inventing Internet protocols, a breakthrough that formed the foundation of the Web. He was also instrumental in the creation of the first-ever commercial email system.[3] It's fair to say that the Internet and email, as we know them, would not exist without him.

Cerf's work is well documented, but more attention is paid to his accomplishments and less to the man himself: the fact that he has a hearing disability is often overlooked.

Cerf saw, perhaps before anyone, the power that the Web held for creating a platform that was truly inclusive – allowing absolutely anyone, regardless of their disability or access needs, to engage with content. At its very origin, what we now know as commercial email was actually an assistive device that allowed deaf users to send and receive messages. In fact, part of Cerf's motivation when building it was to allow him to communicate with his wife Sigrid, who is deaf, while he was at work. Some 20 years after Cerf helped to develop his email service, Sigrid was using the Web to research cochlear implants that would improve her hearing. After nobody returned her calls (via relay service) to Johns Hopkins University, "she sent an email to the doctor and got a response

A. Firth, *Practical Web Accessibility*, https://doi.org/10.1007/979-8-8688-0152-5_1

the next day."[4] Thanks to him, she had an alternate way of communicating, specifically designed with her access needs in mind. Indeed, this piece of inclusive design was so successful that her doctor was now using it too.

Cerf described email to the *New York Times* as "the great equalizer in that everyone, hearing and deaf, uses the same technology."[5] This is the essence of accessibility. It means removing barriers that might prevent someone from accessing or interacting with something, regardless of their access needs. In the case of this book, this means anything on the Web. Email has become so useful to the world because Cerf considered different access needs, and the fact that everyone – from Sigrid to her doctor, from me to you – still uses his work shows how considering the needs of a diverse range of people helps us design better, more inclusive services.

Unfortunately, if we fast-forward to today, the landscape of the Web doesn't quite match his expectations.

In an interview with CNet, he lamented:

> *It's a crime that the most versatile device on the planet, the computer, has not adapted well to people who need help, who need assistive technology... It's almost criminal that programmers have not had their feet held to the fire to build interfaces that are accommodating for people with vision problems or hearing problems or motor problems.*[6]

His frustration is clear and understandable, especially given his original vision. So, how did the Web go so wrong?

The State of Accessibility Today

Firstly, it's important to note that there *are* guidelines on how to be accessible on the Web. In fact, there are groups that have been working for decades to make it a more accessible place. These guidelines outline how sites can achieve a certain level of accessibility and compliance – built over several years by the World Wide Web Consortium (W3C), a group headed by Tim Berners-Lee, the inventor of the Internet. W3C's purpose is to work together in the development of standards for the Web, and Berners-Lee clearly shares Cerf's ideals:

> *The power of the Web is in its universality. Access by everyone regardless of disability is an essential aspect.*[7]

> —Tim Berners-Lee

With this in mind, the group created the Web Content Accessibility Guidelines (WCAG) – a comprehensive list of requirements that, when met, improve a site's web accessibility. It has three levels of success: "A" (the easiest to achieve), "AA," and the strictest "AAA," with "AA" being widely considered as an acceptable legal standard. These guidelines are organized into four principles:

- That web content must be **Perceivable**

- That UI controls must be **Operable**

- That content and controls must be **Understandable**

- That content must be **Robust**

These are referred to as **POUR**. Within these four principles are a series of guidelines to address these principles, and inside these principles are a set of success criteria.[8] Success criteria are the core of WCAG – clear, testable, standalone technical statements that target specific accessibility issues.

This, at the very least, offers a consistent way to achieve a measurable level of accessibility, as well as a road map for gradually improving your level of compliance (start with A and work up to AA and AAA). Yet despite this, we have a largely inaccessible web. Web accessibility experts WebAIM conducted an evaluation of the home pages of the one million most popular websites and found an incredible **96.3%** of them had detected WCAG failures, with a total of nearly **50 million** distinct errors between them.[9]

WCAG is a good resource and a great idea; however, there are a few issues. The first is just how big it is. The latest full WCAG version (2.2) has a page entitled "Understanding WCAG," which is nearly as long as the update itself.[10] Each point in WCAG is accompanied by a long page to help the reader actually understand the rule and a separate page describing how to meet (or fail) the requirement. Content this size can get in the way of understanding and adopting accessibility, as the solutions are too dense to digest for many.

Another big issue is oversight, as rulesets like WCAG don't *have* to be followed before you can put a site live. Although (as we shall see) the threat of litigation is growing, the fact is that you can, with a server and a basic understanding of code, publish your own website without anything or anyone stopping you from doing so on the grounds that your content is inaccessible. It's seen by many as a voluntary and unenforceable standard.

Then there is the issue of relevancy; WCAG 2.2 was released this year, but the version before (2.1) was released over five years before that. The last **full** version update, WCAG 2.0, was released over 15 years ago.[11] As technology always evolves at a rapid rate, this pace of regulation will always struggle to keep up, leaving large holes when it comes to guiding people to be more accessible.

And after all of this, you're faced with the final boss: **being WCAG compliant doesn't guarantee that you're fully solving access issues**. James Buller, Lead Accessibility Consultant at the UK Home Office, encountered an example of this when he undertook some research into how users apply for a passport:

> *We did some testing with deaf people. Initially the query was "why would you do that, there's no audio involved in the service?" But we decided to check anyway... [The subject] was going through the form, and there had been no big problems until she got to the most boring page on the site – the contact page. It asked her to "provide a phone number," and she did, but also wanted to write "I'm deaf, please don't call me." In this case, it wouldn't let her submit an answer with both numbers and text in it. When we tested this page against WCAG, it passed, but on human terms, it was not accessible because we did not provide her with that option.[12]*

This is just one example of the paradox of being compliant but inaccessible, and why you need to go beyond being compliant and "ticking boxes" to truly understand what users need. You need to "view WCAG not as an end goal, but as a floor"[13] – achieve compliance and then be proactive *beyond* it, in order to build something truly inclusive. To do this, you need to approach things differently.

The "Disability-Driven" Mindset

The good news is, we're slowly starting to see evolution in the guidelines to reflect examples like James' – a slight change in approach in the more recent versions of WCAG.

Rather than just stating a rule, this approach encourages you to imagine a user with a specific access need, the barrier they're facing, and then – using the regulation they've added – consider an appropriate solution.[14] Here's an example of one of the new additions, which states that your site should give a user feedback when an action is initiated:

> *Accountant who is blind and uses a screen reader:*
>
> ***Problem****: I selected a class for a conference, but I can't tell if it got added to my schedule.*

Works well*: When I add a meeting to my calendar, I hear confirmation.*[15]

It's short, simple, and clear. You can understand the spirit of it immediately. This feels like a return to Cerf's idea of designing and developing to address access needs, in the same way he considered deafness while he developed commercial email. This is important because a few things happen when you consider accessibility in this way.

First, by approaching your site from a perspective other than your own, you learn to make other access needs a part of your everyday thought process. This practice helps you begin to see potential constraints and design for them from the outset, rather than coming back to them once the site has been built. Cerf said that accessibility shouldn't be "pixie dust" that designers and developers sprinkle on as an afterthought – it needs to be consciously considered.[16] This is what makes disability-driven accessibility a practical solution.

Through simple scenarios like these, you also see that "accessibility" needs are often also in fact "user" needs. **By designing for disabilities, you start solving issues for everybody**, accounting for requirements you might not have even considered.[17] Video captions, for example, help those with hearing loss, but also those who want to engage with the content without sound in a quiet room.

This reflects the World Health Organization's most recent definition of disabilities, referring to a disability not as a "personal attribute" – as they were described in 1980, but as "context dependent... reflecting the interaction between features of a person's body and features of the society in which he or she lives."[18] Their point here is that disabilities happen during interactions between a person and the world around them on a physical and cognitive level, and this plays out regularly on the Web. The needs of the user are not always reflected in the design or function of a website, and these conflicts prevent a person from engaging, or even interacting, with the content of a site.

Using this definition, **everyone has access needs**, and anyone could develop new ones at any time. They can be temporary, situational, or permanent. Consider this excellent diagram in Figure 1-1 created by Microsoft to showcase examples of what accessibility could be.

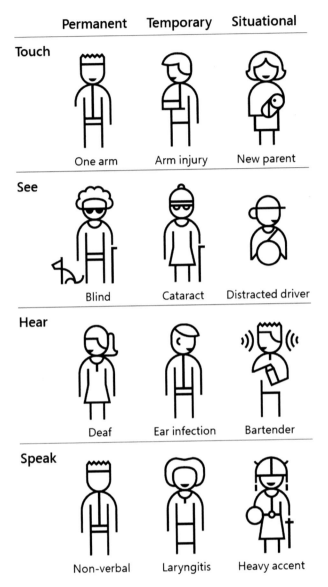

Figure 1-1. *A diagram created by Microsoft to showcase how access needs can be permanent, temporary, or situational. They are categorized into touch, see, hear, and speak. The "touch" example shows the permanent disability as someone with one arm, the temporary disability as someone with an arm injury, and the situational disability as a new parent holding a baby.*

You see these situations everywhere, from interactions with content in a language that isn't your first, with short-term injuries or illnesses, or even from trying to hold a child in one arm and a tablet in the other. As we get older, our eyesight, hearing, dexterity, or mental capacity tend to naturally get worse. These all create needs that can be met by accessible features.

It is therefore our job, as designers, developers, business owners, and anyone involved in running a website, to factor in these cases and create inclusive web experiences that work for the largest number of people possible.

It's not defined by which device has market share right now or what a user's browser of choice is. It's about somebody's experiences of their surroundings. It's about whether someone sees a site or hears it. It's about whether they see your design in a hundred colors or several shades. It's about whether they use a mouse, a keyboard, a head wand, or their voice to navigate everything on their computer and how you can ensure that they all get what they need.

Why Is It Important Now?

As we have seen, the very people who created the Internet knew the moral importance of being inclusive on the Web from the start. An *inclusive* web should give users the ability to access information, services, and entertainment independently, regardless of how they engage with it. For this reason, United Nations Secretary-General António Guterres has called for universal access to the Internet to be a basic human right by 2030,[19] and laws like the UK's Equality Act (2010) are stating that websites are obliged to ensure that their websites are accessible to users with disabilities.[20] It's not enough to be able to get online, everyone should be able to navigate the Web with ease and feel like sites acknowledge the way they do that. Ethics aside, however, there are a plethora of other practical reasons why now is the right time to start thinking about accessibility.

Accessibility Is Receiving More Mainstream Attention Than Ever Before

One reason that this is a good time to begin considering accessibility is because the world is beginning to truly understand its importance. In one of the most widespread accessibility-based news stories in recent years, in January 2019, multiplatinum singer/songwriter Beyoncé's official website was hit by a class action lawsuit. Violating the

1990 Americans with Disabilities Act (ADA), her company has been sued to make their site accessible and seek damages for those who have been subject to unlawful discrimination.

The lawsuit contains a lengthy list of access failings, including but not limited to "lack of alt text on graphics" (that allows screen readers to describe images), "inaccessible drop-down menus" (for keyboard-only or blind users), "lack of navigation links," "lack of adequate prompting and labeling" (for those with cognitive or mental health issues), "denial of keyboard access," "empty links that contain no text," and "the requirement that transactions be performed solely with a mouse"[21] – all barriers that we'll cover.

This may well be the most mainstream case, but Beyoncé is far from the only person to be hit by these allegations – global brands like Netflix, Disney, Target, Harvard, and Dominos have all publicly been subject to lawsuits. The latter made it all the way to the US Supreme Court and lost (more on that later).[22]

The more these cases make the headlines, the more discussion and attention the topic receives, resulting in more cases. In 2018, US Lawyer Caren Decter described the start of an "onslaught of these lawsuits," with cases numbering in the "thousands" after a landmark ruling in 2017 brought against supermarket Winn-Dixie.[23] And yet, between then and 2023, the number of cases brought against websites has, incredibly, more than doubled.[24]

The majority of these cases settle early, with remedial action to fix the inaccessible parts of the site always being part of the settlement. What's more, as there are no official US legal web accessibility guidelines, courts now recognize WCAG as the standard for determining if a site is accessible when cases like Beyoncé's are brought to court.[25] This is also the case in many other countries including the United Kingdom and Australia, the latter having officially adopted WCAG as their benchmark test.

It is worth noting that the threat of legal action is slightly lower in the United Kingdom, but Britain is moving in the same direction. The Royal National Institute of the Blind People (RNIB) has already brought multiple cases against companies for inaccessible websites under the Equality Act that were settled, and "it has long been anticipated that a higher-profile test case will be launched against a noncompliant website."[26]

There is a definite pattern that has emerged over the last few years with regard to action being taken against inaccessible websites. The end result of the case against Beyoncé's website is almost of little consequence individually – it has already drastically increased awareness over the importance of sites being accessible and the potential ramifications if they aren't. Every day, more people are learning what web accessibility is, why it's important, and reading about sites being taken to court for failing to accommodate users. It's damaging to a company's finances and brand to not take this seriously.

Now although the prospect of being sued and having to pay fines or take action to remediate an inaccessible website is a reasonably big motivator, there's also a large commercial *upside* to being among the companies that take accessibility seriously.

Competitive Advantages

You don't always have to be sued in order to make the news for accessibility – there is also the potential to achieve very negative, or positive, press coverage. Upgrades to HSBC's online banking experience inadvertently prevented users with blindness and low vision from properly using their bank accounts. Users complained that what used to be a "simple process has now become unreliable" and forced them to switch to telephone banking, which took much longer.[27]

While this was happening, Barclays capitalized and drew attention to their strength in this area. They contacted the BBC and, in the very same article, were able to demonstrate that Barclays "involves disabled people right from the start, as part of its development and testing process."[28] In this case, Barclays achieved both positive media publicity for being inclusive and also a wave of new customers, all for doing the right thing. Adding to stories like this the rapid rise in awards to recognize excellent accessibility on the Web, mobile, and in video games, and it creates a bright spotlight for those to be recognized and celebrated for doing the right thing.

The possibility of financial gain is also clear. Research conducted by the charity Purple found that in the United Kingdom, the estimated 4.3 million disabled online shoppers who click away from inaccessible websites have a combined yearly spending power of **£17.1 billion**.[29] The BBC reported that retailers could be "missing out on **£249bn** because many are inaccessible to disabled customers,"[30] and in the US, the purchasing power of working-age adults with disabilities is estimated to be nearly half a trillion dollars.[31] A portion of either sum is certainly not the worst outcome for taking access needs into consideration.

With everyone on the Internet competing for users, this gives you a distinct advantage to create excellent experiences for everyone, not just *most* people, as well as making sites easier and more enjoyable to use for everyone. For instance, having an accessible site has been proven to make websites easier to search for, which also increases traffic and revenue.[32] It can also save costs on a retrospective redesign: while it is possible to adapt a site to make it accessible (we'll get to this later), it is always cheaper and easier to build accessibility in from the start, rather than having to go back and change it later. Then there is the added bonus that accessible sites, by being easier to use, typically require less support – people with neglected access needs often make up a significant portion of the audience who typically get in touch for help. Minimizing barriers means fewer phone calls, shorter queues, and lower costs.

Opposition to Accessibility

Unfortunately, despite these mounting practical benefits, in recent years, accessibility has remained an afterthought. Earlier I mentioned that 96.3% of the top one million websites by popularity have recognized WCAG errors on their home pages. That number has remained stable for the last half a decade, only dropping by **1.5%** in all of that time.[33] Clearly, things are not progressing well.

Why this is could be a number of reasons. Lack of knowledge is clearly a factor, as accessibility is rarely taught in coding, design, or business courses. Furthermore, according to Stack Overflow's latest developer survey, less than **2%** of respondents identified as having a physical disability, so representation among those building sites is a clear issue.[34] There are also time constraints for those working on websites. In the fast-moving world of campaigns, product releases, and tight deadlines, people find themselves with a serious time deficit, pressure to deliver, and usually no advocate for building in accessibility. Without knowledge, time, and advocacy, its importance seems to be lost to ruthless prioritization, where it's argued the amount of work doesn't properly match the percentage of users it will cater to.

Hopefully, the past few pages have convinced you that this topic is too important to relegate to an afterthought, and however small the percentage of people you're blocking from your content by being inaccessible, it's still too many – the Web is for everyone, and if you have a website on it, you *have* to consider those with access needs.

On the time commitment required, consider this: Of those 96.3% of errors mentioned earlier, **96.1%** fall into just *six* categories.[35] These most common errors have been the same for years and, realistically, are not hard to fix – they all fall into the lowest and easiest of the three WCAG levels (A). What's more, not meeting this level of accessibility means your site is "impossible or exceedingly difficult for people with disabilities to use."[36] With this low barrier to entry, in both time and effort, it poses a practical opposition to concern about the topic and a starting point that will only generate more interest and momentum for you and your teams after good early progress.

So, Why Approach Accessibility in a Disability-Driven Way?

This book presents a practical approach to accessibility, clearly outlining needs and solutions. It focuses on the hows and whys of barriers users face so that you're equipped to solve a whole host of potential issues, rather than just a few specific scenarios. It is designed to be both a learning experience and a source of future reference for you as you move forward. You can read it from start to finish (which would be lovely), or you can skip to particular chapters if you're currently focusing on a particular access need in your work.

It is worth mentioning that, just as W3C has said that WCAG "doesn't address the needs of people with all types, degrees, and combinations of disability",[37] this book cannot cover every single access need either. It does, however, extend what WCAG has covered and allows you to practice spotting accessibility needs that will allow you to become familiar with a range of them. Obviously, if a particular disability, either permanent or temporary, isn't covered here, that doesn't mean that it's not of consequence.

Thankfully, once you start addressing accessibility from so many different perspectives, you will also begin to notice similarities and consistencies appear – access needs often overlap. For example, longer time-outs on pages where you submit content benefitting people with motor disabilities, severe anxiety, or learning difficulties like dyslexia – but for different reasons. By removing one barrier (in this case a short-timer), you empower and include a wide range of users.

The overlap between access needs and disabilities we focus on in this book means that even if a user has a disability we do not explicitly cover, many of the proposed solutions will still be relevant. It is also always worth remembering that access needs are user needs; accessible design won't just help people with disabilities, it will improve the Web for everyone.

This is where the power of this book truly lies. By the time you finish reading, you'll be familiar enough with a range of access needs (and how to cater to them) to always work with them in mind. It's this mixture of knowing how to identify barriers and then remove them that will ultimately allow you to provide truly inclusive web experiences.

Frequently Asked Questions

Now that we've established the importance of understanding accessibility as well as implementing it into your sites, you may still have questions. The most common question I typically receive is this:

Should I be handling it myself?
This is understandable, as it's a deep topic that can be a little intimidating initially. I would encourage you to give it time. This book can be a constant reference for you in the future as you move forward working with sites, and reading through it will set you up nicely to start engaging with the topic and ensure you're armed with essential knowledge that'll be evergreen.

I consider accessibility to be a topic with a low barrier to entry and a high bar to mastery. This means that you may constantly be working to make the most accessible site possible, as many do to reach the top of their field. However, you can still achieve an awful lot, rather quickly, that has an immense impact on the ability of those with access needs to use your site.

The Pareto principle (known more commonly as the 80/20 rule) teaches us that roughly 80% of consequences come from roughly 20% of the total causes, and this rings true for accessibility. Remember we spoke earlier about an incredible 96.1% of all accessibility errors in the most popular one million websites being caused by only a handful of errors? Handling these in your sites as you make your way through the book won't achieve total accessibility but *will* be an excellent starting point, and help build up your confidence in the topic (I will cover those errors in the chapters to come, and make specific reference to them when we do).

Now I'm not advocating that you stop at 80% (or 96%) – in many ways, those who build sites without accessibility in mind are building for the majority but accidentally ignoring the important minority. However, if everyone engaged with this topic, quickly and at that lower barrier, we'd have a much stronger basis upon which to achieve a truly inclusive web.

The next question I get is usually this:

Are there things that can handle this for me?

Again, a reasonable question. My hope is to change your mind on this idea by the end of the book. There are tools, libraries, and even site builders that attempt to take some of the strain of accessibility off of you. For larger sites with more systemic issues, there are also professional companies that can step in and help remediate a site. I can only recommend the last one on this list, and even then, I believe that most readers will be armed with what they need, and a newfound interest in this topic, by the end of these pages.

Chapter 10, "Outsourcing Accessibility," in this book is written as a slightly more standalone piece about the various trends I've seen rise in popularity over the last few years – everything from building your own site without coding experience using site builders like Wix or Squarespace to frameworks that give you pre-built, accessible "Lego blocks" when building your site, to the grander claim of solving all of your accessibility issues with a single line of code. If you're unsure about focusing your time on accessibility, I'd head over to that chapter and give it a read. Afterward, you will understand why things can't do it for you, and hopefully, you won't want them to.

The natural train of thought for most I talk to then moves here:

Will this book teach me what's actually wrong with my website?

Absolutely. Please make notes of areas you think are interesting or noteworthy as you make your way through, but near the end of the book, you will find a chapter called "Tools and Auditing" (Chapter 11). This chapter is based on the content in the preceding chapters and sets up that information in a way that allows you to complete a robust analysis of how accessible your site currently is. It will feature a mixture of automated and manual testing (as both are necessary to paint a clear picture) and will be laid out in two ways.

First, you will be introduced to the "**FAIR**" framework – an approach I created to help myself (and my teams and clients) engage with existing websites methodically and to know where to start. It creates a way to tackle some of the easy, low-hanging fruit so that you can make tangible progress quickly, but also clear the way to better see the bigger issues.

Second, you'll find my personal accessibility checklist. The list itself is separated into six key areas – aesthetics, content, communication, ease of use, settings, and specifics. Together, these six sections create a list called "**ACCESS**". Now I don't claim that this list covers *every* accessibility issue that exists or that every point will apply to the content on your sites, but it will go a long way. What it doesn't cover explicitly, it will likely illuminate when combined with your own learning as you analyze a site.

Skipping to this chapter before reading the chapters before it will likely be confusing – you will find terms that may be alien or processes that may seem confusing. I'd think of it as a neat refresher once you've done your learning. Finally, the chapter will cover when you may wish to consider external help.

There will always be things to learn on the topic as it grows and the Internet changes. In fact, there are likely multiple issues on the sites I oversee as we speak. I'm not proud of this, but I *will* find them because the key is to stay curious and keep looking.

If your only remaining question is

When do we get started?

The answer is right now!

Conclusion

Hopefully, you can now appreciate the scale of the problem when it comes to a lack of accessible websites, the wave of increased interest in the topic, and most importantly, some of the reasons why making your site accessible is so crucial.

There is undeniably a lot of work to be done in order to improve the general accessibility of the Web. However, this can only begin once we have engagement with the topic – this is what you're doing, so thank you.

The next chapter will start our journey through a range of access needs, showing you how these users typically engage with your sites and content, and the barriers they face. This will set you up well for improving any site you have and give you a strong foundation for making any new site you build accessible from the outset. By the end of the book, I believe that you'll appreciate the value of understanding the various ways that people use your sites and be armed with the knowledge to make them available to everyone, not just some, in the way that the founders of the Internet intended.

Let's begin...

CHAPTER 2

Blindness

According to the World Health Organization, **40 million** people worldwide are registered as Blind.[1] Add to this the rise in age-related disorders like glaucoma and diabetes in aging populations around the globe, and you have a staggering number of people who will need to access content online in a different way. This use of the Web creates a specific set of access needs, as blind and visually impaired users must be able to access the Internet without visual information.

When faced with a site that has neglected those access needs, these users encounter barriers. Not only is this exclusion unfair and discriminatory, but it also contributes to a loss of independence on a platform that can, and should, be accessible to these users. It was this type of exclusion that formed the basis of lawsuits against the websites of Beyoncé, Amazon, and Netflix and the case between a blind customer and Domino's Pizza that made it all the way to the US Supreme Court.

Visual impairments need not be a barrier to using the Internet though. If websites are well designed, built, and maintained, it is easy to include users with sight loss, who can have just as rich an online experience as anyone else. In fact, the Internet is arguably *richer* for blind users when you consider its empowering potential as a previously inaccessible, untapped source of information, services, social contact, and entertainment.

In this chapter, you will learn about some of the main barriers that people with blindness face when using the Internet and the solutions you can implement to help remove them.

This chapter is also unique when compared to most others in this book, as blindness is the only disability that has one fairly unambiguous technology linked with it – screen readers. They're used by people with a range of visual impairments, but if you're able to make your site work effectively with a screen reader, you will empower almost all the blind users who visit your site.

A. Firth, *Practical Web Accessibility*, https://doi.org/10.1007/979-8-8688-0152-5_2

Screen Reader Software

In a survey conducted on screen reader users around the world in 2021, over **90%** experienced blindness or a visual impairment.[2] This shows the captive audience screen readers hold and that they're the best (and only real) means of removing barriers for blind users: designing for blindness currently means designing for screen readers.

First, a bit of context. Screen readers are pieces of software that "read out" information on a page, either through audio or assistive technology, like a braille display. They have become much more prominent in the last decade, and while once upon a time only costly third-party software was available, there is now free software available for every major operating system. This proliferation of screen reading technology has been great for users, but also for developers – allowing them to hear a site they may have only ever seen before. We'll get into the various options available in a later chapter, but at the time of writing, these are the most popular screen readers:

- JAWS

- Voiceover

- NVDA

- Narrator[3]

Although different screen readers have different features, they *all* rely on well-designed and semantically built websites with clear content to work smoothly. There's also a high level of satisfaction with these tools, with nearly **96%** of those polled being happy with their screen reader software. [4] Instead, when screen reader users were asked what would have "the biggest impact on improvements to web accessibility," a whopping **85.3%** said "more accessible websites" as opposed to better assistive technology.[5] Furthermore, over **60%** said accessibility on the Web had either stayed the same or gotten worse for them over the past few years.[6]

This clearly shows that users believe, rightly so, that the responsibility lies with those creating sites and content to take their needs into account when building a website, as opposed to relying on the software to navigate around those mistakes.

So, what can you do?

Perceive, Navigate, and Interact

There is a wide range of things required to make screen readers more accessible, and we will be categorizing them into three key areas:

- **Perceive** – Whether content is accurately displayed to a user

- **Navigate** – Whether a user can effectively move through that content

- **Interact** – Whether a user can freely engage with that content

I've set them out in this order because the process acts as somewhat of a waterfall – to **navigate** through content a user must first be able to **recognize** it, and in order to **interact** with content, they must first be able to **navigate** it properly.

Before we start, a quick note: our focus on making sites screen reader friendly means that this chapter will contain a few code examples. Therefore, please don't be alarmed if you can't engage with every suggestion here or understand the code – you will still be able to understand the principles and intention behind it, and there will also be links to practical examples you can try out for yourself. All examples in the book are available at inclusive.guide/examples.

For those interested in the code behind them, you will be able to find both examples mentioned in this chapter in the "Chapter 2" folder of the GitHub repository (`https://github.com/Apress/practical-web-accessibility`).

Accessibility Tree

First, let's begin with a very quick note on how web pages are built. They're constructed using elements from a programming language called HTML (HyperText Markup Language). Some elements are interactive, like form fields (`<input>`) and buttons (`<button>`), and others are structural, like a `<div>` tag that is purely used to group content. Together, these tags build what's known as a "tree," and it's *this* tree that's then displayed on a web page so it can be seen on a browser window – usually after it's had some styling applied to it through a language called CSS (Cascading Style Sheets).

Now *visually* a user is typically unaware of all of the decorative tags that are used to build a page and its layout, and that's fine – they just want to see the content. Equally, a screen reader user doesn't want to know about these either – they too simply want to access the content. But how does that work when someone is listening to the page instead of looking at it? For this reason, there's another "tree" – the **accessibility tree** (Figure 2-1). This tree only takes *some* of the tags from the full tree – ones that allow a user to understand the content or **navigate** it – and ignores the ones it deems have been added for visual purposes. This tree is then used by assistive technology like screen readers to provide information to a user who *can't* see a page visually.

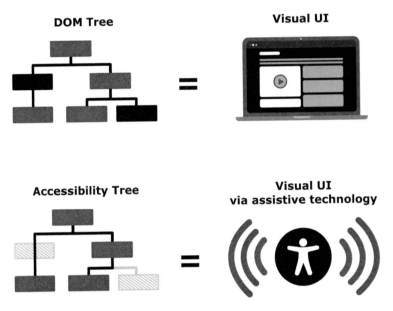

Figure 2-1. *A flowchart depicting how content from code reaches users through visual and audio. In the first flow, the DOM tree created by HTML tags is displayed on a browser window for users to interact with visually. In the second flow, only the informative tags are taken from the full DOM tree to create the "accessibility tree." This is then used by screen reader software to read the contents of a page to the user.*

If you're ever interested, right-click a web page and click the "Inspect" option. You'll see a suite of tools appear, but you'll be able to see both trees – the "DOM tree" with all of the elements of the page on the left and the accessibility properties of selected elements on the right (that you can see by clicking the "accessibility" tab) (Figure 2-2). You can also view the full "accessibility tree" of a page from here. These tools will give you a great indicator about what elements a screen reader user will hear and what the content of those elements will be.

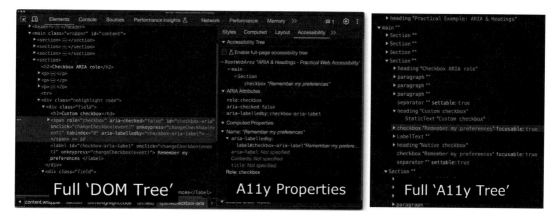

Figure 2-2. *The Developer Tools within Google Chrome's browser allows you to see the elements of the DOM tree that make up the website you're visiting (pictured left). You can also view the accessibility properties of an element you select (pictured middle) and view the whole accessibility tree a screen reader will use (pictured right).*

Screen Reader Information

Depending on which elements you click throughout the accessibility tree, you may see different properties and content. This isn't a surprise as a heading gives you something different to see (or hear) compared to a form. Typically, there are four main pieces of information that the browser exposes about an element in the accessibility tree:

- It's **role** – What the thing is (button, link, etc.)

- It's **name** – What we call it (a button's text, a form field's label)

- It's **description** – What more we can share, if necessary (e.g., a description of what a form field requires, or what clicking a button will do)

- It's **state** – What's happening to it (is a checkbox checked, a button disabled)

19

Here's an example of this information, shown in code in Figure 2-3, for a simple button.

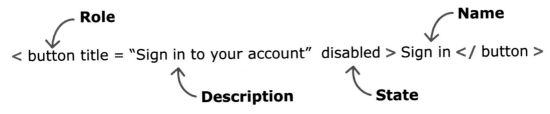

Figure 2-3. An annotated HTML button tag, showing the various information extracted by a screen reader. The name is taken from the tags name, the description is taken from the "title" attribute, the name is taken from the text inside the button, and the state is taken from the "disabled" attribute it has, indicating that it can't be clicked.

So there's a lot to consider in order to give screen readers an experience that's as usable and enjoyable as it is for sighted users. However, there's an easy place to start – it may seem obvious, but using the right HTML tags for the right content goes a long way toward achieving accessibility. Let's explore that.

Native HTML Elements

Native elements are tags that browsers understand to do a particular job. There's a full list at w3schools.com/tags, but you may have seen a few before:

- `<button>` – A button

- `<a>` – A hyperlink (link)

- `<input>` – An input control (or form element), like a text or password field

- `<img>` – An image

These tags have a host of accessibility built into them. For example, when you use a button tag (`<button>`) on your site, it will show up in the accessibility tree with a role and title without having to specify them (so screen readers can announce them), will be recognized as an action that a user can quickly jump to, and can be "tabbed" to by users using only a keyboard or other assistive technology.

You may be wondering, why wouldn't you use the right tags?

As the design of sites progressed over the years, new ways to display and interact with content became popularized. This took people away from what was possible through native tags, which always looked and behaved the same, into making custom components and styled versions of elements like buttons and form elements. These often required building them using tags that are *not* the native ones. In doing this, you may be able to build something that **looks** like a cool button or checkbox visually, for example, and perhaps can be interacted with using a mouse, but for assistive technology, it's useless – it often can't be focused to, and a screen reader has no idea what it's even supposed to be. Take this checkbox component, shown in Figure 2-4 – one is made using the native `<input>` tag that a screen reader understands and will read out as one, and the other is made using a purely visual tag (`<span>`) that a screen reader simply won't recognize as a checkbox.

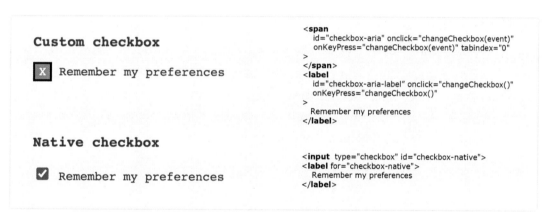

Figure 2-4. *Two checkboxes are pictured left. The bottom one is a native HTML checkbox that's blue when active. The top one is a custom checkbox with an orange style when active and is built using a combination of HTML and JavaScript to achieve the same functionality. On the right is the overview of the code required to build them. The custom checkbox takes nearly three times as many lines of code and is still unusable for screen reader users.*

Now, it *is* possible to make the custom checkbox usable for screen readers using techniques you'll learn in this chapter, so we'll come back to this. But as you can see, it takes a lot more code, including interactive code using JavaScript not shown here, to replicate the behavior you can get with a couple of lines using the right tags. Furthermore, any component you make using a custom implementation has its own fundamental WCAG rule: Success Criteria 4.1.2 (Name, Role, Value). It states that the name and role of a component can be understood by assistive technologies and that states, properties, and values can be set by them. In the documentation, they actually specify that the rule is aimed at people "who develop or script their own user interface components" because "standard HTML controls already meet this success criterion when used according to specification."[7]

Building a site on a foundation of sensible tag choices that reflect the content and interactions available on a page may not always look the flashiest, but they're genuinely inclusive.

Native tags aren't perfect – even when using native elements, there're also still ways to *improve* the information they provide to screen readers. However at its core, *how* you write your HTML will determine how (and even if) screen reader users can engage with your content.

Named Tags

For the same reason, the latest version of HTML (HTML5) introduced "named" tags with predefined meanings. These allow developers to use tags like `<header>` and `<nav>` to represent areas of their site, which help screen reader users understand the layout, help them navigate it easier, and mean your site can handle part of your a11y challenge for you. Take this simple page layout in code, for example:

```
<html>
    <header>
        <nav></nav>
    </header>
    <body>
        <main></main>
        <footer></footer>
    </body>
</html>
```

It's easy by looking at this to see which tags in the code relate to which parts of the content of a web page. Well, when you're using these tags, the same is true for those using screen readers! It's among the easiest and best changes you can make for the accessibility of your site for screen readers, so start there! You may already be using them, but it's worth a check – older websites that were built before these tags were introduced may well be dividing content up in a similar way, but using vague tags like `<div>`, that provide no context whatsoever.

Semantic Markup

Validity is a good first step towards accessibility.

—W3C[8]

Having used the correct tags, it's worth checking if you've used them, well, correctly! Code is prone to human error, and errors such as unclosed tags and incorrectly ordered heading tags can result in the page being displayed in strange and unexpected ways, but also being confusing and even broken for those using screen readers. Validity helps create a consistent experience for all of your users.

There are many online checkers that allow you to submit a page's URL, or upload a file directly, and it will return any validation errors and warnings that it finds – the W3C even provides one themselves.[9] Checking your pages as you build them, and periodically after you've built them, is key to making sure that your hard work isn't being undone accidentally. The easiest way I've found to do this is to add an "extension" to your browser of choice so that you can test the markup of any page with a single click. I've found the extension "Validity" to work well, and you can find more information about it in Chapter 11 "Tools and Auditing." It's important to note that these tools won't flag up poor *choices* of tags (e.g., if you've used a `<div>` tag when you should be using a `<nav>` tag), only whether the markup of your site is valid. Therefore, you still need to be mindful of these markup choices yourself and keep checking to be sure.

So, now that you understand a little more about what goes into a page and how screen readers extract that information, let's start going through some other barriers blind users may face with content and tips to overcome them and improve your sites.

Heading Structure

Headings on web pages are *very* important. Users with visual impairments use headings both to understand what is on a page (**perceive**) but also where they are on a page and to actually move around it (**navigate**) – the first two of our three requisites for screen reader accessibility. Recent studies show that nearly **70%** of the screen readers users that were polled said they used headings to navigate a site, making it by far the preferred way for them to navigate. It shouldn't come as a surprise then that over **85.7%** of respondents find proper heading levels very or somewhat useful.[10] And yet, over **40%** of the one million most popular websites had a problem with their headings, and nearly **8%** had no headings whatsoever.[11]

To make this as easy as possible, all headings on a web page should have a hierarchy, beginning with the most important header and moving down, and a site's code should reflect that. In HTML, the most important title is an `<h1>` (heading level 1) tag. This is usually the title of the page as it's the single most useful piece of information, and there should only be one per page. These numbered heading tags can go all the way down to `<h6>`, and you should drop down to a lower heading tag each time you display subheadings inside a section that already has a heading. Most importantly, you should **only drop down one heading level at a time** – going from a heading 1 (`<h1>`) to a heading 2 (`<h2>`) is fine, but a heading 1 (`<h1>`) to a heading 3 (`<h3>`) is inaccessible. Doing this prevents usability issues and facilitates navigation and understanding of the overall page structure. Skipped headings are a *very* common a11y error – there were over 1.1 million instances of skipped headings in the most popular one million websites, with it being present on over **42%** of all pages.[12]

Figure 2-5 provides an example of a semantic heading structure.

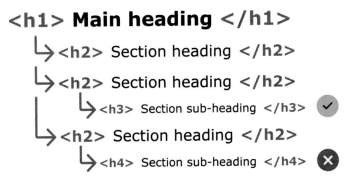

Figure 2-5. *A diagram of how the heading hierarchy on a web page should work. There's typically a single h1 tag acting as the page title, followed by section headings that drop by no more than one heading at a time.*

As you can see, not every heading requires subheadings, but it's important that every heading with an **equal or higher rank** starts a new section and that headings with a lower rank start new subsections that are part of that higher-ranked section. You can use as many or as few headings on a page as you like (I'd recommend leaning on the side of using more), but they *must* start with an `<h1>` and should always be used in order.[13] This is because heading tags denote importance to screen readers, and disordered headers may well confuse a user about what content relates to what section. For this reason, there are two WCAG rules that relate to having a strong heading hierarchy: 2.4.10 (Section Headings) that requires section headings be used to organize content and 2.4.6

(Headings and Labels) that requires that those headings be descriptive. Proper heading structure also benefits the SEO of your page, so there's an added bonus for getting this right.

Styling Headers

With this in mind, it's important that you use these heading tags to display page headings rather than using other tags and relying on where you position them or how you size them to infer meaning. For instance, if you're adding a title above some text, it needs to be in a heading tag followed by text as seen in Figure 2-6.

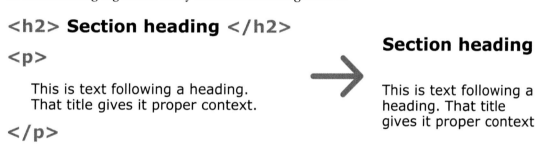

Figure 2-6. *An HTML heading tag, followed by a paragraph tag (pictured left). The right then shows how that would display visually on a browser window, with a bold title with larger text than the paragraph text below it.*

This both displays the hierarchy of content visually and provides the distinction between the title and the paragraph correctly to a screen reader. However, if an incorrect tag is used, but it's placed in the same spot, a title would go and be styled to look like a header, like in Figure 2-7.

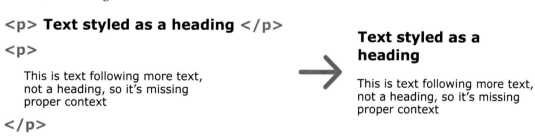

Figure 2-7. *A paragraph tag acting as a heading, followed by another paragraph tag. As the first paragraph tag has been styled to look like a heading, sighted users will not notice an issue. However, this section will not show up as part of the page's heading hierarchy, meaning that it'll be hard for screen readers to find.*

It displays the same visually in a browser, but for screen readers, there is no difference between this "styled" heading and any other piece of text – it would just read the fake "heading" out as text without explaining that it's the heading of the whole section. The result is a potential lack of context for those listening to the page. Using the wrong tag also inhibits proper navigation for those that like to move around a page by its headings – the screen reader won't recognize it as a header, and so the content could be completely skipped over. For this reason, there's a WCAG rule (1.3.1 Info and Relationships) that requires any text styled like a heading needs to use a heading tag.[14]

You may be asking, why would someone not simply use the heading tag? Fair question. The most common reason I've seen is that the design may have called for a smaller heading size-wise than would be semantic. By this, I mean that the heading *should* be an <h3> based on where it is on the page, but the design someone made for the page calls for it to be smaller visually. In this case, I always recommend starting with the correct tags and then styling them to match what the design calls for rather than just choosing the tag that matches the design best. Your sighted users probably won't know the difference either way, but you'll be accessible.

Testing

Just like testing the validity of your site's HTML, you can check your heading hierarchy with one click using a heading map generator. When run on a page, this generates a tree based on the headings on your page (similar to the visual example I displayed earlier) and highlights any that are out of place or have been skipped. Here is an example (Figure 2-8).

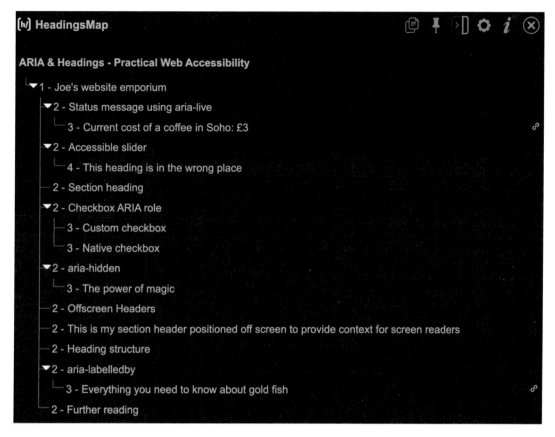

Figure 2-8. *An example of a web page's heading structure, visualized as a heading map with a treelike layout thanks to the HeadingsMap browser extension. The heading hierarchy is semantic, apart from a single h4 tag that is flagged in red.*

The tool pictured is the browser extension "HeadingsMap", and it quickly shows you how a lot of screen reader users will navigate the content of your site, so you can check if

- All the headers that *should* be there from your page content *are* there

- Whether the headings make sense in isolation

- Whether any are in the wrong place so you can fix them (these are marked in red, as shown earlier)

Off-Screen Headers

After you've tested the heading structure of your website, you may have found that certain sections are missing from the hierarchy shown, as they don't have (and in some cases, don't need) a header. From a design perspective, it's fine to have areas where contextual information is inferred visually through the content around them rather than explicitly stated, but you *will* need to add explicit context for screen readers.

To achieve this, you can create a header that is **visually** hidden but will still show up on a screen reader. This preserves the useful signposting that allows screen readers to **navigate** a page as we've covered, without impacting a page's design.

To achieve this, you first create the title with a regular heading (that keeps the heading hierarchy semantic) and a class you can reference in your styles:

```
<h2 class="screenreader-only">This is my title</h2>
```

Then, you add styles to position the header off of the page. This means that the title will never be seen visually but *will* be read out by a screen reader in the position you've placed it in your code. Just in case you need the styles, this is what you'd need to do that:

```
.screenreader-only {
  position: absolute;
  width: 1px;
  height: 1px;
  padding: 0;
  margin: -1px;
  overflow: hidden;
  clip: rect(0, 0, 0, 0);
  white-space: nowrap;
  border-width: 0;
}
```

This isn't always necessary, but some sections accidentally end up without headings because sighted users can recognize the wider meaning of a piece of content without the need for consistent visual headers. A designer may also omit a header because they make that same visual connection between content and context that sighted users do, without realizing the consequences for blind users. For screen reader users though, these headers are always necessary.

Note   If you use a framework for your front end such as Tailwind or Bootstrap, they often have utility classes such as this built in, allowing content for only screen readers and allowing only assistive devices to focus on it. It's always worth checking the documentation of your framework of choice before adding your own, as these projects are actively maintained and so adapt as the Web changes.

Linear Layouts

Now that we've looked at the choice of tags and structure of headings, let's explore how we lay out the content itself on a page. Understanding how screen reader users **navigate** a page often requires sighted users to use their imaginations. Blind users generally move through a page in one direction – as it is read out – from the beginning to the end, which typically differs from that of sighted users.

How Users Navigate

Navigation using a screen reader is dictated by the various ways in which users typically prefer engaging with the content of a page. You can have a screen reader simply read the content of a page to you as it finds it, which is handy for long-form text and articles. Users can adjust something called "verbosity," which is speech feedback that gives information about where they are on a page and describes features like tables that might help build up a mental picture. Screen reader users can also choose whether content is read out a line, word, or letter at a time – which is useful as people might need to hear the same thing several times.[15]

Users, however, hardly ever sit through an entire page in order. Think about how you typically navigate a page. You don't normally engage with every single piece of content from the top to the bottom. Instead, we're always trying to extract key information, like links or actions, that give you an indication of what point the page is making or what is being asked of you. Screen reader users are no different. They can navigate by "content type," such as headings, landmarks, links, and actions, as well as using the "Tab" key to move between the important and interactive content of a page. Recent research found that nearly **92%** of all screen reader users find information on a page through some form of shortcut or navigation, as opposed to just listening to the page.[16]

Interestingly, users with refreshable braille displays navigate pages in much the same way that other screen readers do, and so the same design solutions we'll cover apply. They use small "rocker switches" above each refreshable braille character to send the cursor to a specific space on the page. This is one of the main ways that deafblind users can browse the Internet.

Ultimately, navigation preference varies from user to user, but all methods require that the layout – the order of the page – makes sense. This is best achieved when that layout is linear.

What Is a Linear Layout?

You can get a very literal understanding of what order a page is naturally read out in by removing the styles from that page and seeing what you're left with. For instance, here in Figure 2-9 is the same site with and without styling applied to it.

Figure 2-9. *A comparison of the site layout of the **Financial Times**, first with CSS applied, then without. The first image has a free-form layout, with sections of content laid out around the page. In the second image, the content is simply ordered from top to bottom in a single column.*

The second picture roughly shows the content a screen reader user would experience. When you navigate this way, you begin to realize the order in which content is read out can often differ from how it appears visually, often in ways that make it more confusing to **interact** with, as it hadn't been considered by the designers. CSS makes it possible to create intricate layouts and designs in order to make a web page more attractive to its audience, but taking this idea too far can end up excluding certain users.

A good rule here is that, before any styling takes place, content on a page should follow a simple, linear layout. When building a site, many developers simply place the content on the page in a sensible order, using the correct tags, and then start styling it to match a design. In my opinion, this is the right order. If you led with the styling instead, it's possible to unintentionally lose this logical flow, and you wouldn't know unless you were using a screen reader. As a test, try removing the style from a page on your site. Does it still make sense? Can you discern the sections from one another? Does following the content from top to bottom create a confusing order? Can you identify the core actions you're asking your users to perform? It's key that these things still make sense.

You need to avoid the assumption that it's obvious that two pieces of content are related, or that one follows another, simply because they are close to one another *visually*. Content is read in an order that makes sense, so it needs to be ordered to promote easy reading.

Mobile Devices

A more linear layout can be especially useful for mobile screen reader users.[17] After all, they have far less space to work with! A survey by WebAIM shows that **90%** of screen reader users also used screen readers with their mobile devices.[18] There are a series of gestures that mobile screen reader users employ to navigate a page instead of tabbing: for example, flicking two fingers down the screen to hear content on the page read out from the beginning, a single tap to bring a button or link into focus, and a double tap to activate a button or link. Notably, rather than listening to the page in order, one command involves tracing a finger (or assistive tool) around the screen, either top to bottom or side to side, to explore the interface – hearing the screen reader speak what's underneath.[19]

This last point shows that the physical placement of content on the screen can be just as important as it is for sighted users – related content should be placed close together on the page. Similarly, having a linear order that you can scan through quickly works well.[20]

In June 2019, mobile usage overtook desktop usage globally and has stayed that way ever since.[21] Therefore, it's just as important to consider accessibility for mobile sites too. Indeed, designers are starting to think about it before anything else.

"Mobile-First" Design and Development

"Mobile first," as the name suggests, means that designers start designing a website for mobile devices, which have more restrictions in terms of screen size, and then expand its layout to take advantage of the larger screen real-estate available on tablets, laptops, and desktops. This is visualized in Figure 2-10, where the site's content is stacked on a smaller mobile device and the layout then adjusts to make use of the increased screen space on a laptop. It has become a prominent layout strategy for designers but also aids accessibility a lot, as it forces you to decide what the most important pieces of information on your page are and to lay them out in a way that works well from top to bottom. This lack of screen real estate actually allows all users to focus on one piece of content at a time rather than having to digest a complicated layout.

Figure 2-10. *A representation of a linear, mobile-first design: a layout that stacks top to bottom on a mobile device (pictured left) and a more complicated layout on a bigger desktop screen (pictured right).*

This is another good example of how designing for accessibility can help all users: creating a simple, unambiguous layout that is capable of adapting to all screen sizes will ensure *everybody* avoids confusion.

While we're thinking about page layout, consider this: there is a *lot* of common content on the pages of your site. Things like the header and menu can be small and discreet visually but can be frustratingly repetitive for screen reader users navigating your site from top to bottom. For this reason, a huge quick win for these users is to add a "skip to main content" link.

"Skip to Main Content" Link

As the name suggests, this link allows screen reader users to skip past common, repetitive content in a site (usually a header and/or menu) so they can get straight to a page's unique content. These are a great little tool – helping users **navigate** a page and **interact** with the content quickly and intuitively. Over half of screen reader users regularly use the "skip to main content" feature,[22] and they have the added benefit of also helping people with motor disabilities who navigate using a keyboard.

Most web users are unaware of these links because they are usually only obvious when you need them – they are hidden visually but suddenly appear when you "tab" to them (as users navigating a page via keyboard typically do). They're also positioned as the very first piece of content on a page and so are read out first by screen readers. If you're interested, try heading to some sites you use frequently and hitting "tab" once you arrive. In many examples, you'll see a previously hidden link appear from nowhere and offer to send you down to the unique content by pressing "Enter" or "Space".

Sites usually have a common navigation or header at the start of every page, so not having a skip to content link can leave blind users listening to the same content again and again as they move around your site or having to skip through elements and guess where a page's unique content starts. In cases where a navigation element contains many submenus and items, a user could be waiting for minutes at a time while the screen reader runs through them all. For this reason, there's a WCAG rule dedicated to allowing users to bypass repeated content in this way (2.4.1 – Bypass Blocks).[23]

Instead, you can make a simple link to bypass all that common content in three easy steps (you can skip these steps and head to the practical example I've built for you if you'd prefer – available in the "Chapter 2" folder of the Github repository, or live at `https://inclusive.guide/examples/skip-to-content`):

Step 1

Add your new link as the first piece of content inside your page's body, and have that link point to a section containing your page's main content:

```
<a class="skip-to-content" href="#content">Skip to main content</a>
...
<main id="content">
    ...
</main>
```

Notice that in the preceding figure, the link is navigating to "#content." Links that begin with a hash symbol allow you to navigate to part of the same page with a matching ID attribute – in this case a <main> tag with the ID of "content."

Step 2

Now the link exists, we want to hide it visually. We achieve this by positioning the link off the screen – the same technique we used for off-screen headers:

```
.skip-to-content {
        left: 50%;
        position: absolute;
        transform: translateY(-100%);
}
```

At this point, only screen readers will be presented with the option to use the link.

Step 3

To finish off the link, we need to make a small addition for those only using a keyboard to navigate. To do this, we style the link so that when you focus on it (the state that occurs when you "tab" onto content), it will reappear on the page ready to be used:

```
.skip-to-content:focus {
    position: relative;
    transform: translateY(0%);
}
```

That's all there is to it! You just satisfied a WCAG rule, made your site a bit more accessible, and *much* easier to use, in a few steps and with a few lines of code.

As with all practical examples in this book, I've created a working example for those who would like to insert it directly into their site or use it as a proposal or conversation starter with their teams. As I mentioned earlier, it's available in the "Chapter 2" folder of the GitHub repository, or you can view it at `https://inclusive.guide/examples/skip-to-content`. For this example, I've created two pages with the same menu: one has a "skip to main content" link, and one doesn't. I'd recommend opening the page without the link in your browser first and using a screen reader to listen to the page. You'll quickly discover just how long it takes to get to the main content. Then, try out the page with the preceding feature, and see how one link and the push of a button can save you trouble and time!

Link Placement

This link is usually placed in the top left-hand corner of a web page as that is the first thing a keyboard or screen reader would engage with. It's important to make the link or its focus style obvious because it could well be missed by sighted motor-impaired users; they're forced to tab through common content anyway (we'll discuss focus styles in more depth in Chapter 4 "Motor Impairments").

Alt Tags

Let's talk about images. Roughly **3.2 billion** of them are uploaded to the Web every day, which represents 3.2 billion pieces of content that are, by default, inaccessible to those who are blind and visually impaired.[24] In the top one million most popular websites on the Web, **43 million** images were present, with nearly a quarter of those (9.6 per page on average) missing something that's *very* easy to add, and the thing that would help make them accessible is an `alt` tag.[25]

Alt tags are a property that you'll hear about several times throughout this book because they are useful to so many users. They are added to images in order to describe to users what's going on in the image – what they are unable to **perceive** or **interact** with visually, particularly if you're using a screen reader. This is a simple but fundamental point. If you display imagery, or in any way rely on imagery to convey meaning, you need to provide what's called `alt` text, which is text that a screen reader can read out for those who can't see the image itself. Take this image as an example:

```
<img src="images/stock-graph.jpg" alt=”A graph about stocks”/>
```

This is the tag so many images are missing. Now this example only provides a small, vague piece of information about the image, but if you went on to speak in detail about information held in the graph on the page without providing better `alt` text, screen reader users would still end up quite confused.

This is a common trap that people working on a site can fall into – it's not enough to simply provide `alt` text. It needs to be *useful* text. You may not actually *notice* the mistake you've made when testing your site because providing *any* `alt` text will satisfy the very first WCAG rule (1.1.1 Non-text Content).[26] However, what you've added doesn't always help explain the image. As we've talked about, you sometimes need to go beyond compliance with a WCAG rule and think about what's actually going to help a user.

With this in mind, here is a further improvement to our earlier image:

```
<img src="images/stock-graph.jpg" alt="A graph showing the steady increase
in stock price for Apple month by month over the last 5 years. It peaked
at $192.82 IDS in July 2023 but dipped slightly in the three months that
followed. Its lowest was $37.68 in December 2018. Over this time, it has
increased by 325.78%"/>
```

Now we've ensured that the text actually *describes* what is in the image rather than a simple *declaration* of what the image is. The latter is a common mistake and something you should watch out for in your sites. Other important things to consider when writing `alt` text are as follows:

- **Be succinct and specific** – Say what's in the photo, without editorializing.

- **Aim to keep it around 140 characters** – There's no limit to what screen readers can describe, but it's important to be conscious of the user's time.

- **Don't start alt text with "image of"** – Screen readers announce that the element is an image, so it's thoroughly unnecessary.

- **If there's text in the image, write it in the alt text** – This prevents it from being trapped for screen reader users.

- **Use punctuation** – The text will be read out by a screen reader, so using commas on longer sentences and ending with a full stop will make it more pleasant for those listening.

- **Consider SEO** – Alt text is used by search engines too, so adding it can help grow the visibility of your site online but will be read by an audience larger than just those using screen readers.

If you consider these things when adding your `alt` text, you'll unlock a lot of hidden content and context for blind and visually impaired users and be better than the millions of images out there with `alt` text like "image," "graphic," a file name, and even "blank"![27]

A lack of `alt` text was a consistent problem on Beyoncé's website in the lawsuit brought against her company and is particularly important on ecommerce sites – if the user can't see an image of the product on sale, they need it properly described.

Image Context

Alt text is always worth auditing and checking as it requires a slight shift in thinking to write well. For example, content creators will often place relevant images next to text. They will then sometimes make no direct reference to that image's contents in the text while simultaneously relying on that image to help explain the meaning of those words. This is because they can *see* the image, so for them, the connection is present visually. When that visual connection doesn't exist, it can cause confusion.

Take this example text, placed next to an image that hasn't been described with `alt` text:

"The shaft is one of the longest in recorded history, and can move back and forth at impressive speeds."

What do you think this is talking about? There are a few obvious answers, but none that I'd commit to print. This text refers to an image, but without an `alt` tag specified, a blind user would have none of that important context (they may even think that they've stumbled onto a different site unintentionally...).

This particular example is actually talking about the elevators in the Empire State Building.

Adding Alt Text

Alt tags, as you've seen, are very easy to add, even if you're dealing with existing content. This helps if you're maintaining an existing site with a content management system, such as WordPress or Wix, because there's usually a field to add a description when you upload or edit an image. This can be done retrospectively on any site and makes such a difference to a blind or visually impaired user's experience on your site.

When Not to Add It

This will sound counterintuitive given what we've just covered, but there are times when *not* providing `alt` text is better. Of the images added to a site, there are two broad categories: informative and decorative. Informative images relate to the examples we've covered – information inside an image that is trapped for those who are blind or visually impaired unless we provide a useful description of it. Generally, it's best to think of most images as informative and err on the side of providing good descriptions. The main exception is "decorative" images – images provided for the sole purpose of visually enhancing a site and that don't provide anything useful or contextual that a screen reader would miss. Figure 2-11 shows an example of this.

Figure 2-11. *An image that is purely decorative and has HTML text next to it, and so wouldn't need* `alt` *text adding to it. It is a cartoon globe smiling and holding a trophy. The text below it reads "Award-winning customer service".*

In instances like these, there's an important rule: **provide the attribute, just don't provide the text**. In practice, that could look like this:

```
<img src="images/cute-illustration.jpg" alt=""/>
```

Doing this provides two things:

1. It satisfies the WCAG rule (1.1.1 Non-text Content) of providing an `alt` attribute on any image in a site.

2. By providing an *empty* attribute, it allows a screen reader to ignore the image altogether and move on, making for a less disjointed, more seamless experience as they navigate your page.

The last point is one of the many paradoxes of accessibility and exactly why understanding the topic is so important – there can be times when providing `alt` text is most accessible **and** times when not providing any is best.

So, a final word of warning: make sure you're **certain** that the image provides no useful information or context before effectively hiding it from screen readers.

Social Networks

Of the *many* images added to the Internet each day, most of them are uploaded to social media. The good news is that these sites are now encouraging content creators to think about `alt` tags more frequently. You may have noticed that when you upload an image to sites like Instagram or Twitter, it offers you the ability to provide proper `alt` text before sharing it, thereby making its core media more accessible. Meta has followed suit and has even developed an algorithm to try and describe what's in an image if a user doesn't provide `alt` text.[28] It's not perfect, and even they advise users to check what's been added to ensure accuracy, but it's an excellent attempt to combat human error that can cause inaccessible content. With large social networks placing an emphasis on this, it's more likely than ever to become commonplace on all websites. So, check the content you share, and get familiar with that as a step when you share images online – socially, or on websites you build. Don't get caught out!

The lang Attribute

Another quick win for your sites. In order to **interact** with content, blind users have to be able to understand what language is being read out. This may sound obvious, but the relevant attribute is often forgotten. The lang (language) attribute is used to specify the language that the text on the page is written in. For example, in order to explain that the following text is written in English, we would set the lang attribute to "en" – this is because the tag relates to the ISO language code for the language you're representing (you could even extend it to "en-gb" to represent British English):

```
<html lang="en">
    <body>
        ...
        <p>This content is written in English and, thanks to the language
        tag, a screen reader knows this!</p>
    </body>
</html>
```

This feature is consistently overlooked because it makes no immediate visual difference to a web page when it is added – it doesn't change the language of your text, nor how you read it. However, for a browser, setting the lang of a page does a couple of things. Firstly, it will ensure it offers to translate the content if it doesn't match the user's specific language. This prevents both blind and sighted users from having to try and read content written in a language they don't understand. Secondly, setting the attribute tells a screen reader which accent and pronunciations it should use for the content, thereby avoiding content from one language being spoken with the accent and pronunciation of another. Imagine hearing French from a native speaker, compared to that of an English person! Again, it's often overlooked because it's not how the person who coded it is used to engaging with content. It's also a fundamental WCAG rule (3.1.1 – Language of Page), so make sure you consider it.

Handling Multiple Languages

If a piece of text is *purposefully* written in a different language to the rest of your page, you can simply specify a different language for that section using the same attribute. Here is a piece of French writing inside of our English page, marked up, so a screen reader user will understand when they reach it:

```
<html lang="en">
    <body>
        ...
        <p>This content is written in English and, thanks to the language
        tag, a screen reader knows this!</p>
        ...
        <p lang="fr">J'ai des petites jambes comme un pingouin!</p>
    </body>
</html>
```

In this example, setting the extra `lang` attribute allows a screen reader to provide correct pronunciation and accent for the English text and then switch language profile to French – rather than attempting to read French with English pronunciation (like me in my French lessons at school). It's an incredibly simple thing to add but a big win for users and helps you meet a AA level WCAG rule (3.1.2 – Language of Parts).[29]

Forms

Whatever the purpose of your website or app, you're likely to be using at least one form, whether for gathering information, allowing sign-ups, or carrying out a transaction. A badly designed form can have a huge impact on the experience of every user and cause particular problems for people with accessibility needs.

In a highly competitive online market, an inability to receive customer information through a screen reader, and/or by using solely a keyboard, could result in a heavy loss of traffic and business to competitors. Chris Moore, who is Digital Accessibility Champion at HMRC and a regular user of assistive technology due to access needs, describes this difficulty in the blog series "accessibility and me" and shares a story that reflects our earlier discussion about checkboxes:

Some of the other barriers I face are unlabelled form elements or items that can't be reached without a mouse. It is very frustrating when you start a transaction like online shopping and you are not sure what needs to be entered into a form field or you are unable to activate the button to checkout. Situations like that force me to close the window and then find a more accessible competitor.[30]

Remember the estimated 4.3 million disabled online shoppers who click away from inaccessible websites having a combined yearly spending power of **£17.1 billion**?[31] Well, forms are a key place where users abandon user journeys, and an easy, accessible form will massively increase conversion rates, across *all* customers. This should be more than enough to convince someone that testing this user journey for accessibility issues is a worthwhile endeavor – showing colleagues that certain users can't actually *make it* through – a form on your site is usually a big wake-up call. What's more, many sites are legally required (particularly those in government) to make their forms accessible.

The issue here is something called tabindex, which is a simple attribute that can tell a page that it should be possible for a user to focus on, and interact with, a feature via the "Tab" key and help you create a sensible order and flow within your page for those that navigate this way. We will focus on this more thoroughly in Chapter 4, "Motor Impairments", so if you're experiencing real problems with this, I would recommend consulting there. For now, it's important to know that by default, native form elements have tabindex applied to them. This means that, without adding any custom code, a form on your page will allow a user pressing Tab to move sequentially through your form and interact with the elements there, as long as they have been marked up correctly. This is exactly what we covered earlier – choose the right tags, and you've made an excellent start on accessibility.

Proper Labeling/Identification

Returning to barriers for blind users, as you may have noticed from Chris Moore's comments earlier, he also mentions "unlabeled form elements." What this means is that users should be able to understand what a form field is asking for through a screen reader; otherwise they'd be left simply guessing what they should input. A "lack of adequate prompting and labeling" prevented users on Beyoncé's website from accessing the "goods and services" on the site – purchasing merchandise in this instance.

If you don't properly label form elements, a screen reader will try and guess what is required to prevent confusion. It will go and look for text to the left and above form fields to see if nearby text can indicate what's needed. However, the screen reader is only *guessing* and might associate the wrong form field with the wrong information. Why leave it to chance?

Linking Labels to Form Fields

A common issue I've seen is that a label for a form element *has* indeed been provided, but there has been no **coded connection** to make this obvious to blind users – again, like other barriers we've covered, the connection is purely visual.

The solution here lies in something called the `for` attribute, which pairs a form field with a `<label>` tag to describe it. It does this by adding a value on a label that matches up to the id attribute of a form element to create a connection, like so:

```
<form>
  <label for="first_name">Enter your first name</label>
  <input type="text" id="first_name">
</form>
```

Doing this ensures that the code is aware of the connection, so the screen reader can be aware, so the user can be aware. Again it's simple to fix, and again it makes a large difference. It's one of the many examples where improving a11y improves *all* users' online experience – knowing exactly what each form field needs you to enter prevents a lot of annoyed users!

Bonus: Large(r) Click Areas

An added bonus is that when the `for` attribute is properly set, a user can then click the label to interact with the form field as well as the field itself. This larger hit area is easier to interact with. Take Figure 2-12, for example: If the label is linked to the checkbox correctly, a user would be able to check or uncheck it by clicking, tapping, or tabbing the text as well as the checkbox itself:

Figure 2-12. *A ticked checkbox, next to a label saying, "I accept the Terms & Conditions"*

This change also helps those with low vision, or even people with hand tremors, use form elements by preventing the need to be precise in their tapping or clicking. It also allows you to be compliant with WCAG's minimum target size for inputs (2.5.8 – Target Size) and can even satisfy a AAA rule for even larger target sizes (2.5.5).[32]

Up until now, we've covered good a11y wins for blind and visually impaired users that follow a theme – implement the basics well, and you'll have an excellent foundation. Things like using the correct tags, providing `alt` text, and building sensible heading hierarchies and well-coded forms all take advantage of what native elements can do and what the browser can understand. But as the Web develops, and people create more complex features and pages, how do we tell the browser what it should tell users when the answer isn't as clear? For that, we have ARIA.

Using ARIA

ARIA (Accessible Rich Internet Applications) was a spec, created by W3C, to improve the accessibility of applications by providing extra information to screen readers through code. Screen readers are already quite good at understanding regular HTML, but adding ARIA roles provides screen reader users with more information, more context, and greater interactivity.

ARIA roles and properties are a useful thing to know about because they allow blind users to **identify** what part of the website they are on. If they didn't exist, as screen reader users moved through a site, they could hear lots of content, but with little context. ARIA roles are therefore especially relevant to making sure readers can **perceive** content.

At the start of this chapter, we spoke about the importance of choosing the correct tags on a website to ensure screen reader users can understand the *context* of the content they were hearing. ARIA can provide even deeper, more granular information to these tags, along with vital info and signposting in areas that have *no* context (particularly due to those pesky `<div>` tags). It's a tool more and more developers are starting to use, with ARIA code usage increasing **29%** between 2022 and 2023 and has nearly quadrupled since 2019.[33]

It's great to see ARIA being used by people more and more, as it holds a lot of power when it comes to making the experience online more enjoyable. However, *only* if they're used correctly. The same study that measured increased ARIA usage found that home pages with ARIA present averaged **68.6%** more detected errors than those *without* ARIA – the more ARIA attributes that were present, the more accessibility errors could be expected.[34] Now this does not necessarily mean that ARIA *introduced* these errors, but pages typically had more errors when ARIA was present. Therefore, using it correctly is vital.

Now, ARIA is a large topic, and I won't be able to cover *all* of its uses here. If you're interested to know more after reading this chapter, W3C has a fairly extensive document that goes into more detail.[35] What we will do though is run through some practical instances where the simple addition of correct ARIA use can improve blind users' experiences. You'll therefore be able to see just how easy ARIA attributes are to add, and because the implementation is so consistent, you'll also know how to add others you come across that are relevant to your work.

ARIA is split into two main sections – the first being roles and the second being states and properties. Roles are added to help users understand the purpose and importance of content within a page. They can help identify large, important parts of a page; provide context for common site features that HTML doesn't understand (like a Tab panel); or alert users when other content is added to a page (like a modal dialog). States and properties are known collectively as "ARIA attributes" and are used to give information about how pieces of content are related to each other, highlight changes in status, and generally provide more granular information (we will get to this later).

The important benefit of using all of these is their ability to alter how a screen reader recognizes a page's content and give far greater context to the user. As we know, correct HTML tags are a good start to provide preliminary information. However, enhancing the quality of what's provided using ARIA will make for a much better experience. Let's start with a simple example – you can add an ARIA role by simply assigning a role attribute to a tag like so:

```
<header role="banner">
```

And just like that, a screen reader will announce this section as a "banner" (the place where you'd store your logo/menu/search bar, etc.) – something HTML previously wouldn't have recognized.

The preceding example is known as a "landmark role" because they're recognizable parts of a web page and complement the use of correct tags, a good heading hierarchy, and a good linear layout to make navigating with a screen reader more inclusive and enjoyable. Once you've added them to the page, a lot of screen reader users will use them to navigate, as they can help show where important actions and information will likely be.

Here are a few common roles that you can add to areas of a page in the same way:

- **Banner** – Typically the "header" of your page

- **Region** – A significant part of the site containing content

- **Main** – The primary area of content on your site

- **Form** – A collection of items that make up a form

- **Navigation** – Used to identify groups or a list of links that are intended to be used for navigation

- **Search** – For highlighting search functionality on a site

- **Contentinfo** – Typically the "footer" – containing information such as copyrights and policy documents (such as accessibility statements!)

An important thing to note here is that you cannot make up your own role values and expect a screen reader to read it out – it will only announce roles that are part of the list of ARIA roles. You can find the full list at inclusive.guide/reading/chapter2.

Earlier in the chapter, we covered the use of "named" tags through HTML5, as they have inbuilt information that can be passed onto screen readers without you needing to specify anything. You could replace the need to add most of the preceding roles by using the following tags instead:

- **Banner** – `<header>`

- **Region** – `<section>`

- **Main** – `<main>`

- **Navigation** – `<nav>`

- **Contentinfo** – `<footer>`

There are still instances when using role attributes instead of these tags makes sense. For example, a banner that *isn't* a header and so shouldn't use the `<header>` tag, or setting a role of "search" on a search form, as there's no native `<search>` tag. As a result, I'd advise that you look at the content you intend to place on a page, use native HTML tags for as many parts of the site as possible, and then explore how applying roles could provide extra information to blind and visually impaired users. I highly suggest looking through the "ARIA Authoring Practices Guide" online to explore all the possible additions you can make, as you make new features and experiences. The link will be available at `inclusive.guide/reading/chapter2`.

Adding either of these areas to your page could be done in a couple of minutes and instantly provides info that helps a blind user know where they are and what they are looking at. This is a powerful tool but has to be used carefully – announcing an element as something it isn't could create more confusion than if you'd done nothing at all. For instance, if you stated that an element was a menu and it didn't contain a list of menu items, a screen reader user would be rightly confused.

Much like the tags we covered earlier, these roles are common parts of a site that a browser can understand. However, there's also more we can give that a *user* will understand, and we can accomplish this using ARIA attributes. Let's look at an example of this – in the following, we have a `<nav>` tag. Now we don't need to provide a "role" attribute like the ones earlier because the browser already *knows* it's a navigation thanks to the tag. However, there are many types of navigation that could exist on a web page, so it's useful, but still a little vague. To solve this, we can use ARIA to enhance what a screen reader can share about our `<nav>` tag, using ARIA attribute "aria-label":

```
<nav aria-label="Breadcrumbs">
</nav>
```

Now it's not simply a nav to a user using a screen reader – it's a breadcrumb menu! This makes it so much easier to **navigate** and **interact** with what they're looking for. Let's explore some more uses of ARIA attributes and why you often need them.

Applying ARIA Attributes

Now you may have come across sites with beautiful versions of site elements you've seen a lot – checkboxes, menus, and toggles, for example. These visual changes are typically achieved through "styling" *other* elements to look this way rather than using the correct, native elements. This is because unique, custom site design catches user's attention and makes sites memorable. However, if you do this without applying ARIA attributes, screen readers will only be able to read out the tags that you've used – they won't read the feature out as a checkbox, for example, because it's not. They can only comprehend the tags that have been used. What ARIA does is provide a screen reader, and its user, with a way to **perceive** and **interact** with that feature.

Therefore, if you're creating a design that contains a unique or custom way for a user to input information or a decision such as this, you need to ensure that you have the correct ARIA tags and attributes to allow *all* users to do that. Let's look at a couple of basic examples of ARIA use so you can keep an eye out for them on your own sites.

aria-label

We've already seen what ARIA labels can provide in terms of additional context on areas of websites. However, they can also be very useful for allowing users to **perceive** the effect of an action being taken before taking it and so **interact** with it with confidence. For example, let's accomplish this by adding a simple description to an otherwise vague button action using the `aria-label` attribute:

```
<button aria-label="Submit information and move to next page">Submit
form</button>
```

The user will have already been able to navigate to this button and interact with it using a screen reader, thanks to the use of the correct `<button>` tag, but the extra context from the label being read out makes that interaction easier and more enjoyable. Try going through your common site actions, like links and buttons, to see whether you could provide more useful context to users through the use of `aria-label`. These messages won't be visible and so won't affect your page design but will vastly improve the experience for screen reader users.

aria-hidden

Sometimes it can be just as important to *hide* content as it is to label or annotate it. `aria-hidden` is really handy for hiding components that are on a page for purely visual purposes (like we learned to do with empty `alt` attributes on images earlier). It can also help with text related to that content, so people using screen readers don't have to spend time listening to it needlessly. For this example, here is the code required to display a "tweet" icon, using the popular icon library Font Awesome:

```
<button>
  <span class="fa fa-tweet" aria-hidden="true"></span>
  <span class="label"> Tweet </span>
</button>
```

We hide the icon itself from assistive technologies with `aria-hidden="true"` as exposing it would only waste the user's time, given that the text next to it describes the action. Furthermore, if the icon *didn't* have the same content as the visible text, it being read out to the user could cause confusion.

It's important to ensure that this content provides absolutely no important information for users using assistive technology before hiding it as a screen reader will then make no attempt whatsoever to read it out.

A quick note about this attribute in relation to `alt` text: if you've added `aria-hidden="true"` to an image, it would be contradictory to then add `alt` text. This is because decorative images must be coded in a way that can be ignored by assistive technology and the accepted method is to actually leave the `alt` text blank in order to not cause confusion.

aria-live

You may have experienced a scenario like this before: you fill out a form and hit submit, only to find that you stay on the page and nothing seems to have changed. You then investigate the page to find that there is an error message displayed somewhere else on the page that you didn't expect and weren't navigated to. Now imagine this scenario but without being able to see the screen. In this situation, screen reader users are left to simply try and find out what happened by searching around. This, again, will often drive users elsewhere.

Thankfully, you can use ARIA to provide useful information as it changes with the `aria-live` attribute. It can be added to tags that you *know* will contain content that will change, perhaps based on certain actions that a user should be notified about. Adding `aria-live` will inform assistive technology as soon as its contents change, so users can **perceive** the change without physically seeing it.

For example, you often see messages, like the one shown in Figure 2-13 below, appear as alerts at the top of the page to let users know that an action has succeeded or failed.

Figure 2-13. *A green status banner with the text "Success: This details success information." The component is typically used to reflect either a positive or negative response to a user action.*

However, a blind user will often be listening to, or interacting with, another part of the page when this happens and so will often be unaware of the status change. With this tag in place though, a screen reader will interrupt the content a user is listening to in order to inform them of the change:

```
<div aria-live="polite">
  <span>Status: Uploading</span>
</div>
```

`aria-live` accepts two values, so it's important to know which one to use depending on the content you're sharing. When the attribute is set to `polite`, a screen reader will notify the user of updates but generally does not interrupt the current task. When set to `assertive,` however, assistive technologies **immediately** notify the user, potentially clearing the speech queue of previous updates. You should aim to use the latter only when absolutely necessary.

The section's position on the page doesn't matter, only the attribute, which means that you can position it wherever you would like visually without negative a11y effects. You can also provide both positive and/or negative feedback in the same place ("Form submitted successfully" vs. "there was a problem submitting your form"), and the user will hear it immediately.

This is a very useful attribute, but it's important not to overuse it as it could lead to a very disjointed experience riddled with interruptions. It's also key to avoid applying `aria-live` to large areas of content and reserving it for small, specific, and important page changes. There's an example of this attribute being used in the practical example at inclusive.guide/examples/aria-and-headings if you'd like to try using it with a screen reader.

aria-labelledby

Earlier we covered the importance of a clear heading hierarchy to make navigation for screen reader users easier. However, a header can *also* help provide a good signpost for a piece of content larger than itself. Using `aria-labelledby`, you can tie a heading to a larger section to act as its accessible description for screen readers. You can do this by matching the value of your `aria-labelledby` attribute with the ID attribute of the element you want to use to name it:

```
<section aria-labelledby="goldfish-header">
    <h2 id="goldfish-header">Everything you need to know about
    goldfish</h2>
    <p>More content here</p>
</section>
```

The result is that when a screen reader reaches the section, it will now read out something along the lines of

> "Section. Everything you need to know about goldfish"

That provides a lot more context for users who wish to navigate quickly in this way. This attribute isn't just for headings and sections either – any text can act as the accessible description for nearly any tag when using `aria-labelledby`.

Components

Let's return to our custom checkbox example from earlier, shown in Figure 2-14 below, and use what we've learned in order to make it accessible for screen readers.

Figure 2-14. *A custom checkbox that's selected and has an orange background and white cross for its active state. The label is "Remember my preferences."*

```
<span
    role="checkbox"
    aria-checked="true"
    id="checkbox-aria"
    onclick="changeCheckbox(event)"
    onKeyPress="changeCheckbox(event)"
    tabindex="0"
    aria-labelledby="checkbox-aria-label">
</span>
<label
    id="checkbox-aria-label"
    onclick="changeCheckbox()"
    onKeyPress="changeCheckbox()"
>
    Remember my preferences
</label>
```

I've highlighted the use of ARIA that we've added, but let's go through them:

- **role** – We've assigned an ARIA role of "checkbox," which will allow a screen reader to announce it as such.

- **aria-labelledby** – With this, we've tied our custom checkbox to the text in the `<label>` tag, meaning that it will be announced as a checkbox to decide whether the user wants our site to remember their preferences.

- **aria-checked** – An ARIA property that defines the state of the checkbox, which a screen reader can announce.

Now our checkbox is more accessible than it was, thanks to us providing more context to the accessibility tree, and therefore, the screen reader and the user. It will still require extra code though – JavaScript will be required to notice when a user interacts with the checkbox in order to change the state of the `aria-checked` value so that screen readers can announce that the user's change has been applied. As a result, it's again worth considering whether the customization in style is worth the extra effort to keep your components inclusive for everyone to use. At least now, you know how to.

Checkboxes are of course not the only custom components we see on the Web. The W3C maintains examples of other common components that websites tend to utilize in order to showcase how they can be made more accessible, which I will link to in the reading list of this chapter at `inclusive.guide/reading/chapter2`. You will also find this custom checkbox, along with a custom slider component, in the "ARIA and Headings" practical example at `inclusive.guide/examples/aria-and-headings`. Hopefully, this collection of examples will help you moving forward.

Support and Testing

Every role in ARIA is generally well supported across modern browsers, and when they aren't, they don't pose any harm to a website's layout – they're simply ignored. This means that, when added correctly, they take only a few moments to implement and have no downside. Due to the ever-changing nature of sites on the Web though, you may find that ARIA attributes you've added become incorrect or less helpful as your content changes and others on your teams make changes without realizing the consequences. Don't worry though if you end up using an ARIA attribute incorrectly, it will be picked up by tools when you test a page, which we'll get into in Chapter 11 "Tools and Auditing."

Conclusion

Hopefully, the areas we have covered here will have helped you to understand more about how blind users use the Internet. At the end of each chapter, I will encourage you to do one thing: try the solutions out for yourself. As I mentioned in the introduction to this chapter, blindness is unique among the disabilities we will cover because there is one main tool used by most users to engage with a website, and a version of that tool is available on every major operating system for free. This makes engaging with the technology, and interacting with the Web the way a blind user does, very easy to achieve. Indeed, 77.8% of screen reader users see free or low-cost screen readers as viable alternatives to commercial screen readers, which shows the high level of usage these free versions have. We'll cover a range of different screen readers in Chapter 11 "Tools and Auditing."

In the meantime, UI Engineer Sara Soueidan has written an incredibly thorough setup guide for installing and setting up screen reader software on a range of platforms and devices. I'd encourage you to follow the steps so you can start to take what you've learned here and see it in action as you make your site more accessible. You can find it at `inclusive.guide/reading/chapter2`.

Testing with a screen reader can be a shock at first. It's a completely new way of navigating the Web and requires complete concentration (when you only receive audio information, distractions like phone calls can cause you to completely lose your place). Despite this, I encourage you to put yourself in the same position as your users – perhaps seek some screen reader training, or spend a bit of time with a screen reader user. At the very least, you should go to some of the sites that you use most regularly and see how screen reader friendly they are.

The secret here is little and often. The more you practice using a screen reader, the less daunting they become to test with. Through practice, you should also experience for yourself some of the main barriers we've covered and be motivated to make sure that they can **perceive**, **navigate**, and **interact** with everything on your site.

We certainly haven't covered every corner and caveat of this topic, but you've now had your first taste of approaching web content from a truly different perspective and engaging with the challenges that can bring. Even though you might not know every solution, you will now be able to spot and fix large and common problems in this area and think consciously about what you can do to help empower and include blind users.

CHAPTER 3

Low Vision and Color Blindness

We've covered a lot of work on accessibility for blind users, but the vast majority of users with sight-based access needs actually have other forms of visual impairment. The World Health Organization estimates that at least **2.2 billion** people globally have a near or distance vision impairment, and in at least 1 billion cases, this impairment has yet to be addressed.[1] There are an estimated **39 million** people living with blindness in the world, but over **250 million** people with low vision (significant visual impairment even after treatment) – **86%** of all significant visual impairments.[2] These impairments interfere with a person's ability to perform everyday activities, including using the Web.[3]

The figures are so large because there are many different variants of visual impairment with many different causes, and this means it's something you really need to consider when building and maintaining your websites. In this chapter, we will continue with our functional, disability-driven approach – focusing on these users' various access needs, the barriers they face, and what you can do to help them.

First though, let's begin with the obvious: not everyone sees in the same way. A famous example of this was "the dress." As shown in Figure 3-1, it was an argument that gripped the Internet.

© Ashley Firth 2024
A. Firth, *Practical Web Accessibility*, https://doi.org/10.1007/979-8-8688-0152-5_3

Figure 3-1. *A photograph of "the dress" – an image that became a viral Internet sensation when viewers disagreed over whether it was colored blue and black or white and gold (it was blue and black)*

This image prompted endless debates online and caused members of the scientific community to investigate the photo for fresh insights into color vision. Now, the confusion wasn't caused by a form of visual impairment, but what it did was turn mainstream attention toward the idea that people can view the same image in *different* ways. It gave many people (myself included) who saw the dress as yellow and gold a direct insight into what it's like to view content differently from the way it appears to others (it was eventually revealed that the dress was black and blue).[4]

Visual impairments present a wide range of challenges to both those who use websites and those who make them, and this chapter will draw attention to five main areas of them that you should keep in mind:

- **Clarity or acuity** – Many users experience problems with the clarity of their vision, which means it can be foggy, blurred, or unclear.

- **Impaired contrast sensitivity** – Those with conditions such as diabetes and diabetic retinopathy have problems perceiving content with a low contrast between foreground and background colors.[5]

- **Field of vision** – Many users experience impairments that restrict certain parts of their field of view (e.g., glaucoma leads to peripheral vision loss, and macular degeneration leads to central vision loss).

- **Perceiving color** – People with various types of color blindness, for example, often have no problem with visual acuity or their field of vision but can miss out when designs rely on color to convey meaning.

- **Light sensitivity** – Users with conditions such as albinism, as well as those with eye injuries or inflammation, can experience "photophobia" and find it extremely difficult to work with bright screens and bright content.

In order to cater to these impairments effectively, there are two main themes that underpin this chapter. First, we'll look at how to provide a strong accessible foundation for all users with low vision. By tackling this, you'll see that there are a plethora of design choices that will, for example, make text clearer, contrast better, and feature less color-dependent for these users. This, in turn, will also help ensure a base level of accessibility for *everyone*.

The second thing you can do to dramatically improve accessibility – our second theme – is to allow a degree of customization. Because there are so many types and combinations of visual impairment, sometimes there is simply not a one-size-fits-all solution for users. Low vision is one of the rare areas of accessibility where fixing one barrier can actually *create* another for a different user. The solution, as we shall see, is to facilitate a degree of customization – enabling users to make choices that, with the help of your site, allow them to navigate in their own way and create their own solution.

Accessible Text

Let's begin with text, as it forms the vast majority of every site on the Internet. Having a sensible base font size can help relieve a source of ongoing pain for users. To do so, we first need to learn about the "pixel."

A pixel (written as "px" in code) is a unit of measurement, created specifically to be used on the Web. Although there are many different measurement options available when making sites, pixels became popular because they offered a degree of consistency. Rather than trying to deal with inches, centimeters, points, and picas that people had used before the Web, people began using pixels as standard. The W3C once described it as the "magic" unit when it was released because users could treat **one pixel in code as one pixel on a screen**.[6]

Through this, everyone knew what size things would be, and that size would be the same in every browser your website was viewed in. Figure 3-2 shows a title, sized using pixels, that will display as 16px in size regardless of where you viewed it.

This is a 16px title

Size: 16px

Figure 3-2. *A 16px title, with the size labeled underneath it*

And so everyone began to use pixels for everything, and they never stopped. As of 2022, the Web Almanac found that **71%** of all web pages used pixels for font sizing, which had risen **2%** from the year before.[7]

Relative Units

However, even when W3C introduced the pixel, they didn't recommend using it for *text*. Instead, they recommended using "rem" or "em" units. These are known as "ephemeral units," – units whose sizes are relative to the default font size of the **device** or **browser** that content is viewed on. For example, one "em" is equal to 100% of that default font size, so if you have a browser with a base font size set to 16 pixels, then 1 "em" would equal 16 pixels. Two ems would then be 32 pixels, as it's 200% of that base size, and so forth. By doing this, you can ensure that your text size is, at the very least, a reflection of what a user has decided is appropriate.

This point is really important. Most modern desktop browsers now have the same default base font size of 16 pixels (about the same size as text printed in a book, accounting for reading distance),[8] which would be the "root" size that ems or rems would take into account. What's important is that this number can be **changed by the user** (e.g., by changing their browser or mobile device font size), and by using relative units, your sites can adapt to that user's decision *automatically* – something pixels simply can't do.

Let's use our title example from earlier to show the difference. As shown in Figure 3-3, here are two titles, one using pixels and the other using ems, where the user's default font size is set to 16 pixels. Here it is reflected in code:

```
.pixel {
    font-size: 16px;
}
.em {
    font-size: 1em;
}
```

User's default font size: 16px

This is a 16px title
Size: 16px

This is a 1em title
Size: 16px

Figure 3-3. *Two titles both sized at 16 pixels, one created in pixels and the other using relative units (ems)*

In Figure 3-3, the two titles, one set in px and one in em, are the same size. However, if the user decided to *increase* their base font size to 20 pixels to make content easier for them to read, based on the same code as earlier, the two titles would start to display *differently* as shown in Figure 3-4.

User's default font size: 20px

This is a 16px title

Size: 16px

This is a 1em title

Size: 20px

Figure 3-4. *A title sized at 16 pixels that hasn't scaled with an increase in a user's font settings and a title now sized at 20 pixels using ems that has*

The "em" sizing has factored in the user's preference and altered its size, but the pixel layout was completely unaffected by the user's choice. So, it's clearly more useful for those with access needs that text is sized in websites using **relative** units, as opposed to fixed ones. Despite their flexibility and usefulness though, relative units are used in less than a quarter of sites (**15%** for em and **6%** for rem).[9]

Stop Using Pixels

Because pixels have absolute size, they don't scale in response to user preferences. Setting text in pixels means that it will ignore *any* type of user preference set on a device or browser. If the user's browser has a default font size of 16px and you set some text on your website to be 14px, it will display as 14px. If the user's mobile device has a default font size of 18px, it will *still* display as 14px. If the user has chosen to increase the default text size on that device to 20px, it will ***still*** display as 14px. Using pixels ignores all of it.

This lack of flexibility applies to all font changes, not just increases:

> Some people need larger text in order to perceive letters. Although increasing size is most common, some people with tunnel vision and good visual acuity may prefer smaller letters so they can see more words at a time.[10]

Either way, using pixels for text sizing would clobber every change someone attempts to make through their device settings, leaving them to resort to the more manual task of zooming (which we'll get to) or just leaving your site altogether, which people genuinely do when they find your site to be inaccessible or unusable. WCAG states that users should be able to "change the text size (font size) of all text, without zooming the entire interface".[11] If you're setting all of your font sizes in pixels, you're not catering to this user need. Try changing your device or browser's font size and navigating to your site. If you don't see a change, it's time to start using relative units!

As a quick note in case you were wondering: the base font size of devices and browsers being set in pixels is OK – it's *websites* that need to ensure that they're setting sizes relative to that root size rather than their own explicit pixel values.

Screen Sizes

Now that hardware is changing and pixel densities are growing, pixels are struggling to find relevance as the stable unit they once were.[12]

Back when the W3C was referring to the pixel as the "magic" unit, people were told to think of one pixel in code as one on the screen. Although this may have been true many years ago, screens have advanced *significantly*, and pixels have not. The truth is: **pixels in code are no longer equivalent to real screen-size pixels** and haven't been for a while.

There is now a much wider variety of devices, resolutions, and display ratios available. The idea initially put forward to simplify things with pixels has now done the opposite – it's set a bad rule that people continue to follow. As such, you'll see devices with high pixel density display a page significantly smaller than it's shown on a desktop browser if the sizes are set in pixels because explicitly defined sizes simply will not adapt to larger screen resolutions.

The result of these two points is this: pixels don't make sense as a stable unit of measurement on the Web anymore. Once again I'd highly recommend using relative units instead, as they give users the freedom to adapt your content to best suit the way they enjoy browsing the Web.

Raise Your Base Font Size

With all of that in mind, our first task is to ensure that the standard font on our sites is a good size, meaning that many users may not need to resort to resizing.

It's fair to say that not everyone knows how to change their browser's font size, let alone do it on their mobile device, tablet, or any other device they happen to own. Yet these people would often benefit *most* from a change in font size – older people, for example, have naturally degraded sight, but also lower than average tech literacy.[13]

If the process of transforming your whole site from using pixels to relative units such as em or rem in one go is too much, a good first step is simply increasing the font size you're currently displaying if it's below the **16-pixel benchmark** most research deems to be a reasonable reading size. If you set this as your base font size, you can make it easier for most people to read it.

Indeed, research conducted by Google and IBM showed a marked increase in reading speed and ease of reading as font sizes on pages increased, so increasing this value on any existing site is a great quick win.[14]

Line Height

Line height is the vertical space between two lines of text. Specifically, it's the exact distance between two adjacent baselines, and it can be *just* as important as font sizing. Imagine trying to read multiple lines of text where each line blurs and overlaps with the text below and above it? It would require an unnecessary amount of extra concentration.

To give just one example, a study about typography and accessibility noted that "Increased line height did significantly reduce the error rate for simulated macular degeneration (central vision loss)."[15] Most users will immediately notice that there's something wrong with your text, even if they can't put their finger on what it is.

Line height is usually best defined as a percentage of the font's size in order to ensure readability,[16] with somewhere between **140%** and **180%** being optimal for accessibility – WCAG sits neatly between this bracket, suggesting **150%** at least (1.4.12: Text Spacing).[17]

Remember, you need to set line height using *relative* units like em or rem for the same reasons we discussed with font sizes – if the font size on your site was increased through a user's change in settings but the line height was set as a fixed pixel size, lines of text would start overlapping with each other, and it would render the text completely unreadable. For example, Figure 3-5 shows some text where the font has been increased to twice its original size through user settings but where a line height was set explicitly with pixels that therefore didn't scale.

"Space is big. You just won't believe how vastly, hugely, mind-bogglingly, big it is. I mean, you may think it's a long way down the road to the chemist's, but that's just peanuts to space.

Figure 3-5. *Text on multiple lines overlapping with one another, due to having a font size much bigger than its line height. This makes the text unreadable.*

Instead, we should use the em unit again but set it to be a percentage greater than the font size:

```
body {
    font-size: 1em;
    line-height: 1.5em;
}
```

Using the preceding code, if a user's default font was set to **16px**, their font size would be **16px** (as we mentioned previously, one em unit is equal to the base font size of a browser or device by default, so in this scenario 1em = 16px), and their line height would be **24px** (150% of the default 16-pixel font size). However, if a user increased their default font to **20px**, their font size would be **20px**, and their line height would be **30px**. It's worth noting that, by default, browsers set a line height value between **110%** and **120%** of any text size, which ensures a certain degree of readability. Like many aspects of styling a website (including text size), the accessibility issues occur when we set our own values that aren't adaptive or inclusive. For this reason, it's worth considering if you need to alter the line height of your text *at all*. If you do, lean toward bigger rather than smaller.

Word and Letter Spacing

The spacing between your letters and words is usually less of an issue than font size or line height, as they're handled by default by the font that you choose and aren't edited as often (although they can be edited using the word-spacing and letter-spacing CSS properties).[18] On the word spacing front, it's most important to avoid aligning text in a "justified" style. This is a styling option that involves stretching each line so that it reaches both edges of the space it's been given, rather than having the same sized space between each word, and then letting words that won't fit on the line wrap on to the next one. The difference is shown by the blocks of text in Figure 3-6, with left-aligned text shown in the left block and justified text on the right.

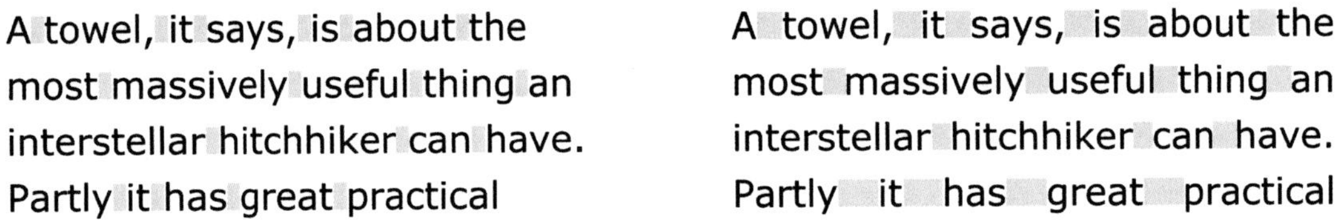

A towel, it says, is about the   A towel, it says, is about the
most massively useful thing an   most massively useful thing an
interstellar hitchhiker can have.   interstellar hitchhiker can have.
Partly it has great practical   Partly   it   has   great   practical

Figure 3-6. *Left-aligned (pictured left) and justified text (pictured right) side by side, showing the inconsistent spacing between words that the latter causes. The spaces are highlighted in yellow.*

Justified text looks neat when viewed as a whole, but it creates different sized spaces between every word and between certain characters on every line of text. Having no consistent gap between these makes it more challenging for users to read, as it can force the reader's eyes to "jump" between words when reading, in a way that isn't required with left-aligned text. With left-aligned text being the most common way to lay out text, and the way text is presented on the Web by default, justified text introduces additional friction for users when reading that doesn't provide an upside. Because of this, text aligned to the left (shown on the left in the preceding figure) has been proven to be easier to read.[19]

This becomes a more serious issue when using assistive technologies though. Many people with vision disabilities use screen magnifiers or enlarge web content by "zooming in" on the page (which we'll go into more detail about soon). This creates a smaller **field of vision** that, if text is justified, means these users may see large, empty spaces between (or within) words when reading a sentence, indicating the sentence has finished abruptly. They may also see words run together in a confusing mess of characters.

For this reason, the W3C published a supplemental guide, outside of their rules, to inform people about justified text. It warns about the impacts on readability and tracking as we've covered, but also that "the problems with full justification are usually much worse when users increase the text size".[20] They also mention avoiding justified text in their WCAG rule on Visual Presentation (1.4.8).[21]

Justification may seem harmless based on how *you* read content, but it can be a barrier in many circumstances.

Font Choice

The final takeaway, and perhaps the easiest, is that you are less likely to run into issues of readability if you've chosen a "commonly" used font – a font available in all modern operating systems. Users can become accustomed to reading text in certain styles after being exposed to them on many different sites and in popular word processing software like Microsoft Word and Google Docs. For use online, Sans Serif fonts are generally used as they are easier to view on a screen, whereas Serif fonts are better suited for printed mediums on paper.

Here is a list of some widely available, and therefore commonly used, fonts that have scored well for accessibility and readability in research:

- Arial
- Georgia
- Tahoma
- Times New Roman
- Helvetica
- Verdana[22]

This is not an exhaustive list of the fonts you can use. Instead, it's a good chance to assess the fonts you're using on your sites, along with *how* you're using them. Doing so can improve the readability and experience for everyone, but especially those with visual impairments, learning difficulties, and dyslexia and those who suffer from migraines. Here's a good list of things to consider:

- Use simple and familiar fonts (like those listed earlier).
- Limit how many fonts and font variations you use (one for headings and one for body text is usually sensible).
- Avoid blocks of text in *italics*.
- Avoid using all UPPERCASE letters in text.
- Try to use **bold** sparingly.
- Ensure characters in the font look distinct from one another.

The last point is important because when certain characters look similar, the brain has to work harder to distinguish between them. This affects reading speed and general comprehension. Some font families use practically identical letter shapes for different characters. An example is Figure 3-7, which shows this problem in the Gill Sans font. The uppercase "I" character, lowercase "l" character, and the number "1" look the exact same next to one another.

I l I   **I l 1**

Gill Sans   **Verdana**

Figure 3-7. *A comparison of the Gill Sans and Verdana fonts, through how they render the uppercase "I" character, lowercase "l" character, and number 1. The former (pictured left) displays all characters nearly identically, whereas in Verdana (pictured right), all three look unique.*

Try this quick test with your site's font and see what happens!

Custom Fonts

It's estimated that there are over 200,000 fonts available online for use on websites, and that is a *lot* of variety. Now there is nothing wrong with experimenting with different typefaces; it's just important to consider other factors beyond whether it looks nice aesthetically.

Having a custom font for your headers, for example, can add a unique dimension to a brand or page design, but adding that same font to the main body of text can throw up barriers that simply don't need to be there. Indeed, many typefaces are made for the sole purpose of being used for headlines and titles, so using them for general text would throw up avoidable issues.

Accessibility-Specific Fonts

One challenge that may come up when selecting fonts is the fact that an option that could be easier for *some* people to perceive may be *more* difficult for others. For example, the simplicity of one font may improve the readability of text for a user with a visual impairment, while a user with dyslexia may find the characters difficult to tell apart.

There are some fonts that have been designed *specifically* for that reason, such as OpenDyslexic and Dyslexie. These fonts feature bold lowercase characters and wider letter spacing to help make the text easier to read and interpret – an example where using a custom font could actually benefit users. You can check them out in this chapter's reading list at `inclusive.guide/reading/chapter3`.

Research has found that common options such as Arial, Helvetica, Open Sans, and Verdana are also solid choices compared to fonts like these though, so overall when it comes to site text, keep it simple!

Contrast Ratio

Contrast is the difference in luminance (the intensity of light emitted from a surface) between two adjacent or overlaid colors. For online accessibility purposes, it's the difference between the color of your text and the color of the background it's shown on. By comparing the difference in luminance (brightness) between these two colors, you can work out a contrast ratio. The more dramatic this contrast is, the easier it will be for most users to perceive that content. On the Web, this ratio ranges from **1:1** (white text on a white background) to **21:1** (black text on a white background).

Strong contrast is incredibly useful for everyone but particularly helps people with impaired **contrast sensitivity**, which includes some users with cognitive impairments, and many types of low vision: from those with **visual acuity** impairments like cataracts to **field of vision** issues, like macular degeneration and glaucoma, to those with color blindness.[23]

Contrast issues can be tricky to spot sometimes, especially if you've been designing for, or working with, a certain brand or color scheme for any length of time. Luckily, contrast levels are easy to test, and there is a widely accepted benchmark for what is accessible. For regular site text, WCAG states that the contrast ratio between foreground and background colors should be at least **4.5:1** for AA compliance (1.4.3 Contrast (Minimum)), and **7:1** to be AAA compliant (1.4.6 Contrast (Enhanced)).[24] A low contrast ratio means that users have trouble reading your content, particularly if it's a large body of text. Consider these three levels of contrast for the standard text size of 16 pixels shown in Figure 3-8: failing (3:1), AA compliant (4.5:1), and AAA compliant (7:1).

3:1

"Time is an illusion. Lunchtime doubly so."

4.5:1

"Time is an illusion. Lunchtime doubly so."

7:1

"Time is an illusion. Lunchtime doubly so."

Figure 3-8. *Three examples of text and background color contrast levels – the first is a failing level (pictured top), the next is AA compliant (pictured middle), and the last is AAA compliant (pictured bottom). The text reads "Time is an illusion. Lunchtime doubly so".*

Just like font size, accessibility here is also tied to the size of text, so it's important to consider both. For example, larger text requires a slightly lower minimum contrast ratio to be accessible – a **3:1** ratio instead of **4.5:1**. Large text is defined as *at least* 14 point (typically 18.66px) and bold or 18 point (typically 24px).[25]

Despite the ease with which we can test, low contrast text (lower than the WCAG AA threshold of 4.5:1) was found on **83.6%** of the one million most popular website's home pages, making it the most commonly detected accessibility issue. On average, each home page had over *30* distinct instances of low contrast text.[26] More broadly, less than **23%** of *all* websites on the Internet today actually pass automated contrast checks.[27]

It's important to walk the line between maintaining the aesthetics of a design or brand that you've created, while also not compromising the content or experience for those with visual impairments. In this scenario, the two following points are worth thinking about.

Good Contrast Helps Users *Without* Visual Impairments

As we've said before, if you design for users with a specific access need, you almost always end up benefiting all users. Situational barriers like users who suffer from migraines, those trying to read content with a glare on their screen, or even those who are very tired will all benefit from a stronger contrast ratio. As we get older and our vision starts to naturally deteriorate, this consideration becomes all the more valuable. Accordingly, having a low contrast ratio will negatively impact *all* your users.

As the contrast between text and foreground increases, so too does the ease at which *anyone* can read it. For that reason, it's worth noting that the contrast ratios earlier are merely the *minimum* contrast that you should aim for – having a contrast level over 7:1 is not only completely possible but good news!

Testing

As I mentioned, contrast ratio accessibility is especially easy to test for. This is covered at length in Chapter 11 "Tools and Auditing" when you're ready to test your sites. For a first test though, I'd recommend putting your brand colors into WebAIM's online color contrast checker. It can tell you instantly whether your colors pass WCAG checks at all levels and lets you try small adjustments to see whether you can tweak them to make them accessible. You can find the tool at webaim.org/resources/contrastchecker.

You Could Always Offer a Change

One approach that requires work but can have brilliant results is allowing for **customization** within your design. This way you don't end up alienating your users for the sake of design but can still maintain your brand. This can be especially useful because

> there may not be one solution that fits [with] regards to visually impaired users. Accommodations for the needs of one user may work against the needs of another user.[28]

For example, we've spoken about the benefits of having a high contrast ratio, but because contrast relies on levels of light, people who suffer from **photophobia** (light sensitivity) can feel discomfort or pain from clashing bright colors.[29]

The W3C (who wrote WCAG) has attempted to address these contradictions. Their findings, and their suggestions, are somewhat vague though. They state the importance of providing high contrast for legibility and recognize there can be situations where, for example, a user can both require high contrast to engage with content and simultaneously experience photophobia. They encourage offering customization as a solution, but when explaining what shape that customization should take, they suggest

> Any strategy for remediation of the functional limitations caused
> by low vision must employ a multi-treatment approach to address
> sets of functional limitations that have contradictory treatments
> when addressed singularly.[30]

Got that? Me neither.

Thankfully, steps can be taken to reconcile these different access needs. In this case, accessibility is preserved by offering users a choice and control over their experience.

I once tackled this issue on a project I was working on. When speaking to customers who had low vision (and some who had dyslexia too), many mentioned that they didn't enjoy reading the regular communications that we emailed them. The typical design style for this project was white text on a dark blue background. Now although this color scheme passed AAA WCAG standards for contrast ratio, customers had reported trouble reading or focusing on the content. This was contradictory to our research about darker color schemes being easier to read, but it was proof that no one color scheme will work for everyone.

It's also another example of a website being WCAG compliant, but still not fully addressing the access needs of users – customers were still having trouble engaging with our content, so we had to make a decision.

The line of thinking we took was this: These emails were being sent to customers regularly, asking *them* to either engage with their content or perform an action. It was also content going to *their* inbox for only them to view.

Our solution was to allow each customer to invert the colors of the communications they were receiving, meaning they could choose an alternative option of dark text on a light background. The contrast levels between the two were essentially identical, but the former created a barrier that wasn't there in the latter. More importantly, it helped them engage with the communications more freely. Figure 3-9 shows an example of an email we send our customers in both light and dark mode.

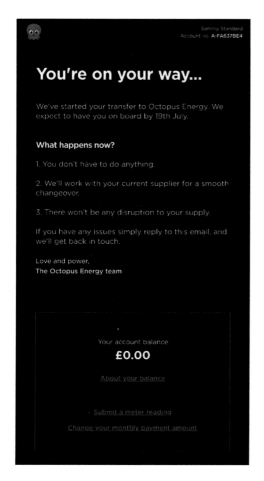
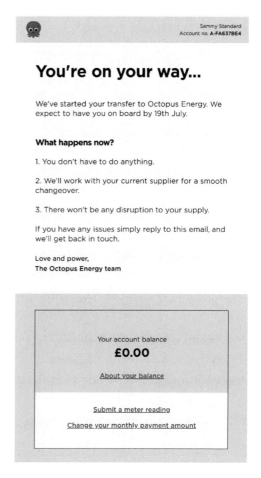

Figure 3-9. *Two examples of the same customer communication: one with the standard color scheme of light text on a dark background and the other with an inverted color scheme of dark text on a light background*

The feedback was hugely positive, and we've since had many users without low vision enable the mode simply because they preferred receiving their content in that style. It also resulted in more users engaging with our emails and performing the actions we needed them to. Now, although customization to increase accessibility is good, your regular brand should still have WCAG-compliant contrast ratios – you shouldn't use accessible alternatives as an excuse to neglect your original design.

Dark Mode

More commonly than this example, we've seen a less intense version of aversion to brightness on web pages through the rise in adoption of offering "dark modes" on websites. These optional dark themes reduce the light emitted by device screens while maintaining good contrast ratios and have become very popular.

Both Windows and Mac operating systems allow easy switching to a dark theme if users prefer it. Dark mode is also available on many of the most high-traffic sites on the Internet – from social media giants Facebook, Instagram, and X to Google's search engine, Gmail, Slack, and more. All of these examples show that the idea of customizing to meet user needs is becoming a consideration in every facet of our online lives for *everyone*, not just those with access needs.

The changes mentioned previously, and settings that provide light text on a dark background, create a strong contrast but with a *lower* level of luminance because the dominant background color becomes darker, placing the stronger white light on smaller, individual pieces of content. Users with **light sensitivity** issues (like those with albinism) or **field of vision** restraints (like those with macular degeneration) often benefit from these settings as it provides a far less light-sensitive environment while still being easy to navigate and read.

Importantly, the ability to change settings at any point allows users to adapt their experience depending on what impairments they are experiencing most strongly at the time (e.g., albinism can often have more of an impact at the beginning of the day, whereas macular degeneration is typically more prominent at the end of the day). This tracks with medical advice for all of us though. The American Academy of Ophthalmology recommends you "set devices to night or dark mode in the evening".[31] This reduces your exposure to blue light that can disrupt your sleep pattern. It's also supposed to reduce eye strain and has been linked to reducing headaches and migraines.[32]

We mentioned earlier that many who could benefit from a larger default font size may not know how to set one, and the same is true with color schemes. Why not avoid the risk and preemptively provide this consideration for your users in a way that's visible on your site? You can do this through adding a "theme switcher" to your site, and it's one of my personal favorite accessibility considerations. I've created a simple example of this functionality for you in the practical example for this chapter, shown in Figure 3-10 below. It is available on GitHub in the "Chapter 3" directory, and viewable at `https://inclusive.guide/examples/theme-switcher`.

Figure 3-10. *Two screenshots taken from the "theme switcher" example for this book – first of the standard theme of the page (pictured left) and the second with the inverted theme (pictured right)*

Providing a toggle on your site to allow users to switch between a light and dark theme puts the choice and control in the user's hands. It can be especially useful on pages with long-form articles or blogs that involve a lot of text and therefore a lot of time spent on your site.

For those maintaining an existing site, this may seem like a time-consuming rewrite; however, it could be a lot easier than you think. This is because CSS has a `filter` property available that can create a whole range of different visual effects on a page. One of those is the `invert` filter, which, as the name suggests, inverts the colors of any section you apply it to. Therefore, we can make use of it to provide a new color option on our website with only a few lines of code:

```
body.dark-mode {
    filter: invert(100%) hue-rotate(180deg);
}
@media (prefers-color-scheme: dark) {
    body {
        filter: invert(100%) hue-rotate(180deg);
    }
}
```

Now when the user opts to change the theme and clicks the toggle, or if they've set in their browser or device settings that they prefer dark mode, every color on the page will be immediately inverted, offering an oppositional theme with only a couple lines of styling. The `filter` property used is supported by all modern browsers, and we'll get to more queries like this in a future chapter. [33]

There are a couple of considerations when adding this functionality, all of which have been added to the practical example for you to use:

- Ensure the toggle is visible on the page in a prominent place.

- Look for whether the user has set a preference for dark mode on their browser or device, and switch to that theme by default.

- Remember any theme selection the user makes and ensure that choice remains when they reload the page, or revisit your site again.

Now, I wouldn't consider this a "robust" dark mode solution. Instead, it's more of an interim step if you intend to eventually implement a more complete one. This is because the colors may not match how you'd like your brand to be perceived in dark mode – it's simply inverting what's there. To build your own, you'll want to use the same code as the example for detecting user settings and switching between themes, but start the process of deciding how you want the *specific* elements and components of your site to look when that mode is active. For example, the following code would dictate the background color and text color when in dark mode:

```
@media (prefers-color-scheme: dark) {
    body {
    background-color: #111111;
    }

    p {
        color: #F0F0F0;
    }
}
```

Dark mode takes time to get right, but there's a great guide to all things dark mode created by CSS tricks, which I'll link to from the theme switcher example. It's also on the reading list for this chapter, which you can find at `inclusive.guide/reading/chapter3`.

Adding this feature to your site is a great opportunity for designers, developers, product managers, and business leaders to work together on an accessibility problem. It will provide an extra dimension to your site for *all* your users but also provide a tool for many to overcome barriers they may have had when engaging with your content.

High Contrast Mode

Prior to the advent of dark modes, Windows High Contrast Mode was the go-to solution for those struggling to engage with content online due to color. However it remains popular today – some recent research with users who have low vision found that it was used by **30%** of respondents, and in a talk, Melanie Richards of Microsoft mentioned that around **4%** of all active Microsoft devices use High Contrast Mode.[34] Users with **light sensitivity** or **impaired contrast sensitivity** can benefit greatly from using High Contrast Mode on their computer, as well as people in low-light environments.

This tool allows users to choose from a range of color schemes that will override the color scheme used on a web page but also allows them to create custom ones themselves. This means that they can view sites across the Web in a way they prefer to view them and enforce a consistent browsing experience where it could have otherwise been jarring or impossible when moving from site to site.

This is good news from an accessibility perspective, as it provides users with the control they deserve to dictate how your site is displayed to them – like a dark mode, but with greater control. It also means that you have to worry a little less about this subset of users. However, much like any assistive tool, I'm going to encourage you to try it out for yourself. There is almost no learning curve when using it, and by trying High Contrast Mode on your website, you'll be able to find out what becomes unclear or unusable when you radically change the contrast and branding. This may well be something you've never had to consider before, but you'd be surprised how commonly testing in this way uncovers improvements you can make for these users. Typical things I've seen are

- Images that work well on your standard color scheme but may become completely unreadable in a different contrast mode (this is also true in dark mode). A logo with dark text may work well on a light background, for example, but that won't be the case when the background is inverted.

- Form elements that don't have borders may display as text, or completely disappear, in High Contrast Mode.

- Equally, buttons that have a color background but no border tend to just look like text when that background is removed by a high contrast theme. This could make actions very difficult for users to find.

Some of these things may *only* apply when a user is in High Contrast Mode, and luckily, there is a way to only apply styles in this situation. Just like the code for applying styles when dark mode is set in a user's settings, the following CSS query allows you to specify changes for High Contrast Modes:

```
@media screen (forced-colors: active) {
    button {
        border: 4px solid;
    }
}
```

Since the first edition of this book, the CSS syntax for targeting High Contrast Mode has actually changed. With the introduction of the "Edge" Browser replacing Internet Explorer, Microsoft worked with the CSS Working Group and the Chromium project to standardize the high contrast rules so that **all** browsers could support the setting.[35] The result is the use of the preceding forced-colors: active. Here is an example of the *old* code, in case you're using it in your sites and would like to update it so that a user's high contrast settings can be respected on any browser they use:

```
@media screen and (-ms-high-contrast: active) {
    button { border: 4px solid; }
}
/* Black on white theme */
@media screen and (-ms-high-contrast: black-on-white) {
    ...
}
/* White on black theme */
@media screen and (-ms-high-contrast: white-on-black) {
    ...
}
```

You can also specify areas that *shouldn't* have their color overridden, which is handy in cases where color is important to convey something without changing, such as displaying the color of a product – a red T-shirt option shouldn't look pink, for example:

```
@media screen and (forced-colors: active) {
    .product-swatch {
        forced-color-adjust: none;
    }
}
```

Note that there is old syntax for this rule too – `-ms-high-contrast-adjust: none;` – ensure that you've switched to `forced-color-adjust: none;` anywhere you're using this.

I would avoid using this too much though, and indeed there are only so many rules you **can** apply to this media query to ensure that users retain control. Now although High Contrast Mode is not covered by WCAG, it's still used by a lot of users, so it's certainly worth testing how your site works with it.[36] If you would like to explore this area further, Smashing Magazine has an excellent guide to Windows High Contrast Mode, which you'll be able to view on the reading list for this chapter at `inclusive.guide/reading/chapter3`.

Color Blindness

Color-based barriers are especially important because they frequently exclude a specific group of visually impaired users. Color blindness (also known as color vision deficiency) is common, affecting approximately 1 in 12 men (**8%**) and 1 in 200 women in the world. Worldwide, it's estimated that 300 million people are color-blind, and in Britain, approximately **4.5%** of the entire population are.[37] Color also affects contrast ratio, and many users with low vision also experience dull colors, so this section is important for them too.

Different Types of Color Blindness

To understand color blindness, and how it affects those who have it online, you first need to understand a little about how the eye works. Your eyes' retinas contain two types of light-sensitive cells called "rods" and "cones." Rods work in low-light conditions to help your vision at night, whereas cones work in daylight and are responsible for color discrimination. Scientists believe that issues with one or more of the three cones we have in our eyes (red, blue, and green) cause color blindness.[38]

The result is a wide range of ways in which someone may perceive color on your site, so it's important to ensure that your features and color scheme work in as many scenarios as possible. There is a wide range of color blindness types, but we'll focus on two of the most common – red–green and yellow–blue confusion.

Red–Green Confusion

This is the most common, and well-known, type of color blindness.[39] Despite the name, red–green confusion doesn't necessarily mean that these people *only* confuse red and green, or can't see them. They simply have a harder time differentiating between them. They can also confuse *any* color which has some red or green as part of it (an example of this is shown in Figure 3-11 below). Within this spectrum, there are four main types of red–green confusion:

- **Deuteranopia** and **deuteranomaly** (also known as green-blind) – Reduced sensitivity to red light and missing or reduced ability to see green hues. Deuteranopes are more likely to confuse:

  - Mid-reds with mid-greens

  - Blue–greens with gray and mid-pinks

  - Bright greens with yellows

  - Pale pinks with light gray

  - Mid-reds with mid-brown

  - Light blues with lilac

- **Protanopia** and **protanomaly** – Their "L-cones" are missing or defective, and so the user cannot see reds. Protanopes are more likely to confuse:

  - Black with many shades of red

  - Dark brown with dark green, dark orange, and dark red

  - Some blues with some reds, purples, and dark pinks

  - Mid-greens with some oranges[40]

  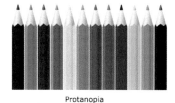

| No colour blindness | Deuteranopia | Protanopia |

Figure 3-11. *A collection of colored pencils is shown in three states. The first (pictured left) displays a full spectrum of colors, as someone without color blindness would see them. The second (pictured middle) reflects how someone with deuteranopia would see them, with pencils featuring red and green taking on a gray and brown hue, respectively. Finally, the third (pictured right) shows the same pencils from the perspective of someone with protanopia. This appears similar to deuteranopia for those without color blindness, but the blues are more pronounced, as are the browns.*

So, how does this affect how someone may use your website?

Color to Infer Status

The biggest challenge here is that red and green are commonly used to infer positive or negative messages. Take the following status messages in Figure 3-12 from a form submission, for example.

You have added an item to your basket

We couldn't add the item to your basket

Figure 3-12. *Two alerts, one positive and one negative, both where color is the primary way in which status is displayed. The top message informs the user that they have added an item to their basket and has a green background, and the bottom one tells them that the site couldn't add an item to the basket and has a red background.*

If you're able to view reds and greens correctly, you can easily make the distinction between the positive and negative messages at a glance. However, this is roughly how a user with deuteranopia would see the messages in Figure 3-13.

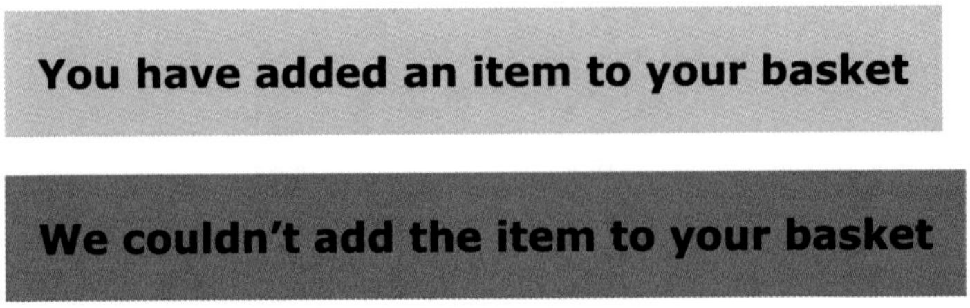

You have added an item to your basket
We couldn't add the item to your basket

Figure 3-13. *The same two alerts, but how they would be seen by someone who has deuteranopia? The lack of a clear green or red makes the alert's meaning harder to discern and the messages look similar.*

Now although someone with red-green deficiency *can* tell the difference between these colors, the quick positive (or negative) feedback users without color blindness would get just by glancing at it is lost, and suddenly the contents of the alert could be misconstrued given the similar wording (particularly if it's negative and unexpected).

Another example would be the "color swatch" mechanism on an online shop's product page. Without a text label to accompany the swatch, it becomes incredibly hard to differentiate between options, or even know which color an option actually is, for someone with color blindness. This is pictured in Figure 3-14.

Without Deuteranopia
Deuteranopia
eight Running
eight Running

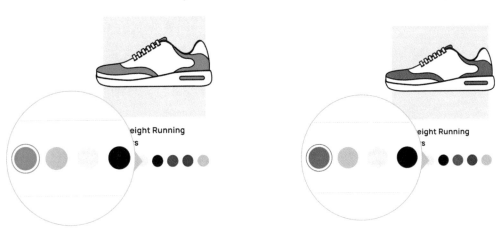

Figure 3-14. *An online shop's "product selector" widget is displayed twice. Both offer a series of color options for a running shoe but only use a small circle of color to showcase the options available. The left shows how these colors are typically perceived by someone without deuteranopia, and the right shows the same colors as someone with deuteranopia would see them. The two color swatches appear very different to someone without deuteranopia.*

Adding labels in this instance is useful for *all* users, as subtle differences in tones, such as dark colors like black and navy, can be hard for *anyone* to tell the difference between visually.

The key in both examples is to use color as a compliment and not a crutch. A reliance on color can create a hugely confusing experience for users who have difficulties *perceiving* color and sometimes result in a complete loss of contextual meaning. This makes it more important to provide additional information, such as text in our color swatch example earlier, or to elevate a color-based status with a message and/or icon. Both options provide immediate feedback to a user without relying on color. Figure 3-15 shows how that would work in our earlier alert message example.

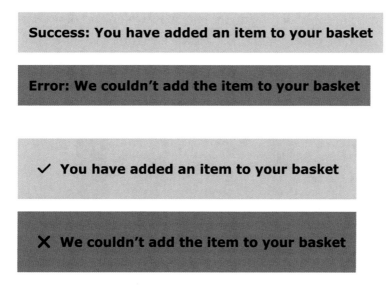

Figure 3-15. *The status messages now use either "Success" and "Error" before the alert text or a "tick" and a "cross" icon, so the meaning of the message doesn't rely on color*

Yellow–Blue Confusion

- **Tritanopia or tritanomaly** – Users have typical red and green vision but have trouble distinguishing yellow and red from pink, and blues appear greener.

Color to Distinguish Sections

The ramifications of yellow–blue confusion are worth keeping in mind, particularly for content that uses **many** colors to differentiate between content. A good example of this would be a bar chart, where color is used to differentiate between sections, and match bars up to a legend of names.

> Colour is often used to signify different segments of a graph – include adequate labelling where colours are necessary. Diagrams and infographics are common offenders.[41]

If you tested many graphs against various strains of color blindness, you'd likely have trouble determining which segment represents which part of the data, even with a legend there to provide more context. For instance, Figure 3-16 shows what a bar chart using a range of colors may look like to someone with and without tritanopia.

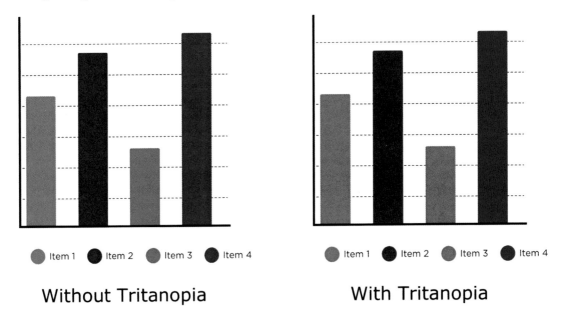

Figure 3-16. *A comparison of how a bar chart using multiple colors looks with and without tritanopia. For those without it (pictured left), the colors of the bars are clearly distinguishable. However for those with it (pictured right), items one and three look nearly identical, as do items two and four.*

Some colors don't change, but it's now much more difficult to distinguish *between* certain ones. There is a broad rule from WCAG on this, set at a fundamental level, that dictates that content cannot "rely solely on sensory characteristics of components such as shape, color, size, or sound."[42] To combat this barrier for everyone, you can again provide an additional way of differentiating between data sets rather than relying solely on color. The graph then becomes immediately more accessible. Figure 3-17 shows the same graph as earlier but with different patterns added to each bar and legend item so that they each appear unique, even without color.

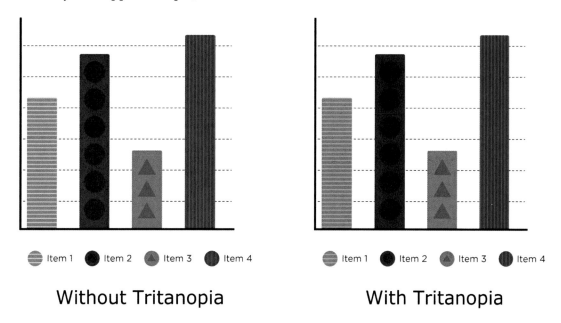

Figure 3-17. *The bar chart now uses patterns to help all users discern between the different bars and legend items without the need for color. This addition means those with and without tritanopia can engage with the content freely.*

Monochromacy

Monochromacy is the rarest and most severe form of color blindness and prevents the user from seeing anything but black, white, and shades of gray.[43] These users are worst affected when we choose to convey meaning solely through color.

> If the purpose of posting the image is to communicate something about the colours in that image, then it is important to provide some other way of understanding the information.[44]

The best example I've seen is the standard London Underground route map when you view it with and without color, shown in Figure 3-18.[45]

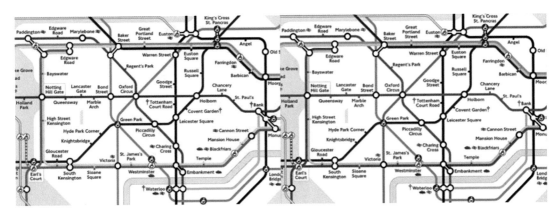

Figure 3-18. *A small piece of the London Underground map. First without a visual impairment would see it (pictured left) and then how someone with monochromacy would see that same image (pictured right).*

Here, a user with monochromacy must rely on techniques we've covered such as descriptive alt text, differentiating the different lines through patterns (such as different types of "dashed" line), annotation, or text next to the image to help them distinguish between the routes.

It's worth noting that, although this map is shown at every station in *this* format, Transport for London has created an excellent range of accessible maps to combat this and many other barriers. If you're facing a similar issue, the link to those can be found in this chapter's reading list at `inclusive.guide/reading/chapter3`.

Links

It's worth mentioning a particularly common color-related issue that impacts multiple color-blind users: links. By default, link text is underlined on a web page, making it accessible, but underlining is often removed using CSS for *aesthetic* reasons by designers, and the distinction is lost. Because of this, you **must** ensure that your links are visibly different to the rest of your text. Best practice would be keeping your underlining, but you can also make your text bold or italicized in certain situations. There is a WCAG color contrast requirement specifically for link text (**3:1** ratio – 1.4.1: Use of Color), and they also specify that the rule will be failed if you remove underlining from a link without providing another visual cue besides color.[46] Figure 3-19 shows the effect of removing underlining, where links without it often rely on color for identification.

Without Tritanopia

There is a link in this text but where?

With Tritanopia

There is a link in this text but where?

Figure 3-19. *Two sentences, both with a link in them. However, as only color is used to display the link, its presence is lost for users with tritanopia.*

Testing

My personal favorite when it comes to accessibility testing tools is a piece of software called Sim Daltonism.[47] When installed, it allows you to quickly see what people with multiple types of color blindness likely see, allowing you to test your sites *as* you're building them, and act on the insights quickly. You can head to Chapter 11 "Tools and Auditing" to read more about it, or check it out in the reading list for this chapter, which you can find at `inclusive.guide/reading/chapter3`.

The Compounding Effect of Accessibility Fixes

As with more and more examples you'll find in this book, accessible solutions you implement to solve a *specific* barrier faced by those with a *specific* disability or access need end up helping those facing completely different barriers. We're only a couple of chapters into the book, but here are a few examples of fixes we've already covered that can help those with access needs that are *different* from the ones we initially designed for:

- Those with low vision may turn to a screen reader and an image's `alt` text if what they're looking for isn't clear from the image itself. Therefore, the great `alt` text you've written for those who are blind is also helping partially sighted people.

- Strong foreground/background contrast is essential for those with low vision but also *really* helps those with color blindness if colors look similar – a strong, vibrant green will be easier for them to discern than a more muted, lower contrast tone. This could be the difference between understanding an important graph and noticing an important status message.

- Our focus on accessible and adaptive text sizing in this chapter to help those with a lack of **visual acuity** also *massively* improves the online experience of those with a limited **field of vision**. Alongside changing font size, these users also utilize zooming and magnification, which we'll get into next – both of which are easier thanks to relative units and consistent letter spacing.

It's a simple point, but one worth reiterating. When it seems overwhelming to tackle so many barriers and consider content from so many perspectives, keep in mind that making *any* change to make your site more accessible will likely open it up to more users than you know, in ways you wouldn't have perhaps considered when doing so. I'll keep raising these overlaps and compounding effects as we make our way through the book, so keep an eye out for them!

Magnification

We've seen how relative units in text sizing can help low-vision users to read text more easily, but also that *not* using them leaves them with one choice – magnifying the whole page. Magnification is used by users to increase the size of content, either by zooming in on an entire page or into a particular area. This feature is available in all major browsers, but specialist software can extend this functionality to other areas of computer use.

This has become a common part of many visually impaired users' setups because they have different needs than most other people, and having some control over how a website appears for them can be incredibly useful. Being able to "zoom" – choosing how large the features of a website appear – is a great example. It can be helpful for those with **visual acuity** problems (blurry vision) from conditions like cataracts and diabetic retinopathy, and zooming *out* can help users with glaucoma – which causes a loss of **peripheral vision**, sometimes described as being like "looking through a straw." Without zooming, content will appear at sizes many can't engage with. These barriers can similarly impact people intermittently and situationally, such as those who suffer from migraines and the natural deterioration of vision as we get older. Addressing these barriers will therefore empower a lot of other users.

So, how do we go about this? To start with, there are some typical issues that can occur when using magnification on a web page that do need to be checked and solved.

Horizontal Scrolling

When users increase the size of content in a browser and the page layout *doesn't* adjust to fit the size of the screen, that content spills over the side of the screen's viewport, forcing a user to scroll horizontally to read text, in addition to the usual vertical movement. This is shown in Figure 3-20.

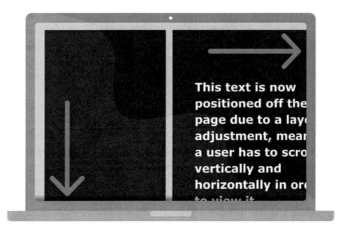

Figure 3-20. *Contents of a web page have been increased in size on a desktop. Instead of resizing, the content has simply gotten bigger, meaning that it now trails off the page both horizontally and vertically. This means the user now has to scroll in both of these directions in order to view the content.*

This is a major cause of frustration and is by far the biggest barrier associated with "unresponsive websites" – websites that don't adapt to the size of the screen, even when magnified. For this reason, WCAG has a rule called "Reflow" that states that content should be presented without "requiring scrolling in two dimensions."[48]

Let's look at what else suffers when zooming isn't accommodated on sites.

Tracking

Horizontal scrolling interferes with "tracking" – our ability to follow lines of text, including getting from the end of one line to the beginning of the next. This dictates how quickly and freely we can read content, and having a page that fails to adapt to larger content affects tracking ability immensely. Accessibility consultant Molly Watt (who has a visual impairment) explains:

> If a website layout is spread out horizontally after I zoom in, it becomes extremely exhausting to scroll across and back and forth every line to read one paragraph. I often give up with this.[49]

This turns something that is already problematic for many users *visually*, given their visual impairment, and adds to it a *physical* element that could prove exclusionary. No wonder users like Molly opt to leave the site and get their content or goods elsewhere.

Text Overflow

Horizontal scrolling is arduous, but **not being able to do it at all** is even worse. When users choose to zoom, some sites can even **cut off** text altogether based on how they're styled. This happens when sites use CSS to intentionally *prevent* horizontal scrolling. If the property overflow-x: hidden has been applied to a site, it tells the page to hide any content that may be outside of the screen's viewport on the x axis, making it impossible to scroll to it.

This has been a popular technique employed in the past to avoid *accidental* horizontal scrollbars that may have been caused by issues with a page's layout. This could be due to a piece of content that is accidentally bigger than the screen width, which in turn creates a permanent horizontal scrollbar that is visible to the user. This is an unfortunate user experience, but it is in no way worse than applying this overflow rule that hides that scrollbar *but* renders the content inaccessible to those using magnification. Have a quick search in your code base for this rule, and if you find it, I would recommend removing it and fixing the underlying layout issue instead.

Testing Zoom

To check whether this happens on your site, try using your browser to increase the zoom to **200%** (Cmd + on Mac, Ctrl + on Windows). This is what WCAG deems as the acceptable **minimum** you should allow your users to zoom to in order to be compliant (1.4.4 Resize Text).[50] What you will hopefully see is your content made twice as large, with headings and text resizing accordingly. The page layout may have shifted around a little, but the content *should* all still be on the page and only require vertical scrolling to navigate. If it is, then hooray! This site is using at least one aspect of what is needed to support users who make use of zooming – responsive web design.

Responsive Web Design

Responsive web design is an approach that aims to ensure pages adapt to users' browsing choices – as opposed to users adapting to them. This type of flexibility eliminates the horizontal scrolling issue by delivering "fluid" web page layouts, rather than a static layout with one defined size. By making your website responsive, it allows a page's content to adapt to the screen size of **any** device. Remember our example about linear layouts in the previous chapter (shown in Figure 3-21 below)?

Figure 3-21. *A representation of a linear, mobile-first design: a layout that stacks top to bottom on a mobile device (pictured left) and a more complicated layout on a bigger desktop screen (pictured right)*

This is an example of the layout of a website adapting to the size of the screen it's on, in a way that's usable everywhere. However, the *zoom* on a site should also be able to trigger this adaptation. For instance, if you zoomed in to **200%** on a desktop, you should find that the layout of a responsive site starts to resemble what it would look like on mobile without zooming (an example of this is shown in Figure 3-22 below).

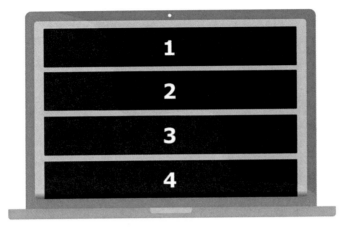

Figure 3-22. *A zoomed in website on a desktop computer. The layout now resembles what's typically seen on mobile devices due to the increased size of the content, with sections stacked on top of each other. Content still stays within the browser window and only requires vertical scrolling to view more content.*

A user may see less on the screen, but it also remains within the confines of the screen that they're using, without needing to scroll both vertically and horizontally to read it or, in the worst cases, not being able to reach it at all.

Ensuring a Responsive Layout

Ensuring your website is responsive provides optimal viewing across a wide range of devices – it adapts as neatly to a mobile or tablet as it would on a desktop. It takes the good work of relative text sizing you've learned about already and extends that flexibility to all content.

You can create a responsive site through actions like

- Setting the size of content as a **percentage** of the page rather than a fixed width or height, which could end up being too big for the screen when zoom is increased. For example, setting an image to be 50% of your page means it will always adapt regardless of screen size.

- Using "**breakpoints**" to size content and alter layouts but *only* at certain screen sizes, such as an image taking up half the width of the screen on desktop but the whole width of the screen on mobile.

- You could simply **not apply sizing at all**. Without an explicit size set, content naturally adapts to fill the space by default. It's only when we give content a fixed size that issues around overflow begin to arise.

These approaches help cater for nearly every access need that we'll cover in this book in one way or another because it prevents trapped or unusable content. For this reason, there's no good argument for a site to not be "responsive."

Thankfully, responsive web design is an area that has come a long way in the last few years. In 2015, Akamai found that only **12%** of the top 10,000 sites on the Web (based on traffic) were responsive, with that figure dropping to **10.5%** for the top 100.[51] If we look at statistics now though, **90%** of all websites are responsive, according to a study conducted by the World Economic Forum.[52] However, due to the sheer amount of sites online, many of which haven't been updated in years, it's still estimated that roughly a quarter of the most popular sites aren't responsive.[53]

It's also clear that *users* have driven this change more than anything else – **94%** of people normally judge a site based on how responsive its web design is, and Google research has estimated that **72%** of people prefer a mobile-friendly website.[54]

This is another example of accessibility needs being user needs. The proliferation of mobile devices with smaller screens has meant that *all* users began to require the ease of use that comes with a site that can adapt to smaller screen sizes or larger content – the exact same requirements that users of zoom need. A responsive website is pleasant for *everyone* to use and therefore more likely to encourage engagement with your content, or the purchasing of your goods and services.

If you're maintaining a site that isn't responsive, perhaps due to its age, I would recommend thinking about how to change that – be that through rebuilding the site or porting the content over to a new site with a responsive layout. It will undoubtedly take some effort, but the reward for doing so, in inclusivity, user trust, and revenue, will far outweigh that effort. If you'd like to read more about the basics of responsive web design, I've added a great guide by web.dev to the reading list for this chapter, which you can find at `inclusive.guide/reading/chapter3`.

Preventing Zoom

There was a dangerous notion going around a few years ago that said: if you had a responsive design, it was perfectly alright to **prevent** users from being able to zoom on that page.[55] I mean why not? You've gone to the trouble of adapting your site for all screen sizes after all, following all the preceding steps. This unfortunately meant that many sites went on to implement responsive web design but *also* to block all zooming with a variation of the following tag:

```
<meta name="viewport" content="width=device-width, initial-scale=1.0,
minimum-scale=1.0, maximum-scale=1, user-scalable=no">
```

The problematic attributes are `maximum-scale=1` and `user-scalable=no`, as both tell the browser *not* to allow the zooming of content. I initially wrote about this years ago, and unfortunately, the problem has failed to go away. According to data from the HTTP Archive Web Almanac, **23%** of desktop home pages and **28%** of mobile home pages attempt to disable zoom.[56] The problem becomes even worse when you look at the one thousand most visited sites, where **21%** of desktop sites and **40%** of mobile sites are using code to prevent user zoom.[57]

This is the embodiment of the two themes we discussed earlier and why allowing custom magnification is still important even *after* you've implemented accessible features: making your site responsive provides a good base level of accessibility that will help users with a range of barriers, but it in no way *guarantees* that you've solved all access problems for every person. You must still allow users a degree of control over their experience on your site – in this case, the option to zoom.

For this reason, if you spot this tag in any site that you work on, I'd recommend removing it; you simply can't guess what users want to do, and they may be viewing your site on a device that you've never tested. If you use the following version of the same `<meta>` tag, you'll ensure that zooming on your site is possible:

```
<meta name="viewport" content="width=device-width, initial-scale=1">
```

In my experience, many sites likely have this troublesome tag and are simply unaware of it, so here's a reminder that you should check! Luckily, browsers like Safari are now beginning to ignore `maximum-scale=1` and `user-scalable=no` attributes, but not all browsers do. It's time we stop disabling a very useful feature by default. Nobody can be *that* confident their layout works for everyone.

Point of Regard

There are a handful of other things you can do to help users once they *have* zoomed in. The "point of regard" or "focus area" is the area of a screen that a user is focusing on. If a user has a low **field of vision** and needs to zoom in order to view content, that point of regard becomes focused on a much smaller area. If an action then *alters* that point of regard, but only temporarily, it can cause the user to lose their place on the page and become confused and frustrated.

A good example of this is content that only appears when you **hover** over a certain area. Imagine you were zoomed in and hovered over an acronym to view its meaning. If the pop-up that appeared was bigger than the view you currently had (due to zooming), you would then have to scroll to read the new content. However, because the content *only* appears on hover, as you scroll, the mouse ceases to hover over the acronym, and so the content disappears. Another example would be trying to fill in a form where the question being asked is on the very left, the input field is beneath, and the submit button is on the far right – when "zoomed in," the user will struggle to locate the button.

To combat this, try and avoid interactions that rely solely on hovering. You could show content to the user with a click, tap, or toggle, as these states require an **action** to dismiss them as well as initiate them. This means the user will be able to scroll to view content without it disappearing as their focus shifts.

Navigation

Given the wide range of visual impairments, the ways in which people with low vision navigate a site are incredibly varied.[58] Nevertheless, there are a few things you can do to make navigation easier for a large portion of users, especially people with impaired **visual acuity** who have opted to use large text and so have room for little else in their field of view. Responsive web design allows content to adapt to a smaller screen size, but this reordering could accidentally isolate some content. You should therefore ensure that you place related information close together and place common features like menus in **consistent positions** to ensure that finding and understanding them is easy. In most cases, it is best if you also make sure that the following is true:

- Feedback is in close proximity to the user's visual focus (i.e., form validation next to the form itself rather than, for instance, at the top of a page).

- Dialog boxes and pop-up messages appear within the user's point of regard (close to where the user opens them from).

- Users are informed of new information that may be outside of their view – such as a new browser tab opening in the background or an alert message in response to an action.

Once again, these solutions help remove barriers in another area of accessibility – they are very similar to those we suggested in the last chapter to help blind users navigate mobile sites (see Chapter 2 "Blindness").

Conclusion

Contrary to the previous chapter, where we had a single assistive technology that we could cater to in order to overcome barriers for most users, the sheer range of visual impairments we've covered here means that simply isn't possible. This is an equally important lesson to learn about accessibility though – there is usually no "one-size-fits-all" solution. It's very likely that users are seeing your site from *thousands* of different perspectives, and the reality is that you won't be able to find a single color scheme or content layout that works for everyone.

Because of this, it's important that we're diligent in checking the effects of what we're building and constantly asking questions we're perhaps not used to asking during the process of building or maintaining a website: Questions like "if I take color away from this, does it still make sense?" and "if I view this content zoomed at 400%, will it even be possible to engage with it?"

This can feel like a tall order at times, but this certainly doesn't mean there isn't hope for accessibility. We've now covered some of the biggest barriers those with low vision and color blindness face, and just by considering these questions, you're already contributing toward a more accessible web. By instilling accessible solutions to as many barriers as you can and by providing users with the tools to customize their web experience to suit their needs, you will have ensured that your site caters to its users and not the other way around.

CHAPTER 4

Motor Impairments

People with motor impairments generally experience a partial or total loss of function of a body part and can be affected by chronic pain, muscle weakness, lack of muscle control, or paralysis.[1] These impairments impact **millions** of people, but there has been very little research into the exact number. Microsoft commissioned the last major study and found that roughly **7%** of working-age adults have a severe dexterity difficulty that would likely force them to seek alternative methods for navigating the Web.[2] The total now is almost certainly more.

Motor impairments can have many medical causes, from physical trauma like spine injuries or amputations to neurological and nervous disorders like strokes, multiple sclerosis, cerebral palsy, Parkinson's, and motor neuron disease. The result is often a need to engage with content online in a *fundamentally* different way – changing everything from how they **navigate** pages to how they **interact** with content. It's our job to make that as easy as possible.

People typically recognize the keyboard and mouse combination as the "common" form of interaction with a computer, but the creation of the first mouse came *long* after that of the first computer. In their inception, computers had no mouse. Instead, all interactions were achieved solely through a keyboard – the **exact** way that many users with motor impairments interact today.

Given that a keyboard-only interface was the first method of interacting with computers, it's disappointing that today many websites don't support keyboard-only interaction as well as they should. We'll start this chapter by looking at how you can identify this problem and then discuss how to fix it.

However, we're now at a point when a user is nearly **twice** as likely to visit your site on a mobile device compared to a desktop.[3] Touch screens condense all external input sources such as the keyboard or mouse into one interface that accepts multiple forms of interaction. This increases the importance of tackling barriers faced by users whose setups are based on "pointer-based" interaction, which includes touchscreens and mice but also joysticks, head wands, and more.

© Ashley Firth 2024
A. Firth, *Practical Web Accessibility*, https://doi.org/10.1007/979-8-8688-0152-5_4

From physical interactions to vocal ones, we'll also cover voice-to-text software (also known as dictation software), which offers users the ability to make their *voice* the primary source of input for their device. We will also look at helping users who, like the late Stephen Hawking, travel the Web using a single switch. We will then finish by examining some solutions that remove barriers for **all** motor-impaired users. Let's begin.

Keyboard-Only Navigation

Have you ever tried using a website without a mouse? It's harder than you might think, particularly when trying to perform a number of actions across multiple pages. Some users that have motor disabilities often *only* use a keyboard to interact with a computer: this includes amputees, many users with Parkinson's disease, which affects roughly **ten million** people worldwide,[4] and some of the **5%** of the population worldwide who experience tremors.[5]

The most common method of keyboard-only navigation relies on the Tab key, which moves the user sequentially between elements on a page that can be **focused** on and **interacted** with. Every native element that requires user input in some form, such as a link, button, and form field, can be "tabbed" to. This is shown in Figure 4-1.

Figure 4-1. *A visual representation of how focus should move between interactive elements on a page when the user hits the "Tab" key (pictured top right). The arrows show how the focus moves: shifting between form fields from top to bottom and finishing on the button at the end of the page.*

When an item is tabbed to, it has keyboard "focus" and can be activated or manipulated with the keyboard. Depending on the element, the action itself is handled in different ways:

- A button can be "clicked" using the Enter or Spacebar keys.

- A link can be "clicked" using the Enter key.

- Radio buttons or drop-down options can be moved between using the arrow keys.

One of the most crucial things you must do in order to make your site accessible is to ensure that all content on a page is operable using *only* a keyboard interface. Many other assistive technologies tap into the keyboard to initiate actions, like physical "switches" that are often attached to wheelchairs and operated by head or tongue movement. Ensuring your site is usable via only a keyboard also helps these users.

Try this on your own site: if you use a mouse, place it away from you, and instead use **only** your keyboard to move between elements and pages. Checking whether your core journeys can be accomplished without the use of a mouse is a great access needs test case that you can carry out without the need of any special applications or test suites.

There is a fundamental WCAG rule that states that this should be possible (2.1.1: Keyboard).[6] If it's not possible, or it's confusing or unclear what's going on when you attempt to, your site is failing, and it's time to fix it.

So, let's start with the issue most sites have: when a user is focused on an element, can they even tell?

Focus Indication

Now that you've (hopefully) tried navigating a website using only a keyboard, imagine going back to using a mouse, moving around a web page using it, but **without being able to see the cursor**. You may occasionally see some elements change color or style to indicate that your cursor is over that element and ready to be interacted with, but others may stay the same. You end up at a loss: you have no idea where you are on the page, and the interactions you attempt to make only make it more confusing.

This is frequently what a keyboard-only user experiences when trying to use a web page.

What's more, only *certain* parts of a page can be focused on, so a keyboard user's movement depends on how *many* interactive elements are present on the page and how far apart each of them is. If they're spaced out, and you have no focus style, the result is *really* confusing.

It's one of the most simple things to add to a web page and yet is often overlooked by those building and maintaining websites: what do my elements do **visually** when they're ready to be interacted with?

Too often we take for granted the presence of the cursor because that's how so many of us use the Web to interact with it. It tells us we're in the right place *regardless* of whether the element changes in a noticeable way visually.

To combat this, we need to ensure that we style for a particular *state* an element can be in: **focus**.

Focus Styles

Elements on a web page can have various states. It's possible to style each state to reflect the action a user is doing or has done. The main four are

- **Hover** – When a user's mouse is positioned over an element but hasn't yet clicked it

- **Active** – The state at the moment a user clicks an element

- **Visited** – Used for links the user has previously clicked

- **Focus** – When an element is receiving keyboard focus (usually by navigating with the Tab key)

The one we're interested in is **focus**. When you're focused on an element using the keyboard, by default a visual indicator appears to reflect that. This is something the browser handles without you needing to do anything. Figure 4-2 shows a button with and without a focus style.

Figure 4-2. *A picture of a button (left) and then that same button with keyboard focus style applied (right). The default browser focus style is typically a slightly blurred blue outline.*

You may have seen this before. The outline indicates that a user can perform an action on the element using either a keyboard or mouse. This is what we call a **focus indicator** – its main purpose is to indicate to a keyboard-only user where on the page they're currently focused, so they can navigate a page with greater context and ease.

The focus indicator is to keyboard-only users what the cursor is to mouse users.

It's so central to their ability to use a site that there is a WCAG rule (2.4.7: Focus Visible) dedicated to ensuring that keyboard focus is visible to users when navigating a site.[7]

No two sites are designed in the same way though, and content is often placed in varied locations. Given this inconsistency, having a clear focus style is invaluable – if users are unsure of where they've just moved to, having a focus style that stands out provides landmarks on the page, which can help users focus their attention on the right content.

Focus State Issues

One big change since the first edition of this book is how focus is handled by browsers. A few years ago, browsers would use the focus state for most elements, and so the outline shown in Figure 4-3 would appear on buttons, links, and a number of other elements.

Figure 4-3. *A picture of a button currently receiving keyboard focus with the default focus style (a slightly blurry blue outline)*

The issue with this was that the focus state is triggered not *just* by keyboard focus but by clicking or tapping as well. This meant that many users would briefly see this outline when clicking a button or tapping on a drop-down, so it was seen often by those who didn't necessarily need it.

In many ways, this was an error – while focus styles are *always* required when users are navigating the page with a keyboard, focus styles are **not** required when the user *knows* where they are putting their focus, such as when they use a pointing device such as a mouse or finger.

Although it was only seen fleetingly, and it was useful for accessibility, many found it ugly. Because of the appearance, some designers and developers removed it altogether, using CSS code similar to this:

```
*:focus { outline: 0; }
```

This hid the blue outline but hid it for **everyone**. For those that needed it to understand their position, they were left with no idea where they were on the page.

Contextual Focus

To further highlight what a bad idea this is, focus styles are not just useful in the context of a whole page – they can be equally helpful when identifying position in a small area or within an element with multiple actions. For example, Figure 4-4 shows two identical menus currently focused on the *same* item. The only difference is that the second menu displays a focus style on that element.

 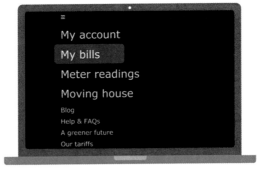

Figure 4-4. *A picture comparing two menus where the user is focused on the same item – one with a focus style (pictured right) and one without (pictured left). The lack of a visual style to indicate focus in the left menu prevents keyboard users from knowing which link is selected.*

Imagine you're a keyboard-only user and you're aiming to interact with one of these menu items. In the first example, you're left to guess which link you're on and could potentially end up heading to pages you weren't trying to navigate to.

The good news is that browsers no longer use the focus state for this functionality, so the blue outline doesn't show up with *every* interaction. Instead, they only show it **when it's needed** – it doesn't show up when you click or tap an element, for instance, but it *does* show up when you tab to it with a keyboard, thanks to a new CSS selector.

Focus Visible

To combat the sheer amount of websites that had hidden focus styles completely, a new state was created that we can use: focus-visible. The focus-visible selector is a more **contextual** version of focus. Specifically, it only activates when an element receives **keyboard focus**. In CSS, it's very similar to focus:

```
:focus-visible {
    border: 2px solid purple;
    border-offset: 4px;
}
```

This ensures that a clear state change is in place for those who navigate by keyboard, *and* it no longer appears for those interacting by tap or click, so designers don't feel the need to hide or override it. Figure 4-5 shows this.

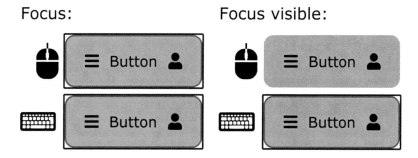

Figure 4-5. *A series of buttons showcasing how the focus and focus-visible states apply focus. For the focus state (pictured left), focus indication appears when users both click and tab to a button. However, with focus-visible (pictured right), focus indication only appears when the button receives keyboard focus.*

At the time of writing, all major browsers support `focus-visible`, so it's safe to use on your sites.[8]

For backward compatibility (e.g., supporting Internet Explorer), you can use a combination of `focus` and `focus-visible` so you can ensure that nobody is left confused:

```
button:focus {
    /* regular button focus styles */
}
button:focus:not(:focus-visible) {
    /* undo all the above focused button styles
    if the button has focus but the browser wouldn't normally
    show default focus styles */
}
button:focus-visible {
    /* some even *more* exciting button focus styles */
}
```

So, we now know how to implement focus styles into a site that are both inclusive and invisible to those who don't need them (thereby ensuring designers are happy).

Next, we need to cover the various ways that you can **highlight** focus so that you can decide which ones work best for the instances in your site – it's one thing to have them, but another for them to be usable.

Custom Focus Styles

We know that browsers provide a focus indicator to interactive elements when a keyboard user tabs to them. However, a focus style being present doesn't *guarantee* that users will always spot them.

Depending on the color scheme and styling of your sites, even default focus indicators may be hard or even impossible to spot, and so you're still left with an inaccessible experience for those navigating by keyboard.

For example, the default outline color in many browsers is blue. This may contrast well against your site's colors, but the user can, on many operating systems, also **choose** the color of the focus outline they use. Figure 4-6 shows how this is possible in the settings of MacOS.

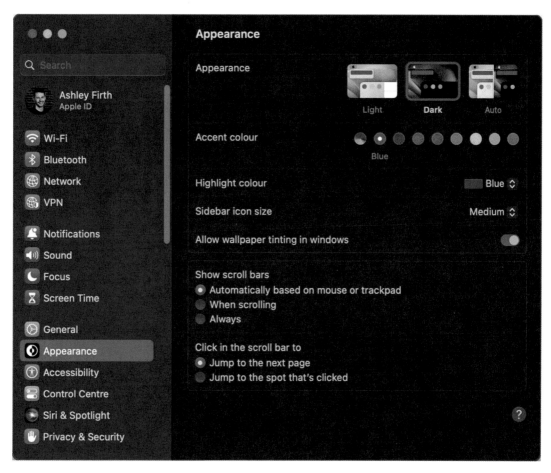

Figure 4-6. *In the settings of MacOS, it's possible to change the "accent" color that is used as the default focus indicator in browsers*

Suddenly the outline is pink, and it becomes hard to spot on the same website that worked well with blue ones.

Given that we can't guarantee a clear focus style by default, we have to sort it ourselves. The answer lies in the root of the problem – **you** style a web page to look the way you want and to reflect your brand. Do the same with your focus styles!

How Visible Do They Need to Be?

We covered foreground/background contrast ratios in Chapter 3 "Low Vision and Color Blindness," but the contrast for focus indicators is the same as for text at WCAG AA level – **3:1**. This is covered in its own WCAG rule (2.4.11: Focus Appearance).[9] In this case though, how we measure contrast depends on *where* the focus style is. For example, if it's **outside** the component (like a drop shadow or outline), it needs to contrast with the background color, in the same way text has to contrast with its background.

However, if it's **connected** to the element (like a border), it needs to contrast with both the background color *and* the element color. Figure 4-7 shows how it's measured this way, with a passing and failing focus color.

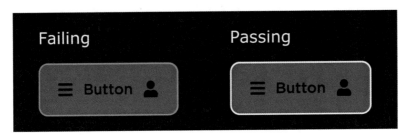

Figure 4-7. *Two buttons with focus applied to them side by side. The first button (pictured left) has a border that contrasts well with the background color, but not with the color of the element, and so it fails WCAG checks. In contrast, the border of the second button (pictured right) contrasts well with both the button and background colors, and so would pass.*

So the challenge is making sure your focus state is clearly different from the default state of your element, but also that it still passes color contrast checks. The larger the change in style between these two states, the easier it'll be to spot.

Examples

Although many sites use the standard outline style to indicate focus on every element, you don't *have* to. Focus styles can be unique to the element and to your site. Let's go through a few examples.

Clear Change in Background

This is a popular option with designers. With some elements having a distinct color filling them, changing that **background color** when focus is placed on it would constitute a clear and obvious change in state. Figure 4-8 shows two examples of components where this works well: a "toggle" component where a user chooses from a series of options (usually made with either a series of buttons or radio buttons) and the "stepper" component that shows the steps of a journey.

Figure 4-8. *Two components, the "stepper" and "toggle" components, are shown in their default state (pictured left) and focused state (pictured right). On the right, there is a clear change in background color for the active step and toggle option, indicating focus.*

In these examples, the change in background of the active option or step is clear to identify. I've used these specific examples to highlight a point: your "focus" background color needs to be different from your "active" background color as they do two different things and can often be used in conjunction with one another. For example, a user may have one option from the "toggle" component *selected* but also be *focused* on another option with their keyboard (shown in Figure 4-9).

Figure 4-9. *A "toggle" component is shown. The option on the left has a dark blue background to indicate that it's currently selected, and the option on the right has a light blue background to indicate that it currently has keyboard focus.*

Having this difference prevents users from being unsure whether they're focused on the component or not.

Clear Change in Border

Another popular option is changing the color of a **border** that an element already has to indicate it has keyboard focus. As common page elements like buttons and inputs typically have borders when they've been styled, this option fits in with most designs. Figure 4-10 shows this.

Figure 4-10. *Two components, the "button" and "input" components, are shown in their default state (pictured left) and focused state (pictured right). On the right, there is a clear change in border color and thickness for when the user is focused on it.*

I'm often cautious of using only borders to highlight focus as it's not always clear, especially when there's only one button on a page – if a user can't see *other* buttons in their default style, they will perhaps be unsure whether the border is a focus state or just a default style.

The most common way people get around this is by **offsetting** the border from the button itself. This creates an outline around the element similar to the default browser behavior, and so users are used to seeing it and knowing what it means, but this time it's in a color scheme that works for your site. You can see the code required for that in the following, along with an example (shown in Figure 4-11).

```
:focus-visible {
    border: 2px solid purple;
    border-offset: 4px;
}
```

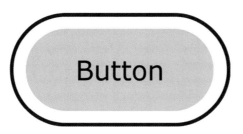

Figure 4-11. *Using the* `border-offset` *CSS rule, you can position a border to be away from the element itself. This created an outline-like style.*

Border changes also work really well in components that have actions the user can complete *inside* them, like a drop-down or the earlier "toggle" component example.

When adding any border or outline for the sake of focus, it needs to be at least **2px** wide in order to pass WCAG checks – anything less and it's likely to be missed. If you make the border *much* thicker (say, 8px), it also doesn't have to be present on all sides of the component. For example, Figure 4-12 shows a thick border on only the left and right hand sides of a button, and this would pass WCAG checks.

Figure 4-12. *Two buttons are shown. The first (pictured left) is a button with a 2px border on all sides, which passes WCAG checks. The second (pictured right) displays a focus style where the border becomes much thicker, but only on the left and right sides. This change is significant enough, despite not being on all sides, that it would also pass WCAG checks.*

Overall, make borders thick!

Outlines

Outlines look similar to offset borders, but they operate in a different way. Unlike borders, the outline is drawn *outside* the element, whereas the border, even when offset, is still *within* the element. Figure 4-13 visualizes this.

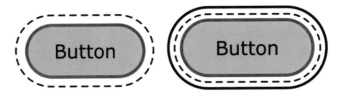

Figure 4-13. *In this example, two buttons are shown, each with a dashed line around them to indicate the size of the actual element. The first button (pictured left) has a border, which sits within the size of the element, as borders always do. However, the second button (pictured right) also has an outline, which always sits outside of the element.*

Depending on your preference, this can be a good or a bad thing. On the one hand, the outline being outside means that when a user is focused on an element, that outline may overlap other content, which some designers do not like visually. On the other hand though, being outside the element *also* means that the user won't see any visible layout "jumps" when a user focuses it, which can happen sometimes with borders:

```
button:focus-visible {
    outline: 4px solid black;
}
```

Furthermore, for those using forced colors mode (like Windows High Contrast Mode) that we covered in Chapter 3 "Low Vision and Color Blindness," things like borders and background colors often change and sometimes are possibly even *removed* depending on the theme, whereas outlines *always* remain.[10]

I'd recommend trying both, especially as the code for them is very similar, and testing to see which one you prefer for your site in a few modes. Both will provide clear focus indication though.

Other Options

If neither border nor background color changes work for the component you're trying to apply focus to, it's worth thinking about the specific details of what you're sharing with a user and how to highlight a state change in a way that's most noticeable. "Shadows" are being used more and more for this purpose, as they tend to cover a larger surface area than borders, but are also more subtle at the same time – encircling part of the element but dissipating as it moves out.

Let's use an example of a "slider" component, shown in Figure 4-14.

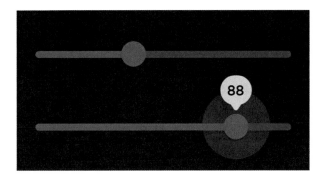

Figure 4-14. *A slider component is pictured – first in its default state (pictured top) and then in its focused state (pictured bottom). In the latter, there is a pink shadow around the slider point, along with a tool tip hovering just above it, displaying the value currently set by the slider.*

```
button:focus-visible {
    box-shadow: 0 0 0 6px pink;
}
```

In this example, you *could* have a border around the whole component to indicate focus, but having something visual on the **point** of focus makes the interaction more obvious and feel more deliberate. As keyboard users then navigate the component using the arrow keys, the slider moves while keeping the drop shadow, and the number above updates.

I've also seen shadows used on buttons to indicate focus sometimes, but using them carries a couple of potential pitfalls. Firstly, a shadow will always be less obvious visually than a sharp border or color change. We're aiming for **immediately** obvious when it comes to showing a user where they are on the page, and these are usually less effective at achieving that.

Secondly, if you're using *only* a drop shadow to indicate focus, be sure that you test how this looks in dark mode as they can often appear to "disappear" if a black shadow is used on a dark theme, for example. Also as I mentioned earlier, some settings in forced colors mode can remove certain styles, and this happens with drop shadows by default. This removal of styles is done in order to increase contrast but in this case would also inadvertently remove focus styles. Luckily, in our preceding slider example, the tool tip is there as a backup to ensure that focus is still obvious to the user. This leads me nicely to…

Using a Combination of Focus Changes

Overall, the more you do to emphasize the change between an element's default state and focus state, the more likely it is that a user will notice it.

For this reason, many sites use a **combination** of style changes to increase that emphasis, such as a background *and* border color change for the focus style of a button, for example. They may even change the text color too in order to maintain a good contrast ratio. You don't have to change only one aspect of the styling of an element.

Another style that is becoming popular is having both a border **and** an outline on elements – one being white and the other being black (shown in Figure 4-15 below). This creates a double border effect and ensures that the contrast between the focused element and the page around it is always high. Microsoft pioneered this with their "high visibility focus indicators" in Windows.[11]

```
button:focus-visible {
    outline: 3px solid black;
    box-shadow: 0 0 0 6px white;
}
```

Figure 4-15. *A pink button, with a white border around it and a black outline around that. This "double border" technique ensures that focus styles are visible regardless of the color scheme of the website.*

The reason I mention these examples is that, just like users being able to change their native focus color, we already know that they can *also* change the color scheme of your whole website through the use of forced colors mode, or dark mode if you have it. Because of this, you won't be able to test every color combination or focus style a user might see on your button, but you *can* ensure that the level of contrast is high and that the visual change is noticeable.

Using Hover Styles as Focus Styles

The hover state is often more thought about by designers and developers compared to focus, so adding the same style for *both*, although not always ideal, is certainly better than nothing and much easier to add and remember.

With the introduction of focus-visible, you can add that on to any hover styles with ease to cater to different needs with the same style, as shown in the following code:

```
button:hover,
button:focus-visible {
    /* Hover and Focus styles */
}
```

Mouse users don't need focus styles, and keyboard users don't need hover styles, so it works perfectly.

With so many options, there's no excuse not to implement clear, visible focus styles. Similarly to when we covered contrast ratio on site colors in Chapter 3 "Low Vision and Color Blindness," we need to tread the line between creating an aesthetically pleasing site and providing an acceptable degree of usability for users who interact with content in a different way. Remember to always consider the **states** of your elements rather than just their default style.

Now, not *all* elements receive keyboard focus, but that doesn't mean that they don't need to be interacted with. Indeed, many custom components you may have made will **require** the user to complete some form of action, but it may not be **possible** without a cursor. In these instances, there's an attribute you can apply to elements to help ensure that this isn't a blocker – tabindex.

Tabindex

I mentioned earlier that if a user is unable to navigate and interact with your content using only a keyboard, it falls under WCAG's "denial of keyboard access," which was one of the major issues raised in the lawsuit against Beyoncé's website.[12]

The good news is that if you use correct markup, certain interactive elements are focusable by default. For example, if you use a `<button>` tag to represent a button (as opposed to a `<div>` styled to look like a button with custom markup), the computer will recognize it as a focusable element. Using the correct tags for interactive elements throughout means that a user will be able to move through a page, from top to bottom, without you having to make any changes to your code for those using a keyboard. Here is a list of some essential elements that receive focus by default because they require an action from the user:

- **`<a>`** – A link in HTML. As long as it has somewhere to go (defined with an `href` attribute), it can be focused through tabbing.

- **`<button>`** – A button.

- **`<input>`** – A field inside a form is defined as an input, and they all have focus set by default.

- **`<select>`** – A drop-down (when focused using the keyboard, you can navigate through the options using the arrow keys).

- **`<textarea>`** – A text box, often used for long-form comments.

It's comforting to know that keyboard-only users already have the power to engage with all of the typical features of a web page, but there *are* certain scenarios where adding, altering, or even removing focus from certain elements can **improve** the experience.

So What Is `Tabindex`?

Tabindex is an attribute you can use to **manage focus** – for elements that *don't* have it by default and elements that have it but need it temporarily removed. We mentioned it briefly in Chapter 2 "Blindness," but don't worry if you've never come across this before. It handles two things, both of which are in the name

- **Tab** – Determines whether an element is "focusable" or not for a user using the Tab key to navigate

- **Index** – The order in which focusable content is presented on a page

With this, you can ensure that motor and visually impaired keyboard-only users have access to *all* the relevant information on a page.

Tabindex Values

Let's go through when and why you'd use `tabindex` through the three values that the attribute takes:

0

The 0 value lets the page know that the element you have set this attribute on should be focusable but in "sequential" order – wherever it is on the page in relation to other elements, it'll be available via "tab" as it reaches it. This means your custom components (like a button) made from tags that aren't interactive by default (like a `<div>` tag) can now be focused just like a real button. Figure 4-16 shows this – here there are two `<div>` tags that can't be "tabbed" to by default, but one has become part of the tabbing order as it has the `tabindex` attribute. The numbers reflect the order in which they will be "tabbed" to.

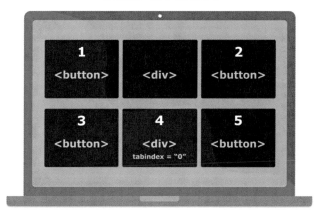

Figure 4-16. *A diagram showing the tabbing order of buttons. One `<div>` tag is ignored, while the other is added to the order as it has the `tabindex` attribute added to it.*

The first `<div>` tag is ignored and passed over as it isn't an interactive element by default. The second, however, with `tabindex="0"` applied, now joins the tabbing order. The order is set based on where elements are in the code, from top to bottom.

1 or greater

This is an option, but I wouldn't recommend doing this. Providing a positive number to the `tabindex` attribute dictates that elements should be both focusable *and* focused on in a **specific order** that you've chosen, regardless of where the element is positioned on the page. Tabbing priority is set in ascending order (so 1 means it's the **first** thing to be navigated to, and a number bigger than 1 would be navigated to after). Figure 4-17 shows an example of how this can be used to create custom tabbing orders.

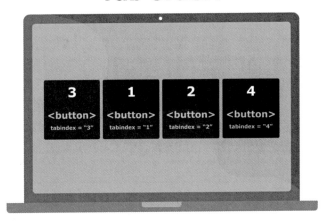

Figure 4-17. A diagram of a custom tabbing order being dictated by the `tabindex` attribute. The order is not sequential (left to right) due to the use of positive `tabindex` values dictating the order they should receive focus.

In the preceding example, a user tabbing this series of elements would find themselves jumping around the page rather than moving sequentially, which is highly unexpected behavior. Simply reordering the buttons would remove the need to set a custom `tabindex` order and prevent users from having to move through content in a nonlinear way.

In my experience, there isn't a good reason to dictate a custom tabbing order – doing so can create a confusing or even unusable experience. WCAG's "Focus Order" rule (Success Criterion 2.4.3) requires that components receive focus "in an order that preserves meaning and operability," and anything other than moving linearly from top to bottom fails to achieve that.[13] Every accessibility expert I've come across has said the same thing.[14]

-1

A negative `tabindex` value **removes** the element from the sequential flow we just mentioned, so a user can't tab to it. However with this attribute applied, when the element *is* needed by the user, it can still have focus applied to it through **code**. This is very useful for elements that should not be tabbed to *all* the time but that may need keyboard focus in certain situations depending on a user's behavior on the page.

The classic example of this is a modal or dialog window, as shown in Figure 4-18.

Figure 4-18. *A picture of an active modal. It's overlaid on top of the web page's contents, along with a semitransparent "mask" to obscure the content below.*

As a modal usually only appears when a user opens it, the content is hidden when they first arrive on the page. We therefore don't want the content to receive keyboard focus by default as the user may end up tabbing to content they can't see.

However, when a user opens the modal, causing the hidden content to appear, the contents should now receive keyboard focus, allowing the user to tab around it and not the rest of the elements on the page below. This is only possible in code if the element already has a negative `tabindex` value set. We'll cover this in more detail later.

Obscured Elements

Once you have your focus styles in place, and they're clearly visible to users, the next step is to ensure that no other part of your website can *interfere* with that visibility. That may seem obvious, but over the years, more and more common elements and features have appeared on websites in ways that cause elements to be partially or completely invisible, even when a user is ready to interact with them.

This is why there are two WCAG rules that relate to ensuring that the focus a user has on an element isn't obscured visually by anything else. There's 2.4.11 (Focus Not Obscured (Minimum)) that allows focused elements to be **partially** obscured as long as they're still visible and 2.4.12 (Focus Not Obscured (Enhanced)) that doesn't allow them to be obscured at all.[15] The former is a AA requirement (the middle of the three levels), and the latter is a AAA requirement (the strictest).[16]

Fixed Elements

The most common way I've seen partially obscured elements is the introduction and popularity of fixed elements that take over part of a page and remain there. It's used a lot with headers and menus at the top of the page and, more recently, at the bottom of the page for cookie consent banners.

Due to them being positioned in a way that makes them immovable regardless of whether you scroll or tab up or down, it's possible for a keyboard user to tab between elements and find that the one they're focused on is **behind** this fixed content – they're focused on it but can't always *see* it. Figure 4-19 shows an example of this.

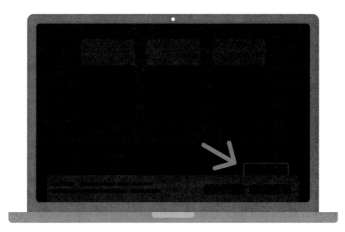

Figure 4-19. *An illustration of how a fixed element can obscure another element that is receiving keyboard focus. In this example, a fixed cookie banner is positioned at the bottom of the page, and a button in the footer has keyboard focus, but you can only see half of the element.*

As this is only partially obscured, this would pass a WCAG AA check but fail the stricter AAA check. If the focused element was completely obscured, it would fail both.

Solutions

For cookie banners, the best bet is to try and reduce its size – the smaller the surface area of the fixed element, the less likely it is to obscure another element. Many sites have taken to positioning it as a smaller element in the corner of the page to limit the possibility that it could get in the way.

For menus, it's worth considering whether it should even be fixed in its position. Users are used to knowing where on the page the menu is, even if it's out of sight visually as they move down the page, so not fixing it in place can free up more screen real estate for the user to make use of.

If you're a big fan of fixed menus, consider having the menu disappear as the user scrolls or tabs *down* the page but reappears when they attempt to move *up* the page.

Research has found that when moving downward, users are exploring and engaging with the content. However, when they're moving upward, they're beginning to look for a way to navigate elsewhere or engage with an action they've already seen. This is highly likely to be something from your menu as it's typically the first element.[17]

Setting it up in this way achieves the best of both worlds – you limit the chances that you obscure a focused element for a keyboard user but retain the usefulness of a fixed header **when** the user needs it.

Overlays

Different to a menu or most cookie banners, overlays take over the **entire** page when they appear. Often they are initiated by the user by clicking a link or button, but there are times when they can appear *without* that interaction, thereby catching the user by surprise.

When this happens, they can completely obscure the page you were viewing and the element you were focused on, creating a clear WCAG failing. Worse than that though, keyboard-only users can be left completely unable to close the overlay and get back to what they were looking at, even *if* they initiated the action.

To understand this more, we need to go through how this happens and, most importantly, how to avoid it yourself.

Accessible Overlays

Overlays like modals are common features (and accessibility pitfalls) online. Keyboard-only users can hit barriers when they're presented with new content, whether through their actions or not, but find it impossible to interact with.

Let's take a look at some of the challenges these actions pose and how we can make them more accessible. We'll go through the process of creating a modal that can be triggered, interacted with, and closed, using a keyboard-only setup, thereby ensuring that the process of displaying new content can be achieved in an accessible way.

Before we get started, I have already created this modal example for you to play with in the practical example for this chapter (found in GitHub under the "Chapter 4" folder and live at `inclusive.guide/examples/modal`). The following sections will focus on the functionality we're aiming for rather than the code itself, but you can follow that link to look at, or use, any of it.

Changing Focus When the Overlay Appears

The first, most obvious challenge is to make sure that any new content receives focus when it appears on the page so that the user can both navigate and close it if they're not interested. Figure 4-20 is an example of this.

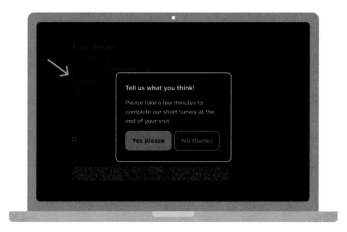

Figure 4-20. *A picture of a feedback modal overlaid on a page but with keyboard focus still on the content beneath it (highlighted by an arrow pointing to the element with keyboard focus). Because of this, it's impossible to close it using only a keyboard.*

While browsing the site, an overlay was added to the page without prior warning. What's more, once it had appeared, I couldn't interact with it using the keyboard. As you can see in the image, my keyboard focus remained on the button behind the modal – pressing "tab" was still cycling me through the content of the page *beneath* it. Ironically, the message is asking for feedback on the site and its ease of use.

You need to be wary of changing focus when you overlay content on a page. If you don't, keyboard-only users won't be able to navigate it. This amounts to taking over the user's page without their permission and then, without keyboard focus on the overlay, refusing to give it back. This is what is known as a keyboard trap.

Keyboard Traps

A keyboard trap happens when a keyboard-only user is caught within a specific piece or group of content that they can't get out of. This leaves them trapped without a way to continue and usually means they have to leave your site altogether. This most commonly occurs when content is added to a page, either through a user action or without warning, and keyboard focus is not *moved* to that new content.

Modals have been around for a long time, but the problem has become increasingly common over the last few years due to the GDPR (General Data Protection Regulation) on data protection. These rules require sites using cookies to prompt users to accept that behavior when they first visit the site, and this is often accomplished by presenting an overlay modal that the user must accept in order to dismiss it. From a design perspective, it ensures that the rest of the user's time on the site can be free of pop-ups, but the unfortunate truth is that, when created incorrectly, these overlays can stop some users from engaging with the content at all.

Because of how common this is, WCAG actually has a fundamental success criterion in its spec for how to avoid creating a keyboard trap (2.1.2: No Keyboard Trap). Their spec states that you have to be able to move to and from a component using only the keyboard, and if you can't achieve this through the Tab key, you need to explain how to do so.[18]

You can solve this problem by using code to apply focus to the modal when it's opened, thereby preventing the issue with the feedback modal shown earlier.

What Should I Move the Focus To?

What specifically you decide to focus on *within* the modal is up to you, but it should be steered by the purpose of the modal and the content within it. For example, if it holds information that doesn't require interaction, perhaps assigning focus to the button that closes the modal is the way to go.

Alternatively, if it's an overlay containing an action that the user needs to complete, like a form, it's more beneficial applying focus to the first form input. Figure 4-21 shows both examples.

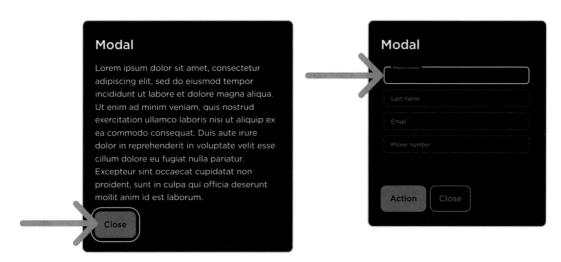

Figure 4-21. *Two examples of modal content are shown. The first (pictured left) is a text-only modal, and so keyboard focus is given to the only interactive element within it: the "close" button. The second modal however (pictured right) contains a form with multiple inputs. In this instance, focus is given to the first form element.*

For simplicity in code, you should move the user's focus to the **first** element in the modal that can receive it, regardless of the content in it. This will either be the first form element or action button or the "close" button if there's nothing else interactive in there. Either way, the user's focus has been moved, so they now have control.

We achieve this in the practical example by setting `tabindex="-1"` to the modal, so it isn't part of the tabbing order when you load the page. Then, when the user initiates the modal by clicking a button, focus is given to the first interactive element within its content. This is possible thanks to the `tabindex` attribute we set, which allows us to then place the content **back** into the sequential flow of the page. Again, you can try this yourself at `inclusive.guide/examples/modal`.

Keeping Tab Focus Inside the New Content

Being able to move through the content in the overlay makes it accessible and prevents a keyboard trap. However, we still have a problem: the modal has become *part* of the elements that the user can now tab to rather than the *only* thing they can tab to.

As a result, a user may end up tabbing through the content in the modal and continue onto the content below the overlay. If they do this, they won't be able to see that content due to the overlay, and so the user still ends up losing their place and isn't sure why.

To combat this unexpected behavior, we need to ensure that we keep keyboard focus within the modal until the user decides to close it. Strangely, you actually want to form a kind of temporary keyboard trap here: cycling through the interactive content in the modal while it's open. Figure 4-22 illustrates how this would work.

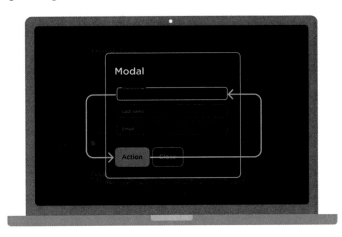

Figure 4-22. *In order to retain keyboard focus within a modal, you must ensure that tabbing only cycles between interactive elements within the modal rather than moving to the rest of the page. The arrows in the illustration show where focus would move to next if a user tabbed from the last element in the modal or shift-tabbed from the first element.*

This means that if a user is focused on the last focusable element in the modal and hits tab, instead of shifting them onto the content underneath, it would place focus back on the *first* focusable element of the modal. Likewise, if someone tabbed backward (by using Shift + Tab) while focused on the *first* focusable element, it would shift their focus to the *last* focusable element.

Allow the User to Close the New Overlaid Content

We've touched on this already, but once the user is in the modal, they must be able to close it **without using a mouse**. You can offer this behavior in a range of ways to cater to everyone:

- **A "close" button** – This is the obvious first option. With one button and keyboard focus within the modal, users can close a modal and return to the page content with a single key press. The button is often seen as an "X" icon positioned in a corner, but a "close" button is more explicit.

- **Hitting the escape key** – This has become a very common user behavior to close content, and so adding it to our modal, even if many people don't use it, is still of value. In the practical example, we have our code listen for the escape key being used when the modal is **open** and close the modal if it's hit.

- **Clicking outside of the modal content** – Now although this approach doesn't work for keyboard-only users, it certainly helps provide a way of closing the modal without the need to accurately press a specific button; clicking anywhere outside of the modal content will close it. This is incredibly useful for "pointer-based" users who suffer from motor impairments but still navigate with a cursor in some way. You can achieve this by closing the modal whenever a click occurs on the overlay, *except* for when that click happens on the modal content.

These pieces of functionality are shown in Figure 4-23 and are in the practical example I've added for this chapter.

Figure 4-23. *There are multiple ways to close an accessible modal when it has been opened. This illustration points toward a "close" button in the modal itself that can be interacted with via keyboard or mouse/finger, as well as a click or tap that can occur anywhere outside of the modal in order to close it. Finally, not pictured here is the ability to hit the "Escape" key and close it.*

Allow the User to Return to Where They Were Before

Finally, once a user has interacted with your modal and closed it, the focus should be returned to the place they initiated the modal from. This way, they can continue on their journey through your site from the **same** point. WCAG's rule on this (3.2.1: On Focus) states that when an interface component receives focus, it does not initiate a **change of context**. After being on the modal, sending them to *anywhere else* other than where they were would fail this.[19]

This is easy, as when the user first opens the modal, you can make a note of the element that initiated it in your code. Then when the user closes the modal, you simply return focus to that same button. This is illustrated in Figure 4-24.

Figure 4-24. *When a user initiates a modal opening via keyboard, it's important for your code to make note of which element they were focused on when they did so. Then, when they're done with the modal and decide to close it, you can place keyboard focus back where it was.*

Now, if you've overlaid content **without** user interaction, returning them to where they were is tricky as the user didn't cause the content to appear, and in order to be accessible, you will have moved the keyboard focus to the overlay, and you may be unable to tell where their attention was.

One thing you can do is get the code you're running to check if the user was focusing on *any* content at the time the modal appeared. You can then store that and return their focus to that element once the modal has been closed. However, they may not have been focusing on *anything* at the time, in which case you may need to resort to applying focus to the first focusable element on the page. This is better than nothing but has the added possibility of annoying users by taking over the page and then returning them to a completely different part of it. This raises the broader question of whether it's a good idea to inject content unannounced into the page in the first place (I believe the answer is "no").

Third-Party Software

This is a good point to finish this section on, as it's worth noting that barriers like this could be present on your site *without* you realizing it. Many sites choose to add third-party software to their site, perhaps to handle their GDPR-compliant cookie pop-up or to gather feedback as we saw in the example earlier. If you do this, you could be inflicting a keyboard trap on your users that *you* didn't create, but that can lead to negative feedback about the accessibility of *your* site from users. For this reason, it's good to check if any third parties you use are injecting content into your site and, if so, whether they're doing it in an accessible way. If they're not, then this issue is likely happening on many more sites than just your own, so it's worth raising.

Now that we've covered a few ways to make content more accessible for keyboard-only users, let's look at some *other* ways in which users with motor impairments interact with the Web.

Pointer-Based Gestures

Some motor-impaired users prefer to navigate and interact with content on the Web using pointer-based gestures. This *might* involve pointing and clicking with a mouse, but this action often causes users to tire quickly, be less precise, and become prone to making mistakes. Other users (like those with milder **arthritis** or **tremors**) may use specialist mice or joysticks to mitigate these problems.

It's worth noting that although using the mouse has become the most traditional way of navigating the Web in a pointer-based manner, it's far from the only way. The introduction of touch screens opened up a plethora of other options, whether operated by hands or feet, or like some of the **18 million** people with **cerebral palsy** – using head wands and mouth sticks.[20]

For those involved in making websites, all of these "pointer-based" forms of touch interactions are *indecipherable* from one another – all we can see from analytics is that the user is on a mobile device. This is equally true for those using computers, where point-based navigation can be achieved with a mouse alternative, like a joystick, or even eye tracking.

This is why we must think about interactions in a **holistic** way, much like we did with keyboards – if you can ensure that all of your actions are clear, easy to use, and error-tolerant, then you can be confident that you're catering to *all* of the people who initiate them, regardless of the different tools they use to do so. We're not aiming to make actions easier for head wand users specifically, for example. Instead, we're aiming to make actions easy for **users**.

To that end, let's cover some considerations you can make to ensure that it's easy to complete pointer-based actions.

Large Hit Areas

The first thing you can do is to check that the areas where users perform actions, such as clicking buttons or checking checkboxes, are big enough for everyone to operate easily. The key is to reduce the need for **precision** in the actions you ask users to make.

This is another design pattern that would help the Web as a whole. All users would have a much larger margin for error, avoiding a great deal of frustration.

This is especially important on mobile devices where fingers, or other methods of input, offer even *less* precision than a mouse cursor and use much smaller screens than standard monitors. Furthermore, interactions on a mobile device using assistive equipment (like a head wand tapping the screen) can obscure part of the screen from the user's view as they're performing the action.

WCAG has two rules that specify a minimum target size for actions: 24 pixels x 24 pixels for AA compliance (2.5.8: Target Size – Minimum)[21] and **44 pixels x 44 pixels** for AAA compliance (2.5.5: Target Size – Enhanced).[22] Now this doesn't mean that everything on your site should be square – if you use 24 or 44 pixels as a minimum for *one* axis, making the other axis even larger will make the target easier to hit. An example would be buttons on a mobile screen that designers often style to fill a high percentage of a screen's width while ensuring the minimum pixel height – as Figure 4-25 shows.

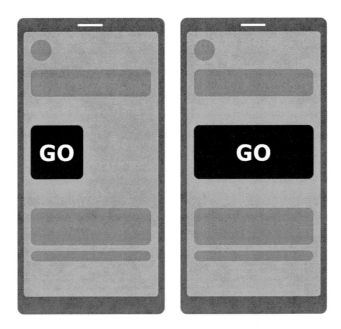

Figure 4-25. *An illustration of two target areas on two mobile devices – the first (pictured left) as a 44 pixels x 44 pixels square and the other (pictured right) whose height is 44 pixels but whose width adapts to fill the screen.*

Both the preceding buttons satisfy WCAG criteria, but the latter clearly has a much larger margin for error when trying to interact with it. Given how easy it is to implement as part of typical responsive design, and the obvious benefits of doing so, these are easy rules to comply with and consider when designing and building a site. Large buttons more clearly advertise actions on your page you want a user to complete, which is particularly useful for users with low vision.

Pointer Gestures

It is always worth remembering that some users, although capable of completing a click or tap, may not be able to make certain gestures that require a more involved movement, like clicking and dragging or pinching to zoom on a touch screen. These gestures are so commonplace in popular apps like maps and games that you may not have considered how you'd complete the same actions *without* that ability. As a result, we need to again avoid the assumption that interactions are *always* carried out by common tools like mice and fingers.

Therefore, the next point is ensuring that interactions you have on your site don't rely on a gesture as the *only* way to complete an important task. WCAG uses the following example in their "Pointer Gestures" rule (2.5.1):

Comic with cerebral palsy who has limited movement in fingers:

- **Problem** – I can't move my fingers like that. I need another way to zoom in on the map.

- **Works well** – Good thing there are buttons to zoom in and out.[23]

Figure 4-26 shows an example of this.

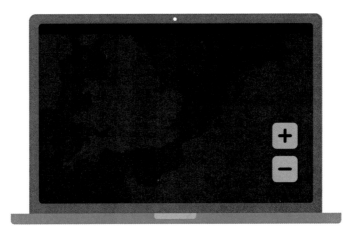

Figure 4-26. *In this illustration of a map website on a laptop, buttons are provided in the bottom right hand corner of the screen in order to allow users who can't perform gestures like "pinching" in order to zoom in on part of the map.*

Pointer Cancellation

This leads us nicely on to "pointer cancellation" – another great rule added in WCAG (2.5.2).[24] Now this rule may have been added to ensure that there is support for pointer-based users with impairments, but it *also* safeguards a much wider group of people by allowing for a very common degree of human error. Indeed, nearly everyone who's used the Web has likely experienced this without even realizing it. Imagine the following scenario:

You're on a website purchasing a new book (after you've finished reading this one, naturally). You reach the final page of the checkout journey, and just as you click the "submit order" button, you realize that the delivery address is set to your ex's house.

Awkward. However, you haven't lifted your finger from your mouse/phone screen just yet, and so you slowly slide your finger/cursor away from the button and then slowly lift it off. The interaction on the button didn't register, and you've saved yourself an unpleasant phone call.

How is this possible? The answer is that actions like "click" or "tap" are made up of both an "up" event and a "down" event. A "down" event is registered the moment a pointer-based interaction is *initiated*, and if this type of event activated the "submit order" button above, the order would have been submitted instantly. Figure 4-27 showcases how this might look visually.

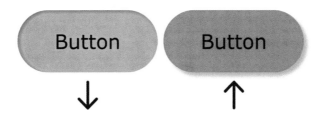

Figure 4-27. *Buttons have two "events" when a user interacts with them using a pointer-based input like a cursor or finger. The first (pictured left) is the "down" event and fires as soon as the click or tap has happened. The second (pictured right) is the "up" event and fires when the user releases the mouse click or lifts their finger.*

This is why the second "up" event exists. Unlike the down event, this event only happens when the "up" motion of *finishing* a tap or click is complete – it waits for the user to finish the whole action. Having this allows users to cancel unintended actions midway through.

For this reason, the following things are needed for your site to pass the rule:

- The first "down" event should **never** execute functionality, only the "up" event.

- The "up" event can **reverse** any action from the "down" event.

This is how the native <button> element behaves by default, so if you're using this, you have nothing to worry about. If however you're using custom elements to build functionality as we covered earlier in the book (such as a button built using a <div> tag), you'll need to ensure that the corresponding code you write to initiate actions on that element *only* occurs on the "up" event.

Undoing the Action

Even after initiating actions on an "up" event, users may *still* wish to cancel the action.

For example, if that sudden moment of clarity had happened on the checkout page *after* they'd clicked the "submit order" button, they might still want to undo it. Furthermore, users interacting through a keyboard don't get the benefit of an "up" and "down" event, as keyboard interactions happen immediately. Luckily, part of the same "Pointer Cancellation" rule mentions that it should be possible to "undo the function **after** completion".[25]

This happens frequently: Buttons can be pressed accidentally by someone with tremors while trying to scroll, or by someone with a head wand who has missed their target, which reminds us to think about human error even after interactions have passed.

A good example of this is Google Mail, which introduced a great example of this. Immediately after clicking send on an email, the following notification appears (displayed in Figure 4-28).

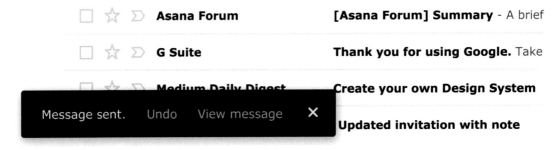

Figure 4-28. *An example of Google Mail's "undo sent message" feature. It appears in the bottom left hand corner of the user's inbox after an email is sent, which gives them the chance to undo the action.*

This small (keyboard-accessible) box provides users with the ability to swiftly undo this action. It's also becoming more common for ecommerce sites to let people know exactly how to reverse the purchase they've just made on the order success page. It's also possible to extend the amount of time this box appears for, which is especially handy for those who can't complete actions quickly (more on that later). I've added a guide on how to do this in the reading list for this chapter, which you can find at `inclusive.guide/reading/chapter4`.

Now, both keyboard and pointer-based inputs are types of **physical** interaction, but not all motor-impaired users operate in this way. In fact, there are those that use only their voice.

Voice-to-Text

Voice-to-text is another increasingly common form of navigation as it enables users to control devices without any physical input. This is the latest example of an accessibility feature that the whole world is now adopting due to its convenience and efficiency. Through messaging apps like WhatsApp, searching and writing through companies like Google, and voice assistants like Apple's Siri and Amazon's Alexa, writing through speech to text is becoming ubiquitous. At the time of writing, it's one of the fastest growing markets, with the global speech and voice recognition market size expected to be worth around **$83 billion** by 2032.[26]

Away from its mainstream appeal and specific use cases though, it *greatly* empowers a range of motor-impaired users to be able to control a device themselves. This includes those with paralysis (like those with **quadriplegia**), **chronic pain**, or **arthritis** (which affects over **18 million** people globally).[27] Rani Nayyar, who experiences **osteoporosis** and **fibromyalgia** (which causes chronic pain), explains:

> I use Dragon Naturally Speaking software due to the problem with my hands. It was recommended to reduce the use of the keyboard and mouse.[28]

Dragon is a popular speech recognition software, but there are a range of others. This software responds to voice commands that allow you to scroll, activate links, dictate text, move the cursor, and also move through content in the same way a screen reader would.

Given that voice-to-text users often navigate in a similar way to keyboard-only users ("tabbing" between content), a lot of the accessibility solutions we've covered earlier in this chapter and in Chapter 2 "Blindness" apply here. Here is a quick checklist if you're currently focused on optimizing for speech software:

- **Focus styles to indicate position** – If a user explicitly states which link to navigate to, displaying a focus style that shows that the command was successful is important.

- **Ensure a linear page layout** – With voice-to-text software navigating similarly to keyboards and screen readers, there's another good reason to provide a logical visual and tabbing order for content.

- **Display clear form labels** – Many voice command users complain about difficult forms, and correctly labeled form elements make this interaction much easier. Without this, the user is forced to rely on the "tab" voice command or guess what the designer or developer has called that form field so they can move directly to it.

- **Use semantic markup** – As we mentioned in Chapter 2 "Blindness," you should make sure that you are using the right HTML tags to reflect the feature that you are building. For example, if a user says the command "click button" on a button that was made using a `<div>` tag instead of the native `<button>`, nothing will happen.

- **Avoid content that *only* appears on hover** – Voice commands are usually used to initiate a **full** interaction such as a click. A hover action, however, isn't as deliberate and is more fleeting – it disappears the moment a user moves elsewhere, intentionally or not. For example, if a menu opens on hover, it may close before the user can engage with one of the links inside of it.

- **Making target areas larger** – You may think that, much like keyboard-only navigation, the target area for an element such as a button wouldn't matter if you're using speech software. However, some voice-to-text users also use a feature called "MouseGrid." After using this command, a numbered 3 x 3 square grid will appear on the page, as you can see in Figure 4-29.[29]

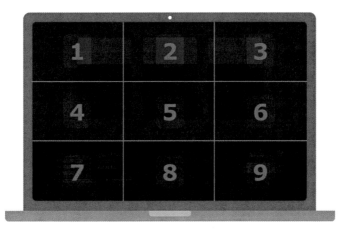

Figure 4-29. *An illustrative example of an active MouseGrid on a web page. A transparent 3 x 3 grid appears over the page, and the user can say one of the numbers to zoom into that part of the page.*

The user will then say the number **closest** to the content they want to interact with. Once they've done that, a new 3 x 3 grid appears in their chosen square, and they can select again. Figure 4-30 displays an example of this enhanced view.

Figure 4-30. *An illustration of a MouseGrid on a web page after a user has chosen a number from the first grid. The same grid appears but this time on a smaller part of the web page. The user continues with this exercise until they're close enough to their target to initiate an action.*

This verbal magnification continues until the grid is small enough that the user can click their target. If you'd like to see this feature in action, I've added a short video of it to the reading list for this chapter, which you can find at `inclusive.guide/reading/chapter4`.

MouseGrid can be used to overcome one or more of the barriers we've mentioned earlier, but more simply, some motor-impaired users may just prefer to navigate in this way. Again, we want to avoid making assumptions about how users choose to interact with content. As a result, making target areas for interactive elements such as buttons, links, and forms bigger proves very useful. Bigger targets are also a big win for voice-to-text users who use specific commands to **steer** the cursor, like "move cursor 50 pixels left" because it increases their accuracy.[30]

Beyond element sizes, ensuring that those elements are spaced apart in a sensible way will really help with this process. The closer elements are together, the more magnification will need to take place in order to successfully click the element they're targeting. Adequate gaps between elements may save one or two magnification steps *every time* they attempt an action that, over many pages and actions, can save a lot of time and effort.

One final big improvement, which will also help blind users, is to ensure websites don't ever play audio or video **unexpectedly**. This typically means avoiding autoplaying content, and that any audio on it is muted by default. As you can imagine, this can severely interfere with voice recognition software – even the act of trying to pause the noise on the page can be tricky in this situation. Instead, you should always mute by default and provide a link or button to activate the audio. WCAG's original spec has a rule about how to handle content like this, and we'll be covering it properly in Chapter 8 "Imagery".[31]

Support for All Motor-Impaired Users

The more barriers we cover, the clearer it hopefully becomes that changes you make that impact *specific* user needs also help a wide array of users with *different* needs. In this section, we'll cover several improvements you can make that assist *all* motor-impaired users and many other users too.

Of course, some people naturally stand to benefit more than others, and so it is quickly worth noting that the following solutions are some of the most useful fixes you can put in place for an often neglected group of the **millions** of motor-impaired users worldwide – people who use switch devices.[32] If you haven't seen a switch device in action before, I'd recommend watching the short video demo that Todd Stabelfeldt gave at the WWDC to showcase this technology – I've added it to the reading list for this chapter, which you can find at `inclusive.guide/reading/chapter4`.

Stephen Hawking, who had **amyotrophic lateral sclerosis** (**ALS**) – a form of motor neuron disease, famously used a thumb switch and a digital, on/off, "blink switch" attached to his glasses to interact with devices. He wrote at a rate of about one word a minute until autosuggest came along and doubled his writing speed. Besides sensory switches, switches can be buttons, like those on the side of your phone, sip-and-puff machines, or even camera switches in iOS products, operated by tilting your head.

If you want to imagine how switch users navigate and interact, a focus outline slowly moves across the screen (or across the onscreen keyboard), and you need to wait until it's at the element (or letter) you want to click and *then* activate the switch.

If Stephen Hawking were to have scrolled down a page on an iPhone using the switch device that he wrote **17 books** on, there's a good chance that he would have had to do the following:

- 2 quick clicks to bring up an interaction menu

- 1 click to select the row with scroll button

- 1 click to select the scroll button

- 1 click to select the row with scroll down button

- 1 click to select the scroll down button

- 1 click to go back to the main menu

- 1 click to close the interaction menu[33]

Switch users can use the Internet like anybody else but obviously find it incredibly time-consuming. Given the patience required, the following solutions become *especially* important, but everyone holds value for all users too.

Short Timeouts

Timeouts can generally occur after a certain period of inactivity on a page or journey and are important in preventing fraud or unauthorized access (in the case of a user's account) or in allowing for items in a basket to be made available to others (in the case of an online shop). The action after a timeout often results in progress in a journey, or inputted information, being lost – unfortunate, but not inaccessible.

However, an inability to **alter** or **extend** the time allowed to complete actions is worse – leading to hastily completed actions, inviting human error, causing frustration, and excluding motor-impaired users (and others) who work more slowly. It's therefore worth considering the following accommodations if you impose time restraints on users in any way.

Extend a Timeout

The main issue with timeouts for motor-impaired users is that they usually fail to accommodate those who cannot complete the action before the predefined time limit is reached. All users may be indecisive about purchasing what's in their basket, for example, but some users need more time to finish the journey once they've decided. This includes motor-impaired users with head wands and switches, cognitive-impaired users who require longer to comprehend and complete tasks, or even those using screen magnifiers, mentioned in the last chapter, who take longer to scroll.

Now, there are varying degrees of "success" when it comes to extending timeouts. WCAG states that you should provide the ability to extend a deadline by at least **ten times** the initial time you provided, with a prompt at least **30 seconds** before the end of the timer.[34]

Inside this prompt, there should be a way to choose to **extend** the timer; otherwise, the same problem could occur – this is required for basic compliance (level A). A more involved solution (to achieve AAA compliance) could be allowing the user to reauthenticate after a long time away and continue their journey without having lost the data they've already submitted.[35] This is ideal but of course is a bigger job. It's worth evaluating the nature of your journey and the effort required to complete it to determine which solution would be most applicable. Either way, it's imperative that you allow users to extend any time constraints you place on them.

Motion Actuation

Motion actuation describes the performing of certain actions by **physically** moving a device and is the subject of success criteria for accessible websites introduced in WCAG (2.5.4: Motion Actuation). This is because there are certain features that occur when a device is moved rather than by interfacing with the screen.

For example, the iPhone has a feature where shaking the device will undo something you've just written. This presents an accessibility issue because the feature may be unintentionally activated by turbulence, for example, a mounted wheelchair on a bumpy bus. This also poses problems for users with Parkinson's, for example, who experience hand tremors and other unintentional movements.

To remove this access barrier, there must be a way to switch the feature off, either on the web page or the device (to prevent "accidental triggering of functions"). You must also be able to achieve the same behavior using another method and undo what the motion-based feature does.[36] For the iPhone example, this is the cancel button that appears when the "shake to undo" feature occurs and prevents a situation where users are punished when this happens unintentionally.

This criterion is aimed at devices, but there are many ways that websites can leverage a device's mechanisms such as the accelerometer or camera, and it's been used on sites to provide features based on gestures such as tilting or shaking. These are fun for those who can engage with them, but they often exclude users with motor-based impairments. It's important to design customer journeys that don't rely on them to complete an interaction.

Orientation

I want to briefly touch on orientation. A few years ago, when responsive sites were not as commonplace as they are now, people would ask users to *rotate* their device in order to view the content of their site. This was because their content hadn't yet been optimized for the screen size. Instead of fixing that, they instead used CSS to detect a device's orientation and showed them a message encouraging them to tilt their screen. It would look something like what's shown in Figure 4-31.

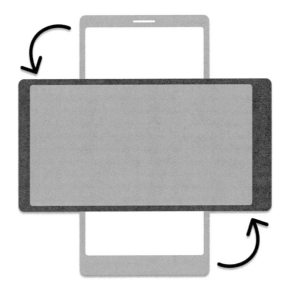

Figure 4-31. *An example of a web page illustration, displayed in portrait mode, asking the user to rotate their device to view the content. This is because, as the message states, the site is "optimized" for landscape mode. This makes it impossible for a user to engage with the web page in portrait mode.*

This was wholly inaccessible, as it made the dangerous assumption that rotating a device was even *possible*. For many motor-impaired users whose devices are mounted to their wheelchair, for example, it would be impossible for them to rotate its orientation. This meant that if they were unlucky enough to visit the site in an orientation that wasn't supported, they would be locked out of the content. It's for reasons like these that there is a WCAG rule **prohibiting** content from only being visible in a single orientation (1.3.4: Orientation).[37]

These days, this is hardly a problem on a site level, but this is still a good reminder to ensure that your site is capable of responding well to *any* screen size. There will certainly be instances where one orientation isn't as optimal as the other, such as displaying a video in portrait orientation compared to landscape, but that's certainly better than preventing users from seeing it *at all*.

Skip Links

For the first time in this book (but not the last), we're going to talk about a feature we've already covered in detail. This is because it applies so well to those with another set of disabilities or access needs.

In Chapter 2 "Blindness," we covered "skip to main content" links and how to add them. This was because they allowed those using screen readers to interact with the link and skip right to the main content of the page rather than having to listen to long navigations or headers beforehand.

The **same** barrier is true for those who use a keyboard to navigate (or other tools that tap into keyboard technology, like switches). These users tab through rows of interactive content from the top of the page to the bottom. Therefore, to get to your main content without a "skip" link, they would have to tab once for every link, button, or form input that's present *before* the unique content of the page – if your menu has ten items, that's ten "tabs." If it's a larger menu with subitems, it could be dozens.

At least for those using screen readers, they can *also* navigate by headers or landmarks if a "skip" link isn't present. Keyboard users don't have that option – without a skip link, their only other option is to utilize search and hope they find what they're looking for. This is why we implemented focus styles to ensure that the "skip" link was **visible** when it was tabbed to in the practical example for Chapter 2 "Blindness" – available at inclusive.guide/examples/skip-to-content. Figure 4-32 shows an example of how a "skip" link typically looks when tabbed to.

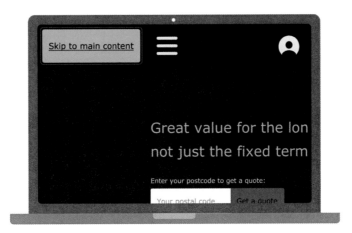

Figure 4-32. *When a user reaches a page that has a "skip to main content" link and presses "Tab," the skip link becomes visible, usually in the top left hand corner of the screen. The link is usually a bright color to make it noticeable and has keyboard focus to allow them to skip to the unique content of the page with one key press.*

With the same feature created to overcome barriers for screen reader users, keyboard users can reach a page, hit Tab once, and then interact with the link to send them straight to the main content. If they need to use multiple pages on your site, this can save minutes.

If you're here before reading Chapter 2 "Blindness," I'd recommend heading back there to understand how to implement a "skip to main content" link.

Autofill

Not to be confused with autocomplete, which we'll cover in Chapter 6 "Cognitive Impairments," autofill is a common browser feature that pre-fills a form field automatically with details a user has previously saved. This could be an email or home address and can save a user time.

The usefulness of autofill is actually more heavily debated than you may think. On the face of it, autofill seems entirely useful – it allows users to store information that they input frequently (most commonly addresses and passwords), which prompts them every time they arrive at an address or login form, allowing them to paste that content rather than rewriting it every time.

This cuts down time for a lot of users and holds an added benefit for those who find typing difficult, strenuous, or time-consuming – such as those using head wands or switches. By default, browsers allow this, and from the perspective of many users with motor disabilities, it can be a big win. Figure 4-33 shows what a common autofill looks like on Google Chrome.

Figure 4-33. *An illustration of how a browser's autofill feature works – displaying previously filled and stored options from common sites or form elements. This feature aims to avoid the needless repetition of filling in the same content again and again.*

So why is there a debate?

Well, although autofill can save some typing time, many people have raised the argument that browsers frequently store data in incorrect fields which, when inputted, can either force users to have to delete what was autofilled and replace it or end up submitting data in the wrong fields without noticing (thereby causing potential delivery or billing issues). Furthermore, having browsers hold sensitive information becomes a problem if a user's device is stolen.

From an aesthetic perspective, any input on a form that has been automatically filled switches its background color to let the user know which inputs have received information. This color usually clashes with most color schemes in order to stand out and so has the potential to negatively impact a design. You might think that people would be hesitant to remove this useful feature for the sake of a color scheme, but remember people *also* frequently removed the small blue outline caused by the focus state.

Then, there are times that autofill appears when it's clearly **not** helpful. The UK government did some interesting research into times when autofill appears, obscuring part of the page, and yet offers no value. These include

- Registering for something on someone else's behalf, yet your own details are constantly provided by autofill.

- Searching for a location (like a school) by address, but *your* address details appear via autofill. If the input has an autocomplete feature (that offers options below the input as you type), autofill styles will always cover the top results, making it unusable.[38]

To combat this, those who build sites have the power to completely remove autofill using one attribute:

```
<input type="text" name="address-line-1" autocomplete="off" />
```

Just like that, the user's browser will not allow autofill in *most* browsers. However, Google Chrome, the most popular browser in the world, won't respect this attribute – it will show autofill options regardless.[39] All of this creates a difficult situation around a feature that's supposed to be useful.

My personal opinion is that autofill should be encouraged simply because the potential annoyances and visual barriers are *far* outweighed by the benefit they bring to those who struggle to input content. There is also a reasonable solution for most of the concerns previously raised:

- Each user can choose not to store their information in autofill, but turning it off through code makes that choice for **every** user.

- It's reasonable not to want the wrong information in the wrong form fields. However, a combination of good form validation (e.g., ensuring a postcode can't appear in a telephone number field) and allowing a user to check both after the initial autofill *and* on a review page means that this isn't a good enough reason to turn it off for people who may rely on it.

- I wholeheartedly agree that sensitive data shouldn't be stored in a browser, and I include passwords in that category alongside credit card information. This is why password managers are so important and on the rise in terms of popularity. Keeping data in an application specifically designed to keep it safe is the safest choice.

- In response to the change in input background color that autofill creates, you can use CSS to alter its appearance to a more palatable color, just as we mentioned that you could for the focus style. The following would change the background for autofilled inputs:

```
input:-webkit-autofill {
    filter: none;
    background-color: black;
}
```

It's worth noting that it's important to choose a color with a high-enough contrast that the user can *read* the prefilled information displayed by autofill without issue. Otherwise, you're potentially trading one accessibility issue for another.

There is more we could cover around autofill, but we won't go deeper into that in this book. If you're interested, I've added a comprehensive guide to autofill to the reading list for this chapter, which you can find at `inclusive.guide/reading/chapter4`.

Conclusion

Motor disabilities create a range of access needs that require careful consideration. You should now understand the way many users interact with a page, other than with a mouse and keyboard or a finger on a screen. You know how to test your site using only a keyboard and the importance of the `focus` state, as well as how to make it something that is both beautiful *and* usable rather than simply removing it.

You've also learned how to avoid trapping motor-impaired users in content (and out of it) when features like modals and overlays take over a page and how to avoid excluding them from content that they might not be able to interact with using the `tabindex` attribute. We covered navigating by voice, as well as how to avoid a reliance on gestures or motion-based actions like tilting and shaking that many users may not be able to perform. All of these practical steps will help make browsing your site as effortless as possible, and giving them control over the time constraints you impose on them will make it far more enjoyable.

Much like considering whether your users *hear* your site rather than see it, or whether they only see *some* of the colors on its page, you have to consciously consider the **physical** barriers many of your users may face when engaging with your content and, in doing so, accommodate for them in order to make your sites as accessible and inclusive as possible.

CHAPTER 5

Deafness and Hard of Hearing

Hearing loss is extremely common. It's estimated that around **20%** of the world's population – **1.5 billion** people – are affected by hearing loss in at least one ear. More than **5%** of the world's population – **430 million** people – are hearing-impaired, and more than **70 million** people are deaf.[1] It's thought that by 2050, over **700 million** people (1 in 10) around the world will be affected by disabling hearing loss.[2] With deafness being such a common disability and set to become even more prominent, we need to ensure that more attention is given to the barriers that these people could face online.

Deafness affects people of all ages and does so in different ways. For instance, some people are born without the ability to hear, while others lose their hearing later in life. As a result, the latter may learn to read and write while being able to hear. The former often find this much more difficult, however, and so might instead be more proficient at sign language (communicating through visual gestures) or reading lips. There are also several forms of hearing impairment that don't constitute a *complete* absence of hearing, including conductive hearing loss (where sound is muffled), perceptive deafness (where sound is distorted), various types of tinnitus, and auditory agnosia (where it is difficult to distinguish *between* sounds).[3] At a glance, these users experience the same barriers – auditory information must be communicated in alternative ways. In reality, there is far more to it, and it's important to remember that different deaf users have different preferences about *how* they receive this information. This is very similar to the range of visual impairments, and their differing preferences, that we covered earlier in the book.

Since 1970, sign language has come to play an increasingly central role in the cultural unification of the deaf community.[4] Around half a million people in the United States use American Sign Language (ASL) to communicate, and of the 11 million people in Britain

© Ashley Firth 2024
A. Firth, *Practical Web Accessibility*, https://doi.org/10.1007/979-8-8688-0152-5_5

who are deaf, over 150,000 use British Sign Language (BSL) as their preferred language.[5] I spoke to Áine Jackson of the British Deaf Association, and she explained that

> These users often do not feel disabled and argue that they run into barriers due to a lack of understanding and services delivered in their **first language**. Deaf users can be considered a linguistic and cultural minority, a part of a community with a rich heritage and identity.[6]

Remember that in the introduction, we discussed the World Health Organization's change in the definition of "disability" from a "personal attribute" to a conflict between a person and the *society* they live in. This is the perfect example of that. Many BSL users don't want their deafness to be treated as a disability; they instead want people to understand that they have a different (and neglected) set of access needs when compared to hearing people, and this speaks to the essence of this book.

Therefore, in this chapter, we will look at how to design with these access needs in mind and help to remove those unnecessary barriers. The solutions in this chapter will empower deaf users, other hearing-impaired users, as well as more situational access needs, from people who speak another language to those who simply find reading difficult.

The good news is that many of these solutions can be added to content that already exists. We'll begin with, and largely focus on, creating and adding accessible subtitles and captions – tools that hold the greatest potential for providing access to previously inaccessible content. As the way to achieve this now has global adoption across different browsers, we can provide this content in a way that better caters to the needs of deaf and hard of hearing users than was possible before.

We'll then look at the importance of the content *itself* and how to include options that cater to the various preferences of different deaf and hard of hearing users, such as the importance of transcripts and the process of creating videos that are inclusive to those with sign language. Then, we'll examine advancements in automated accessibility from video streaming sites like YouTube. From communicating with customers to dealing with autoplay, barriers for deaf users often crop up unexpectedly, and this chapter will prove that it's important to be proactive when addressing common pitfalls that make understanding information harder than it should be.

Subtitles and Closed Captioning

Video and audio have grown online massively in recent years, with 92% of all Internet users worldwide watching digital videos each week.[7] Therefore, ensuring that yours are accessible has never been more important. If your videos have any sort of audio that holds meaning, then deaf and hard of hearing users are missing out on that information. Do you remember how we fixed existing inaccessible images in Chapter 2 "Blindness" by adding `alt` tags as another way to interact with them? It's time to do the same for videos!

You'd be forgiven for thinking that updating existing videos would be significantly harder than adding `alt` tags to images, but really it only involves adding one tag and creating a file with a format that's easy to build. The main difference is that the amount of content you must describe depends entirely on the length of your videos. Just like with `alt` tags too, there are fundamental WCAG rules that require you to provide captions/subtitles to your video content to be compliant (1.2.1: Time-based Media and 1.2.2: Captions).[8] Before we get into the implementation though, it's worth briefly getting to know the different methods for describing audio content in written form. These are **captions** and **subtitles**, and understanding the difference can be tricky. This is because, in many instances, the two words have often been used interchangeably, with captions sometimes referred to as subtitles for the hard of hearing. However, elsewhere, people draw more concrete distinctions.

What's the Difference?

Typically, that distinction is that captions provide an accessible way for viewers who cannot hear audio to watch video, whereas subtitles provide an accessible way for speakers of any language to watch video.

The W3C describes captions as a word-for-word transcription of what is being said in the same language as the audio. They also contain auditory information that isn't *spoken*, but that helps the user to understand the context of the video. This could include indications of actions, music, and sound effects. They're described as being intended for deaf and hard of hearing users. Subtitles, on the other hand, **only** include words that are spoken and can be translated into **other languages**. W3C argues that subtitles are designed for hearing users who want the dialogue provided in text form as well.

The problem is, while it is useful to make a distinction between the two, these definitions make some unnecessary and confusing assumptions.

One big problem is that this definition assumes that subtitles are "for" hearing users and captions are "for" deaf users. Lisa Herrod, a user experience consultant who has written extensively about designing for deaf users, disagrees. She argues that both options are useful for deaf *and* hard of hearing users in different ways:

> As a transcription, captioning is simply the written form of spoken words and sound effects, including slang, colloquialisms, modifiers, and wordplay—which... can be very difficult for deaf, and Hard of Hearing people who struggle with English as a second language.[9]

In other words, captions are not "for" all deaf users because, as we shall see in a moment, the word-for-word language can be confusing.

Similarly, Herrod goes against the W3C to point out that subtitles should not *always* be a word-for-word transcription of what is spoken – they should be considered translations, which allows us to change the text:

> Subtitling, which is a translation, provides an opportunity to use words that are closer to the signs a Deaf person would use. However, it is important to note that typically, native sign languages have no natural written form.[10]

Here, subtitles can help *some* deaf users who prefer altered English, especially those who understand English poorly, or as a second language (we will explain how to write like this in more detail later in the chapter). Just as captions shouldn't be considered "for deaf users," subtitles shouldn't be seen as existing "for" hearing users.

So, how do we avoid this confusion? Instead of emphasizing a distinction based on who they are "for," we instead need to emphasize a difference in **purpose**. It's better therefore to think of these processes as "**translation**" (changing text – sometimes into a different language – so it can be better understood) and "**transcription**" (writing down text word for word). Moving forward, we will use these terms when the distinction should be clear and "captions and subtitles" when talking about the more general idea of providing text for audio and video content.

User Preference

So we have captioning providing extra contextual information (**translation**) and subtitling containing the spoken content (**transcription**) but with the option to translate that content into another language, or more accessible text in the same language, using the most appropriate words for the task (**optional translation**). These options should be seen more as user preferences: some deaf users, for example, prefer "deaf-friendly" subtitles, while others are more comfortable with word-for-word transcribed English captions. Todd Wright, a bilingual deaf user, explains:

> I would prefer all subtitles and/or captions be more like literal translations with transcribed sound effects – I view media with full English captions as I do understand English very well.[11]

So, there's value for users in thinking beyond **transcription** and into the **translation** of what's happening. This gives users a richer understanding of the content and makes what they're engaging with through text more accessible. Let's explore some ways to achieve that.

Caption Actions

You often see an indication like this in captions, wrapped in square brackets, like so:

```
[spits milk]
```

This infers information that isn't spoken but helps the user better understand the context of the video. An example of this is shown in Figure 5-1 below.

Changes like these are intended to provide a catered experience to users who cannot hear and break through barriers that aren't solely tied to the words in the video. Imagine each of the following scenarios while watching a movie with no sound:

- Characters in a movie have their backs to the camera, and so it's not clear who's speaking.

- A glass smashes off-screen that draws attention, but the viewer cannot hear the sound.

- The soundtrack in a movie scene turns ominous, but there is no dialogue.

Figure 5-1. *Two people are dancing on a video. The captions read "[You Never Can Tell" Plays], informing them what they're dancing to in order to provide extra context.*

Here, subtitles alone would leave a user with only part of the experience. You can easily see the difference captions make in these examples and equally what would be *lost* in the experience without them.

Both captions and subtitles are available in two forms: open and closed. Open means they are overlaid permanently on the screen and cannot be turned off, whereas closed means typically they are off by default but can be turned on at will by the user. We will be focusing on the "closed" method as they can be added to existing content without remaking the video. After reading this chapter though, you may want to consider which of the two approaches best serves your users based on your content.

The Rise of Captions

A theme that comes up throughout this book is the idea that access needs are user needs – that when building a site or feature with accessibility in mind, it creates a more usable and improved experience for everyone. I think subtitles are one of the best recent examples of that.

Research revealed that **85%** of Facebook videos are watched with closed captions on and sound off.[12] In 2022, Netflix revealed that **40%** of its global users have subtitles on *all the time*, while a staggering **80%** switch them on at least once a month – stats that far exceed the number of viewers who need captioning because of a hearing impairment.[13]

When research was conducted about why, the examples given were incredibly varied. Here are a few:

- Watching in a loud environment (commuting)

- Trying to maintain a quiet environment (baby sleeping)

- Engaging with content made in another language

- A thick accent from an international actor

- Understanding a subtle moment some people might miss that's integral to the plot

- Helping you follow what's going on while doing other things, like using your phone

- Improve comprehension of a language you're learning (genuinely – many people have taken to using them as a means of testing themselves).[14]

These are circumstances many of us can relate to, and some *may* be considered situational access needs, but largely they're being used to heighten the viewing pleasure, either enabling you to do other things or enabling you to better understand the content. What's more, subtitles are most popular with those between 18 and 25 years old, who are almost four times more likely than older viewers to watch TV shows with subtitles, despite having fewer hearing problems.[15]

Moreover, as with most a11y features, they can help with multiple access needs. The W3C has argued that subtitles can also help some cognitive-impaired people because they provide content in more than one format. When used simultaneously, multiple formats increase the likelihood of understanding and positive engagement, as users don't have to rely on a single source of information.[16]

What all this tells us is that they're useful for a wide range of reasons, popular with an ever-growing group of people, and most importantly, make content accessible to everyone that wants to engage with it. So, let's look at how to add them to our videos!

<track> Element

As I mentioned earlier, we added `alt` tags to images in Chapter 2 "Blindness" to provide a description of images for people who can't perceive them. Now, we're faced with a similar challenge but for audio and video. Luckily, HTML5 allows us to solve the problem by adding subtitles or captions for a video using the `<track>` HTML tag. Let's take a quick look at the code:

```
<video controls>
    <source src="videos/video.webm" type="video/webm">
    <track label="English" kind="subtitles" srclang="en" src="vtt/subtitles-
    en.vtt" default>
    <track label="Deutsch" kind="subtitles" srclang="de" src="vtt/
    subtitles-de.vtt">
</video>
```

For those who haven't seen this type of code before, this is how a video is added to a page in HTML. The three main tags that are being used here are

- **<video>** – The main element that wraps the other tags. It tells the browser that it will be displaying a video.

- **<source>** – This tag holds the path to the actual video file that the video player will play. A video can have multiple sources to account for different video formats because some browsers will only display videos with a certain format.

- **<track>** – The tag we're most interested in. This is what allows us to add our own subtitles and captions.

Now let's take a closer look at the attributes of the `<track>` tag we're focusing on and the ways you can customize it:

- **label** – This provides the title for the caption or subtitle you've provided. Users will see this when they select a caption option.

- **src** – The path to your caption file.

- **kind** – Quite simply specifies the type of file. As we mentioned earlier, there is a difference between subtitles and captions, and so you can specify which type your file is through this ("captions" and "subtitles"). Other notable types are "chapters," which are provided to help users navigate to particular parts of audio or video, and "descriptions," which provide an overview of the visuals of a video if it's obscured or the user can't see it due to blindness or low vision. This is more useful when there is little to no dialogue in the video.

- **srclang** – The language that the captions or subtitles are provided in. For this, you provide the same ISO country code format we mentioned in our work with the lang attribute in Chapter 2 "Blindness." Our preceding example has en for English and de for German. This is an important point to make as you can provide multiple <track> files in order to provide captioning for a range of languages, including "deaf-friendly" captions. By doing this, you can also remove an access barrier present for users whose first language is not the one that your content is presented in. If the kind attribute is set to "subtitles," you **must** set a srclang.

- **default** – Following on from the last point, you can specify the **default** language that captions should be provided in (if you have supplied multiple options). This comes into effect if the user's preferences indicate that another track would better suit them – such as language preferences on their device/browser.

Much like going back through your site and adding alt tags to images, <track> is a big win for sites that already have video or audio on their site. For content that cannot be remade in order to overlay captions onto it, due to time or cost restraints, you can simply create your own and add them retrospectively. Despite this, the <track> element is included on the <video> element less than **1%** of the time online.[17] We've seen how the file is added, so let's look at how to make the file itself that we need to display captions and subtitles.

WebVTT Files

The HTML video player requires captions in a WebVTT (.vtt) format. WebVTT stands for Web Video Text Tracks Format and is just a simple text file. They follow a specified format and can be made without any knowledge of coding in an application like TextEdit or Notepad. Here is a basic example of the format to create two lines of captions for a video:

```
WEBVTT
00:00:00.500 --> 00:00:03.500
Run run run as fast as you can
00:00:03.600 --> 00:00:05.000
You can't catch me
I'm the gingerbread man
```

It's genuinely as simple as that. You start the file with WEBVTT, specify the start and end time for the part of the video you want to annotate, and then add the words spoken within that time frame directly underneath. You can also place this text over multiple lines if you want, as shown earlier. You could save the preceding code as a .vtt file, add it to our video example earlier using the <track> tag, and the first 5 seconds of it would display your text during those times. Figure 5-2 shows what this should look like.

Figure 5-2. *An illustrative example of how WebVTT captions would be displayed on a video player. The text reads "Run run run as fast as you can" on the bottom middle of the video.*

As of 2023, WebVTT is supported in over 97% of browsers worldwide[18] and is recommended by the W3C, making it both very easy to create and maintain and helpful to nearly everyone.[19]

Styling Subtitles

Providing text tracks for audio and video is a good first step, but much like a web page itself, styling with CSS can really elevate both their aesthetics and usability. You may want the text to match your site's style or for the captions to work a little harder to help those using them to better understand the content. Thankfully, WebVTT has a broad set of features, allowing you to customize captions and subtitles to fit your content, and user's needs, better.

cue

The first rule that can be styled is the cue rule – this is what each line of text in a .vtt file is known as. Using cue, you can add styling rules that will apply to **every** caption or subtitle shown. Figure 5-3 shows the result of the following code – turning the caption text red and the background white:

```
video::cue {
    color: red;
    background-color: white;
}
```

Figure 5-3. *The same caption as our first example, but now styled with red text and a white background*

Formatting

On top of changing the style of entire lines, we can also format *parts* of text. There are a few simple tags that WebVTT recognizes, which work on every major browser:

- **<b> (Bold)** – Allows you to place emphasis on certain words

- **<i> (Italics)** – Allows you to italicize parts of a text

- **<u> (Underline)** – Allows you to underline areas of a sentence

However, you can take this a little further and apply styling changes directly to these tags, thereby allowing you to change their appearance beyond these default styles. In the following code, you can see a line from a WebVTT file with bold (<b>) and italic (<i>) tags. The following CSS targets those tags to *change* their styles. Figure 5-4 shows these changes taking effect:

```
/* CSS */
video::cue(b) {
      color: indigo;
}
video::cue(i) {
      color: green;
}

WEBVTT
00:00:08.100 --> 00:00:10.500
<b>I'm</b> not the monster here. <i>You are</i>.
```

Figure 5-4. *Parts of the video's captions are now styled using the bold and italic tags. The bold text is now indigo, and the italic text is now green, thanks to our preceding styling.*

Positioning

Beyond the aesthetic changes to captions, you also have control over *where* text is displayed on your video. You can achieve this with a range of attributes, so let's go through them.

Position and Line

You'll often see captions positioned in different places over the course of a video to indicate who is speaking at a certain time. The "position" and "line" rules allow you to do this as they let you decide where captions are positioned on the video. The position attribute is responsible for the x axis, and line is responsible for the y axis. You can see this in Figure 5-5.

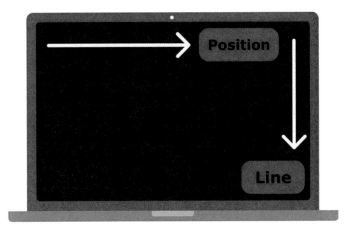

Figure 5-5. *A diagram showing how the* position *and* line *attributes affect the placement of captions or subtitles over a video.* position *adjusts movement on the x axis, while* line *affects the y axis.*

You can set both attributes as a percentage from 0% to 100%, with 0% being far left for position and top for line. However, line can also be a number that represents how many lines from the top (if the number is above zero) or bottom (if the number is below zero) the caption should be. These rules can be applied to every caption through CSS, **or** on a per-caption basis. In Figure 5-6, you can see how different percentage values change the position of several captions.

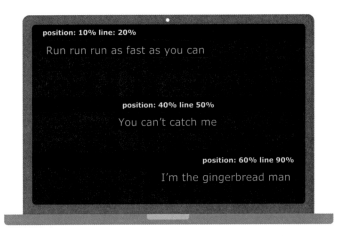

Figure 5-6. *A visual representation of captions positioned in different places on a video using the* position *and* line *attributes as percentages. Low percentages place the captions top left, numbers around 50% place them in the center, and higher numbers place them in the bottom right.*

This isn't useful if you're adding "translations" without captions (subtitles) as they're **always** positioned in the center and at the bottom of the screen, but it *is* useful when positioning captions. These rules allow caption content to be closer to the person who is speaking if there's more than one person visible in the video, or if the mouth of the person speaking isn't visible, for example.

Align

This attribute specifies the alignment of the caption text *within* the caption window. This is different from `position` that sets where the caption window *itself* is positioned. It can be set to `start` (left), `center` (middle), or `end` (right) and can be applied to each cue individually. Figure 5-7 shows how each of these three options are displayed:

```
00:00:04.100 --> 00:00:06.000 align:center
You can't catch me
```

Figure 5-7. *Captions aligned left (pictured top), center (pictured middle), and right (pictured bottom) based on the* `align` *attribute that has been set. The captions read "Run run run as fast as you can," "You can't catch me," and "I'm the gingerbread man" and are all colored green.*

Size

The `size` attribute dictates how *much* of the screen your caption window takes up and is also specified as a percentage from 0% to 100%, with 100% being the default. For example, the following code **reduces** the size of the caption box to 10% of its possible size, with the result shown in Figure 5-8:

```
00:00:06.300 --> 00:00:012.600 size:10%
You can't catch me
```

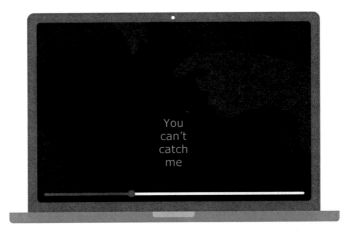

Figure 5-8. *A caption displayed as one word per line due to the size of the caption window being set to 10% of the screen. The caption reads "You can't catch me".*

It's worth considering whether you *should* reduce the size of your captions or subtitles though, as research has shown that it can be difficult to read more than two lines at a time while also engaging with video.[20]

Future Features

The following features are part of the WebVTT spec and are supported in the Google Chrome and Safari browsers on both desktop and mobile but have varied support elsewhere. They are however worth thinking about because of their potential to provide greater benefits for *all* users in the future. Moreover, given that Chrome and Safari hold nearly 85% of the browser market share globally at the time of writing, making use of them would enhance a *lot* of user's experience and combat a lot of access needs.[21]

I have provided an example of each of these features in the practical example for this chapter, which you can find at inclusive.guide/examples/webvtt. If a browser *doesn't* support one of these features, it will simply ignore it and display the text normally, so they're safe to implement.

Voice Spans

WebVTT allows for "voice spans," which help to distinguish certain subtitles consistently. For example, consider the following markup:

```
00:00:00.000 -> 00:00:08.000
<v Walter>I am the danger
```

This will allow you to consistently style text spoken by a particular person, such as a character or narrator (in this case, Walter). This is especially useful for dialogue as you won't have to apply the same styling rules to every part of the file in which a certain character speaks. To make everything Walter says appear light blue, for example, the CSS for the preceding code would look like this:

```
video::cue(v[voice="Walter"]) {
    color: lightblue;
}
```

Classes

Applying a class will allow you to style a piece of text in the same way that you can use CSS to style any other element on a web page. The syntax is a little different from the other examples, but the results are the same:

```
/* CSS */
video::cue(.my-class) {
    color: purple;
    text-transform: uppercase;
}

WEBVTT
01:23:00.000 -> 01:23:04.000
<c.my-class>Get busy livin', or get busy dyin'</c>
```

You can assign multiple classes to a line *and* use "voice spans" at the same time, allowing you to create layered and rich style combinations as shown in Figure 5-9:

```css
/* CSS */
video::cue(.first) {
    font-style: italic;
}
video::cue(.loud) {
    font-weight: bold;
}
video::cue(v[voice="Walter"]) {
    color: lightblue;
}
```

```
WEBVTT
00:00:00.500 --> 00:00:03.500
<v.first.loud Walter>I am the danger.
```

Figure 5-9. *An illustration of captions that have been styled using a mixture of voice spans and multiple classes. The text is now light blue, bold, and italic.*

:past and :future Pseudo Elements

These two selectors allow you to style captions that happen either **before** or **after** the video's current playtime. A good example of this is karaoke, where it's handy to have a sense of timing related to a line of text. Take the following example:

```css
/* CSS */
video::cue(c:past) {
    color:gray;
}
video::cue(c:future) {
    color:pink;
}
```

```
WEBVTT
00:00:19.500 --> 00:00:22.300
<c>I've tried</c> <00:00:19.500><c>to be</c> <00:00:20.000><c> fair</c>
<00:00:21.000><c>to</c> <00:00:21.750><c>you</c> <00:00:22.250>
<c>creatures</c>
```

Here, you can see timestamps assigned to certain *parts* of a sentence in the WebVTT file. As the video or audio reaches a particular point, the text that came *before* that time will be gray, and the text *yet to come* will be in pink, which Figure 5-10 shows.

Figure 5-10. *Captions displaying text in gray that is in the past (based on the point in the video) and pink for words in the future. The caption reads "I've tried to be fair to you creatures".*

Karaoke is quite an impractical example here though. A handier use for this functionality is that you can more accurately match words as someone is saying them so that deaf users can engage with physical gestures as well as the text. This is useful because it helps users build up a greater sense of context. For example, deaf and BSL users "rely heavily on facial expression to convey essential meaning and emphasis."[22]

The key is utilizing this styling but also having shorter and more frequent captions rather than bigger ones that last longer. This allows users to understand gestures, follow with greater ease, and not focus *too much* on just the text because they're unsure how long it'll be present on screen – preventing them from getting overwhelmed.

Captions or Subtitles: Which Should I Apply?

It's worth thinking about the **content** of the video and ensuring that any important context wouldn't be lost if you were to purely **transcribe** speech and nothing else. The best solution when you're not sure would be including a captioned track that "transcribes" the contents of media, one that "translates" the text into "deaf-friendly" language, and a hybrid that includes both. This takes more work but creates choice for the user and caters to the widest possible set of access needs.

The good news is that, despite their different purposes and benefits, accessible subtitles, captions, and a mix of the two are implemented in the same way technically, and the change in how you format the content between the two types is minimal. So, whichever challenge relates to your site, we'll be tackling it.

Audio Captions

Let's return briefly to the concept of karaoke, which wasn't a relevant example when we were dealing with video. A better example would be providing captions for an *audio* track and not video – let's go through how to handle that now.

Providing captions for audio files is especially important, as this form of media *only* conveys information via sound and would otherwise be *completely* inaccessible to hearing-impaired users – video at least compliments audio with visuals. However, there is one **big** problem – at the time of writing, even years on from the first edition of this book, captions don't really *work* at all with the `<audio>` tag. Even though it's an accessibility requirement to provide captions for the `<audio>` tag[23] and despite recognizing that they're there when provided, they have no native way to display them.[24] This is likely why the `<track>` tag is only present on a meager 0.06% of all `<audio>` tags online.[25] In a way, this makes sense – the "V" in WebVTT stands for "video" after all. However, this technicality does nothing to help deaf and deafblind users engage with this content.

The good news is that we can work around this problem using the `<video>` tag. What we can do is provide an audio file such as an MP3 *instead* of a video file, specify that as the type, and the `<video>` tag will simply **play audio** from a video player:

```
<video class="audio" controls>
    <source src="media/audio.mp3" type="audio/mpeg">
    <track label="English" kind="captions" srclang="en" src="vtt/audio.vtt"
    default />
</video>
```

This makes sense as the `<audio>` and `<video>` tags both use the same `<source>` tag and **both** extend from a native media element. This is great news for accessibility but does come with a slight drawback: as captions and subtitles display at the *bottom* of a video by default, and because an audio track has no video to display, the captions can often end up displaying *underneath* the browser's native video controls.

There are a couple of ways to combat this issue. First, you could provide a thumbnail or "poster" image for the video player. This image is the still frame you typically see before you press "play" on a video but is also shown as a fallback when no video is present:

```
<video class="audio" controls poster="images/poster.jpg">
```

This is useful for us because it gives the `<video>` tag the height it needs to avoid displaying captions below the controls.[26]

An alternative if you're looking for a smaller, less visual audio player is to explicitly set a height for the `<video>` element serving the audio and then using the `line` attribute we mentioned earlier to position the captions at the top of the `<video>` instead of the bottom. The result of this is shown in Figure 5-11:

```
/* CSS */
.audio {
    height: 120px;
}

WEBVTT
00:00:08.100 --> 00:00:10.500 line:1
I'm not the monster here. You are.
```

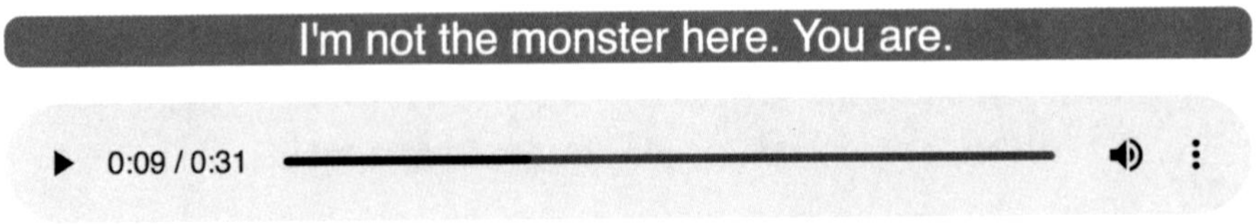

I'm not the monster here. You are.

▶ 0:09 / 0:31 ━━━━━━━━━━━━━━━━━━━━ ◀)) ⋮

Figure 5-11. *A custom audio player using the* `<video>` *tag, with a fixed height and positioned captions. The captions sit above the timeline and controls of the player, and they read "I'm not the monster here. You are."*

Remember `line:1` means that the caption should be displayed **one line from the top of the video**. I have created both implementations in the practical example for this chapter so that you can see both in action and decide which works best for you. Whichever you choose though, you will have ensured that you've both provided captions and subtitles *and* displayed them in a meaningful and accessible way.

Practical Example

What is hopefully clear from looking at all of these attributes is that there are ways to cater to pretty much every preferred style of displaying captions and subtitles. You can now have full control over positioning, styling, colors, and the direction the text is read – even allowing users to follow along word for word as they're spoken. There should, therefore, never be an issue where you are unable to accurately describe what is happening in audio or video by using WebVTT.

I have added examples of each of these features into this chapter's practical example, including a demonstration of how this works for audio as well as video. For those who are interested in the code, you can check it out on GitHub in the "Chapter 5" folder or, if you just want to see it in action, you can view it at `inclusive.guide/examples/webvtt`. Again, what's great about this implementation is that you don't necessarily have to *change* anything about the content you already have – it's really easy to add captions or subtitles as an extra file, and your site will immediately become more accessible.

Now that you know how to add captions and subtitles for both video and audio yourself, let's briefly cover how users can control them and how they're handled on a global scale by a large video-based website like YouTube.

Closed Caption Buttons

When you supply a `<track>` file, all modern browsers will automatically display a button to toggle the subtitles/captions on and off (or choose between the multiple options if you have provided more than one). This is the same behavior as sites such as YouTube or Vimeo. This means that you don't have to build this functionality yourself – you're rewarded with it for providing a `.vtt` file! Figure 5-12 shows the expanded version of the "caption" button on a video player.

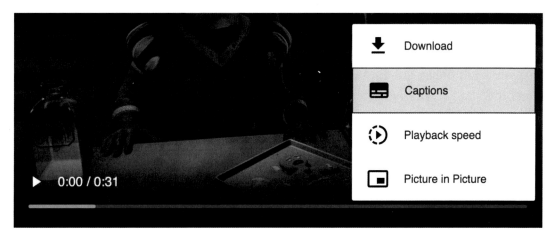

Figure 5-12. *When opened, a browser's default "closed captions" button offers the chance to download the media file, choose between the various languages that have been set as captions, adjust the playback speed (for video and captions), and reposition the captions to a "Picture in Picture" view.*

This is a brilliant accessibility gain, but you may not always want to display captions *by default* – overlaying captions or subtitles on your media for every user automatically may not be necessary. Fortunately, this is easy to handle and can be controlled by one attribute on the `<track>` tag – `default`. If you *don't* provide a default track, the video won't display the captions by default and instead require the user to turn them on via the "closed captions" button.

Other Caption Formats

It's worth noting that `.vtt` isn't the only format that can provide captioning for video and audio. There are a range of different formats that were created and adopted by different video platforms, but they all *mostly* follow the same format with a couple of minor style tweaks. For instance, this is an example of an `.srt` (SubRip) caption – another widely known format:

```
1
00:01,000 -> 00:04,000
-This is the common sloth in its natural habit
2
00:05,000 -> 00:09,000
-It moves very slowly along a branch
```

It's nearly identical to our earlier WebVTT example – the main differences are the formatting of the times (`.srt` uses commas between seconds and milliseconds, instead of full stops), and numbering captions is mandatory. Popular sites like YouTube, Vimeo, and Netflix all support `.srt` and `.vtt`, so you can't really go wrong with either.[27] If you'd like to read more about the various caption formats that exist, I've added a robust guide to the reading list of this chapter, which you can find at `inclusive.guide/reading/chapter5`.

YouTube

As we mentioned before, major streaming platforms such as YouTube and Vimeo and media players such as VLC and iTunes support the ability to upload the WebVTT captions we just created. This means you can make your content more accessible even when it's **not** hosted on your own site using the `<video>` tag. But do you *need* to upload captions to YouTube, the biggest video website in the world? As of 2023, there are over **800 million** videos on YouTube, with videos being watched **1 billion** times a day.[28] That's a lot of potentially inaccessible content, but thankfully YouTube actually creates captions for videos that are uploaded to their system themselves automatically:

> YouTube can use speech-recognition technology to automatically create captions for your videos. These automatic captions are generated by machine-learning algorithms.[29]

You can view these by clicking the "CC" button next to the full-screen icon on a YouTube player, and Figure 5-13 shows how the captions are displayed, along with the message to clarify that they're autogenerated.

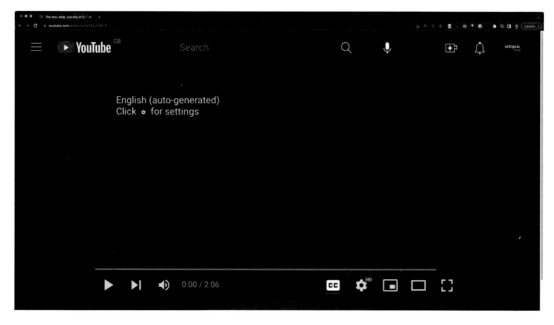

Figure 5-13. *A visual of captions being displayed on a YouTube video. It informs the user at the beginning of the video, in the top left hand corner, that the captions have been autogenerated.*

This is seriously impressive and provides an excellent baseline of accessibility on one of the most visited websites in the world. However, YouTube does state that "the quality of the captions may vary" as the algorithm gets smarter. It's therefore worth going over the captions that have been created for your content and making any necessary changes if some have been incorrectly created. At the time of writing, they also don't generate things like caption actions that we covered earlier, making it more important to review and improve them.

It's possible to do this through YouTube's "Studio" page (shown in Figure 5-14), where you can edit both text and timings that have been generated automatically.

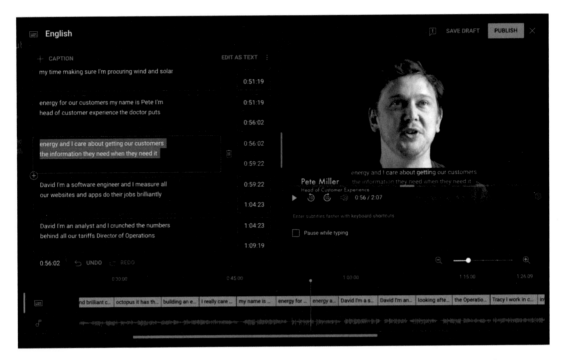

Figure 5-14. *The YouTube "Studio" page allows you to alter the generated captions for your video. The video is positioned on the right, with the captions and their beginning and end times on the left. You're able to remove the captions, add more, and change the text of existing ones.*

You can also choose to download and edit the captions YouTube has generated, which are provided as an `.sbv` file, but bear a heavy resemblance to the `.vtt` files we made earlier. Here's an example of the format for `.sbv`:

```
0:00:03.529,0:00:08.970
We started Octopus Energy to be
fairer to customers
0:00:08.970,0:00:13.380
to make energy digital the way it should be
and because it's so important we move to renewables
```

Equally, you can upload caption and subtitle files you've already created to YouTube to replace the ones they generate for you, again through the "Studio" page. At the time of writing, the best-supported file format for YouTube is `.srt`, but it's *very* easy to convert `.vtt` files into this format. If you need it, there is a link to a conversion website to do this in the reading list for this chapter, which you can find at inclusive.guide/

`reading/chapter5`. I'd advise you to start by editing the generated captions YouTube provides, unless you've already written them yourself, to both save time and allow you to download them if you need to make a transcript or use them elsewhere.

Accessible Subtitle/Caption Content

We've talked about how to implement subtitles and captions for video and audio, so the next challenge is to ensure that the text itself is *also* accessible.

Some deaf users who can read English comfortably are happy with word-for-word captions. However, as we mentioned earlier, it can be incredibly useful to **translate** (as opposed to **transcribe**) your subtitles, providing the option to have them in a version of English that many deaf users will find easier to understand. This is especially important to American Sign Language (ASL) and British Sign Language (BSL) users because "typically, native sign languages have no natural written form".[30]

There are several reasons that native ASL and BSL users often find it difficult to understand word-for-word transcribed English. For example, it is more difficult to learn English without sounding out the words, something many deaf users are unable to do. Moreover, BSL, for example, is very different from written English – words that sound the same in English will often have very different BSL signs, and BSL also has its own grammar structure. For example, a phrase like "How old is your friend?" might be expressed as "Friend yours how old?".

How a deaf user prefers to receive accessible information often depends on what they consider to be their **first language**. As we mentioned at the start of the chapter, many native sign language users consider that their first language and so would benefit most from onscreen signing. This is the gold standard for sign language captioning and is an AAA level WCAG rule (1.2.6: Sign Language).[31] This is achieved through a person being overlaid on your video, typically in the bottom right hand corner, and signing the content of the video as it's played. Figure 5-15 shows this.

Figure 5-15. *An illustration of where a sign language interpreter would be overlayed on a video in order to sign the contents of the video as it's playing*

Signed Captions

There are many organizations that you can commission to create sign language titles for both your video content and larger blocks of text, as this approach isn't as easy to implement as closed captions and subtitles. The result, as Áine Jackson of the British Deaf Association explained to me, is that many simply don't do it:

> Most web content accessibility guidelines do not make adequate provision for sign language users to access content in sign language as a first language. While there is limited good practice happening with some organisations and charities, this is very much the **exception** and not the rule.[32]

Therefore, your first task here is to decide whether you can engage with a company to create sign language-friendly content for you. If your site is video-heavy, you are an essential service provider, or you maintain high-traffic websites, this process would certainly be worth the expense. If this translation is *not* an option, perhaps due to cost, then Lisa Herrod recommends:

> A combination of captioning (to transcribe sound effects) and subtitling (written translation, with a focus on users with sign as a primary language) is most effective.[33]

This is the exact approach we covered earlier. Therefore, let's now explore techniques to accomplish writing this content in the most accessible way possible.

Sign Language-Friendly Content

There are some important steps you can take yourself to ensure that your subtitles are more accessible for native signers. These all revolve around writing in a way that is more considerate of, and **accessible** to, these users. Just like using a screen reader, or considering content without color, this process involves you considering content from a perspective you may not have done so from before. When doing this, it's also important to remember that deaf users for whom English is their first language often still struggle with written English and as a result typically have a lower reading age (a common way to estimate someone's reading ability, measured against the average ability of people of different ages).

Research about this is disappointingly rare, but a famous report in 1979 found that deaf school leavers had an average reading age of around nine years old. A more recent report from 1996 found that with modern teaching techniques, this had only risen to around 13 years old.[34] Therefore, the solutions we are about to propose are extremely useful for removing barriers for these users, as well as those with learning difficulties who might not sign but will still benefit from more accessible written English:

- **Avoid puns** – Words that mean the same thing in English tend to have very different signs, and puns rely on understanding the **sounds** of the words to make sense. Unless a deaf user has a very strong grasp of written and spoken English, hearing puns can become quite confusing. For example, the phrase "time flies like an arrow, fruit flies like a banana" could be difficult to understand due to the different meanings of the word "flies" – especially for BSL users who have different signs for flying and insects.[35]

- **Synonyms** – English has more synonyms than almost any other language, while sign language uses very few gestures to describe the same thing. It can therefore be useful to avoid them where possible or use a more common synonym regularly rather than using a range.

- **Text speak** – (i.e., **C U L8er** or **m8**). Again, to understand what the letters mean here, you have to understand how they *sound*, which isn't an option for many deaf users.

- **Avoid colloquialisms/idioms** – A lot of idioms, like "once in a blue moon" do not carry over to BSL well – it is difficult to know whether they should be taken literally, and therefore they might not be understood.[36]

- **Clear simple speech** – This is especially important due to a lower average reading age in deaf users. We will talk in more detail about writing plain English in Chapter 6 "Cognitive Impairments" as this is also relevant when catering for various cognitively impaired users.

Where possible, deaf and sign language-friendly English should be used across your **entire** site. This is part of a much wider, but admittedly vague, accessibility requirement – writing clearly. Sign language-friendly language includes several aspects of "plain English." Writing accessible English is especially worth it when you consider that it will make your writing much easier to understand for those with disabilities like dyslexia and autism, but more generally for those scanning content quickly, or engaging with a new topic for the first time.

Writing accessible English shouldn't be mistaken for "dumbing down" content though, it's more about making content clearer:

> There seems to be a perception by some people that subtitles for the Deaf use dumbed-down language. However, I've always perceived the language to be based on the English equivalent of the signs that would have been used had an interpreter been present. Of course, this means that the grammar continues to follow an English pattern, but it seems to me that the subtitles are likely to be more accessible to a wider audience.[37]

Transcribing and Summarizing Audio and Video Content

Providing a short summary of what is in your media can be just as useful as adding captions and will allow all users to decide whether they want to engage with it or not.

Here's an example from a hearing-impaired user called Ruth, talking about watching an Aretha Franklin performance on Facebook:

> I see her playing the piano and I think, What song is she playing? There's absolutely no description. It's not that I need to hear every word, but sometimes I have no idea what's happening.[38]

This is the same process as adding `alt` text for images, but instead placing it visually on the page, next to the audio or video, so everyone can see it. This shows that it's **connected** to that content and holds particular benefit to those with a hearing impairment. On a Web where people browse quicker than ever, and so stay on your site for short amounts of time, providing a summary may help capture the attention of users for longer, as well as being accessible.

Providing a Transcript

Another way of providing media in a way that includes deaf users is to provide a **full transcript** of any content that contains audio. There are multiple WCAG rules that specify that prerecorded audio and video content needs to be accompanied by another suitable format to prevent it from being inaccessible to some users (1.2.1 Audio-only, and 1.2.8 Media Alternative).[39] It of course has the potential to be quite a lengthy body of text depending on the length of content, but it can have its benefits – users can read it in their own time and, in the case of video, read each part of the transcript in isolation while watching the media. Therefore, providing content in another way that doesn't exclude users offers them the freedom to choose.

Often, transcripts are kept in some form of drop-down so that they're not initially visible. This helps to keep the web page short but still make it easy for those who want that content to engage with it. This is what I've done with the transcripts in the practical example for this chapter (`inclusive.guide/examples/webvtt`), and the drop-down feature itself is *also* accessible, in case you'd like to use it elsewhere.

You can actually get a full transcript without doing any extra work by generating it from the contents of your WebVTT file, meaning that you get two accessible features for the price of one! There are a range of converters available online that accept `.vtt` as a format (which I'll cover in more detail in Chapter 11 "Tools and Auditing," but I'll also place one in the reading list for this chapter, which you can find at `inclusive.guide/reading/chapter5`.

Unexpected or Automatic Audio

Deaf and hard of hearing people may have a hard time gauging how loud videos are, particularly when they play automatically or unexpectedly. "You see a video on your Facebook feed and there's no sound," explains Ruth in the same interview. "If you click on it to make it big, the sound plays, but you don't realise. Sometimes I have my hearing aid off and I feel like the video is blaring out sound".[40]

Interestingly, autoplaying video on mobile devices has been prohibited for a long time largely due to the user being inadvertently forced to download the contents of a video using their roaming data the moment they arrive on a page. However, this suppression doesn't extend to desktop computers, where it's still very much possible through the `autoplay` attribute on videos.

When this happens, it can cause embarrassment for anyone, with or without a hearing impairment, so if you intend to autoplay video on your site, you should couple it with another attribute: `muted`. Doing this ensures that even if a video has started playing without the user's knowledge, it won't blare out sound too:

```
<video autoplay muted>
    ...
</video>
```

Users will be able to unmute the video themselves if they choose using the video player controls.

Linear Layouts

Deaf users are used to relying almost entirely on their sense of sight and are therefore more susceptible to being confused by badly or illogically designed websites. We covered linear layouts and clear heading structures extensively in Chapter 2 "Blindness" to help those who cannot interact with the visual aspect of a site, but the same solutions apply to users who rely **solely** on visual information.

Double-checking that your headings are descriptive and have a clear structure reduces the risk of a deaf user encountering problems with the only means that they have of interpreting content on web pages:

> I rely so much on visual information... If they weren't [clearly
> structured], I'd feel very lost because I completely rely on reading
> for understanding.[41]

I won't cover the same ground again; if you want to check you're catering for this issue, head back to Chapter 2 "Blindness," but I wanted to raise this as a consideration in this chapter as it's not a barrier that many would associate with users who can "see" a site.

Indeed, when content in its various forms (headings, paragraphs, lists, etc.) becomes harder to interact with (through either incorrectly coded sites or because their default style has been altered through design), those using screen readers may still use ARIA roles to help appropriately signpost and highlight types of content. For those interacting through sight *alone* though, these properties don't help.

Correctly coded sites, and layouts that display content in a linear, unambiguous way, are good practice and help everyone, especially people who are reliant on a single input for their information online – be that auditory or visual.

Now, it should be clear that a major barrier appears when a user's need for visual information isn't respected. A prime example of this happens when a company only allows them to get in contact via the telephone – a medium that simply doesn't accommodate that. We'll now discuss what you can do to combat this access need.

Servicing Customers Without a Telephone

Barriers can crop up in unexpected places, and sometimes you have to be proactive to spot them. For example, customer contact pages are one overlooked area where deaf users are often excluded. Here, placing your company's phone number, or requesting a user's, can be useful for some people, but if it is the *only* channel of communication, it can exclude the deaf and hard of hearing. We covered the following example in the introduction, but to recap, here's James Buller again (Lead Accessibility Consultant at the UK Home Office), talking about testing the United Kingdom's online passport registration process:

> We did some testing with D/deaf people. Initially the query was
> why would you do that, there's no audio involved in the service?
> But we decided to check anyway... [The subject] was going
> through the form, and there had been no big problems until she

got to the most boring page on the site – the contact page. It asked her to "provide a phone number" and she did, but also wanted to write "I'm D/deaf please don't call me" In this case, it wouldn't let her submit an answer with both numbers and text in it. When we tested this page against WCAG it passed, but on human terms, it was not accessible because we did not provide her with that option.[42]

You should therefore ensure that you offer **multiple** means of communication so as not to exclude a certain demographic. This also involves avoiding a reliance on vocal communication and any voice recognition which will often disrupt an otherwise accessible user journey.[43]

Providing Alternatives

In research conducted by experience management firm Qualtrics XM, they found that **77%** of consumers consider the difficulty of reaching an agent to be the biggest issue with customer service.[44] Nobody likes a long wait on hold, and customers are getting used to having multiple options when it comes to getting in touch – ranging from email and live web chat to communication through popular social networking sites like Facebook.

Your customers should be able to contact you in a mode of communication that is accessible to **them** and meets **their** needs. Email seems like the natural alternative to the phone as it doesn't require an audible interaction. However, some people still want the instant responses that phones offer. In this case, live chat, or even a Facebook or WhatsApp Messenger integration can provide the best of both worlds, and it's been proven that younger customers feel more comfortable and familiar with live chat than they do with phone support.[45]

Implementing these options allows you to more effectively communicate with your customers but also allows them to do the same with you. This freedom often results in them taking the time to provide more feedback on how you're doing, which is invaluable, and significantly lowers the amount of complaints companies receive.

Text or Video Relays

Research by PwC found that, despite the trickiness of reaching them, 75% of consumers will *still* choose to interact with a real person, even as the technology for automated solutions improves.[46] So although offering a range of communication options is a positive, you must still ensure that you **keep** that personal touch, including for those with access needs. For this reason, another available option that many deaf users find useful, and that is growing in popularity, is Text and Video Relays. This service either connects a hearing person on a standard phone line with a deaf person using a textphone (a special type of phone with a keyboard and display) or places them in a video call with whoever they're contacting and an interpreter. In both instances, "an operator acts as an intermediary and will relay what is signed or typed".[47] However, Áine Jackson explains that

> It is common when using text relay or BSL video calling to contact a service provider that frontline staff are not aware of this service and that it can be used, and will refuse to accept or interact with a call.[48]

If your website or service relies heavily on customer contact, you should ensure that your staff know that this is an option. I will place links to companies that offer this service in the reading list for this chapter, which can be found at `inclusive.guide/reading/chapter5`.

Conclusion

In this chapter, we've looked at catering to users with hearing-based access needs. We've learned about subtitles and captions, the differences between them, the preferences that different hearing-impaired users have, and how to implement **both** yourself using WebVTT. We've discussed how to make the most of these technologies by sizing, styling, and positioning captions for added effect and how to add these improvements for audio as well as video. Through this, my hope is that you now feel equipped to review your own content and make the simple, practical enhancements that will help unlock it for so many users and make even more *want* to engage with it.

We then turned our attention to the *content* of these subtitles and captions and focused on how to make the words you use accessible through plain language and deaf-friendly text. Finally, we moved away from captioning and explored an array of other accessibility issues – from preventing unexpected audio by muting videos that autoplay to making sure that you can communicate with deaf customers in real time effectively and personably.

More than **5%** of the world's population are deaf or hearing-impaired. Having read this chapter, you're now in a good place to improve their experience online through the sites you build and the content you share.

CHAPTER 6

Cognitive Impairments

For most people, technology makes things easier. But for people with disabilities, technology makes things possible.

—Mary Pat Radabaugh

A study by University College London has found that cognitive impairments have more than **doubled** in the last decade.[1] This number is staggering, albeit a little misleading, because we now *understand* more about these disabilities than we've ever done before. We now know, for example, that over **55 million** people worldwide live with dementia, and there are around **10 million** new cases per year.[2]

Alongside this increased understanding, more people than ever are *living* longer. By 2040, the US Census Bureau estimates that **80 million** US citizens – about one-quarter of the population – will be 65 or older. The older we get, the more cognitive challenges we face, and impairments that typically affect us later in life are becoming more prevalent.[3] For those facing these impairments from a young age, this also applies – the longer people live, the more they face these barriers – which, in turn, increases our understanding of them.

With both average age and understanding of cognitive impairments increasing year on year, we now have a much greater appreciation for just how many people these are affecting and the importance of catering to them. This is good progress from when Robert McDowell, author of the "Neurodiversity and Digital Inclusion" report, explained to me a few years ago that they are sometimes referred to as "hidden disabilities" due to the sheer difficulty in understanding and identifying them.[4]

However, he also explained that "not only are cognitive differences **hidden**, they have in many ways been **ignored**," and despite being given more attention in recent years, this *still* rings true. According to him, cognitive-impaired users are still "woefully neglected when compared with the work done for other users online."[5]

© Ashley Firth 2024
A. Firth, *Practical Web Accessibility*, https://doi.org/10.1007/979-8-8688-0152-5_6

This is partly why one of the main goals of the latest version of the Web Content Accessibility Guidelines (WCAG 2.2), which was released in October 2023, was to improve accessibility guidance for users with cognitive and learning disabilities.[6]

What Are Cognitive Impairments?

Generally, a cognitive impairment is when a person has trouble remembering, learning new things, concentrating, or making decisions that affect their everyday life. They can take many forms – clinical diagnoses include **autism**, **Alzheimer's**, **Down's syndrome**, **dementia**, **dyslexia**, **ADHD**, and a whole host of other impairments and learning difficulties. Each disability can mean that someone experiences one or all of these symptoms, and they range from mild to severe. This creates a wide variety of things we need to consider in our online journeys to be inclusive.

Luckily, around the same time as WCAG 2.2 released its first draft, the Cognitive and Learning Disabilities Accessibility Task Force (**COGA**) published a document entitled "Making Content Usable for People with Cognitive and Learning Disabilities." This is more great progress that has happened since the first edition of this book, but it's a *very* long document that, much like the latest version of WCAG, will always limit the amount of people that engage with it. It's also only a *guidance* document and not something enforceable. Because of this, it remains somewhat vague on the **practical** details of features that could help users.

It did however offer an excellent summary of the main areas that any website should focus on to make life easier for this cohort of users – users that, despite us understanding more about their impairments, still find troubles online. To help web content creators meet the needs of people with cognitive and learning disabilities, they identified these key areas:

- **Use clear content**
- **Help users understand what things are and how to use them**
- **Help users find what they need**
- **Help users focus**
- **Help users avoid mistakes**

As this area may grow in the future, in this chapter I'm going to overlay **practical** improvements and suggestions over this COGA framework. This way, you can assess and improve your websites for those with cognitive impairments right away but transfer that knowledge into anything new that builds upon this layout in the future.

Now, some of the access needs in this chapter may be a little more difficult to understand than in prior ones and so present a slightly different challenge. For example, it is much easier to understand that somebody might have trouble perceiving a shape because they have low vision, or experience color blindness, than it is to understand that somebody might have trouble actually recognizing and understanding what a shape *is*, or *means*, because of a visual cognitive impairment. This is part of what Robert McDowell meant by these being "hidden disabilities."

What's more, it's sometimes more difficult to clearly *categorize* these access needs. Again, when we talked about visual impairments, it was easy to tell the difference between needs based on blindness and color blindness. However, as we shall see, this is harder with cognitive impairments, with overlap between barriers and some users experiencing more than one of the preceding categories. To make it easier to consider cognitive impairments in your sites and to make it easier to *identify* the types of barriers they face and learn about them, I have grouped them into five main areas of symptoms that you'll see throughout the chapter:

- **Language comprehension**

- **Visual and visual-spatial comprehension**

- **Learning difficulties**

- **Executive function and focus**

- **Memory**

This list is based on the latest reading and reports, supported by suggestions from charities, and inspired by existing work from the W3C and COGA. It won't presume to include every possible cognitive impairment, but it *will* strengthen your understanding of the areas we have the clearest understanding of at the time of writing.

Let's get into it.

Use Clear Content

Let's begin with a point that may seem obvious but many sites often struggle with – providing content that is simple to follow and read for as many people as possible. Doing so holds the potential for you to help a huge range of cognitively impaired users, particularly those with issues around **language comprehension** – it's estimated that **15%–20%** of the population has some form of difficulty with reading, writing, or speech.[7]

COGA categorizes the use of clear content as "easy words, short sentences and blocks of text, clear images, and easy to understand video." We've covered video in the previous chapter (Chapter 5 "Deafness and Hard of Hearing") and will cover imagery more directly in Chapter 8 "Imagery," so let's focus on the wording side of things. We'll talk about how to structure that content, choose the words that make it, and how best to display them.

Plain English

The most valuable of all talents is that of never using two words when one will do.

—Thomas Jefferson

Ironically, this quote is a little wordier than it needs to be, but the sentiment still stands.

Using plain English means writing clear, concise, well-organized content – essentially writing in an accessible way.[8] It is especially useful for those with **dyslexia**, who represent around **10%** of the population worldwide, making it the largest cognitive impairment that we know of,[9] and **aphasia** (a language-based impairment that often results from a stroke).[10] Its impact also extends to users with impairments that impact language less directly though, as having fewer words to read helps those with **visual impairments** or those with other forms of comprehension and reasoning difficulties (like some users with **Alzheimer's** or **Down's syndrome**).[11]

The importance of accessible writing may seem like one of the most obvious points raised in this book. After all, who wouldn't write in plain English? Unfortunately, this happens surprisingly often – in trying to share as much information as possible, we often lose the ability to be concise and direct. At some point, you will have come across text that feels harder to read or engage with than usual. The fact that you can *tell* that there's something wrong without knowing exactly what it is draws attention to the importance of being clear and concise and shows that exclusionary prose can have an impact regardless of expertise or how comfortable someone is with reading.

Moreover, despite a rise in literacy rates in the past few years, they still remain a problem. In the United States, **54%** of adults have a literacy below sixth-grade level (11 years old).[12] In England, over **7 million** people (1 in 6) have what are considered to be poor literacy skills.[13] Given how ubiquitous the Web is in these countries, these numbers represent a large portion of people reading your content.

Interestingly though, the benefits of plain English aren't confined to those who find reading difficult. A study by language expert Christopher Trudeau found that **80%** of participants, including those considered to have high literacy skills, *preferred* sentences written in plain English. He found that this preference was true no matter the country, literacy level, or industry.[14]

When we encounter a subject we are not familiar with, there can be a lot of specialist terms and phrases. We can get bogged down in understanding the words themselves rather than the point they're meant to be making. Surprisingly though, the study also found that even experts in those areas, who understood these specialist terms, *vastly* preferred the writing to be plain and jargon-free for ease of reading too. It seems it's what everyone prefers and makes us more productive.

So, let's explore how to create writing people *want* to read. There are two main areas to look at when we talk about plain English. The first concerns the structure of the text and how it's organized, and the second has to do with word choice.

Structure

Research has found that people on average only read **20%–28%** of text on a web page, and the pressure on the brain to understand content increases for every 100 words you put on a page – even on pages with as little as 100 words of content, on average a user will actually only read **half** of that.[15] Therefore, paying attention to how you structure your content, especially on longer pages with more of it, can really help keep users focused.

The Center for Plain Language is a nonprofit that helps government agencies and businesses write clear and understandable communications. They explain that

> When you create material in plain language, you also organize it logically for the audience. You consider how well the layout of your pages or screens works for the audience. You anticipate their questions and needs.[16]

This is largely because a clear structure prevents your readers from becoming overwhelmed and allows them to understand contextual information clearly – they can easily see where one of your points ends and another begins and identify the most important information on the page. It allows them to easily pick that 20%–28% they *want* to read, rather than struggling to engage with it all to find what they're looking for.

This is also tied to the creation of a linear page layout, as it organizes content logically, from top to bottom. Let's now explore what forms this layout – from a section's heading to the paragraphs within it, down to the individual sentences within those paragraphs.

Headings

If you write headings that help readers predict what comes next, it creates a structure that allows readers to quickly and confidently find the information they are looking for. We've mentioned this before when talking about how screen reader users often **navigate** using headings, but the same is true for those with attention deficit disorders who struggle with continued **focus**. With a header, they can reanchor themselves to what they were reading more easily. Good examples include

- Questions that the user may ask themselves – **"What is the purpose of plain language?"**

- Simple statements that aren't ambiguous – **"The purpose of plain language"**

Whereas the following styles of heading make it harder for users to navigate:

- Headings that are dozens of words long instead of a succinct statement – **"Everything you need to know about how to create good headings as part of using better plain English"**

- Vague headings that don't help the user understand what a section is about – **"Exploring the effects behind the nature of headings"**

- Introducing new terms for the very first time in the heading (unless it's part of a question)

Paragraphs

Underneath these headings, the content should be broken up into short sections as opposed to large paragraphs. This offers stopping points for the reader, allowing them to digest what they've read or to take a break. Forcing a user to read through a twenty-line paragraph takes a toll on both **focus** and **memory**. As a guide on how large to aim for though, research conducted by the UK Government suggests a paragraph shouldn't be more than **five sentences** long.[17] Equally, you should take into account where the "natural" stopping points are – you shouldn't cut a paragraph midway through an idea or point.

Sentences

Inside your paragraphs, your sentences should be short but logical. Doing so increases readability and understanding as it avoids the need for the user to hold too much information in their head at once. This makes them less likely to get confused by content, or how it's laid out. Over a century's worth of research backs up this premise, and a study from the American Press Institute created this neat table comparing the number of words in a sentence to the level of difficulty for the average reader to understand it.[18]

Words per Sentence	Difficulty Level
8 or less	Very easy
11	Easy
14	Fairly easy
17	Standard
21	Fairly difficult
25	Difficult
29 or more	Very difficult

Even if plain language is not used, the sentence can still be accessible if it's reasonably short as "people with moderate learning disabilities can still understand sentences of **5 to 8 words** without difficulty."[19] A good test is to read a sentence out loud. If you run out of breath reading it, it's too long.

Guiding Sentences

You can also achieve better sentence comprehension by trying to write what is known as "guiding" sentences (or "front-loading content"). This involves placing the most important content at the beginning of a sentence, so you know what is being talked about right away, which makes it easier to grasp. An example is that the following sentence

> "Designing Accessible User Experiences" is a new course that will be offered this August.[20]

is typically easier to read than

> There is a new course offering coming this August called "Designing Accessible User Experiences."

As the course itself has been introduced first, a reader knows what is being talked about from the outset, as opposed to finding out that *something* is starting in August. This approach has been proven to improve **memory** retention of the whole sentence.

Supporting Content in Multiple Formats

In the last chapter, we talked about how captions can help users understand audio and video by introducing another channel for them to receive information. The same principle applies to all types of content.

If you can provide content in a range of formats other than just text, you can *significantly* increase the likelihood that a user with **language comprehension** difficulties like dyslexia or aphasia will be able to engage with it, as well as those with **visual comprehension** difficulties, who use visual mediums like pictures and graphs as sense-making tools.

Good examples include using images (as long as they have `alt` text added) and diagrams to compliment written content, rather than inadvertently creating a wall of text in only one format. Not only does including other formats make pages look more appealing to engage with, but the variety makes reading them more manageable – it breaks up a page in a similar way to headings, providing a clear journey through the page and regular places to stop.

Having looked at how to structure written content, let's look at the changes we can make to the text itself. To do this, it's useful to know how users typically interact with words and why word choice matters.

Word Choice

When we're children, we quickly learn to read common words and become familiar with a primary set of **5,000** words and a secondary set of around **10,000** words. We use these words every day and are comfortable with most of them by the time we're nine years old.[21] Once we've become familiar with these, we actually stop *reading* the words and start *recognizing* their shapes instead, which allows us to read much faster.

This is because research suggests, however, that cognitive-impaired users read in a different way. For example, people with both moderate **learning disabilities** and **visual comprehension** impairments find it more difficult to recognize the *shape* of words – those with **dyslexia** and **visual processing disorder** (VPD) are prominent examples (this issue is common enough that a font called Dyslexie has been specifically designed to aid reading and comprehension online by changing the shape of some letters).[22] Users who experience these issues are "more likely to read letter for letter – they do not bounce around like other users."[23] Using plain language can therefore have huge benefits.

We mentioned earlier that many cognitive-impaired users can understand a standard sentence of five to eight words; however, by using common words, you increase this dramatically – helping these users understand sentences of around **25** words. This could significantly offset the barriers usually faced by **language-impaired** users.

Now, although your vocabulary will grow, you will always be comfortable reading from those base 5,000 words. When writing content, you can make the most of this ability by using these more common words and using them in a plain, concise way to ensure that users will not encounter barriers with your text. I've added this word list to the reading list for this chapter, which you can find at `inclusive.guide/reading/chapter6`.

Use Familiar Language

We talked about using familiar language a little in the last chapter (Chapter 5 "Deafness and Hard of Hearing") when it came to writing BSL-friendly English, and many of the same ideas apply. You should try and avoid complicated words, jargon, idioms, and figures of speech (such as "once in a blue moon"). The last point is especially useful because users with **autistic spectrum disorder** (ASD), for example, struggle to comprehend figurative language and so are more likely to attempt to interpret these phrases literally.[24]

Also, try to think about shorter words and less obscure synonyms for other words, and don't be afraid to leave out details that don't help or may distract readers, even if they are interesting. This is good practice for all writing and will make your written content clearer.

Avoid Using Lots of Large Words

Research into content design found that when you use a longer word of eight or nine letters, users are more likely to skip the shorter words that follow it.[25] As a result, if you make a habit of consistently using longer, complicated words, they are likely to require unnecessary attention and increase the chances of users skipping large parts of your content. This affects comprehension and encourages disengagement. Take this sentence, for example:

> The recently sanctioned alterations to Transport for London's seasonal timetables should not be displayed before 1st January 2024.[26]

There's a lot going on here, but the most important word in the sentence is "**not**" – you should **not** display the new transport timetable before this time. However, because of the lengthy words that precede it, that vital word is more likely to be overlooked. The "not" is far more obvious in a sentence like this:

> Do not display the new Transport for London timetable before 1st January 2024.

This is because the sentence is now a guiding one (as the important "not" is now at the beginning) but also because the more complicated words have been removed.

Use an Active Voice

Sentences that use an active voice are especially clear. This happens in sentences where the subject performs a stated action – thereby placing a clear **focus** on that action to readers. A sentence such as "You must create an accessible website by Friday" is more comprehensible than "An accessible website must be created by Friday" as it clearly involves the reader as a character.[27]

Pay Attention to Text Style

There are a range of text styles that can be used to draw attention, such as **emboldening**, CAPITALIZATION and *italicizing* to denote meaning, and <u>underlining</u> to advertise an action of some sort (a link or a description of the word).

Styling like this can be used to make sure important words are not overlooked. Take the transport timetable example from earlier:

> Do **not** display the new Transport for London timetable before 1st January 2024.

Now the "not" is far more obvious. It should be noted that excessive use of these text styles can be confusing to users with **visual comprehension** issues, as we mentioned earlier, as they can make words look less familiar – they're useful but in moderation. It's important to note here that you shouldn't overuse these text styles; otherwise, they lose their power. They can also affect the user's ability to read content — a paragraph of capitalized text is much harder for someone to read compared to regular text.

Testing How Easy Content Is to Read

Hopefully, all of these techniques are clear and practical so that you can keep them in mind when creating content that is accessible to all users. However, it's always handy to **test** whether your text is easy to read once you've written it. One interesting way to test this – the **Flesch-Kincaid readability test** – was developed under contract for the US Navy in 1975. It was first used by the army for assessing the difficulty of technical manuals in 1978 and afterward became a military standard.[28]

The test scores content from 0 to 100 (with 0 being the most difficult to read and 100 being the easiest). Anything over 60 is considered a good score. This tool will also let you know where your content is letting you down with a scoring system based on factors like

- Sentences with more than 30 syllables
- Words with more than four syllables
- The amount of adverbs and clichés you include

Score	Ease of Reading
100–90	Very easy to read. Easily understood by an average 11-year-old student.
90–80	Easy to read. Conversational English for consumers.
80–70	Fairly easy to read.
70–60	Plain English. Easily understood by 13–15-year-old students.
60–50	Fairly difficult to read.

(continued)

Score	Ease of Reading
50–30	Difficult to read.
30–10	Very difficult to read. Best understood by university graduates.
10–0	Extremely difficult to read.

It's not a perfect test but, combined with the preceding suggestions, can act as a comprehensive guide to ensure that your text is as inclusive and readable as possible. For those using popular word processing tools, a reading ease test tool based on this test is available directly within programs like Microsoft Word and Grammarly, so you can grade your content as you write it.[29]

Tech company Readable has also created a free online tool using this test, which allows you to paste in text you've written, and it will score it. You also have the opportunity to edit your text within the website, and it will update as soon as you make any changes, so you can instantly see if your score has improved or not. For more granular editing, the online "Hemingway Editor" highlights the specific parts of the text that are causing issues, and provides guidance on how to reduce the complexity. I've added both to the reading list for this chapter, which you can find at `inclusive.guide/reading/chapter6`.

Help Users Understand What Things Are and How to Use Them

According to COGA, people with cognitive and learning disabilities massively benefit from common behavior and design patterns when understanding and interpreting content online, so they don't have to learn new ones. For me, this feels like a fair ask for *any* user, but it's often not what they find.

In order to help users understand what things are, we need to provide clear information and set clear expectations. We'll go through some examples of how you can do that for the content you've created and then highlight the struggles that ambiguity can cause, particularly in the world of icons.

Provide Definitions

Acronyms and long, difficult words are sometimes unavoidable, particularly when talking about specialist subjects. When using them though, you should remember to **explain** what they mean – if not in the text itself, then through a simple interaction for the user. Not doing so can be confusing for readers, particularly those with **learning difficulties**, causing them to disengage out of frustration. For this reason, there are WCAG rules that require you to provide easy ways for users to identify and understand the meaning behind both acronyms and "unusual" words (3.1.3: Unusual Words and SC 3.1.4: Abbreviations).[30, 31]

Luckily, you can do this very simply with code. It involves wrapping an acronym or specialist term in an "abbreviation" tag – allowing you to provide an explanation of it:

```
<abbr title="Accessibility">a11y</abbr>
```

Once you've done that, the word will display with a small dotted underline (as shown in Figure 6-1) by default. Then when the user hovers over, taps on, or tabs to the word, the meaning will be displayed in a tool tip next to the cursor (as shown in Figure 6-2).

Figure 6-1. *An example of how an abbreviation tag displays on text. The word "a11y" has a dotted line underneath it.*

Figure 6-2. *When a user hovers over an abbreviation tag, the meaning appears in a tool tip next to the cursor. Here, hovering over "a11y" shows a tool tip with the text "accessibility".*

Alternatively, you can simply write the definition next to the word or acronym in brackets or in prose such as "otherwise known as...." This is better suited for those of you who control the content of a site but don't typically have access to the code, such as a CMS (otherwise known as a Content Management System). See what I did there?

Reading Time

In the same way, it's useful to explain the *meaning* of words you've used, explaining how *long* it will take a user to get through what you've written can provide important context. The "reading time" feature lets people know quickly how long it would normally take someone to get through what's on the page (as shown in Figure 6-3).

Figure 6-3. *An example of Medium's "read time" feature, shown at the top of each article. The post shown can be read in five minutes.*

Everyone reads at different speeds, but the rough agreed-upon average for an adult is **183 words** per minute.[32] For those with lower **language comprehension**, they can still use this average to determine how long it will take. It's also useful for setting user expectations and allows those with **learning difficulties** to decide when and how they interact with your content.

Beyond helping those with impairments, research has proven that having one increases engagement with your content by around **40%**. It also reduced bounce rates and increased page views and time spent on the site.[33]

On top of providing up-front information about how long your text may take to read, you can also provide a visual representation of their progress as they make their way *through* it. Progress indicators have become popular as they create a sense of movement, progression, and achievement, as well as a reduction of uncertainty. Because of this, they've been proven to increase the likelihood of people getting through content, as they can see that they're getting near the end. This helps those with **memory impairments** remember how far they've gotten and aids **visual comprehension** as it provides another measure of progress beyond the (often hidden) scrollbar of a page. An example of this is shown in Figure 6-4 below.

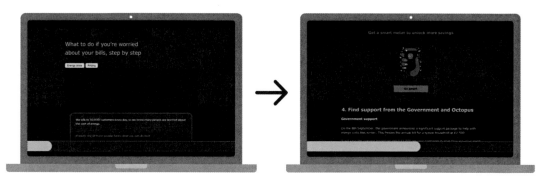

Figure 6-4. *A progress indicator is an element on a page that displays live progress to the user of how far through an article they are. As a user scrolls down, the progress indicator updates (pictured right).*

Of course, words are not the only content on a page that a user can engage with to understand information or perform actions. Let's talk about the power of using clear iconography on your sites and the potential drawbacks for users if you get it wrong.

Clear Iconography

Using icons can be a neat way to display a status or action without the need for excessive amounts of text, and their frequent use throughout sites has created a strong understanding of certain ones. Notable examples include symbols like a cog to represent "settings," a magnifying glass to represent "search" functionality, or the "hamburger" icon to represent a menu.

However, an *overreliance* on icons can lead to exclusion, as it is difficult to connect many icons that are used online to their associated action, despite it being clear to those who added them. This barrier is felt keenly by users with impaired **visual comprehension** (e.g. **visual processing disorder** (VPD) and **dyscalculia** – which can affect a user's ability to imagine, understand, and remember shapes).

Users with these access needs have trouble identifying images, comprehending the meaning behind them, and associating them with a given action. What's more, not all sites use the same icons to represent the same actions, and this inconsistency can create a lot of barriers – if a user's understanding of an icon is based on previous experience, and each experience is different, they're left unsure as to whether the meaning they *believe* an icon represents is accurate.

Let's look at a few common examples, starting with Figure 6-5.

Figure 6-5. *A speech bubble*

The speech bubble icon is used quite widely. Although its style is tweaked slightly between sites, its meaning changes far more drastically. It means "View post and comments" in an Instagram feed but then means "Add a comment" when a user is on an individual Instagram post. It also means "View messages" on Facebook, "Reply" on Reddit, and "Start a thread" on Slack. Next is the "pencil" icon, shown in Figure 6-6.

Figure 6-6. *A basic "pencil writing on a piece of paper" illustration*

This icon is used inside a square to mean "Create a note" in Apple notes but means "View drafts" in Outlook. It is also commonly used to represent an "edit" action on many sites (and in Google's "Material Design" library).

Now it could be argued that these two examples represent *similar* actions, and so there's a degree of cognitive connection that can be made by a user between them, but that argument doesn't account for a user's cognition being impaired. Impaired **memory** could prevent associating an icon with multiple actions, as well as those with **low tech literacy** (also known as **digital literacy**) who aren't exposed to the Web or web-based icons often enough.

To that end, let's look at the third and final example, shown in Figure 6-7: the "arrow" icon.

Figure 6-7. *An arrow, pointing upward and left*

This is my least favorite icon, used to represent "Share a post" on LinkedIn, "Undo an action" in word processing programs like Google Docs and Microsoft Word, "Back" on social media sites like Twitter, and "Reply" in email platforms like Outlook and Google Mail. Although some of these actions are somewhat related and you *might* be able to guess what the icon means from context, it'd still be a guess, as the actions represent a much wider array compared to the speech bubble or pencil examples – it would be an incorrect assumption that **everyone** would be able to make that intuitive leap.

Custom Icons

What's worse than common icons with slightly different actions are uncommon icons where the action is unclear.

This happens when using custom icons you've created yourself. Untested, these are often open to interpretation and misunderstanding, meaning that your attempt to make a page *less* cluttered can cause *more* confusion. They cause all of the same issues as the ones mentioned earlier, but they happen a **lot** more frequently when the icon is unknown.

I would caution that if you look at one of your own icons for long enough, its meaning can seem obvious, but it won't be to others. This idea isn't confined to the Web either – it's visible everywhere and a problem for everybody. Household appliances, for example, are a gold mine of ambiguous icons. Figure 6-8 shows a dial on a washing machine.

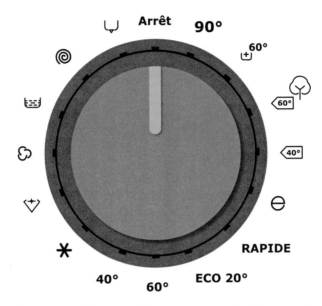

Figure 6-8. *A dial on a washing machine, surrounded by completely ambiguous icons and numbers. It would be hard to decipher what any one of them represents.*

I genuinely have no idea what some of these mean, and icons are supposed to *remove* the need for extra text.

How Do We Combat This?

This ambiguity means that custom icons cannot be relied upon to convey meaning by themselves, certainly not for all users. You should therefore ensure that there is another way to understand what an icon means. This is commonly handled with a label underneath or next to the icon. A study found that when users were presented with icons that were also labeled, they were able to correctly predict what would happen when they tapped the icon **88%** of the time. As soon as the label was removed, the comprehension of those icons dropped to **60%**.[34] Again, this problem gets exponentially worse when you create icons yourself. The same tests found that for unlabeled icons that were unique to the app, users only had a **34%** success rate when guessing what they were for.

Aim for stylized versions of common icons over custom ones, and always provide another way to understand what they mean. It's also important that we know how to make icons accessible. We'll be covering all of this in Chapter 8 "Imagery."

It's now time to think about how the mixture of content and visuals can come together to create a site that is overwhelming and even damaging to users with cognitive impairments. We'll look at what makes a "complex" page, what you should avoid having on your pages for this reason, and ways in which you can provide a sense of control and ease to your users.

Help Users Find What They Need

Make navigating the system easy. Use a clear and easy-to-follow layout with visual cues, such as icons. Clear headings, boundaries, and regions also helps people understand the page design.

—COGA Task Force

Accessibility experts WebAIM conducted research that discovered that, on the whole, home pages are becoming more complex. The home pages tested had over **one billion** page elements. This equates to an average of **1050** elements per home page in February 2023 – a **10%** increase from 2022 and an incredible **34%** increase over the last 4 years.[35] Let's explore how to ensure that your pages and your users' experiences with them aren't overly complex.

Avoiding Complex Pages

As we mentioned in Chapter 2 "Blindness," most users primarily engage with the Web using visual information – by looking at the screen. It's clear that when designing for users with **visual comprehensive** impairments (like **dyscalculia** or **dementia**), iconography can cause trouble in understanding actions that are represented visually. If we take a step back though, entire layouts and experiences are also interpreted in a visual way, and so when badly designed, they can cause even greater difficulties for users. There are two sides to this: the complexity of a page's **layout** and the complexity of its **experience**.

Complex Layouts

If your layout forces users to work hard to follow or identify content – because of irregular positioning, direction, or size – you create unnecessary barriers between your users and what they want to engage with. This relates to the point we made earlier about how users only read a fraction of a page's content because complex layouts prevent them from "skimming" comfortably. Figure 6-9 shows a screenshot of the home page for the clothing website Zara.

Figure 6-9. *The home page layout of clothing brand Zara's website. Content is scattered everywhere without a particular order or linear flow, with some parts overlapping crucial elements.*

Zara is one of the biggest fast-fashion brands in the world, and their site receives between **90 and 100 million** visits per month at the time of writing.[36] What those users find when they reach the home page is shown in the preceding image and is needlessly complex. Content does not flow in a linear manner. Instead, information is scattered everywhere, which draws a user's attention from place to place in a confusing manner. Key elements like the menus and account actions are so small that they're difficult to engage with even on a large screen, and sometimes they're actually hard to *spot*. This is because a moving video is constantly playing in the background, which obscures the view of them – part of the search bar is covered in the preceding screenshot, and an entire menu item isn't visible due to part of the video. Users are confronted by a page that's complex despite not having a lot of content and, in many ways, looks broken.[37]

To briefly return to something we covered in Chapter 2 "Blindness," a clear linear layout has been proven to help users navigate your site and find what they're looking for with greater ease. This is part of why a mobile-first approach to design really benefits accessibility and those susceptible to the cognitive effects of complex layouts. Learning to make the simplest layout (thanks to the smaller screen size of mobile devices) and then scaling your design up forces the site to take on a simpler feel and provides users with only one or two things to **focus** on at a time – guiding them naturally from one piece of content to the next. Once that's done, designers can then ask serious questions about whether components really *ever* need to be sprawled all over bigger screens simply because there is room to do so.

Coherent Navigation

Beyond the unique layout of any one site, there are a few generally accepted principles that you can find on almost all web pages, and that you should try to follow. For example, we're used to finding main menus at the top of the page, both on mobile and desktop devices. Research has proven that users with impaired **visual comprehension** benefit most when you consistently position these features where they would commonly expect to find them due to "subconscious searching patterns" we tend to follow when looking around a site.[38]

Despite menus accounting for over **half** of the elements on Zara's home page, it's a principle they haven't followed – three types of menu are all in different positions, and those positions change from page to page. This inconsistency between pages affects users who experience **visual-spatial impairments** such as **dyscalculia** and **visual processing disorder** (VPD), which can affect orientation, as they can easily become lost when moving around and between pages.

Realistically, consistent and coherent navigation helps everyone. The W3C says we should aim for "clearly structured content that facilitates overview and orientation," which is why it's a WCAG rule (3.2.3: Consistent Navigation).[39] A good start involves making sure your main source of navigation is consistently placed and easy to engage with. It should prioritize core tasks, features, and information and hero those rather than presenting too many options. Take a look at the two menus shown in Figure 6-10.

Figure 6-10. *A visual comparison between two menus – one with high-level menu items and several submenu items shown at once (pictured left) and one with just the high-level items (pictured right)*

The latter provides a much clearer initial overview, whereas the former – showing both items and subitems from the outset – makes it harder to know where to begin and could be overwhelming for users. This is the difference between "flat" and "deep" navigation patterns. You can still have subitems, but only make them available when you *interact* with a main item (through a click or tab). This is more effective because users would be able to understand the subitems within the context of the main item they engaged with.

Another good point is to highlight a **single** navigation item if it is the most common action that your users take, as shown in the second menu of Figure 6-11. This could be starting a journey they're likely looking for (i.e., "get a quote") or a useful reference point if they want to engage with your site ("get in touch" or "search"). This helps with orientation to key parts of your site across *all* pages.

Figure 6-11. *A visual comparison between two menus – one where all menu items are the same and the other where one item is singled out visually*

If you have a lot of menu items, then a great feature to accompany the downsizing of it can be making a clear "Help" or "frequently asked questions" section. A robust help section should mirror common user queries, with pages like "I can't understand my bill" or "where can I change my card details?" The added responsibility that you must be aware of here though is ensuring that the content you add remains up to date and relevant as you move forward – there's no use having an easy way to reach incorrect information. A regular audit of content, particularly popular content that receives a lot of traffic, can mitigate this issue.

Giving users access to a search function that can provide these answers, rather than forcing them to navigate a help section, is even better. When writing about dementia, a condition that can significantly impact **visual comprehension** and **memory**, Ability. net identified the "search box" as an essential navigation item for these users.[40] By anticipating needs like this, you create a flatter site structure and also make your pages easier to find if someone were to search for that same question through a search engine instead.

Complex Experiences

Overcomplicated or unpredictable experiences can also impact cognitively impaired users who are easily overwhelmed. In a world of pop-ups, adverts, cookie banners, and multimedia content, the core content of a page can be obscured or overshadowed, even if the layout is simple. For some users with **executive function impairments** who can be easily distracted, all of this visual "noise" can render content inaccessible. For those with **autism**, for example, providing too much information at once can potentially cause stress, anxiety, and even physical pain:

> If I get sensory overload then I just shut down; you get what's known as fragmentation…it's weird, like being tuned into 40 TV channels at once.[41]

Busy pages with a range of different pieces of content vying for attention can prove especially overwhelming, and it's the most common form of complex experience I see online. In the first edition, I used the example of gaming site "GamesRadar." Unfortunately, I have to do the same again. The site receives tens of millions of visits a month and still represents one of the most complex and intense experiences I've come across.[42] Figure 6-12 shows how the site appears when you first arrive.

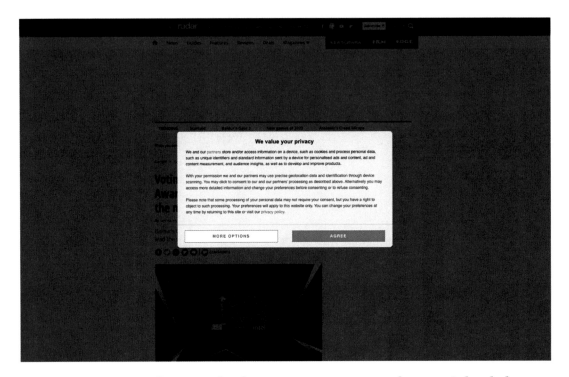

Figure 6-12. *An overlay on a site that appears as soon as the page is loaded, asking the user to accept the use of cookies*

The user is immediately greeted by this as they arrive – not ideal, but understandable given regulations. However, it's followed quickly by that shown in Figure 6-13.

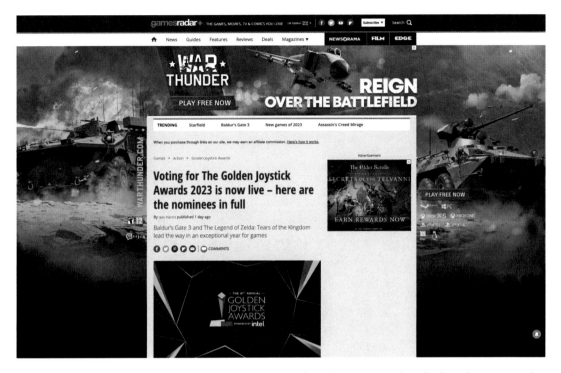

Figure 6-13.   *The same site as earlier but with adverts now loaded at the top and sides of the content in a range of bright colors, alongside multiple images, and an autoplaying video to the right of the content*

An advert has now taken over most of the space on the screen that was previously a neutral gray, posing an intense and unexpected distraction. The delay is likely due to retrieving the advert from an external site, which affects performance.

A few seconds later, two more modals appear automatically – a request for the site to send the user notifications even when they're away from the site and an advert that takes over the page, asking them to sign up for their newsletter. The advert to the right of the content has also transformed into a larger, taller advert than before (shown in Figure 6-14).

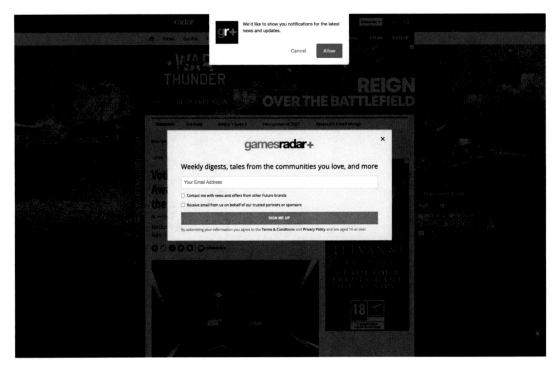

Figure 6-14. *The same site again, but with two new overlays that appeared a few seconds later, asking the user if they'd like to join the site's newsletter and receive notifications from them*

You've probably experienced sites like this before. In this example, all of the following appear within a minute of arriving on the site:

- A "please accept cookies" pop-up

- An advert at the top of the page

- Adverts down both sides of the page showing different content

- A video advert that plays automatically

- A sudden change in background color, from gray to a vibrant range of colors

- A range of images with text, from adverts next to the article

- A pop-up encouraging them to subscribe to their newsletter

- A pop-up asking permission for the site to send the user notifications, even when they're not on the site

That's a lot to take in, and none of it relates to the content they came to the site to engage with.

Of this list, ads are often the most off-putting, as they're usually completely unrelated to the content of the page and take longer to load than the rest of the content. As a result, many users, including those with heightened sensory awareness, often block ads to prevent themselves from being overwhelmed. Unfortunately, sites that display ads often find ways to display *other* ads that load much later on, which prevents ad blockers from picking them up. The result is another delayed and unexpected addition to the experience, shown in Figure 6-15.

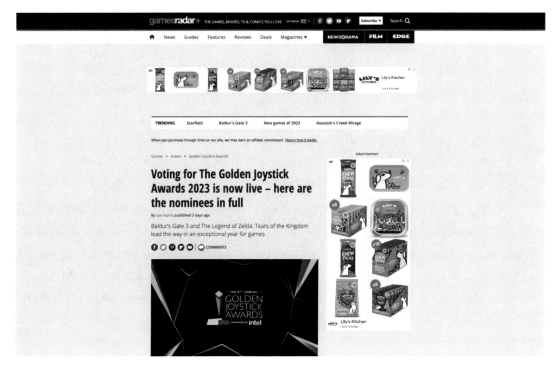

Figure 6-15. *The site now displays a gray background due to the adblocker, but the site has been able to load new adverts a minute later, which appear unexpectedly*

It's a struggle to wade through all these distractions before you even reach the content, and afterward, the layout itself is affected by the need to work around these components. There is often nothing wrong with any of these components individually, and I understand they can impact revenue and conversion, but together they create a seemingly unrelenting assault on your attention, which ultimately prevents users from reading their content. It's frustrating for everyone, but exclusionary for many. A balance therefore needs to be found.

If you *need* to display adverts and pop-ups, some possible compromises include

- Synchronizing the content of the adverts so that they show a consistent message.

- Advertising with just images or videos but removing autoplay as we've covered already in Chapter 5 "Deafness and Hard of Hearing."

- Reviewing whether banner images are necessary alongside other imagery at the top of the page and spreading the rest of those images out as a way of breaking up longer blocks of text.

- More subtle positioning of the cookie pop-up so it doesn't hijack the user's focus.

- Not having any adverts take over the page and instead making sure it appears at the end of the content or more discreetly in the corner of the page.

- Considering whether dynamic adverts are even a good idea – according to statistics from Google, over **half** of users abandon a site if it takes more than 3 seconds to load.[43]

This idea of creating logical, simplistic layouts and predictable experiences with content is relevant when catering to any form of cognitive impairment in some way and realistically applies to almost all users; people visiting sites don't want to be confused or overwhelmed.

Let's turn briefly from the very complex to the very simple. During the advent of website builds, there was always a consistent way for users to see every page that was on a website in one place (although they aren't used in this way as much anymore) – let's talk about sitemaps.

Sitemaps

A sitemap is a file and/or page, written in code, that lists all of a website's pages – providing a complete overview of a site's structure. They were common in the early days of the Web, as a site would only contain a handful of pages and there weren't always links between them. In recent years, though, the number of pages on a typical site has risen drastically, and the rise of online blogs and shops has meant that a sitemap could hold hundreds (or thousands) of pages. This has meant that sitemaps are nowhere near as easy to use as they once were.

This is partly why sitemaps are now geared more toward helping search engines like Google find and index pages.

However, the fact that sitemaps provide every link in the same serialized format without the need to go searching for all of them in different menus and journeys means they're still useful for accessibility purposes. This helps satisfy WCAG's "Multiple Ways" rule (2.4.5), which recommends you provide more than one way to navigate and find content[44] – if users know that they can locate content within a site from the same consistent place (Google requires it to be at the root directory of every website – i.e., mywebsite.com/sitemap.xml), they can easily find what they're looking for. W3C even say so themselves:

> A person with cognitive disabilities may prefer a table of contents
> or site map that provides an overview of the site rather than
> reading and traversing through several Web pages.[45]

A user with cognitive impairments would therefore be able to engage with **one** file to find a page should they have trouble understanding a user flow or traversing numerous menus and submenus they aren't used to. They may well prefer not to do this, but at least they would have the choice. As they hold benefits for search engine optimization and make a site a little more accessible, sitemaps are well worth the effort.

Help Users Focus

The average attention span online is less than a minute. It's around **47 seconds**, which is a third of what it was when research was first conducted in 2004. This is remarkably short, and the bitesize nature of the content users typically consume on social media sites is likely to reduce this further.

For your site and content, this means two things: firstly, the average user has a lower attention span than the length of a standard blog or email you may want them to read, and secondly, those with cognitive impairments are likely under that average – particularly those with **learning difficulties** and **executive function impairments** that affect focus.

Because of this, COGA recommends providing features that avoid distracting a user from their tasks and help them orientate themselves. I'd like to share two techniques: one that can help users focus and one that can help them refocus when they lose it. Let's start with the first – the TL;DR.[46]

TL;DRs

TL;DR is an acronym that stands for **"too long; didn't read"** and is a summary of long-form information. It began its life as a deadpan response to a very long post on an online forum. The point was simple – your content is too long for me to interact with. This is a point we've made throughout this chapter: large amounts of info can be overwhelming and difficult for many users to get through, including people with impaired **language comprehension** and **learning difficulties**. You can help reduce this by putting the recommendations we mentioned earlier into action and keeping content as concise as possible, but sometimes longer content is unavoidable. In those situations, one particularly useful solution involves providing a heavily summarized version of existing content – enabling those with cognitive impairments to still extract useful information from your content.

After its first use, TL;DRs became popular and were commonly seen accompanying long posts in the early 2000s. They were made famous by sites such as Reddit and 4Chan, where content often centers around long-form posts and discussions. Now, you'd be hard-pressed to find a long post without one. They're created by extracting the core information from the content into self-contained sentences and placing them at the top or bottom of any long post, allowing readers to take away the key point(s). An example of how this typically looks visually is shown in Figure 6-16 below.

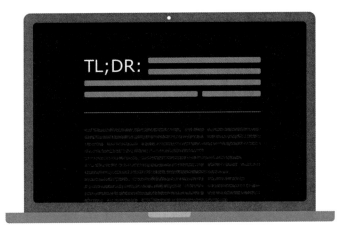

Figure 6-16. *A TL;DR (too long; didn't read) box is positioned above a long body of text. This box contains a series of short sentences that summarize the main points of the text that follows it.*

This is great for any user who is in a rush, but the impact is even greater for those with access needs. For example, users with **autism** or **ADHD** have often been known to want to skip straight to particular actions online rather than read through content in full. Furthermore, those with **low literacy** or **learning difficulties** may not even be able to *read* that length of content. There is even a WCAG rule that encourages you to provide supplemental content, or a simplified version of content, if the content you're sharing requires a reading level above "lower secondary level" (3.1.5: Reading Level).[47] A TL;DR can be that supplemental content due to its far shorter length and emphasis on important points and actions – it requires much less **focus** for those lacking **executive function**.

Implementing a TL;DR

A TL;DR is all about succinct, engaging content. When you're writing one, aim to

- **Identify the key points** – Carefully read through the content and identify the key points you'd like to convey (key stats that would interest someone, an area the content covers).

- **Don't have too many** – Aim for more than **two** points, but no more than **five**.

- **Limit the actions** – Try to avoid your points being a list of actions. It'll be less engaging and also look like a table of contents rather than an overview.

- **Use simple language** – Covered earlier in this chapter: avoid long words, jargon, or technical terms.

- **Keep it brief** – The TL;DR should be short and to the point, so aim for a sentence for each point, and avoid lengthy or complex sentences.

But Ashley, Won't It Ruin the Surprise of What's in the Content?

On the contrary, summarizing content doesn't mean you have to fill it with spoilers or oversimplifications. Instead, they *increase* the likelihood that your content will be read at all – they've been proven to increase the average time a user spends on a page and reduce bounce rate.[48] Therefore, while TL;DRs are supposed to be concise, they can still be engaging and capture the reader's attention.

For example, you could use your TL;DR to explain the main points you'll cover on a page but also raise some new questions that are secondary to the main title that might convince the user to stay and read the content. Think of it as an extended advert for your content that is more likely to convince a reader to stay and read it once they've arrived on the page. Here's an example from an article about Snooker:

- We'll be taking a look at how Snooker is trying to reinvent itself.

- We speak to Barry Hearn, chairman of World Snooker about its progress.

- The key to its revival came from an unusual place...

This TL;DR includes the main point of the article (an interview with the head of Snooker) but also an anecdotal line about a section to grab the reader's attention. Overall, a TL;DR simply shows an appreciation for all users' time – understanding that they may want to know what they're getting into before they start.

Breadcrumbs

Breadcrumbs are a form of navigation that lets users know where they are within a **series** of pages, allowing them to navigate more easily within a wider journey or through sub-pages.

They're mentioned specifically in COGA's document around making content usable for people with cognitive and learning difficulties and recommended by WCAG in multiple rules. One of the main rules is "Location" (2.4.8): breadcrumbs allow you to provide "multiple ways of navigating" a site, which helps when the user is unsure of their location within it.[49] Secondly, the Baymard Institute, who conduct independent web usability research, ran a study with various ecommerce websites and found that breadcrumbs remain a vital tool for helping users navigate. They then studied 50 of the top ecommerce websites and found that, despite their usefulness, **94%** had what they called "sub-par breadcrumb implementation," with nearly a quarter having no breadcrumbs at all.[50]

Earlier we spoke about the importance of coherent navigation to help users find what they need, but navigation can also help with **focus**. If a user gets distracted, breadcrumbs can help reorientate them, helping them restore the context they lost. Providing linked breadcrumbs can help the user undo mistakes.

These two handy uses for those with cognitive impairments represent the two main types of breadcrumbs: **hierarchical** and **historical**.

Hierarchical Breadcrumbs

This is the most common type of breadcrumb. They help show users the position of their current page within the *hierarchy* of the site and are most often used to navigate between items within a certain category, as Figure 6-17 shows.

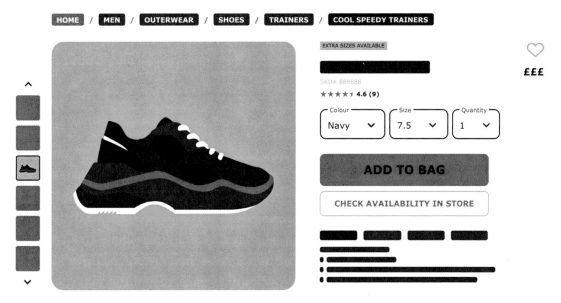

Figure 6-17. *A screenshot of a product page on the Uniqlo website, with a set of hierarchical breadcrumbs at the top. The links, left to right, are home, men, outerwear, trainers, and cool speedy trainers.*

Not only do they provide a clear indication of a user's position within a site, but they help the user understand what *else* is available around them. They also create a contextual menu that helps users navigate content that's more closely related to what they're currently viewing rather than forcing users to use a main menu. In the example image earlier, a user could decide to go and look at other blazers, jackets, and women's clothing more generally or go back to the home page, all without having to search for any of those pages.

This means users with lower **visual-spatial comprehension** don't have to try and picture a sequence of pages, or their path through them in their head – it is always on the page with them. This goes back to the WCAG rule called "Multiple Ways" (2.4.5) that ensures that users can find content on a website in more than one way.[51] A user may have trouble interacting with one method of finding content (e.g. a large main menu) in which case links in a footer, or a set of breadcrumbs, would prevent them from getting stuck.

Without providing breadcrumbs, the user is forced to make what is called "drastic scope jumps" such as going all the way back to the main menu if they want to explore related content. This doesn't make for a great user experience, and for those who become lost easily due to issues with **orientation** or comprehending **visual information**, a lack of granular navigation could be exclusionary. This applies to much more than ecommerce sites – it can help users navigate to related pages of *any* content that may be organized in subcategories. For example, hierarchy-based breadcrumbs could help users discover related content in blogs through tags assigned to posts or in frequently asked questions (FAQs) organized by topic.

Routes into Your Site

Another good reason to add breadcrumbs revolves around helping users who come across your content from **outside** the site. It's entirely possible that rather than reaching certain pages on your site by journeying from your home page to one section and then another, users will have found it via a search engine or advert or another site that's mentioned yours. Given that Google uses a site's breadcrumbs to evaluate and list pages, this seems likely.[52] You can't assume that the user has reached the preceding product page, for example, after visiting the "women's clothing" page, then the jackets section, and finally the product itself.

Therefore, breadcrumbs provide contextual information that a user who has just arrived on the site wouldn't otherwise have. Without breadcrumbs, they wouldn't immediately know what other pages are on the site or their position within those pages. In this way, breadcrumb navigation invites users to explore related content rather than simply leaving your site. It "blends site taxonomy and user behavior into a single functional element."[53]

Historical Breadcrumbs

Now that we've started to think about the different journeys a user could take to *get* to your website, let's think about the different types of journey they can take **within** it. Going back to the example of an ecommerce website, a user going through a checkout process will likely not benefit from a breadcrumb menu that is based on page hierarchy, such as

Home ➤ Shopping ➤ Checkout

Instead, it'd be more useful to have what's shown in Figure 6-18 below

Basket ➤ Shipping Address ➤ Payment Details ➤ Review

Figure 6-18. *A timeline from a checkout process that shows the user how far they've progressed and which steps they have left to complete*

This is an example of a **historical** breadcrumb, which provides quick links to get back to places the user has been while on your site. This is, of course, possible with the "Back" button on a browser, but that's restricted to moving one page at a time, whereas breadcrumbs allow you to go back to multiple steps or stages.

This is particularly useful for users with **impaired working memory** (like those with dementia), who find it difficult to carry information from one page to the next. Breadcrumbs remind them "of the route they've taken to get to a page and [allow them] to see which section they're currently in."[54]

With both hierarchical and historical breadcrumbs providing different but equally useful features and both satisfying the "Location" (2.4.8) and "Multiple Ways" (2.4.5) WCAG rules, the Baymard Institute recommends that you implement both types. It's important that you review the sections and journeys within your site to see whether a breadcrumb menu could be useful.

Help Users Avoid Mistakes

A good design makes errors less likely. Ask the user only for what you need!

—COGA

You could argue that all of the other areas we've covered so far are in service of this: preventing users from making mistakes. Having your site be clear and error-tolerant, both visually and functionally, gives those with cognitive impairments the best chance to get what they need.

Let's finish by exploring two common friction points for users on websites – initiating an action and inputting information – and the practical steps we can take to remove those barriers.

Self-Contained Actions

On many sites, actions may be part of a wider journey or be embedded within the flow of a sentence, and it may not be immediately clear what a particular action is or what it is asking a user to do. With that in mind, I'd like us to touch briefly on how (and *why*) to ensure that your site's actions are "self-contained."

Self-contained actions are links or buttons that users can understand in **isolation** from other content on the page rather than relying on the content *around* them to provide context. The term was raised in a study about web accessibility for users with **autism**, where it mentioned that having information that was self-contained was particularly useful for users with **sensory processing disorders** (SPD) and reduced the time needed to concentrate on a task – an issue that could apply to any user.[55] Links with text like "click here" may make sense as part of a sentence, but seen by themselves, it's difficult to know exactly what would happen if you interacted with them. These findings are backed up by the WCAG rule "Link Purpose," where you must ensure that the purpose of a link or button can be determined from the link text alone.[56] Of the top one million websites online, **17.3%** of pages had ambiguous link text, such as "click here," "more," and "continue." These pages had over five instances of ambiguous links on average.[57]

It's an easy mistake to make when creating a website, but we often don't notice that the action wouldn't make sense by itself. Describing actions so that they make sense on their own can remove barriers for a wide range of cognitive-impaired users. They help those with **reasoning impairments** understand what task they are meant to be doing and *how* to do it and users who have difficulties with **executive function** (planning and execution) identify the next step they should take to accomplish their goal. They also help those with ADHD to **focus** on the task at hand and can remind **memory-impaired** users about what they were doing.

If users come across an action that is vague and nondescript, this can lead to a stressful and negative experience. Take the following two buttons shown in Figure 6-19 – both responsible for submitting details in a form.

Figure 6-19. *A comparison of two buttons by themselves, one with text where the result of the action is unclear ("Go!") – pictured top – and one where it's clearer ("Submit order") – pictured bottom*

Only one of these two buttons makes *any* sense by itself. You need to check if, when read completely in isolation, the action makes sense and informs a user of what will happen if they interact with it. Phrases like "click here" and "get started" may seem obvious given the content and text *around* them but are ambiguous and say very little independently. On the other hand, links such as "Attach files" or "Subscribe to newsletter" are clear, concise, and unambiguous.

Beyond cognitive impairments, they're actually also useful for people using **screen readers**. This is because there is usually a break between a screen reader reading out the content of a sentence and the text in a link (they are two different elements after all), so the context of the sentence can be forgotten. Therefore, having to wait a few seconds and then hearing a link entitled "click here" will almost certainly cause confusion and force the user to reread the previous sentence.

Again, there are many overlaps between access needs despite different reasoning, and paying attention to clarity benefits everyone. With this in mind, let's think about a common issue on the Web for *all* of us – human error.

Autocomplete

Issues with human error are common across the Web. Google shared that **one in ten** searches are misspelled and so spend a lot of time providing search results for words close to common misspellings (as shown in Figure 6-20).[58] However, that's *Google* – this support isn't always available, and so the effects are felt more keenly on an unforgiving website, especially by those with cognitive impairments. Most commonly, it happens to those with **language comprehension** issues, **learning difficulties**, **memory impairments** like dementia, and **low tech literacy**.

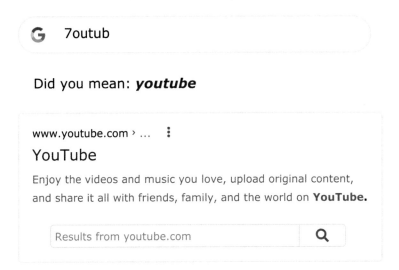

Figure 6-20. *When a user searches for something on Google with text that's similar to a known result, it will provide that result and ask whether they meant to type that*

To combat this, you need your site to be as error-tolerant as possible, and a large portion of these pain points are revealed when content is **inputted**. I often find myself typing too quickly and placing letters in the wrong order, so if a site can compensate for these small and very human errors, it will prevent unnecessary frustrations.

Autocomplete is often seen on form inputs and attempts to "guess" what a user has started to type. It then provides options that they can select from, based on the information the user has already provided, and offers to complete the entry for them. Now, autocomplete is only as smart as the data behind it – usually pulled from a database or a list of potential results in a site's code – but they're most commonly used in instances where the data a user provides is from a **finite** list of options (e.g. a US state, or an address).

Beyond avoiding misspellings, it can often help users find results more quickly, especially if they have trouble remembering what they are looking for or how to spell it. This can help your site avoid punishing human error with a difficult experience and in doing so also help people with **ADHD** or **autism**, who often become overwhelmed by too many options, by offering it as an alternative to a *very* long drop-down. Example like selecting a country from a list is a perfect candidate for autocomplete, as it filters those options the moment a user starts interacting.

This approach encapsulates one of the WCAG success criteria that the Cognitive and Learning Disabilities Accessibility Task Force (COGA) actually helped add. It's called "Identify Input Purpose" (1.3.5) and refers to the ability to programmatically determine the purpose of an input field in order to make collecting data from a user easier.[59] Here, they explain how autocomplete can also help users with **dyslexia** and **dyscalculia**:

> *Supermarket assistant with dyslexia and dyscalculia:*
>
> *Problem: My address is so complicated. There's lots of numbers and long words. It's hard to type it all without making mistakes.*
>
> *Works well: I love websites that can automatically fill it all in for me. Then I don't have to work so hard to get the numbers and spelling right.[60]*

This can be a powerful feature, but there is a catch – not all autocomplete features are created equal. By default, many of the libraries used to add autocomplete aren't great at accommodating **human error**. As a result, their usefulness depends on the way a user searches, and errors inputting content by the user can actually *offset* the time saved by implementing the feature and cause more frustration. This is what I call "strict" search.

"Strict" Search

A good example of this is the most frequently used autocomplete library on the Web – jQuery UI Autocomplete.[61] This is easy to implement and *can* save users time, but importantly, it only returns results for queries that are spelled **correctly**, as opposed to returning results that are **close** to an intended answer. If we were hypothetically trying to search for Croatia from a list of every country in the world, using this library, here are the search examples that would return it as an option:

- **Cro** (typing the start of the word, with the letters in the correct order)
- **Roat** (correct spelling, but with the first letter missing)
- **Croatia** (the country name itself, spelled correctly)

It does what it should when the *correct* information is submitted, but it's not lenient to human error. For example, when typing in the phonetic spelling of the country, it doesn't return any results (as shown in Figure 6-21).

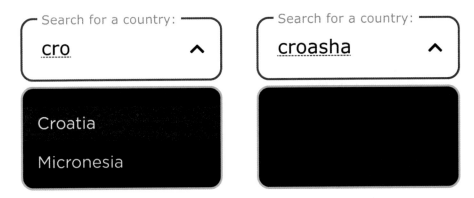

Figure 6-21. *Strict search accurately returns Croatia when the user has entered "cro" but returns no results when the user has entered an incorrect spelling of Croatia – "croasha"*

An accessibility feature that doesn't account well for human error isn't *really* accessible, especially for those with cognitive impairments. You need to factor in the likelihood of those with learning difficulties never being able to spell an option correctly or those with memory issues needing more lenient prompts to help them remember what they were searching for.

Luckily, there's a better way to provide support with this feature – let's talk about "fuzzy" matching.

"Fuzzy" Matching

You've probably seen autocomplete on sites like Google and Amazon and how good they are at "guessing" what you're searching for. This is known as "fuzzy" matching (or approximate string matching to be technical).

Fuzzy matching can search for results in a list like the preceding example, but *also* in a far more lenient way, without relying on an exact match with content that has already been inputted. It accommodates misspelled words, the correct letters that are in the wrong order (accidentally switched letters are one of the most common spelling mistakes), or alternative spellings of a word (something that sounds like you'd spell the word).[62]

Not only that, but fuzzy matching can also take in associated or **related** information for each search result rather than just the word itself. For example, if a user is searching for a book, they may want to search by author or ISBN – not just by title. These are all common user behaviors when searching, and allowing them on your site will make your user experience more accessible.

The following is a series of search terms based on the same list of countries mentioned previously, but with a couple of differences – this example allows for "fuzzy" matching, and it can interpret additional information to help the user find the result they may be looking for. In this case, it allows users to search by **ISO country code** as well as the country itself. Here are just a few examples of entries that a user could write in the form field to return Croatia as the top result:

- **Cro** (typing the start of the word, with the letters in the correct order)

- **Croatia** (the country name itself, spelled correctly)

- **Croasha** (misspelling of the "tia" at the end)

- **Coratai** (all of the letters in "Croatia," but in a completely wrong order)

- **Roatia** (missing the first letter, likely from a quick-typing error)

- **HN** (the ISO country code for Croatia)

- **Crosha** (a misspelling)

- **Crowaysha** (written as the word sounds)

- **Croaysha** (same as earlier)

And many more I likely haven't thought of.

Figure 6-22 shows a few of these scenarios working successfully with a fuzzy matching search.

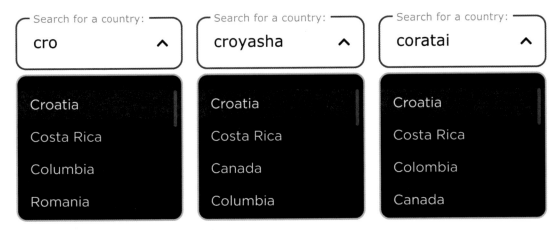

Figure 6-22. *Fuzzy search accurately returning "Croatia" in three scenarios: when the user has entered the start of the word – "cro" (pictured left), an incorrect spelling based on how the word is said – "croyasha" (pictured middled), and when the user has entered all of the correct letters for the word but in the wrong order – "Coratai" (pictured right).*

I've provided examples of both of these approaches in the practical example for this chapter, so you can compare them side by side and perhaps implement one in your own site. There are also a number of other popular libraries for achieving autocomplete, and I've added links to those too, along with an explanation of how they handle result matching. You can find the code for the practical example on this book's GitHub repository (in the "Chapter 6" folder), but if you'd simply like to see it in action, you can visit `inclusive.guide/examples/autocomplete`.

Neurodiversity

I wanted to finish this chapter by highlighting the work that the "neurodiversity" movement has been doing over the past few years to fix the lack of attention toward cognitive impairments. This movement argues that there is no "neuro-normal" mind, and instead there is "a broad spectrum of human minds that interpret and experience the world in different ways."[63] From within their framework, conditions like ADHD, dyslexia, dyscalculia, and autism are simply examples of **neurodiverse** minds – part of a spectrum of minds, in which everybody has different strengths, weaknesses, and access needs. Robert McDowell's neurodiversity report echoed this, explaining that "paying attention to accessibility for neurodiverse users will, by definition, cause you to make things clearer and better, and easier to use."[64]

Both strongly argue that disabilities only arise when users' access needs are ignored, thereby creating barriers. This focus, and the fact that they can arise for anyone, echoes our approach in this book.

Many experts believe cognitive impairments have been *ignored* as much as they have been hidden. In reading this content, you will now find many of the barriers less hidden from you, but you've also chosen not to ignore them.

Conclusion

Through this chapter, you now have an idea of the route that COGA and the W3C want to take when it comes to thinking about cognitive impairments online. This should help what you've learned remain relevant moving forward but also give you some practical steps you can take **now** to help users on your own sites.

We've covered five key areas to think about when evaluating sites and five areas of symptoms that you're now more aware of. Together, this creates five questions you can keep in mind when designing, building, or maintaining a site online:

1. Could my content be shorter, simpler, or easier to read, perhaps testing it through the reading ease test?

2. Could I make what I'm sharing clearer, through tools like average reading time for content, providing abbreviations, or labeling vague icons?

3. Are my pages, menus, or journeys too busy or complex?

4. Can users understand the purpose of my content or actions at a glance, perhaps through TL;DRs or well-named, self-contained actions?

5. Am I helping users avoid mistakes in what I'm asking them to do such as through adding autocorrect or autocomplete?

As I said at the beginning, this chapter is different from others – the barriers between access needs are more vague, and that can make what's helpful harder to determine. However, this lack of clear distinctions has its benefits. In the introduction to this book, I mentioned that through regular practice identifying access needs and barriers, you can become adept at identifying these issues in your work and therefore see how you can cater to a *wide* range of users.

Now that we are a few chapters in, I hope you have started to catch some of the overlaps that have been cropping up. As a small recap, here are some solutions that we've covered in this chapter that **overlap** with access needs we've covered in other chapters:

- TL;DRs can be useful for **screen readers**, particularly if they're positioned at the top of a page or email, as these users can read the summary before deciding whether to engage with the rest of the content. They can also help users in a rush, who don't have time to fully engage with all of the content.

- In Chapter 4 "Motor disabilities," we mentioned the importance of shortcuts like "skip to main content" for **keyboard-only** navigation, and breadcrumbs provide another excellent option. These quick, context-based links allow a motor-impaired user to quickly tab to a related page without searching through a large menu.

- Some users with **dyslexia** have trouble reading on certain foreground/background color combinations (such as white text on a black background) even though it has a high contrast ratio.

- Similarly, we looked at how bright contrasting colors can overwhelm some users with **autism** – a barrier that can *also* exclude users with **photosensitivity**.

- "Unexpected autoplay" was a discussion topic in Chapter 5 "Deafness and Hard of Hearing" but was also relevant in this chapter because of the effect it has on those with **heightened sensory awareness**. It's capable of contributing to the complex experiences that can overwhelm users with **executive function impairments**.

- Sitemaps provide a consistent format for displaying lists of pages on a site and, aside from providing an alternate way to navigate for cognitively impaired users, they can also help **blind** and **low vision** users through their consistent layout for screen readers to digest.

It's worth taking a little time to think about each of these and other crossovers you might have spotted. No chapter is completely isolated from the others in this book, in exactly the same way that no disability or access need is isolated from other user needs. Just as cognitive impairments can be known as "hidden disabilities," many of these overlapping benefits can help you cater to "hidden needs" – things you hadn't considered because it wasn't immediately obvious that they applied to a specific area or disability but that can still improve a user's experience on the Web. The more that you begin to think like this, the more needs you will tackle, and the better you will get at seeing more than one benefit. Accessibility is iterative, and practice is key.

CHAPTER 7

Mental Health

Design is what mediates our interaction with the internet. It's the language we read it in. It's not too much to ask that that language is comprehensible and honest.

—Harry Brignull

Of all the disabilities we have discussed so far, mental health impairments have arguably seen the biggest increase in exposure over the last few years, and yet our understanding of them is very much still forming. Consequently, the way we think about mental health on the Web is in a state of flux. While some mental health disorders, like **depression** and **anxiety**, are fairly well understood, the way we categorize and define other conditions is constantly changing. The definitions of conditions like **schizophrenia** or **psychosis**, for example, have changed a lot over the last few years and can refer to a wide variety of experiences.[1]

While this is happening, our understanding of just how many people these disorders can affect has also grown. The World Health Organization now estimates that mental health disorders make up **10%** of the global burden of disease and **25.1%** of the nonfatal disease burden.[2] In 2020 alone, due to the COVID-19 pandemic, there was a **28%** increase in anxiety and major depressive disorders, and we're yet to see a decrease in those numbers in the wake of it.[3]

What we *do* know is that some of these impairments can come and go and can come on for the first time at any point in our lives. The charity Money and Mental Health estimates that "in any given year, nearly **one in three** people will experience a mental health problem which can affect their cognitive and psychological functioning."[4]

This is a really large number of people, but it *could* be even larger. Because of this state of flux around mental health, our understanding is inhibited because effective **diagnosis** is far more difficult, which results in much lower levels compared to other disabilities. In their "Fundamental Facts About Mental Health," the Mental Health

Foundation said: "Nearly **half** of adults believe that, in their lifetime, they have had a diagnosable mental health problem, yet less than a **third** have received a diagnosis."[5]

Mental Health on the Web

This variance creates a challenging task for us to address. Experiences can vary substantially from person to person, across different conditions, at different times in a person's life, and even differing understanding around whether their symptoms constitute a mental health condition. As Merlyn Holkar of the UK Financial Conduct Authority told me:

> Everybody's mental health will get better and worse over time – it could be that somebody has had a breakup or a financial problem that has recently just made things worse. People might not tell you that they are experiencing these symptoms.[6]

This creates a situation that differs from catering to most other access needs, where we cannot always confidently identify people affected by mental health issues. At the same time, research has found that "consumers experiencing mental health problems are systematically disadvantaged…and are more likely to pay over the odds, experience poorer services, and are more likely to end up in financial difficulty."[7]

So, how do we approach this? Well, the preceding quote raises an interesting question: **what causes some people to pay over the odds, based on their mental health online?**

This question cuts through the inconsistencies around data and the unknowns around when it might affect someone, and it's *this* area I'd like to explore in this chapter. We all use one Web, but as you know, many people interact with it in different ways. Well, we all visit many of the same websites and complete many of the same journeys too – sites made to sell products, and journeys made to get you through them as quickly as possible.

In the art of selling and persuasion, there are a range of tactics to use, and that's no different on the Web. However, there are differing levels to which we are **susceptible** to them, and the effect they can have on those with poor mental health can be profound. Understanding these tactics is key to being inclusive online and protecting a user's mental health by finding practical ways to identify and avoid them. They have had many names since they were first coined in 2010, but I'm going to use the original: dark patterns.

Dark Patterns

Figure 7-1. *A series of illustrations to represent dark patterns we're about to explore in the chapter*

What Is a Dark Pattern?

Put simply, dark patterns are carefully crafted interfaces that trick people into making decisions or performing actions that they otherwise would not. Dark patterns can range from subtle omissions to outright lies, but what they all have in common is that they undermine users' intentions and cost them time or money they never meant to spend. They come in many forms, can be used in combination with one another, and tap into how we typically perform actions online so they can hijack them.

In 2018, the Norwegian Consumer Council published a paper called "Deceived by Design." In it, they highlighted some of the tactics used by the biggest sites in the world – Facebook, Google, and Microsoft – to "manipulate" users into disclosing information and relinquishing their privacy online. This included using certain language to alter decisions, pre-ticking certain form inputs, prompting "take it or leave it" questions, and hiding actions deep inside account menus. The report concluded that these actions were implemented in their online experiences "to a degree that we consider unethical."[8]

Just over six months later, following the advent of GDPR (General Data Protection Regulation), Google was hit with a **£44 million** fine for these tactics.[9] Fast-forward three years, and they were fined ***again***, this time **€150 million** for the use of dark patterns in how they handled letting users control their cookie settings.[10]

Now although these fines focus on regulating privacy, dark patterns can also manipulate users, "nudge" them into behaving a certain way, and cause distress through lack of transparency. Online deceit exploits human behavior, and those with mental health problems can be more sensitive to this exploitation.

Why Are They Used?

These practices are known to increase conversion, retention, and most other metrics that sites measure success by, which explains why they're so popular. It's also difficult to legislate when it comes to leveraging human psychology, and so holding businesses accountable here is hard to do. What's more, not all of them are immediately obvious, but they *are* common. In 2022, the European Council found that a staggering **97%** of sites they tested had some form of deceptive pattern.[11]

Encouraging a user to do something isn't necessarily the problem (all sites do this in some way); it depends on *how* sites do it – ensuring that what you've added is **persuasive**, but not **manipulative**. As the Norwegian Consumer Council explains:

> The use of exploitative design choices, or "dark patterns," is arguably an unethical attempt to push consumers toward choices that benefit the service provider.[12]

Dark patterns create negative experiences that can be amplified for those with mental health–oriented access needs: for example, those who struggle with a lack of **motivation**, those susceptible to periods of **impulsivity** that cause them to make quick (and sometimes poorly judged) decisions, and those who suffer from **anxiety**. Other access needs might even arise from the treatment of these symptoms – the Web Accessibility Initiative (WAI) explains that "medication may have side effects including blurred vision, hand tremors, and other impairments," which can *also* increase how sensitive these users are to dark patterns.[13]

Another problem is that this sort of behavior isn't monitored or regulated consistently. Indeed, despite the recent rise in awareness, there isn't an agreed set of rules for helping those with mental health issues online. WCAG doesn't explicitly mention mental health disorders, and COGA (Cognitive Accessibility Roadmap and Gap Analysis), mentioned in the last chapter, is still working on gap analysis to understand the state of web accessibility and what to recommend.[14] This allows these practices to continue largely unchallenged. However, this issue is *so* pressing that the inventor of the Web itself – Sir Tim Berners-Lee – is taking steps to fight the use of dark patterns online (we'll get to that later).

Now, not all dark patterns are added nefariously – sometimes dark patterns have manipulative consequences that go **beyond** what their creators intended, and some are entirely unintentional when copying other sites or seeking to boost metrics. Either way, it's important to know how to spot them and how to reach and support these users more generally. Fully understanding the effect that certain web features have on users with mental health problems can lead you to make better decisions when catering to these users.

What We're Going to Talk About

Harry Brignull coined the term "dark patterns" in 2010 (which he now refers to as "deceptive patterns"), and since then, it's become ubiquitous. He's also written an excellent book on the topic since the first edition of this book was released. If you'd like to examine more deeply the **psychology** behind the tricks sites use to coerce and control users, I've put a link to his book in the reading list for this chapter – you can find it at `inclusive.guide/reading/chapter7`.

For us, we'll approach the topic from a different direction. Brignull says that "the best defense against dark patterns is to be aware of them," so that's what we'll do.[15] This chapter will approach dark patterns through the dual lens of understanding (and therefore avoiding them) in your websites but also understanding the effect they have on those with a range of mental health issues. By first understanding which features are exacerbating these symptoms online, we can take practical steps to avoid them.

Pulling together work from government bodies, research groups, mental health charities, and users themselves, we will address several patterns, organized by the following themes:

- **Dark pattern** – An example of a manipulative technique used to either illicit or coerce a user's action.

- **The symptom(s)** – The symptoms that a pattern can aggravate and how these are compounded for people with mental health issues.

- **Solution(s)** – Solutions we can implement to combat these issues, or simply actions to avoid. This will also include some examples of those who have approached this in a way that empathizes with users.

You will also see overlaps between this chapter and previous ones, especially around cognitive impairments (Chapter 6), due to these patterns affecting planning, reasoning, memory, and attention. Beyond that though, many of these patterns will be situations that you can relate to directly and may have been impacted by yourself. This helps to put yourself in the situation of these users and ensure that your sites are doing everything they can to make their experience online a positive one – let's get started.

Dark Pattern: Complicated and Obstructing Journeys

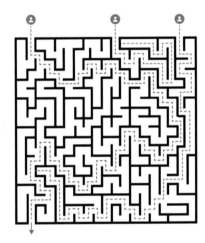

Figure 7-2. *A journey that is very simple to get into, but exceedingly difficult or impossible to get out of, is known informally as a "Roach Motel."*

Dark patterns creator Harry Brignull also coined the term for a particular pattern – a "Roach Motel." This is a user experience that is *very* easy to get into, but very difficult to get out of.[16] A classic example of this online would be the act of deleting an account or canceling a subscription. Businesses often believe it is in their best interests to make these journeys as hard as possible to discourage users. Here are some notable examples of complicated or obstructive journeys so that you can understand what to avoid.

New York Times

The *New York Times* made it very easy to sign up for a subscription, but difficult to cancel, as users have reported being required to call or chat with customer service to cancel, waiting on hold for long periods, or being redirected to other web pages without being able to cancel their subscription. In one test, it took roughly **17 minutes** of conversation with a customer services rep to successfully cancel a subscription.[17] Conversely, it takes a matter of seconds to create a new subscription.

This often leads to users giving up on the process due to the friction and paying for a service they no longer want or need.

Instagram

It's worth noting that the impact on mental health isn't always financial-based. Instagram accounts can be made in **20 seconds** but take minutes to delete, followed by a **30-day** waiting period before it's *actually* deleted. This is not only a difficult journey to go through, but the open-ended nature of account deactivation means that those who struggle with **social media addiction** are far more likely to come back, and *not* get the help they need.[18] This practice keeps user numbers high, which increases ad revenue and stock price, but at the risk of some people's mental health.

This is a widespread problem online – some services merely offer deactivation, rather than deletion, "in case you wish to return." Others require you to submit "requests" for cancellation to be considered. Frequently, you will have to email a customer service team, or even call them on the phone, and then be quizzed on your reasons for wanting to leave. All of these tactics help form the "Roach Motel."[19]

Google

Google was fined €150 million for their use of the "hard to cancel" pattern. They made it easy for users to accept *all* cookies immediately on the first step of their cookie information notice but had an obstructive journey to refuse them, where relevant information was "only accessible after several steps only, implying sometimes up to five or six actions."[20] This constituted hiding information – "nesting" it deep in sub-pages in a way that was needlessly complicated and violated a European Privacy Directive, which requires clear and comprehensive information on the purposes of cookies.[21]

Google also used a "false hierarchy" in its design by presenting the "Accept all" option more prominently than the "Reject" option. This made it seem like accepting cookies was the default and **expected** option, while refusing them was a secondary, less important choice.[22]

Figure 7-3. *A cookie notification showing a primary "accept" button and a secondary "show details" button. There is clear preference in the design for the "accept" option.*

Symptom

Online journeys can be daunting, and companies hope that users will give up and go along with what the site wants. That's what complicated sitemaps and various "dead ends" are designed to do.

Anyone would have trouble navigating deeply nested pages or struggle to remember account security details. However, for those with conditions such as **depression** who are prone to experiencing a debilitating lack of motivation, or users with **panic disorders** who are experiencing high levels of panic and confusion, these actions can be nearly impossible to complete and so prompt disengagement. For example, Money and Mental Health reported that

> For many, this is simply too difficult, particularly when they are unwell. When depressed, people often lack the motivation to pursue hobbies and other pleasurable activities. At these times, engagement with online services can require superhuman levels of effort. Eight in ten (**82%**) of our survey respondents said they found the thought... exhausting.[23]

Complicated journeys also impact users with conditions like **schizophrenia**, who might have trouble mentally mapping out how pages relate (known as impaired **visual-spatial comprehension** – which we mentioned in the previous chapter). Merlyn Holkar describes how this technique can cause "information overload":

> Some mental health problems can affect your "attention switch" and other cognitive faculties that you use when you are scanning between different things to try and find the information that's appropriate to you... if there's a website and...you're trying to find a specific thing but you just don't really know what it is, and there's too many things for you to know what to look up.[24]

So not only does this affect users with these conditions, it can actually make their symptoms worse.[25]

Solutions

A simple benchmark, as said by the President of the United States:

> **It shouldn't be harder to cancel a service than it was to subscribe for it.**[26]

This should be what we all aim for as it shows respect for your users and a sense of transparency about your product – if it's great, you don't need to fight to keep them. Persuasion and offers are entirely reasonable, but once the decision is made, you're only hurting your users *and* your reputation by making it more complicated than it needs to be to cancel.

Highlight the Offenders

We also want to both combat and shine a light on this poor practice. "Just Delete Me" is a fantastic service that makes it easier to delete accounts by letting you know the effort required and offering direct links to pages that are often buried deep in sites. It also acts as an excellent gallery of those who make it impossible to delete an account, which hopefully makes companies rethink this practice the bigger it gets. I've added a link to this site in the reading list for this chapter, which you can find at `inclusive.guide/reading/chapter7`.

Optimize Common Journeys

While journeys like closing an account may only need to happen once, other journeys can take a greater toll because they are used more frequently. Therefore, let's explore some practical ways to make online journeys as a whole more inclusive for those with mental health disorders.

For some users, even the act of logging in can be a barrier, raising questions like

- "What email did I sign up with?"

- "Do I remember my password?"

- "If I reset it, how long would that take?"

- "Will the email end up in spam?"

Sometimes these steps are unavoidable, and that's because the risk of exposing sensitive data is simply too great. However, it's good to actively think about whether common journeys *could* be accomplished in fewer steps than they currently require, even if that requires a little more work on your end.

Digital bank Monzo did this with their login process, which now requires only an email address be remembered by the user to log into the app. Once they submit that, a "magic" link is sent to that inbox that logs them in. Users still need to know their PIN to use the money in their account (which is good for security purposes), but that's easier to remember than a long password.

I've encountered a similar issue at Octopus Energy while reviewing the journey users take when submitting meter readings. It's something that is required monthly, and after receiving an email reminding customers, they would need to remember their login details to access their dashboard, head to the "meter reading" area, and then submit them. We spoke to customers and found that the number of steps involved meant that they weren't submitting readings and therefore receiving potentially inaccurate bills.

We reviewed the journey and realized that no sensitive data was required when submitting a reading. Moreover, the submission page itself also checked that the reading submitted was within a reasonable threshold of the previous one to prevent fake submissions. This meant that a login wasn't necessary to allow the user to complete the journey, so we removed it.

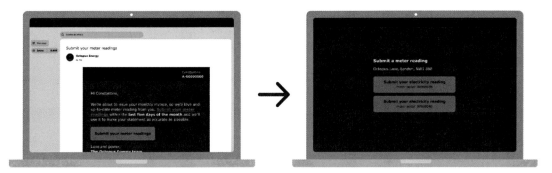

Figure 7-4. *An illustration of how a user can submit a meter reading to Octopus Energy anonymously without logging in, just by clicking the link in the email they receive*

We created an anonymous link that we'd email to users every month with their reminders. By clicking this link, they could submit the reading without login details, reducing the time needed to complete the action dramatically. It particularly helped our users who have issues with memory by removing the need to remember a password (e.g., those with **dementia**). It also aids people with **anxiety**, who often like to minimize the time spent on sites they aren't familiar with, and more generally, any user looking to complete required actions as quickly as possible.

Since introducing the feature, the percentage of people submitting their meter readings increased drastically while also reducing the amount of issues created through inaccurate bills. This makes it best for us **and** best for all users, and we now use this approach for other journeys throughout our site. It's worth considering if there are any opportunities for you to do the same.

Communication Anxiety

Let's briefly return to the journey a user might take when deleting an account on a site. After going through pages and pages of menus, drop-downs, and options to close an account, many services *still* require a phone call with someone to finalize its closure. This is a massive barrier for many users with impaired mental health:

> Many people with mental health problems, particularly anxiety disorders, are phobic about using the telephone. This can be a significant barrier to market engagement, particularly where customers must make a telephone call to cancel an existing contract.[27]

239

Access needs such as **social anxiety** and **panic disorders** mean that many users are not confident communicators and so can experience difficulties communicating with their providers, managing their accounts, and getting support when problems develop. It can also affect those with cognitive impairments, such as **autism**, as it "involves impairments of social communication and interaction abilities."[28]

For some, being forced to use an unsuitable communication channel can trigger **panic attacks** or **suicidality**:

> I have massive anxiety about talking to strangers on the phone. I frequently end up feeling exhausted or at worst suicidal afterwards.[29]

Why Do This?

Many users feel (quite rightly) that the phone process may not be easy – the person on the other end may not immediately comply with what you're asking them to do and instead try to persuade you not to leave – to try a different type of account, to reduce the frequency or amount of the payments you're making, or *anything* to stop you from actually leaving. They often have targets to retain customers and so have the same intention as those who create complicated journeys and dead ends online – it's another barrier designed to wear the user out and make them give up on leaving or canceling.

Reach Users Where They Feel Comfortable

Different people prefer different communication channels. Just as some people cannot answer the phone, some people will not open print mail, and others do not trust web chat. The reasons can be quite personal, and so providing a variety of options gives you the best chance of making it comfortable for users:

> The option of having different ways of getting in touch can really help. Some people get really flustered on the phone, but if they can use a webchat to talk and send other information, they can have a break, they can read back over what's been said – you don't have to rely on your memory and you can take it at your own pace.[30]

Therefore, it's important to offer alternative ways of communication for those unable or unwilling to interact via a specific medium, as we mentioned in Chapter 5 "Deafness and Hard of Hearing." Ideally, you'd have phone, chat, and email as ways of finalizing an account closure. Giving users the freedom to choose provides some comfort and control and helps avoid trapping and negatively affecting those with mental health impairments.

Setting Expectations

Anxiety is the most common mental health disorder, affecting hundreds of millions of people.[31] It's characterized by excessive fear, unease, and worry, all of which can be severe enough to result in significant distress or impairment in functioning. It's something we all feel at some point in our lives.

In 2023, an average of **37.1%** of women and **29.9%** of men reported high levels of anxiety.[32] This number has risen considerably in the last few years, with the COVID-19 pandemic being a contributing factor. Anxiety is felt particularly keenly by those with other disorders, such as **generalized anxiety disorder**, **panic disorder**, **phobias**, and post-traumatic stress disorder (**PTSD**).[33]

Uncertainty is closely linked to anxiety, and uncertainty online can be a big problem – largely due to the sheer volume and variety of content out there. The Web is home to such a wide range of sites – built using different technologies, at different times, during different phases of design and development. As there are no consistencies between these factors, there is no guarantee about how a site is going to appear – one website may design a user journey one way, while another may take a different approach. Of course, some common journeys require similar information (e.g., delivery and payment info will likely be required for an online shop), but even then, this can be asked for in a plethora of ways, over varying amounts of pages and steps.

This makes every experience on a new site a journey into the unknown. For many users, this leads to **anxiety**, which can prevent them from making their way through a journey effectively, or from even starting one. This can manifest in several ways, from a fear that something bad might happen if the user makes a bad decision or does something wrong to confusion about how far along they are in a journey, how much further they have to go, and what information they might need.[34]

The solution to this lies in setting a user's expectations correctly to reduce anxiety. There are two good ways to accomplish this: priming messages and signposting.

Priming Messages

Priming messages are used to set a user's expectations ahead of the next step in a journey. After the user completes the action(s) on a page, it's important to explain what will happen next.

Let's take a look at two buttons (Figure 7-5), each taken from different sites but both at the point in their respective journeys that the next step will be the "payment" page.

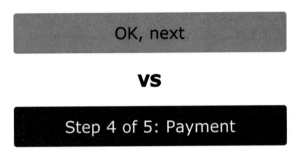

Figure 7-5. *A comparison of two buttons – one that simply says "OK, next" and the other that lets the user know the number and name of the next step in the journey*

The first says nothing. The user doesn't know what "next" means in this context, in the same way that people don't know where a link entitled "click here" will send them. At least in the case of the link, the text that comes before it can provide some context.

Conversely, the second option tells users what to expect in the next stage of the journey and also lets them know how far along in the journey they are. This all helps set their expectations for what's to come. It can also mean that users don't have to work as hard to motivate themselves, which can be an issue for those with **bipolar disorder**. This affects roughly 1 in 100 people, and users with it alternate between depressive episodes and periods of manic symptoms.[35] During those depressive states, motivation is incredibly low, and so breaking down tasks into easily understandable chunks removes some uncertainty about how long a task is going to take, and therefore, the worry that the task could go on for can feel like forever.[36]

Priming Messages Away from Your Site

The UK Home Office created a series of simple "dos and don'ts" posters in 2017 to offer guidance on how designers and developers can make sites more accessible for users with certain access needs. We'll cover these properly in Chapter 11 "Tools and Auditing," but their latest addition to the collection was on designing for anxiety. According to them, your online journeys shouldn't leave users "confused about next steps or time frames" or "uncertain about the consequences of their actions."[37]

We've just covered "next steps," but the reason that time frames are mentioned is because sometimes the steps on your site are only *part* of a user's journey. For example, if a user is trying to reset their password, it could involve receiving an email or SMS they need to interact with to confirm their identity. In this case, you can help to set expectations by letting them know

- What the next step is
- When they should receive these communications
- When they should next expect to hear from you
- What will be expected of them when they hear from you
- What to do if they don't receive a message

This can be especially useful for those with **obsessive-compulsive disorder** (OCD). This affects approximately **1%–2%** of the global population and is a mental health condition where you have recurring thoughts and repetitive behaviors that you cannot control.[38] A primary symptom is pathological doubt, and so they have particular difficulty tolerating uncertainty.[39]

The key here is to be upfront and truthful about time frames – if it'll take an hour, then tell users that. Promising shorter wait times will only result in frustration for users when it *doesn't* happen. It's proven that people are happy to wait longer if they *expect* that to begin with.[40]

Signposting

Beyond priming for the next action, signposting the main stages of an entire journey can also provide a handy reference point, and source of calm, for users making their way through. Providing context in this way, as seen in Figure 7-6, displays progress *and* reduces journey drop-off, as people can set their expectations accordingly.

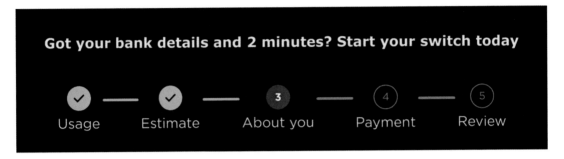

Figure 7-6. *A timeline from a checkout process that shows the user how far they've progressed and which steps they have left to complete*

In the preceding journey timeline, you can see

- What the steps are

- How far you've come already

- How far there is left to go

This can help users make a decision about when to complete the journey, given what's left to do, and whether they have the right information in order to complete those steps – these are some of the main concerns we raised earlier. Sarah Drummond, founder of the agency Snook, which develops design patterns for mental health services, has talked about how you must "prepare people by providing what information is needed for the journey they are embarking on." This allows for a sense of "confidence and readiness."[41] Priming messages facilitate **preparation** for each step, and this simple feature provides it for the whole journey.

Symptoms

This has also been known to help users who suffer from attention impairments – a symptom associated with mental health problems such as **ADHD** and **schizophrenia**, and results in difficulty concentrating. Activities such as comparing products, scrutinizing charges, or filling out lengthy forms require a lot of attention to complete correctly. Knowing exactly what these activities are, and how many of them are present in an online journey beforehand, reduces the chances of them abandoning it out of frustration and not trying again.

This ties into the "historical breadcrumbs" that we covered in the last chapter *and* WCAG's rule on providing users information about their location within a set of pages

(2.4.8: Location).[42] The combination of providing good signposting of progress in your journeys and enabling users to interact with the various steps and navigate between them creates a feature that is both reassuring and practical for those with both cognitive and mental health impairments.

Dark Pattern: Forced Urgency Through Scarcity

Figure 7-7.   Messaging on product pages such as "low stock" and "only 2 left" creates a sense of urgency through placing the idea of scarcity in a user's mind. This scarcity is not always true.

We've just seen how setting honest expectations can help users understand and complete the journey they are about to go on. Now we are going to look at how some sites manipulate users into rushing these journeys, particularly in ecommerce, by creating a false sense of urgency.

As people, we commonly have what are known as **cognitive biases**. These are basically shortcuts in the mind that have been built up over time through completing common tasks. On the Web, this manifests as certain actions in response to visual cues like reviewing inputted content when a form field is red or clicking the more brightly colored of two buttons to confirm an action without reading the text of those buttons.

When sites and journeys *hijack* these biases, they can cause us to make errors in our decision-making without us being consciously aware of them. One powerful example is scarcity – the idea of grabbing something before it's no longer available. This is incredibly prevalent online when you're unsure who else is going after the same product or ticket as you. Companies turn this unknown to their advantage, often in ways that are untrue, to encourage impulsive and risky decisions.

Booking.com

According to Similarweb, one of the most popular choices for booking travel accommodation online is booking.com with more than **675 million** monthly visits.[43]

Now, when searching for hotels, the user is typically not *just* browsing. Instead, they probably need accommodation. These sites know this, and it becomes about **when** they book, not if. For this reason, their aim is to make this happen as quickly as possible because once the purchase is made, it's been proven that they are *far* less likely to critically reexamine their purchase and opt for an alternative hotel through a competitor or directly from the hotel.

Instead, something called "psychological post-decision rationalization" occurs, which paints the decision already made in a favorable light compared to when the decision was made. Businesses have a clear understanding of this behavior, which they leverage to their advantage. In doing this though, they fail to perceive how their aggressive sales techniques create a real sense of **stress** in the user. They may be manipulated into buying quickly, leading them to the fast instead of the best decision and creating a lot of regret.

There are two main things sites like booking.com rely upon:

- Creating a sense of scarcity to force people to act

- Pitting other users against one another to build competition

Some of the tactics they employ to accomplish these two goals can definitely be considered dark or deceptive patterns. Let's explore some of them, thanks to research conducted on how the messages they display aren't *always* what they claim to be.

Creating a Sense of Scarcity

This site has been frequently cited as an example of a journey that unduly forces a sense of urgency on users. After searching for a hotel in London for a weekend, I found all of the following messages on the site:

- "In high demand – only 1 room left on our site!"

- "Booked 10 times for your dates in the last 24 hours on our site"

- "1 other person looked for your dates in the last 10 minutes"

- "In high demand" (in big red letters – two lines below a badge that says the exact same thing)

- "33 other people looking now"

- "Last chance! Only 1 room left on our site!"

- "89% of our listings are reserved on these dates"

- "Prices have been increasing on your dates over the past 3 days"

Alone, these messages could be considered informative. **Eight** of them, however, add up to form an intense experience. To compound this worry and urgency, they also show rooms that you "just" missed (shown in Figure 7-8).

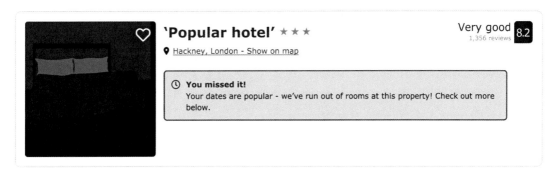

Figure 7-8. *A screenshot from booking.com, where a message is informing the user that they've missed the opportunity to book a certain room*

Even if you had no intention whatsoever of booking the room, you now have a sense of urgency forced upon you, playing on a fear of missing out – look how quickly everything is selling! Imagine if you don't get a great deal![44]

There are examples of this all over the Web. Ticketing websites, for example, often work with even more time-sensitive sales. Many make use of "virtual queues" for ticket releases – loading screens that update every couple of seconds to let you know how many people are queuing behind you. This increases the urge to complete the purchase as you suddenly become aware of a group of people who are ready to take your tickets if you don't act quickly.

Symptom

While these intrusions can be a source of irritation and stress for many people, they can be complete showstoppers for people with mental health disorders that cause them to feel **anxiety** – which include **generalized anxiety disorders**, **panic disorders**, and **psychosis** – who often need to take their time when completing actions. Rushing these can make them "feel pressured to make decisions more quickly than is comfortable for them," aggravating their symptoms.[45,46]

Similarly, features like this also prey on **paranoia**, which can leave you "thinking and feeling as if you are under threat even though there is no (or very little) evidence that you are."[47] It can be a symptom of many mental health problems and encourages people to act instinctively rather than taking the time to consider the wider context.

Finally, these patterns can also encourage impulsive behavior that may be harmful in the long run. This is a symptom of conditions like **borderline personality disorder (BPD)**. Despite it being a lesser-understood mental illness, it is typically characterized by the increased intensity of emotions that someone feels. This is why it's also sometimes referred to as **emotional intensity disorder (EID)**. It can compel users to make decisions, like impulsive purchases, that negatively affect their lives without properly examining them.[48] This is *precisely* what actions with time constraints encourage – a sense of urgency and a fear of missing out.

These journeys can create overwhelming situations for **anyone** depending on the current need of what the site is offering, but these scenarios for those with mental health disorders could lead to mistakes, heavy regret over purchases, and lasting emotional and financial damage.

The Reality Behind Apparent Scarcity

Software developer Roman Cheplyaka actually did a deep dive into booking.com's online practices in 2017 and found that, when you look into the information behind the messaging, there's nothing at all to worry about. It's the nature of the messages themselves – their wording and appearance – that gives the impression that you need to act immediately. There's a particular button on the site that says "someone just booked this" next to a particular listing. However, when interacted with, "just booked" was actually several hours ago. The notification itself appears a few seconds after the page is loaded though, giving the (incorrect) impression that it's appearing in real time.[49] Despite this, it remains capable of alarming users and convincing them to react immediately, perhaps even rashly, in response to the information.

It was these practices, from booking.com and several other sites, that got the attention of the Competition and Markets Authority (CMA). They concluded that giving a false impression of a room's popularity could break consumer protection law and forced these sites to cut down on that behavior. They commented that they will "be watching to make sure that these major brands, used by millions of people in the United Kingdom every year, stay true to their word."[50] At the time of writing though, these tactics are reducing, but remain prevalent.

Shopify

Unfortunately, it's not only large companies that are implementing functionality like this. The significant rise in "build your own website" platforms like Wix or Shopify (that we'll cover more in Chapter 10 "Outsourcing Accessibility") means that more people than ever are running online shops.

On Shopify's app store, there is a program created by HeyMerch. This makes it easy for store owners to show **fake** low stock messages. They can select options that cause it to display fake low stock counters and fake sales numbers (Figure 7-9).

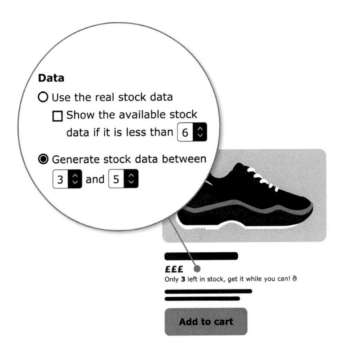

Figure 7-9. *A product page displaying a low stock message to the user. However, this message is based on fake data that the HeyMerch app allows you to create.*

On the page for this app, they specifically mention, in the first sentence of the description, that you can "create a sense of urgency and scarcity."[51] This is one of the effects of large companies engaging in dark patterns – others see it and want to replicate it.

Solutions

Here, our solution echoes a recommendation from Chapter 4 (Motor disabilities) about timers on a site, where giving the users more control over timed tasks made inputting information easier. You need to give users enough time to complete an action, and this applies to decision-making as well as setting impractical time limits. This is why WCAG has a rule to allow users to control or remove any timer placed on them by a journey.[52]

Currently, there is no WCAG rule against this scarcity dark pattern, but if you bombard users with multiple sources of information, even information that you think is useful, they could end up making a decision they're not happy with. This could result in complaints, requests for refunds, and losing repeat customers – you potentially increase conversion but almost certainly trade it for customer happiness and trust as a result.

As I mentioned earlier, these pieces of information are not always added nefariously to manipulate the user. Sometimes it can simply be the unfortunate cumulative outcome of testing lots of small features on a page to see if they increase engagement or conversion and then keeping each one that's successful. As a user on the popular development forum, Hacker News explains:

> This is what A/B testing does to a popular site. You test for immediate customer engagement but cannot (easily) test long-term customer loyalty. This is why booking.com has become the largest online hotel booking site in several continents. Nevertheless, I think it will eventually be their downfall.[53]

It's important to review your journeys and ensure that adding features for the sake of conversion hasn't created a situation where you're pressuring users through your funnel as quickly as possible. You don't want them to regret the decision they've made with you.

You should look at your journeys, and if they overencourage the user to rush an action, then simply choose the single most compelling argument in each scenario and emphasize that – drop the rest. This is similar to the logic behind setting expectations. You should stress the importance of the action and then cede control to the user – knowing that the page's simplicity will give them the freedom to choose.

Dark Pattern: Confirm Shaming

Figure 7-10. *Two options are presented to a user. The choice a site wants a user to make is portrayed in a positive light, whereas a shameful message is associated with the choice they don't want them to make.*

Confirm shaming is the act of framing a decision you want a user to make in such a way that saying no to it could "shame" them or make them feel bad about their choice. It's an approach that has become applied to actions of every kind online, from accepting discount offers to joining newsletters.

The switch from offering a traditional "Yes or No" choice is due to the fact that framing questions in this way can result in more people choosing the option that the business wants – increasing anything from sign-ups to retention rates. However, it can unsurprisingly have a negative impact on users and make you look bad while doing it. Here's an example: Figure 7-11 shows how Amazon frames the option of **not** buying Amazon Prime.

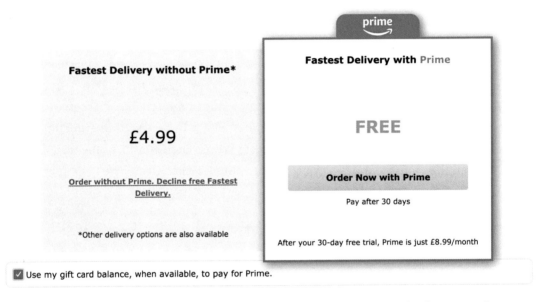

Figure 7-11. *The two choices offered to users when deciding whether to order a product with or without Amazon Prime. A large, colorful box for the Prime option has a big button and the words "FREE" above it, whereas the "decline" message is a simple link that reads "Order without Prime. Decline free Fastest Delivery".*

This design is clear and obvious misdirection. Not only is the option of declining the Prime offer relegated to a much smaller link compared to the shiny sign-up button, but it turns something that shouldn't be hard to avoid (not signing up to a subscription service when buying a product) into something users have to focus on – at a glance, it looks like you're making the *wrong* decision if you don't choose it.

With the user now engaged with the decision, the wording for not signing up associates **negativity** with the choice the site doesn't want them to take, encouraging them to accept the other choice for fear of missing out or making a bad decision. You're not just saying no, you're saying no to unlimited, fastest delivery!

There's more when it comes to this image, but we'll come back to it later.

Extreme Examples

There is an entire site called "Confirm Shaming" that is dedicated to calling out this type of dark pattern and sharing it publicly as a way of dissuading others from doing it.[54] Their examples range from subtle put-downs to outright name-calling. Here are a few examples I found:

Choosing not to sign up for a beginner's guide to gardening:

"No thanks, I know everything about gardening"

Choosing not to enter your email address to get 15% off an order:

"No thanks, I'm not into savings"

Choosing not to disable advert blocking on a website:

"I am a bad person"[55]

Choosing not to receive notifications from MyMedic

"No, I prefer to bleed to death"[56]

Symptoms

Statements like this can deeply affect users with **social anxiety** (also known as **social phobia**).[57] As the National Health Service (NHS) explains, people with social anxiety often fear criticism and have low self-esteem, and every one of these examples plays on that. With it being such a widespread symptom, this can also affect those with **generalized anxiety disorder**, **panic disorder**, and **PTSD**.[58] As Money and Mental Health explains, these users "often find it more difficult to shop around or leave a service that isn't right for them for fear that something bad might come of the decision."[59]

These tactics are also often used to supplement complicated journeys ("Roach Motels"), for example, given to a user who wants to cancel their gaming subscription at the end of the journey (shown in Figure 7-12).[60]

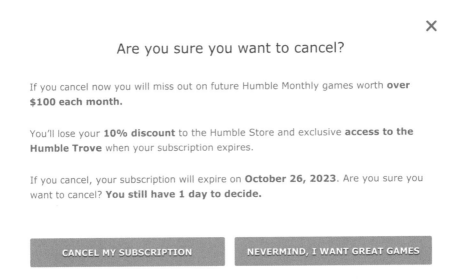

Figure 7-12. *A pop-up asking the user to confirm that they want to cancel their gaming subscription. The "no" option is worded "Nevermind, I want great games".*

Solution

In both cases, you can clearly see how the option that the site **doesn't** want to happen is intentionally worded to either shame or scare the user, whether they mean to or not. Those who are susceptible to feeling embarrassed, humiliated, or judged negatively have their access needs used against them simply because they don't want to sign up for a newsletter or give out their details. Even if they choose not to perform the action, they've still had to face the decision.

We spoke in the last chapter about choosing language that is plain, particularly for actions, but you must also ensure that those words don't shame or manipulate users. The Confirm Shaming website describes doing this as "hot garbage," and I'm OK with printing that in a book and standing by it.

Dark Pattern: "Sneak into Basket" and Hidden Costs

Figure 7-13. *Some sites have been known to sneak something else into a user's basket when they add an item. These are sometimes surprise fees rather than actual items.*

When you add something to your basket, some companies add **another** item automatically, putting the responsibility on you to accept it. This is known as inertia selling or "sneak into basket" selling. In recent years, this behavior has become more prevalent when it comes to hidden charges or fees that are being "snuck" into the final cost compared to what is initially advertised.

We've all been there – you look at a ticket to a concert or an Airbnb listing for a few days, and you're shown a price for it. Then, by the time you're ready to fill out your payment details, your basket has been filled with "fees" – service fees, fulfillment fees, cleaning fees, and admin fees. The list of vague charges goes on and on. Suddenly, the total is alarmingly larger than it was before (Figure 7-14).

Price details

$108.99 x 1 night	$108.99
Cleaning fee	$75.00
Service fee	$25.98
Occupancy taxes and fees	$18.12
Total (USD)	**$228.09**

More info

Figure 7-14. *A breakdown of all of the extra surprise fees in an Airbnb stay. The cleaning fee, service fee, and taxes account for more than 50% of the total cost.*

However, the fee isn't the only thing that's changed. At this point in the journey, you're now only one or two clicks away from purchasing something. It's gone from a browsing exercise to one of **sunk cost** – the idea that if a user has put enough effort into the process already, they'll be lacking motivation and so more likely to accept a surprise charge than leave the journey. You have to decide how much you care about those extra fees now that you're ready to buy. There's a limit to what we'll accept at this stage when it comes to surprise payments, but it's different for everyone. What **has** been proven though is that it works.

Research conducted in 2021 had two groups of people complete a purchasing journey. The first group were shown a price **without** fees, and those hidden fees were then shown right at the end. The second group were shown the **full price** from the beginning, with all fees applied up front. The first group spent **20%** more money in the process compared to the second group and were nearly **15%** more likely to actually go ahead and complete the purchase.[61]

Symptom

This tactic is often combined with the forced urgency that we mentioned earlier. For example, knowing that others are queuing behind you to get tickets and that there are only a few left plays on the users' potential anxiety to increase profit through accepting extra fees. Those with **anxiety** or **panic disorders** sometimes suffer from uncontrollable fears that impair personal function, which then leads to poor decision-making. The fear of missing out based on information they've been provided online has been proven to be a cause. The European Council conducted research that was able to prove a link between this dark pattern on sites and increased heart rate and mouse clicks, thereby identifying them as a cause of anxiety.[62]

All of this makes ambiguous costs such as "management" and "handling" fees – which only appear on the review page – difficult to refuse. There're also those with **learning disabilities** to consider, who may not comprehend or notice the changes that have happened since deciding on purchasing something.

Inconsistent Legislation

It's important to note at this point that, likely due to the trickiness in identifying dark patterns and the damage they cause, countries have different legal laws and regulations around what a site can and can't do.

With hidden fees, the competition and consumer commission in Australia forbids sites from not showing the total cost of something up front. Equally, the European Commission has applied pressure on sites like Airbnb behaving this way (along with the Norwegian Consumer Authority). However, in the United States, as well as other countries, there is nothing that prohibits this.

Companies have been penalized for this practice in the past. In 2018, ticket seller Viagogo was fined **£400,000** for "failing to provide actual ticket prices, misleading customers about ticket availability, and imposing unfair deadlines for claiming refunds under their guarantee."[63]

Solution

The solution to this dark pattern is very simple. Make sure that any charges the user has to pay are obvious up front, and don't put anything in their baskets that they didn't add themselves. In the case of Airbnb, they rolled out transparent pricing globally this year, regardless of what the rules are in the individual countries they operate in (Figure 7-15).[64]

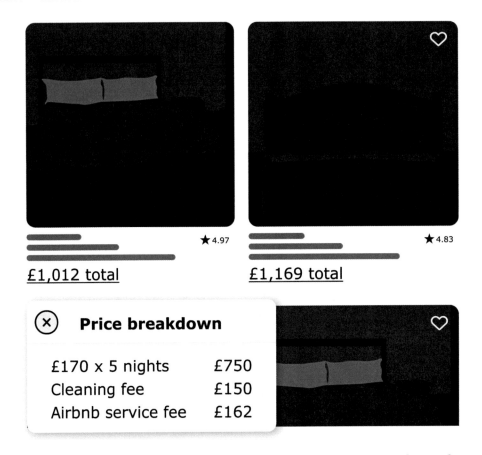

Figure 7-15. A pop-up Airbnb now shows on their search page. It shows the total including **all** fees and a breakdown of what those fees are when the user interacts with it.

Not all sites act in this way though. Given the ability to drastically increase conversion, many sites are changing their behavior based on the laws of each country in order to maximize revenue. These practices, just like forced scarcity, may yield more money in the short term but damage their reputation and revenue negatively in the long term. Trust in transparency when it comes to your site.

Giving Users the Chance to Revert Actions

A lot of physical shops offer easy returns without negative repercussions if the user changes their mind, and where possible, the same should be true of online commitments. Making this easy is also the perfect tonic to any worries a user might have about being mis-sold something, such as completing a purchase without noticing surprise fees. This is an example of where applying friction is actually *beneficial* to the user.

The bank Monzo had some research conducted on their behalf that found that users who experience **bipolar disorder** (something that affects tens of millions of people)[65]

> tended to overspend on needless items – often late at night – while in a manic phase, only when morning came to be faced with this reality. With no way to remedy their mistake, people can then find themselves slipping into a depressive state. That is a dangerous, daunting place to be.[66]

To combat this, Monzo added a feature called "review late-night spending," which notifies the user the next day about purchases made late at night and asks them whether they'd like to review it.[67] This provides users with a degree of control and, in the instances where a return or refund is possible, makes the process easy enough that it doesn't require a lot of motivation to complete.

Dark Pattern: Visual Interference

Figure 7-16. *Visuals can be used by sites to tap into our cognitive biases and present the more costly option (a subscription, an upgrade, etc.) as the "correct" decision*

Hidden charges are not always hidden in a basket though – they can be hidden in plain sight, but trick us **visually**. Take the example shown in Figure 7-17, found by a user on the booking site lastminute.com.

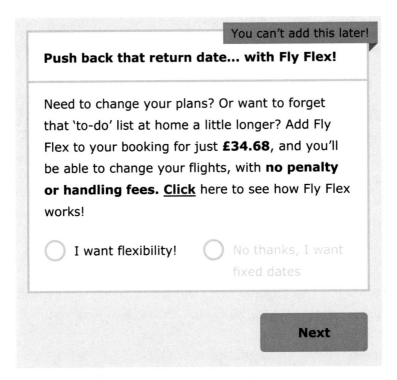

Figure 7-17. *A pair of radio buttons, where one option looks disabled. That option can actually be used to opt out of paying more money for flexible flights.*

At first glance, it doesn't look as though you have a choice – one option appears inactive (thanks to its "grayed out" styling). If you were completing the journey quickly, perhaps becoming tired in the process, you may instinctively select the other option and move on. However, the option that is supposedly "inactive" – not purchasing the upgrade – can *still* be selected, as Figure 7-18 shows.

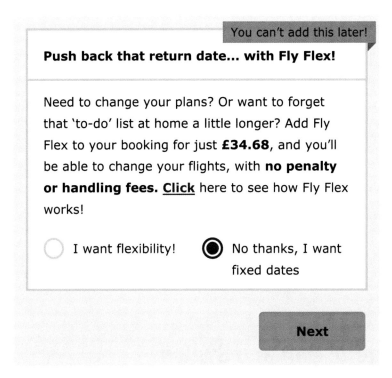

Figure 7-18. *The same pair of radio buttons as earlier, but with the seemingly inactive option selected*[6,8]

This is a small feature, but part of a wider dark pattern called "visual interference": using styling to disguise the **true** purpose of an action. Much like Amazon presenting a subscription button as the "correct" choice earlier, this form is trying to elicit an instinctive reaction from a **user** that benefits the **company** by hiding the action behind what we *expect* to happen when we do it.

In this example, low contrast means we don't focus on the content compared to other elements, which is one of the cognitive biases that's being tapped into here. It's why you see actions a site *has* to display but doesn't *want* you to do, shown in a low contrast, low font, and low position of importance on a page.

It effectively hides it on the page, thereby reducing the chances of users noticing it, interacting with it, or considering it a plausible alternative to the choice that's being given to them in such a visually appealing way. It impairs decision-making and doesn't provide a choice in a fair manner. Given it's actually possible to interact with this element, the low contrast is also inaccessible from a WCAG perspective as well.

Solution

You must ensure that all choices are presented in a fair and consistent manner, with equal weight given to both. This was a big part of the legal action taken against Google and Facebook that I mentioned at the start of the chapter, and unlike some other dark patterns, it's **very** easy to prove. That cognitive bias they're trying to tap into is the same one that can easily tell when something is wrong with an element's layout when we're focused on it.

Intentionally obfuscating the meaning behind a common UI element, in wording, behavior, or styling, is unethical and equivalent to lying to users. If you violate a user's expectations in this way, in the *best* case they spot what you were trying to do, avoid it, and get annoyed at the attempt. In the worst case, you gain money you'll eventually need to give back and potentially find yourself in court. Even the best case doesn't sound very appealing.

Dark Pattern: Bait and Switch

Figure 7-19. *"Bait and switch" is the concept of a user being lured into an action by a site, only for that action to be switched for something else*

For visual interference with a surprising twist, look no further. In 2016, Microsoft started rolling out pop-ups on people's computers, encouraging them to upgrade to Windows 10 (shown in Figure 7-20).

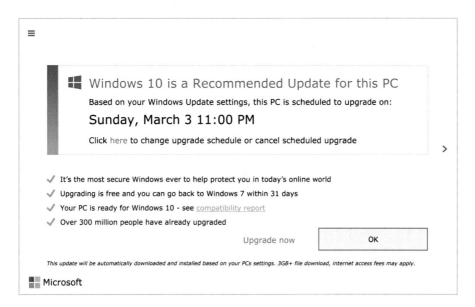

Figure 7-20. *A pop-up that appeared on Windows computers – recommending that they upgrade to Windows 10*

This is a fairly routine call to action, but over time, the frequency of the pop-ups increased. It started appearing as a "recommended upgrade" for users, and unlike the Confirm Shaming we just spoke about, this pop-up didn't have two "Yes or No" style buttons. Instead, it had one button that recommended you start the install and only a small default "X" icon in the corner of the pop-up to close it.

The frequency probably constituted nagging customers, but it was nothing heinous. Despite the increased frequency and change in wording, many users still weren't upgrading and instead dismissing the pop-up when it appeared.

Then, in a particular pop-up, they changed the behavior of the universally known "X" icon that, on every one of the previous pop-ups, closed the window. Instead, clicking the icon this time actually **scheduled** the upgrade process. By doing this, they deliberately cashed in on the action that these users had been performing so consistently for nearly a year: hitting the "X" icon to deny the upgrade and close the window. This tactic, by one of the biggest tech companies in the world, is actually used by viruses, where closing actions can trigger unexpected behavior that does the opposite of what you would expect.[69]

The backlash was massive, and because of this, an immediate patch was created to revert the change. Chris Capossela, Microsoft's chief marketing officer, said:

> Within a couple of hours of that hitting the world, we knew that we had gone too far.[70]

Symptom

The "X" icon represents one of the few universally identifiable online actions, and because of this, people trust that it will behave consistently between sites, browsers, and even operating systems. If this doesn't happen, it can trigger a range of symptoms. The most immediately obvious is **stress**. Stress can commonly occur when we experience something new or unexpected or when we feel as though we have little control over the situation.[71] Although not considered a condition in itself, stress can exacerbate mental health problems like **anxiety** or **depression**, and equally *having* a mental health problem can induce stress itself.

Similar tricks have been pulled without changing the functionality of a site, where the action itself stays the same but the **wording** changes. A classic example involves inverting the option to opt out – using wording like "tick if you do ***not*** want to receive promotional material." People are used to leaving this box unchecked because it typically results in an endless stream of marketing emails, but here, *failing* to do so leads to the same outcome.

Following on from the idea of complex online experiences in the last chapter, parts of a site that compete for your attention and then behave in strange and unpredictable ways when users interact with them can leave users feeling stressed, tricked, and powerless. Users may have already had to expend a lot of effort to get through a journey and be feeling unsure or frustrated. Behavior like this can create an intense sense of panic in **paranoid** users who find online processes stressful – leaving them worried that they may not have understood something properly or feeling like the company is trying to trick them. In the case of Microsoft, they'd have been right.

Solution

The solution here is another slam dunk – actions need to be **consistent** for everyone, especially when they use components or UI elements that users will be used to interacting with already. The result of tricking more people into upgrading their operating system wasn't worth the backlash that Microsoft received, and the same applies to any site that attempts to leverage the learned behavior of a user to make them perform an action they don't want out of pure instinct.

WCAG has a rule simply named "consistent identification" for this reason. It states that

> People who learn functionality on one page on a site can find the desired functions on other pages if they are present.[72]

This refers to actions within your site specifically, ensuring that if you lay out a way of doing something on your site, that behavior is consistent across all pages. You can't have an "opt in" checkbox on one page and then switch to "opt out" on another.

I'd challenge you to look at this principle through a wider lens though: As a site on the Web, I think you have a responsibility to ensure that if you choose to use a common icon, button hierarchy, or form element, that it represents the action that a user would expect *anywhere*. These are known to do specific things – knowledge built up over consistent use across many websites – it's your responsibility to not abuse that.

Dark Pattern: Privacy Zuckering

Figure 7-21. *A user holding a mobile phone, with a series of connected eyes surrounding it*

OK. Mr Zuckerberg, your company recently conducted this massive ad campaign on how far the internet has come in the last 25 years. Great ad. You ended with a statement: "We support updated internet regulations to address today's challenges." Unfortunately, the proposal that you direct your viewers to fails to address dark patterns, user manipulation, or deceptive design choices.

—FTC Chair Lina Khan[73]

This pattern's name is based on the founder of Facebook (now Meta), Mark Zuckerberg, and the revelations that Facebook had been collecting and using user data without explicit consent – most notably in the Cambridge Analytica scandal of 2018.[74]

"Privacy Zuckering" refers to when a company uses cleverly designed interfaces or dark patterns to trick (or sometimes deceive) users into sharing more personal information than they would have otherwise.[75]

In the digital world, users must constantly make decisions about privacy and security. These decisions most often occur at the beginning of use, on the first view of a website, or during the sign-up process of a product. This is also where many of the dark patterns related to privacy occur: often obscuring or overly complicating privacy decisions with the aim of getting the user to disclose additional personal information. A 2020 study of popular consent management platforms found that **88%** of the top 10,000 UK websites contained dark patterns relating to privacy.[76]

Some of these tactics are visual like we've covered, but another recognizable pattern is the use of what's known as "hidden legalese stipulations," in other words writing terms and conditions in complicated legal jargon that can be hard to grasp.[77] Facebook's use of these tactics resulted in the highest penalty ever imposed by the FTC: $5 billion.[78]

Symptoms

Laying out content in this way relies on the idea that people **won't** engage with it. Despite the potential issues and risks, one of our cognitive biases is to quickly agree to large terms and conditions rather than read them. The result of this is that many users skim or don't even read the policies of the product they are signing up for. This can be true for even simple agreements for those with mental health disorders.

For example, the impulsiveness typically caused by **ADHD** can impair a user's ability to properly assess risks before consenting to an agreement. Without a clear point of reflection in the journey to encourage the user to do this, many people will reach the end of a journey without any knowledge of what they've actually agreed to.

Moreover, the potential for disorganized thinking associated with **schizophrenia**, as well as the reduced ability to understand the complicated structure of legal prose for those with **learning disabilities**, leaves both groups of users vulnerable to the whims of a company.

Solutions

It's important to ensure that the main points of *any* agreement you enter into with a user are laid out to them in clear wording, using plain language as much as possible and avoiding jargon (as we discussed in Chapter 6 "Cognitive Impairments"). Where possible, you should also lay out the main points of the agreement in bullet points in order to allow a user to engage quickly and scan the content.

It's imperative that you don't simply highlight the points that suit you – any attempt to hide things that might discourage a user from consenting to your agreement will be certain to provide you with a fine.

By making the terms as easy to read as possible, we are increasing the chance that users will read them in **full**, reducing the instinct to skim. The button to move to the next page should then be labeled "I understand and agree" – again reinforcing the need to comprehend the terms.

Amazon and Combined Dark Patterns

Throughout this chapter so far, I've alluded to the idea that dark patterns can be used in conjunction with one another to be even more potent to users. I'd like to close the chapter by showing you a prime example of that.

I spoke in the first edition about Amazon's awful process surrounding how you delete your Amazon account. It was the perfect example of "hard to cancel." It involved finding various hidden sub-pages and clicking the correct link from a very large and vague list. After that, you *still* had to call them up to confirm the removal of your account.

Since then, they've streamlined it immensely. There's now a link in your settings that specifically mentions removing your account and gives you a checkbox to tick to ensure you understand that the process is irreversible and you're done. It's an excellent improvement from using dark patterns by one of the world's biggest websites, which showed real, tangible progress in this arena – if Amazon can do it, you have no excuse not to.

Unfortunately though, the dark patterns weren't removed, just moved. Only this time they're being sued by a government entity for it.

Amazon vs. US Federal Trade Commission (FTC)

Amazon tricked and trapped people into recurring subscriptions without their consent, not only frustrating users but also costing them significant money.

—FTC Chair Lina Khan[79]

The US Federal Trade Commission (FTC) has recently sued Amazon, alleging the nation's dominant online retailer intentionally duped millions of consumers into signing up for its Prime program and "sabotaged" their attempts to cancel.[80]

The agency even used the term "dark patterns" to explain the behaviors used by Amazon, meant to steer users toward a specific choice and enroll in Prime without their consent:

> These design decisions, commonly known as "dark patterns," push
> customers into acting unintentionally often through misleading
> imagery or intentionally vague offers.

What's more, the lawsuit accuses Amazon of slowing or rejecting changes that would have made it **easier** for users to cancel Prime because those changes "adversely affected Amazon's bottom line." Investigation from Business Insider found that not only is Amazon **aware** that their Prime upselling journey is confusing and "tricks" people into signing up, but they've known **since 2017** and avoided changing it, as it'd reduce subscription growth.[81] Current employees who spoke to Business Insider claimed that "we have been deliberately confusing" with the Prime journey for years in order to maintain growth in sign-ups.[82]

Let's return to the image I showed earlier in the chapter (Figure 7-22), which showed how the Prime service was advertised to users who were in the process of completing a purchase.

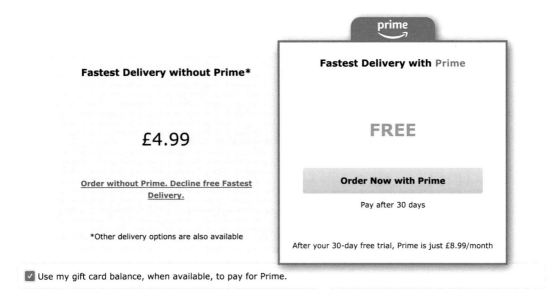

Figure 7-22. *The two choices offered to users when deciding whether to order a product with or without Amazon Prime. A large, colorful box for Amazon Prime has a big button and the words "FREE" above it, whereas the "decline" message is a simple link that reads "Order without Prime. Decline free Fastest Delivery".*

We've been covering dark patterns in isolation, but the effect when a site uses **multiple** patterns to manipulate decisions or coerce customers can be disastrous to the well-being and mental health of a user. From what we've covered so far, you may be able to spot quite a few dark patterns at work here. Give yourself a few moments to analyze the image.

Here is a list of tactics the Prime journey employs, based on the image and FTC lawsuit:

- **Trick wording** – The user is misled into taking an action due to the presentation of confusing or misleading language.

- **Confirm shaming** – The user is emotionally manipulated into doing something that they would not otherwise have done.

- **Visual interference** – Using style and presentation to steer users away from a certain choice.

- **Sneaking** – The user is drawn into a transaction on false pretenses because pertinent information is hidden or delayed from being presented to them.

269

- **Hidden subscription** – The user is unknowingly enrolled in a recurring subscription or payment plan without clear disclosure or their explicit consent.

- **Hard to cancel** – The user finds it easy to sign up or subscribe, but when they want to cancel, they find it very hard.

Let's go through the ones I've mentioned in this scenario:

Trick Wording

In the preceding image, it uses the vaguely named "Order Now with Prime" for the main action button. It doesn't do enough to adequately explain that the user is *also* agreeing to a paid subscription, especially with the massive "FREE" message positioned above it.

I mentioned earlier that sites typically have different messaging or functionality from country to country based on the laws there, and in the United States, the wording was **even vaguer**.

The button read "Get FREE 1-day Delivery with Prime" at checkout. A single click on this button, with no additional confirmation step, automatically enrolled users into a 30-day free trial of Amazon's Prime program, which later converts to a paid membership unless the user cancels it."

If you're unsure whether that's a trick, an internal report at Amazon at the time read:

> The button's label "Continue with FREE 1-day shipping" did not adequately convey that the customer was signing up for a membership...Unintentional sign-ups erode customer trust.[83]

Confirm Shaming

In the first edition of this book, I showed an image of an Amazon Prime advert as an example of confirm shaming. In it, the option to decline read:

> "No thanks, I don't want unlimited One-Day delivery"

Here is what I received when I was offered Prime in late 2023:

> "Order without Prime. Decline free Fastest Delivery"

You *could* argue that the shaming has softened somewhat but would struggle to argue that it had actually gone away. It still frames the choice to opt out as something negative – something we know has the power to guilt or shame those with **anxiety disorders** into making a different choice.

Much like the action button wording, the language for opting against a subscription apparently tends to fluctuate. In the United States, the option to decline a free Prime trial offer switches between a simple "No thanks" and a longer "No thanks, I don't want FREE One-Day Shipping."

Once again, Amazon is aware of what these messages achieve. In another internal email, they stated:

> There is a well established external trend (negatively perceived) called 'customer shaming' and we're even specifically called out in some cases.[84]

Visual Interference

Not only does the language shame someone into choosing the option the company wants, but **visually** it looks like the correct option at a glance. Again tapping into our unconscious bias of what a sensible choice or action looks like, here are the main visuals they use in the image to capture our attention as users and reinforce the idea that we're making the "right" choice by signing up:

- Only one option has a button, something we associate as users with action and proceeding in a journey. The option to opt out of Prime is relegated to a text link.

- The blue outline on the Prime section makes it look "selected" already.

- The green style of the "FREE" text subconsciously associates the option with the "right" option.

- The size of the Prime option on the page is greater than the option to not sign up, which gives it immediate significance to us.

- The white background and range of colors used are more welcoming than the dull gray of the option not to sign up.

- It's positioned on the right, which research has shown draws the eye first on a page.

All of this, working in conjunction with trick wording and confirm shaming, forms a powerful combination. It explains why so many people sign up accidentally – they see so much of what we expect to be normal journey behavior that allows us to proceed with making a routine purchase, which we often act without even considering what we've just done. It's then on us to have to undo it.

Sneaking

The checkbox underneath the delivery options states that I can "use my gift card balance when available to pay for Prime" – a convenient feature perhaps, but an option that is checked by **default** when you reach the page. If you paid no attention to it, this selection would be taken **automatically** as your choice rather than letting someone actually opt in to it.

Selecting something on behalf of your users is generally bad practice. It's similar to the "trick wording" pattern we covered earlier, as both practices make it unclear what their action (or inaction) will result in. This can adversely affect **paranoid** or **anxious** users – seeing a box that's been checked without your knowledge *after* you've submitted a form can be very triggering.

This, plus the dark patterns used alongside it, means a user could be tricked and/or shamed into a subscription they don't want but also lose the value of a gift card they've been given if Amazon took payment before they realized.

Hidden Subscription

All of the preceding patterns come together to hide one thing: that you'll be signing up to a subscription

There **is** text that explains this, but it's underneath all of the visual interference we just covered - relegated to the bottom of the section in small text. Beyond this visual, the biggest thing that hides the nature of the subscription is the lack of a review page to understand what you've agreed to before you continue.

Reviewing Information

Let's return briefly to this image about setting expectations (Figure 7-23).

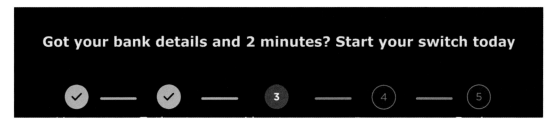

Figure 7-23. *A timeline from a checkout process that shows the user how far they've progressed and which steps are left to complete*

Another point worth mentioning here involves the final step on the preceding diagram. If you are asking a user to provide information over multiple stages or site pages, or you're selling them a product or service, it's important that you give them the opportunity to **review** and alter the information they have provided before they submit it.

Not having the chance to review submitted information or decisions made can cause users to worry. This is partially because unreliable memory is a very common symptom of many mental health problems, like **schizophrenia**, for example, and can also be a side effect of some treatments.[85]

Being able to review and then alter and/or revoke actions empowers those with **obsessive-compulsive disorders** (OCD) or **anxiety disorders** who might wish to check whether they have made a mistake several times. WCAG covers this feature in a rule called "error prevention."[86] They state that this benefits users with "all disabilities who may be more likely to make mistakes," but realistically it should actually say "**all users**." We are *all* susceptible to human error, and while features like autocomplete can safeguard against some incorrect submissions, mistakes can still be made in other areas.

Amazon's internal research on the matter found that the use of an additional confirmation page for all trial services **should** be in place. It said customers were "displeased when there wasn't an additional step" before starting the free trial, calling the current workflow "an unwelcome surprise." "This was a trust buster for these customers, and hints at why accidental sign-ups happen," it said.[87]

No wonder that in the year they launched with this journey and language, "**17,131** of the **25,542** cancellation requests directly handled by the Prime team were related to **accidental** sign-ups."[88]

Hard to Cancel

To top it off, after all of these dark patterns, the act of undoing this action and canceling Prime is riddled with the very same friction and dark patterns I brought them to task for using years ago when trying to delete your Amazon account. It seems as though they've moved the friction from that journey over to their subscription service rather than simply removing it.

When complaints were filed in 2021 by consumer organizations in the EU and United States, these were the processes you had to go through in order to cancel your Amazon Prime subscription:

1. Locate the main menu.

2. Click the "Account" option.

3. Scroll down to click "Prime membership."

4. Click the "Manage membership" text.

5. Click the "End membership" button.

6. Scroll past a number of warnings and graphics about what benefits "you will lose."

7. Click "Cancel My Benefits."

8. Scroll past more warnings and graphics (two different offers from two different attempts).

9. Click "Continue to Cancel."

10. Scroll past a new set of warnings and yellow buttons.

11. Scroll down to the bottom and click one of the two buttons to end the subscription.

12. Cancellation is now confirmed, but you may rejoin at any time.[89]

What's more, all of this friction was **deliberate**. An internal project within Amazon named "Iliad" (named after the Greek poem by Homer, known for its incredible length) was created to make it *harder* to cancel Prime. The project created multiple layers of questions and new offers before a user could cancel their subscription. After the program launched, cancellations dropped **14%**.[90]

As we covered, those with **depression** who are prone to a debilitating lack of motivation, or users with **panic disorders** who experience high levels of confusion, are more likely to struggle with difficult journeys and ultimately give up. However, this journey is a tough ask for *anyone*. When these same struggles were investigated internally by customer-focused teams inside Amazon, reports suggested that

> In several cases, fixes for these issues were proposed and considered, but resulted in lower subscription growth when tested, and were shelved by executives.[91]

In 2022, Amazon agreed to implement a smoother version of this process, with fewer steps and less friction. However, at the time of writing, a version of this process is still live.[92]

It will be interesting to see how the FTC's case builds against Amazon for these practices – their accusations, plus the internal reports and quotes from employees, are damning. Much like accessibility as a whole, high-profile cases like this have the positive outcomes of both drastically raising awareness of the practices companies are engaging in and also deterring others from considering taking the same approach.

The effect that these patterns have on those with mental health issues is still poorly documented relative to the amount of users who suffer from them. It's my hope that this case will shine a light on these access needs and encourage companies to consider the damage they could be doing chasing a higher conversion rate or revenue.

Legal Changes

These practices target the most vulnerable people online for profit – a profit that other ethical companies refuse to make. A fair marketplace requires everyone to play by the same rules, and luckily, progress is being made on the legal front to ensure that. In the EU, both the **Digital Markets Act** and the **Digital Services Act** are now in effect. These laws target large tech monopolies and online services and have a broad set of rules that include preventing them from

- Nagging users

- Interfering with their choice

- Making it more difficult to unsubscribe for a service than it was to subscribe

All dark patterns!

In the United States, there have been fewer new laws, but more successful cases to punish companies using dark patterns. The FTC is currently suing Amazon as you know, but they've had notable settlements in the last couple of years:

- **$100 million** – Vonage[93]
- **$245 million** – Epic Games[94]

Numbers like these make headlines that then dissuade others from following the practices that got these companies in trouble. My guess would be that with Amazon's Prime service having over 200 million members worldwide, and what's come to light about their practices to gain those customers, any potential settlement would be even larger, along with strict reparations to halt their deceptive and damaging practices.

If you would like to read more about the legal side of this progress, I'd again recommend Harry Brignull's excellent book on *Deceptive Patterns*, which I've added to the reading list for this chapter – you can find it at `inclusive.guide/reading/chapter7`.

The Inventor of Web Steps In

The good news is, even the **inventor of the Internet** is joining the fight against dark patterns.

Around the 30th anniversary of the World Wide Web, Sir Tim Berners-Lee proposed a "Contract for the Web." This site featured a range of principles he believes that governments, companies, and citizens should uphold and should be commonplace on the Internet three decades after its inception.

One such principle charges companies to "respect and protect people's privacy and personal data to build online trust," which we know large companies have failed to do of late.[95]

More recently though, he announced the launch of a project to **counter deceptive design**, which will be run by the Tech Policy Design Lab – known for being the "action arm" of the Web Foundation.[96] The Design Lab describes dark patterns in the way this book does and examples of how they've been weaponized by companies that might sound familiar to you now:

> It can be found on travel booking sites, gaming platforms, and e-commerce sites. You might spot it when finding it difficult to cancel a subscription, or understand a cookie consent process.[97]

This lends real legitimacy to both the existence and damaging effect of dark patterns. Their aim to combat them is to

- Build a coalition of stakeholders to mobilize change.

- Create a crowdsourcing tool to report dark patterns.

- Launch a storytelling tool to explore people's experiences with dark patterns.

Through this, they aim to create "new norms and standards for Trusted Design… guiding industry reform and regulation."[98]

This is fantastic news and shows real promise for the goal of protecting those susceptible to dark patterns online moving forward rather than exploiting them as companies have. Time will tell how effective this project will be, but it's the most promising step forward for those with mental health disorders online that I've seen in the years I've been writing about the topic. To have the **inventor** of the Web legitimize the troubles they've been facing and recognize deceptive design as a "human rights issue" leaves no doubt that companies using them will have a real fight on their hands.

I've added the Tech Policy Design Lab's write-up on deceptive design to the reading list for this chapter, which you can find at `inclusive.guide/reading/chapter7`.

Conclusion

Mental health is still an area where the accessibility community is finding its feet. Comments from governing bodies, charities, researchers, and even the Web's inventor are definitely helping to create a consensus, but we're not quite at the point where there is a consistent, agreed-upon set of solutions for fixing barriers to these access needs.

Instead, awareness is growing around what **bad practice** looks like, which shouldn't be the end goal but is still good progress – as people become more adept at spotting dark patterns, their ability to extract profit from users will start to dwindle, making them less attractive. As we mentioned earlier, figures differ regarding how many people suffer from mental health conditions, and one big reason is that

> Access to support continues to rely largely on vulnerable consumers disclosing information about their problems – a factor which is particularly problematic for people experiencing mental health problems.[99]

It is therefore important that you can spot these barriers, as there's no telling how many people they're affecting, but also because there's currently no test or audit to run in order to flag them. Hopefully, in this chapter, you have come across patterns that you can understand and clearly see are frustrating and damaging, especially for those with mental health impairments.

Now, the use of dark patterns is not *necessarily* the result of malicious intent. With these patterns being prevalent, it would be easy to copy strategies that work well for others in an honest attempt to increase engagement or revenue. Luckily, more and more is being done to highlight these patterns and the harmful effects that they have – allowing those who design and build websites to do so with deeper thought and care for the human at the center of their site.

One problem that remains is that dark patterns are still **profitable**. For all the potential legal troubles and public admonishment, Amazon Prime is the second most popular subscription service in the world, with over **200 million** subscribers and billions in revenue.[100] A service that big and successful, filled with wonderful content, still feels the need to attract users in a dishonest way and make it hard to leave, based on the words of its own employees. There's no doubt whatsoever that this practice has aided its growth.

This is what the decision ultimately comes down to. As the Norwegian Consumer Council has said:

> When digital services employ dark patterns to nudge users...
> the financial incentive has taken precedence over respecting
> users' right to choose. The practice of misleading consumers into
> making certain choices, which may put them at risk, is unethical
> and exploitative.[101]

Therefore, it becomes a choice that each business, and site, has to make. Everyone wants their site to be successful, but if you achieve this through deception, and do so in spite of (and often at the expense of) a user's mental health, then you risk damaging your reputation and long-term success.

Please do take the time to check for the ones we've covered in this chapter to ensure that you're not a culprit. With the help of strong product principles and a focus on meaningful, transparent engagement with our users, we can avoid the pitfalls of dark patterns.

CHAPTER 8

Imagery

There are approximately **750 billion** images on the Internet.[1] According to statistics from W3Techs, over **96%** of the 10 million most popular websites on the Internet contain some form of imagery.[2] Images have become an unavoidable component of website design and development – used for everything from sharing experiences on social media to showcasing products. Mirroring their diverse range of uses, visual media can create an *equally* diverse range of barriers for users. Imagery is capable of adding so much to the online experience for so many, but we must ensure the **content** they share is available to everyone.

Because of this, we'll be shifting our focus from specific types of access needs to more general areas of online experience, where a broad spectrum of users commonly encounter difficulties, starting with this chapter. Online imagery comes in a few different forms, but we'll start with **images** themselves – discussing content, color, and several other things to keep in mind when using them.

These ideas are relevant when talking about video too and so are the stakes, with videos watched billions of times online every day.[3] We've covered accessible captions and subtitles for **videos** already, so this time we'll focus on how to implement the videos themselves in a way that accommodates user needs and preferences and how to safely use moving imagery for the sake of aesthetics.

We'll then look at the different ways in which **icons** have been added to websites over the years and how to make each of these approaches accessible. This will help you decide which approach is best for you or how to elevate the implementation you already have. This discussion will culminate in an overview of the Scalable Vector Graphic (SVG) image type and how to ensure that this popular format is as accessible (or even more so) as other formats.

© Ashley Firth 2024
A. Firth, *Practical Web Accessibility*, https://doi.org/10.1007/979-8-8688-0152-5_8

Images

Let's start with images, which are by far the most common type of visual media seen online. In Chapter 2 "Blindness," we mentioned that roughly **3.2 billion** images are uploaded to the Web every day, and we covered how they are inserted into a web page's code through HTML – requiring an `alt` tag in order to be accessible to screen readers and low vision users:

```
<img src="assets/cat.jpg" alt="A cat playing with a large blue ball of yarn" />
```

As a quick recap, when writing `alt` text for images that aren't simply decorative, you should

- **Be succinct and specific** – Say what's in the photo, without editorializing.

- **Aim to keep it around 140 characters** – There's no limit to what screen readers can describe, but it's important to be conscious of the user's time.

- **Don't start alt text with "image of"** – Screen readers announce that the element is an image, so it's wholly unnecessary.

- **If there's text in the image, write it in the alt text** – This prevents it from being trapped for screen reader users (you should avoid text in images wherever possible though).

- **Use punctuation** – The text will be read out by a screen reader, so using commas on longer sentences and ending with a full stop will make it more pleasant for those listening.

- **Consider search engine optimization (SEO)** – Alt text is used by search engines too, so adding it can help grow the visibility of your site online but will be read by an audience larger than just those using screen readers.

If you are maintaining a site's content, this is such a quick win because it doesn't require the image to be remade. It's also *just* as important to ensure that the `alt` attribute is actually there – if the image is purely decorative, leaving it empty will allow screen readers to ignore it:

```
<img src="assets/decorative-image.jpg" alt="" />
```

For those using a content management system (CMS), most give you the chance to add `alt` text when you upload an image, as well as go back into your media library and set it at any time (as shown in Figure 8-1). As a result, you should set yourself the task of reviewing the content already uploaded and in use to ensure you're giving your screen reader users the best experience possible but also so your pages are more visible through SEO.

WordPress, by far the most used CMS in the world, will automatically add an `alt` attribute to any image you publish in a post but won't populate it.[4] This is better than assistive technology reading out a file name or the word "blank" as a description (as other CMSs do), but it *does* mean that it will skip past every image in your post. With there almost certainly being useful information in a lot of your images, this is an important task to complete.

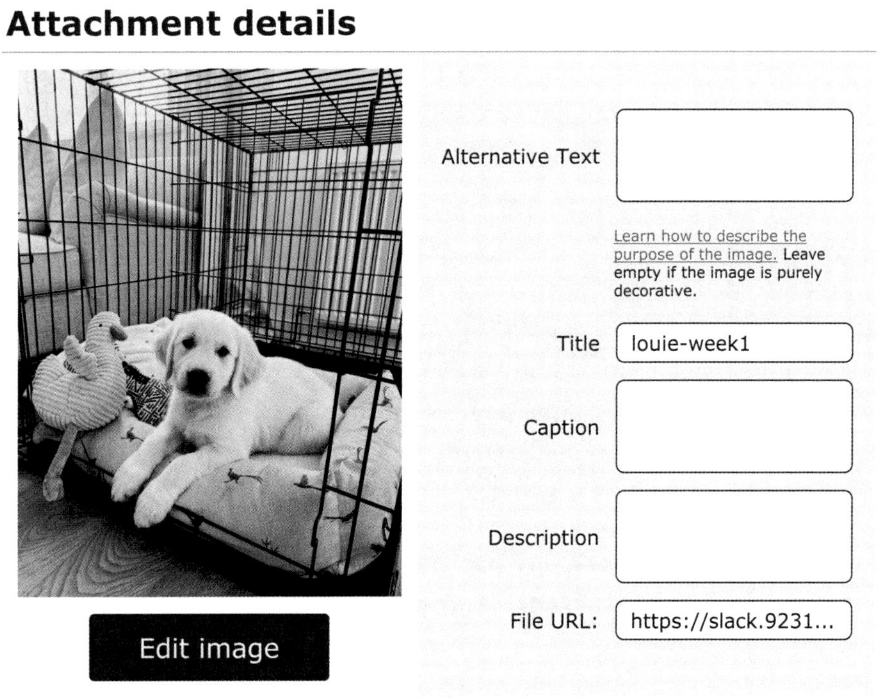

Figure 8-1. *A dialog window in WordPress prompts the user for a description of the image (pictured left), which will become the* `alt` *text content. It also provides a link for a guide to writing good* `alt` *text.*

<picture> Tag

If you remember the code for the <video> tag we covered in Chapter 5 "Deafness and Hard of Hearing," this should look familiar:

```
<picture>
    <source media="(min-width:650px)" srcset="flowers-full.jpg">
    <img src="flowers-cropped.jpg" alt="...">
</picture>
```

The <picture> tag allows you to supply multiple <source> tags for an **image** that will be used when certain criteria are fulfilled, with a standard <img> tag you're used to seeing as the fallback when none apply. With the preceding example, the flowers--full.jpg image will be displayed on screen sizes **over** 650px wide. For those below it, the fallback flowers--cropped.jpg image will be used. This extended functionality compared to the standard <img> tag gives you finer control over the imagery shown in certain conditions, which is good for accessibility in a number of ways. Let's go through the things that may trigger different <source> tags and how that helps us.

Orientation

You can specify picture sources depending on whether a device's display is in portrait or landscape mode. This is most handy to avoid showing wider images (that are easy for users to engage with visually on large screens) on smaller devices, where scaling them down makes it difficult to understand what's in the image. Figure 8-2 shows this:

```
<picture>
    <source media="(orientation: portrait)" srcset="flowers-portrait.jpg">
    <source media="(orientation: landscape)" srcset="flowers-
    landscape.jpg">
    <img src="flowers-default.jpg" alt="...">
</picture>
```

With a version of the image appearing that's better suited to the smaller screen size, those with **visual impairments** will be able to engage with it more freely, without extra effort being expended to do so.

Figure 8-2. *Two mobile phones, one in landscape orientation (pictured left) and the other in portrait (pictured right). Both show the same image of trees and a mountainscape, but the images have different cropping and aspect ratios to better cater to the orientation.*

Screen Size

As mentioned in our first example, you can set images to only be shown when the dimensions of a screen are a certain size. You can specify as many of these rules as you'd like in a `<picture>` tag, and the result is shown in Figure 8-3 below:

```
<picture>
    <source media="(min-width:960px)" srcset="flowers-desktop.jpg">
    <source media="(min-width:650px)" srcset="flowers-tablet.jpg">
    <img src="flowers-mobile.jpg" alt="...">
</picture>
```

Figure 8-3. *Two devices, a laptop (pictured left) and a mobile (pictured right). Both show the same image of trees and a mountainscape, but the images have different cropping and aspect ratios in order to adapt best to the size of their respective screens.*

This is good for those with **visual impairments** just like the orientation example, but it also helps maintain a good linear layout at various device sizes – ensuring that more content is visible and in a clear order without images monopolizing the space.

Color Scheme

You can provide a catered image that will display when the user has specified that they prefer a certain color scheme:

```
<picture>
    <source srcset="night.jpg" media="(prefers-color-scheme: dark)">
    <img src="day.jpg">
</picture>
```

You shouldn't do this unless your **entire page** responds to the preference with a change of theme (like we've covered in Chapter 3 "Low Vision and Color Blindness"). It's also important that nothing is lost in the context or information of the image between themes – the switch should purely be to make it more in line with what dark mode users are looking for, which is a little less brightness and more muted colors – don't show dramatically different images between themes.

Having this in place can make the experience on your website feel less disjointed between content and imagery when a dark mode is enabled – having your text and background accommodate the shift while the images remain the same is really only a job half done.

Now, there are a couple of important things to note about the `<picture>` tag before we move on:

- You must **always** have an `<img>` tag inside a `<picture>` tag – sources are not enough. The `<picture>` element is a container only and so doesn't replace `<img>`.

- The various image sources you use should be the same content with slight deviations, not totally different images with completely different content.

- For this same reason, only an `<img>` tag has an `alt` attribute – a `<source>` tag can't have one. Therefore you need to remember that your `alt` text is describing **every** image, so they need to remain similar enough where the `alt` text works in every situation.

Overall though, this advancement on the `<img>` tag is a welcome evolution and one that does a lot for the accessibility of imagery online.

Background Images

Adding an image in the way we've just mentioned will ensure that it displays directly on the page in the same way as any other content. However, there are many cases where images are displayed as the **background** of certain parts of sites. This could be as part of a banner (as shown in Figure 8-4), a general background, or a repeatable pattern. You can create background images using **CSS** instead of **HTML**:

```
/* CSS */
.banner {
    background-image: url('assets/space.jpg');
}

<!-- HTML -->
<div class="banner">
    <h1>Welcome to my site</h1>
</div>
```

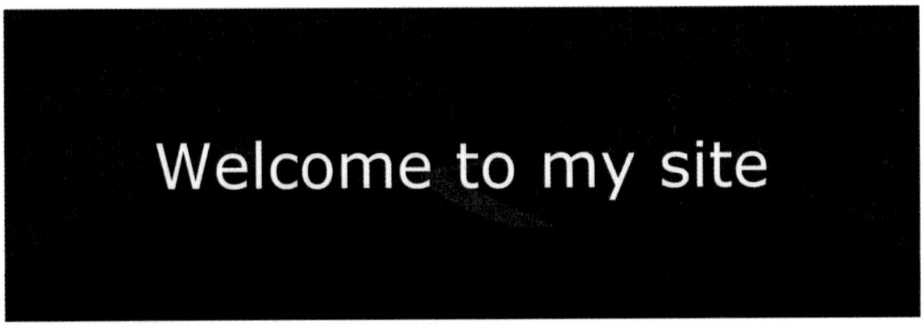

Figure 8-4. *A site banner with a background image applied to it. It shows hills, trees, and wind turbines, as well as the text "Welcome to my site." The latter won't be announced to a screen reader as the text is part of the image.*

This is an entirely reasonable approach for displaying an image as a background, but if the image holds important information that a user would miss if they couldn't see it, then this impacts that image's accessibility. This is because the image itself isn't present in the page's code; you can't apply an `alt` attribute to it and therefore can't provide a way of describing the image's contents to any visually impaired or screen reader users.

It is therefore important to know when to use an image as a **background** and when instead to place it on a **page** and provide an `alt` tag. WCAG's very first rule (1.1.1 Non-text Content) offers a neat distinction:

> When an image is used for decoration, spacing or other purpose
> that is not part of the meaningful content in the page, then
> the image has no meaning and should be ignored by assistive
> technologies.[5]

The test is quick and easy – if an image is purely decorative, then feel free to use it in CSS. Otherwise, we need to relay its useful content to users through code. The easiest way is to remove the contextual info from the image, if possible, so it can *remain* a decorative background image in CSS, and place that info (usually text) in the code. Alternatively, you could move the image *itself* into your page's HTML and provide it with suitable `alt` text. Either way, it needs describing.

Text in Images

Generally, **you shouldn't have images with any text** in them – WCAG rule 1.4.5 (Images of Text) specifies that clearly.[6] However, this approach used to be quite popular, as it allowed designers to manipulate text in a way that wasn't possible otherwise.

For example, they could use fonts that weren't supported by all browsers or position text in ways that would be hard to achieve with CSS. This practice is still common when it comes to email, where the ability to use CSS is limited and less consistent.

The main problem with displaying text inside imagery is exactly the same as with background images – it effectively hides that content for blind and visually impaired users.

For instance, if you were to display a banner image at the top of a page (as shown in Figure 8-5), and that page's title was **part** of the image, and *not* text on the page, that title wouldn't be read out by a screen reader.

Figure 8-5. *A site banner with text as part of the banner image, rather than added in code and positioned over it. This leaves the page without a title that can be read out by a screen reader.*

As a result, the context behind an entire page could be lost. Even if you applied `alt` text to this image, you'd potentially have to describe both the image **and** the text, which can get confusing for users when it's being read out. Furthermore, without this text on the page, your SEO is affected, which makes it harder for users to search for and find your content in the first place.

In this example, as I mentioned earlier, you could still use the image as a background *without* the text in it and instead place the text in your site's HTML and then use CSS to position the text **over** or next to the image – this is immediately far more accessible, as the image in the background becomes purely decorative and the important text is now in your code. With it there, it can benefit from all of the great accessibility wins you've learned so far in this book.

It is important to note though that when overlaying text over images, you must still check that there is a reasonable color contrast between the background image and the foreground text, as we covered in Chapter 3 "Low Vision and Color Blindness." This can be tricky if the background image has a range of colors in it, as one part may make the text easy to read, while another part may make it unreadable. For that reason, you should try to avoid placing text over images.

This is another instance of aesthetics vs. accessibility. You should try and keep decorative and meaningful content separate as much as possible – even if it's difficult to recreate the design you're hoping for in code.

Text in Responsive Images

"But wait Ashley, couldn't I just place an image with text inside the HTML and use the `alt` attribute to provide that same text for screen readers? Problem solved, right?!"

Smart thinking reader, but it's not the *only* issue with text in imagery.

Avoiding text in images is useful from a design perspective as well. This is because any text that is displayed inside an image will scale according to the image, but **not** in the same way as the rest of the text on a page. With so many responsive sites now built to *adapt* to different sized screens and devices, you could be left in a position where the text in an image could be far bigger than any other text on the page (or worse, much *smaller* and therefore unreadable).

Trapping content like this results in inconsistent content sizes – if a user increases (or decreases) the default text size of their browser or device, the text in the image won't adjust like the text around it would. Therefore, this approach can create a real barrier for people with an impaired **field of vision** (like glaucoma), **low vision**, **impaired visual acuity**, or those who prefer to zoom in on content. Figure 8-6 shows an example of a page containing a banner with text in it – both on a desktop computer screen and a mobile.

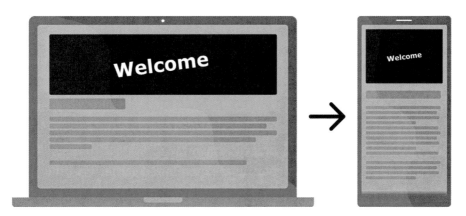

Figure 8-6. *A visual of how a banner with text inside it shrinks on a smaller device, making the text harder to read than the rest of the page's content*

As you can see, thanks to its sizing and style, the text looks like a page header when on a desktop. However, as the screen starts to shrink to fit a smaller device, the title ends up significantly smaller – becoming the same size or smaller compared to the text it's supposed to be introducing.

In addition to this, there's the issue of image quality. With text in code, it will always be sharp regardless of screen size, resolution, or zoom. The same cannot always be said for images. Images will likely be pixelated on newer mobile devices due to the high pixel density (DPI) of their screens. This is also a big problem for **visually impaired** users who use screen magnifiers – as they zoom in, images could become unreadable due to low quality. With so many different sized screens on the market, you could either spend a *lot* of time ensuring that your banner text is readable in dozens of different scenarios, or you could simply place the text on the page with code instead.

Color in Images

Finally, having text inside of images can also lead to inferior color contrast. What's worse, despite there being a WCAG rule for a minimum contrast for text in images (1.4.11: Non-text Contrast), it's something that **won't** show up on the tests that you can perform on your website. This is because, once again, these tests can't recognize text inside images. Low contrast, as we've covered, creates issues for those with **low vision**, **color blindness**, and some users with **cognitive impairments** who rely on text being presented as clearly as possible (e.g., users with autism).

Moreover, images often aren't particularly responsive to users switching their browser or operating system color scheme (which we covered in Chapter 3 "Low Vision and Color Blindness"), such as dark mode or Windows High Contrast Mode. The effects can be quite varied – sometimes images are ignored by a theme switcher and therefore remain unchanged, creating a clash between themes. Alternatively, sometimes the image colors are inverted (which is often true in High Contrast Mode), which can make the contents of the image confusing, or it can appear to disappear entirely if the image color matches the new background color. As we mentioned earlier, ensuring your images adapt to these changes along with the rest of your site is essential for a consistent experience. Look to use the `<picture>` tag for images, and later in the chapter, we'll explore what to do for icons.

All of the preceding factors can create a situation where the imagery that has been added to a site to *elevate* its content can end up *restricting* or subverting it for many. I'd suggest taking the time to check your site's images for instances like these.

Videos

> Many websites now have moving images behind text. This in itself
> is an obstacle for someone trying to read the text. And it can mean
> that the text has no contrasting background to make it easier
> to read.[7]

Moving imagery, such as **videos** or **animations**, can pose just as much, if not more, trouble to users than static images. Not only can they have text in them, but they can contain

- Sound that requires captioning

- Visual elements that need to be described in text

- Constant changes in lighting and color

- Movement that can affect users in a range of ways

Background videos have been popular in recent years despite mixed results from research about the effect they have on metrics like conversion – some companies attribute conversion rate increases of over 85% to their background videos, even while others are saying that they do nothing or even decrease the same metric.[8,9] Because of this division, you may still be asked to add one or maintain a site that has one. Therefore, let's go through some of the pitfalls of foreground and background videos while learning to create accessible versions of both.

I've created an accessible background video for you in this chapter's practical example, which you can find in the "Chapter 8" folder of the GitHub repository or view live at `https://inclusive.guide/examples/imagery`. This practical example contains all of the following features in case you'd like to use it on a site (or just avoid the code examples).

Pausing

First of all, users should always be able to easily stop any moving imagery that appears when they reach the page. Almost all background videos autoplay as soon as they've loaded, and this can have a negative effect on those sensitive to sharp movement or changes in light, such as **epilepsy** and **photosensitive visual impairments**, or those with conditions that can lead to **heightened sensory awareness**, such as autism. For example, research in the Autism in Adulthood journal tells us to

> Avoid textured backgrounds, moving images and decorative
> elements that do not convey information...these types of elements
> may make the site difficult or impossible to comprehend.[10]

In many cases, a video displayed in the background of a home page or landing page doesn't necessarily contain information. This can be a good thing, as we've mentioned regarding text in images. However, it could be argued that when videos sit directly behind content, such as titles or calls to action, they can still interfere with a user's ability to comprehend that information in the foreground.

Luckily, WCAG's spec has mentioned this exact issue in their criteria for WCAG rule 2.2.2 (Pause, Stop, Hide):

> For any moving, blinking or scrolling information that (1)
> starts automatically, (2) lasts more than five seconds, and (3)
> is presented in parallel with other content, there [must be] a
> mechanism for the user to pause, stop, or hide it unless the
> movement, blinking, or scrolling is part of an activity where it is
> essential.[11]

Because of this, the first challenge is creating a way for users to pause and play the video. This is quite easy to add when you're using the native HTML5 <video> tag. Firstly, there is a controls attribute that you can add that will automatically give your users a full range of controls for pausing, muting, playing, moving between parts of the video, and going full screen (shown in Figure 8-7).

Figure 8-7. *An illustration of how the default controls of the* <video> *element look in a browser. It provides users with the ability to pause, play, move between parts of the video, and mute it.*

However, this often doesn't look particularly nice, and you usually end up compromising the effect you were trying to create by adding the video in the first place. For this reason, you'll often see videos with the controls attribute omitted. To ensure it remains accessible, we're realistically only looking to be able to **stop** and **start** the video, and this can be accomplished with one button. You can add this to create your own custom controls that are more discreet and change their behavior through code depending on what the video is doing.

To achieve this, we add a single, small button in our code that sits in the corner of the video, with a class of js-video-button so we can target it:

```
<button class="js-video-button">Pause</button>
```

We can then add the following code to run every time the button is interacted with by the user (shown in Figure 8-8):

```
$('.js-video-button').on('click', function() {
    let video = $('video');
    video.paused ? video.play() : video.pause();
    let buttonText = video.paused ? 'Play' : 'Pause';
    $('.js-video-button').text(buttonText);
});
```

Figure 8-8. Instead of the native video controls, a button is now visible in the bottom right corner of the laptop screen, over our video player. The button reads "Pause" and will allow a user to alternate between playing and pausing the video.

This is written in a JavaScript library called jQuery but can be written in a number of ways. It should also hopefully be very easy to follow, but let's go through it. If the video is paused, we ask it to play when the button is clicked, and if it isn't, we know that it's playing and so ask to pause it instead. We use the same check to alter the button text to reflect the current action that the user can perform on the video (so it displays "Pause" when the video is playing and "Play" when it's paused). We're using a `<button>` tag for this, as it'll mean that it can be tabbed to, and focused on, by default – a useful feature for users with **motor impairments** who typically only use a keyboard to navigate a website.

No Sound

We also want to avoid sound coming from an autoplaying video as soon as a user reaches the site. It's often unexpected, can be very distracting, and excludes users who are **deaf** and **hard of hearing**, as well as those simply browsing on a muted device. You can of course handle this by ensuring that the video you use has no audio, but to be safe, you can add an attribute called muted to the <video> tag to make sure:

```
<video muted>
    ...
</video>
```

Consider the Color Scheme of the Video

When using moving video as a background, problems often arise if the colors change quickly and frequently. This means that any text that you've overlaid can *start* readable but become unreadable. It's a tricky balance to strike, so I would consider one or more of the following when overlaying content on top of a video:

1. Choose one main color scheme for **content** in the video so that text can work consistently over it.

2. Provide a consistent **background color** for your overlaid content. That way, your text remains readable *even* if the background video changes color. This is the approach that W3C recommends, and Figure 8-9 shows an example of their approach.

Figure 8-9. *Content displayed over a background video but with a semitransparent background to prevent potential problems with contrast between the text and the video*

Note that the preceding background color can be *partially* transparent so that you can still see the video behind it to some extent. This is perhaps the safest approach to placing written content over a video. Some other things to consider when creating a video that text will sit on top of are as follows:

- Limit the animation in the background video or restrict animation to a particular part of the video. This allows you to separate the animation from any important content and allows the user to focus their attention more on the latter.

- Blur the video slightly to reduce the chance of sharp clashes between it and the foreground content. Some users also argue that a softly blurred video requires less focus as there are fewer details competing for attention.

It's also worth mentioning that rapid changes in bright color can seriously impact users who experience **photosensitivity** – like some users with low vision or epilepsy. WCAG found that having more than three flashes per second renders a page inaccessible and so made a rule for it (2.3.1: Three Flashes or Below Threshold). Flashes are usually found in badly made banner images, optical illusions, background videos, and effects.[12]

Only Play the Video Once It Has Loaded

Even if you create a background video with minimal animation, your users could still experience unpleasant sharp movements if your video regularly starts and stops. This could happen when you attempt to display a video as soon as the page loads, but it hasn't downloaded completely (perhaps due to a bad connection).

Luckily, you can tell a video to wait **until** that is no longer a problem before playing:

```
video.addEventListener("canplaythrough", video.play());
```

We can do this by "listening" to an event that happens in the video. Once this event occurs, we can run a piece of code. An "event" could be when the video has finished playing or when it's paused, but in this case, we're interested in the `canplaythrough` event. Waiting for this event to occur ensures that a video is only played once the browser has downloaded enough of the video that it can play the whole thing without any additional buffering. This prevents a constant start/stop motion for users with a slower Internet connection – something that could confuse screen reader users or contribute to a complex experience that excludes those with **cognitive impairments** (as mentioned in Chapter 6 "Cognitive Impairments"). More broadly though, it's simply an annoying experience to sit through!

Loading a Poster Image

If you use the preceding approach, you still need to handle what the user sees **until** the video has loaded enough to play. On a slow connection, this lasts for a few seconds, and then suddenly the page will go from displaying nothing to showing a moving video, which constitutes unexpected behavior. For these reasons, loading a temporary "poster" image to display first is the best solution:

```
<video poster="assets/poster.jpg">
```

These are easily attached to the `<video>` tag itself and always take less time to load, as images are a much smaller file size compared to videos. If you don't include one, the `<video>` tag will sometimes try to use the first frame of the video instead, but this is often just a black screen. Adding one provides you with more freedom to specify the initial visual that the user sees and gives users more context around what the video may be about before it loads.

Don't Loop Your Video

This is our final slam dunk, particularly if the video doesn't have a play/pause button. If the video on your site is constantly playing by looping, there is no way for users with access needs such as **autism** and **epilepsy** to avoid it, and they may well be forced to leave your site. Looping a video without a way for the user to control it is also considered a failure of WCAG rule 1.4.2 (Audio Control).[13]

This time, instead of adding an attribute, you need to ensure that the following *isn't* present on your `<video>` tags:

```
<video loop>
    ...
</video>
```

Understandably, you might not want a blank screen once your video has finished playing. A neat alternative to looping is to transition your video to a static image or background color once the video has finished. This lets the user know that the movement is done and ensures that the decision not to loop the video feels deliberate. This flow is shown visually in Figure 8-10 below.

Adding this involves listening for another "event." Here, we're grabbing the poster we displayed before – in case the video hadn't loaded – and setting it as the background image of the element that holds the video. Once this is done, we remove the video:

```
video.addEventListener("ended", function() {
    $(video).parent().css({
        'background-image' : 'url(' + video.getAttribute('data-poster')
        +      ')'
    });
    video.remove();
});
```

Figure 8-10. *Three laptops, showing the series of functionality from the preceding code. The first laptop (pictured left) shows a video with a poster image displayed, ready to be played. The second laptop (pictured middle) shows the video playing, and the third laptop (pictured right) shows the original poster image being displayed after the video is finished.*

Should You Use Background Videos?

It is my personal opinion that videos *can* create a nice effect if they are included correctly. I would, however, generally avoid displaying any information over or in them, as it's usually too difficult to ensure that the content will be visible **throughout** the video and, as we know, the background should be decorative. Again, it's also important to avoid sound entirely, especially if the video is being autoplayed. This can contribute to an assault on the senses and exclude deaf users, and potentially embarrass all users, if there is no clear way to turn it off.

Reducing Movement

I'd also like to touch on the topic of animation inside and outside of videos and the potential effect that this can have on users. Val Head, a specialist web animation consultant, explains that

> As animated interfaces increasingly become the norm, more people have begun to notice that large-scale motion on screen can cause them dizziness, nausea, headaches, or worse. For some, the symptoms can last long after the animation is over.[14]

Users with visually triggered **vestibular disorders** (which usually involve problems with the inner ear that can cause dizziness and balance problems) feel an especially strong sensation of motion sickness when viewing animation with excessive movement.[15] Reports suggest that vertigo and dizziness are common symptoms in the general population, estimated to affect between 20% and 56% of people.[16] The A11y Project describes the impact of these disorders as such:

> Imagine a world where your internal gyroscope is not working properly. Very similar to being intoxicated, things seem to move of their own accord, your feet never quite seem to be stable underneath you, and your senses are moving faster or slower than the rest of your body. Your personal steady-cam is broken. Whatever you look at tends to move regardless of if you are moving.[17]

We've already talked about making sure sites can adapt to user preferences such as color scheme or magnification. Thankfully, there are also other checks that can be made to deal with common image-based barriers, using media rules – a way of including some styling or functional code but only if certain user conditions are true.

Here are a few examples of checks that can be made in code and the user preferences that they represent:

- **`prefers-reduced-motion`** – The user prefers less motion, such as animation, on the page.

- **`prefers-contrast`** – Detects if the user has requested the system increase or decrease the amount of contrast between adjacent colors.

- **`prefers-color-scheme`** – Detect if the user prefers a light or dark color scheme (we covered this in our "theme switcher" practical example for Chapter 3 "Low Vision and Color Blindness).[18]

- **`prefers-reduced-transparency`** – The user prefers a reduced amount of transparent imagery or translucent layering of content (this one is still experimental and so not well supported by browsers).[19]

All of these are worth looking into, but for our purposes, the query that we're interested in here is `prefers-reduced-motion`. This preference can be set by a user on a range of devices:

- **Windows** – `Settings ➤ Ease of Access ➤ Display ➤ Show animations`

- **Android** – `Settings ➤ Accessibility ➤ Remove Animations`

- **MacOS** – System Settings ➤ Accessibility ➤ Display > Reduce motion

- **iOS** – Settings ➤ Accessibility ➤ Motion ➤ Reduce motion

Once this is done, you can make changes in the functionality or styling of your sites to take this preference into account. But how?

Handling This in Code

You have two options. The first is JavaScript, where you can use a function called matchMedia to check if the user has set the prefers-reduced-motion setting and then execute some code if they have. This approach is best for **functional** changes to elements on the page like the following code. For example, if the user has asked for reduced motion, the following code removes autoplay from a video and pauses it (just in case) to intercept and prevent a potentially harmful experience before it happens:

```
if (window.matchMedia('(prefers-reduced-motion)').matches) {
    video.removeAttribute('autoplay');
    video.pause();
}
```

For **visual** changes like animations that are set in CSS, you can also check for this setting there using the @media query. In the following example, there's a rapid and potentially dangerous animation in place as its frequency could trigger a seizure in a user with **photosensitive epilepsy** due to its speed and flashing. No animation online should behave like this, but let's use it as an example of how to remove that worry for users who've opted for reduced motion.

Again like the JavaScript example, we check whether the setting has been set, and if so, we remove the animation altogether:

```
.vibrate {
    animation: flashing 0.3s linear infinite both;
}
@media (prefers-reduced-motion: reduce) {
    .vibrate {
        animation: none;
    }
}
```

Between these two approaches, you're guaranteed to have an easy way to adjust your code to make allowances for that user setting. If you'd like to dive deeper into the specifics of designing accessible animations, the A11y Project maintains an excellent series of sources on how to do that. I've added a link to that in the reading list for this chapter, which you can find at `inclusive.guide/reading/chapter8`.

Now, I'm not suggesting that everyone should remove all animation or movement from their pages. Instead, we can be mindful of **excessive** movement on pages and seek to reduce it – either through changing the original material shown to all users or by tapping into their preferences to tone down the level of animation. Try enabling this setting on your device and see if it has an effect on your typical browsing experience on the sites you use. Try to also go through your site and journeys to see whether there is any movement that could do with being removed or reduced in this way. Finally, this setting is part of the practical example for this chapter, so you can see it in action there!

Parallax

It's worth pointing out that it's not always images and videos that create movement on a web page. Parallax scrolling is a design effect, where the background of a web page moves at a slower rate to the foreground, creating a 3D effect as you scroll. It's a very popular feature of websites as it creates an effect of depth that can make a page stand out immediately. An example of how this appears to the user is shown in Figure 8-11 below.

Parallax takes content that is typically static (with scrolling usually being the only source of movement) and changes it in a way that users often don't expect. Additionally, seeing as scrolling is typically the *only* source of movement and is controlled by the user – altering the effect and speed in this way takes some of that control away.

Figure 8-11. *Three laptops displaying the effect of parallax on a website from left to right. As a user scrolls the page, the content of the page and the background scroll at different speeds. This creates a sense of depth, but people can struggle to engage with it.*

Unlike a video or image, these effects typically apply to the entire page and have therefore been known to cause bigger problems than "smaller" animations:

> Animations that move an object across a large amount of space are most apt to trigger a negative response for someone suffering from a vestibular disorder. The physical size of the screen matters less than the size of the motion relative to the screen space available—so a small button with a 3D rotation probably won't cause trouble, but a full-screen wipe transition covering the entire screen likely would."[20]

Not only is parallax scrolling often a full-screen animation, but it also only stops when the user stops scrolling – if they want to engage with content that is currently off-screen, then the animation resumes the moment they move up or down the page. For this reason, WCAG has a rule dedicated to animations triggered by interactions, stating that it must be possible to disable them unless they're essential to the functionality (2.3.3: Animation from Interactions).[21]

Carrying on from our earlier example – ensuring that your site responds to users' `prefers-reduced-motion` setting – it is easy to use this feature to reduce, or altogether remove, parallax for users who have specified that they have a problem with excessive motion. There is no good reason not to do this, given that the effect is purely for aesthetics and the potential pain it can cause users. By implementing this, you can add the feature knowing that it won't create barriers for these users, without altering your design or experience for your wider audience. This way, you can create a feeling that your site's experience is unique while ensuring that it is not overwhelming either.

Iconography

Let's now turn our attention to icons. Icons on the Web have evolved significantly over the years, and their ability to help keep a design looking clean has seen their popularity soar. In Chapter 6 "Cognitive impairments," we spoke about the perils of creating your **own** custom icons that could be vague or confusing to users. However, even with established icons, **how** you get them onto your site and display them can raise accessibility concerns. Whether you're deciding on an approach for a new site or if you're trying to improve the accessibility of icons in a site you maintain, it's worth looking at a brief history of how icons have been implemented and how to make sure each approach is as inclusive as possible.

<img> Tag

This was the original way of adding an icon to a web page: creating an icon and then linking to it in an `<img>` tag allows you to provide `alt` text for it:

```
<img src="cat.jpg" alt="A cat playing with a large blue ball of yarn" />
```

If you're adding a link around an icon, which is common, the `alt` text should describe the action that clicking the icon would perform, like so:

```
<a href="cat-toys.html">
    <img src="cat.jpg" alt="View our cat toys" />
</a>
```

Many icons are still added this way. The image is in the code with `alt` text, which is good for accessibility, but the image itself is a fixed size and color, making it inflexible when adapting to a user's setting like dark mode, a larger font size, or zooming in on a page while maintaining clarity.

Sprites

Popular in the late 2000s, an "image sprite" is a large collection of images and icons stored in one single file. The thought process behind this was mostly performance-driven as it would only require retrieving one file (as opposed to dozens) from a server to load all the images on a page. This led to quicker load times but meant that you had to use CSS (styling code) to display any one of the images by itself rather than having them in the code like the `<img>` tag.

You accomplished this by setting one "sprite" (containing lots of icons) as a background image and then positioning that background image at the point on the x and y axis that matched your target image. As a quick example, let's try displaying the second icon in this sprite – shown in Figure 8-12.

Figure 8-12. *An image "sprite," containing multiple icons in one file. There's a lightning bolt (pictured left), a flame (pictured middle), and a truck (pictured right)*

What you'd do is work out how big the icon is by itself, then determine its position within the full sprite, and then create a rule in CSS for it. Figure 8-13 visualizes how you would do this.

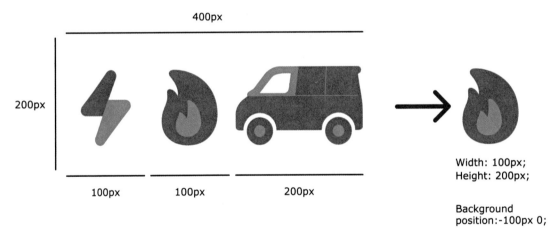

Figure 8-13. *A breakdown of how to work out how to display a particular icon from an image sprite. This takes the chosen icon's width and height into account, as well as the size of the sprite itself in order to determine the icon's X and Y position.*

Here, the flame icon is **100 pixels** wide and **200 pixels** high, and it's positioned **100 pixels** along the x axis. Therefore, we would need to use CSS as follows:

```
/* CSS */
.flame-icon {
    width: 100px;
```

```
    height: 200px;
    background-image: url('sprite.png');
    background-position: -100px 0;
    background-repeat: no-repeat;
}

<!-- HTML -->
<div class="flame-icon">
```

This approach was very popular for a while but was eventually abandoned by developers. It was found that it didn't really help with performance and had restrictions because it couldn't handle multiple image formats. Also, as you could probably tell, it was a nightmare to maintain. The minute you change a sprite, perhaps by adding another icon, the position of the other icons could change too, and suddenly none of your icons work anymore.[22] Relevant to this book, having the icons in CSS instead of on the page means screen readers can't announce them, as there's no `<img>` tag or `alt` attribute, so I highly recommend avoiding this method.

However, you may well be maintaining a site that still uses image sprites, and undoing that can take a fair amount of effort. I would encourage you to move away from it, but in the meantime, sprites can be made more accessible with little effort. The only way to achieve some form of accessibility is to use a solution we covered earlier in Chapter 2 "Blindness." This involved creating a small piece of HTML, hidden visually, to describe the icon for screen readers and other assistive technologies:

```
<div class="flame-icon">
    <span class="screen-reader-only">View your gas meter readings</span>
</div>
```

Theme Switching

I want to touch on this concept again as it pertains to iconography. We've mentioned High Contrast Mode (HCM) in full before (Chapter 3 "Low Vision and Color Blindness"), but it's an accessibility feature built into Windows that assists people with visual impairments by allowing them to change the color scheme of content, at an operating system level, to make it more readable. In the same chapter, we also covered the prevalence of "dark mode" as a setting preferred by many and set at a device or operating system level. When implemented, both features do a great job of automatically adjusting the color scheme of most of your page's content in response to a user's preference, but they do hold a couple of problems where imagery is concerned.

There have been issues with background images not displaying when High Contrast Mode is active (another reason not to use image sprites) but most commonly, images with transparent backgrounds that seemed to "disappear" when the color in them matched the now-altered background color. For example, if this image and text combo (shown in Figure 8-14) was displayed on a page.

Figure 8-14. *An icon of a lightning bolt, as well as some text (Danger: High Voltage) – both displayed as purple on a white background*

Switching to a different theme would invert the background and text color, but the image, as a separate file, **wouldn't update**. This would often result in it appearing as though it's **not there**, as shown in Figure 8-15.

Danger: High Voltage

Figure 8-15. *The same image and text combination as earlier, but with the color scheme inverted due to High Contrast Mode. The text has been inverted, but the image now appears to be invisible as it couldn't be inverted by High Contrast Mode.*

We also mentioned in Chapter 3 "Low Vision and Color Blindness" that there is a CSS @media rule that can be used to explicitly enhance a design in High Contrast Mode and combat the issue earlier. You can set specific styles that will respond if High Contrast Mode is active, as we covered, but we can also take this further. You can specify *which* particular color scheme is active, allowing you to not only make imagery visible in these modes but cater to them:

```
/* High Contrast Mode is active */
@media (forced-colors: active) {
    .bolt { filter: brightness(0.8); }
}
/* Black on white theme */
@media (forced-colors: active) and (prefers-color-scheme: light) {
    .bolt { background-image: url('bolt-icon-black.png'); }
}
/* White on black theme */
@media (forced-colors: active) and (prefers-color-scheme: dark) {
    .bolt { background-image: url('bolt-icon-white.png'); }
}
```

With this information, you could load a different color lightning bolt icon for the given example so that it always remained visible. This is certainly *better*, but far from perfect – although this approach is accessible visually, as people will be able to see the icon, it's no good for screen readers (as you know) as the icon is still a background image. Therefore, the next evolution of icons on the Web needed to be something in the code but *also* customizable with CSS. Enter the icon font.

Icon Fonts

An icon font is essentially a custom font that contains illustrations instead of letters and numbers. They arrived in earnest in 2012, namely, through a library called Font Awesome. This library was initially made for use with Twitter's Bootstrap framework but has since gained massive adoption. Icon fonts as an approach provided some key benefits over older icons:

- They scaled better than regular images, meaning that they would stay sharp if they were made larger, while standard images would become grainy and pixelated.

- They're all contained in a single file, like a sprite, thereby requiring less network calls compared to individual image files.

- With an icon font, icons are added into a page's code, not in its styles, like a background image or sprite. This meant that you could adjust an icon's appearance such as **size** and **color** using just CSS (as shown in the code and Figure 8-16):

```
/* CSS */
.fa-solid {
    color: purple;
    font-size: 18px;
}
.fa-pound-sign {
    color: orange;
    font-size: 24px;
}

<!-- HTML →
<i class="fa-solid fa-dollar-sign"></i>
<i class="fa-solid fa-pound-sign"></i>
```

Figure 8-16. *Two icons next to each other. The first (pictured left) is a purple dollar sign icon. The second (pictured right) is a slightly larger, orange pound sign icon.*

Relevant to our issue about theme switching clashes earlier, you can also change the same icon's appearance in response to user settings, **without** needing to provide a different icon or image, using the code below and shown in Figure 8-17:

```
@media (prefers-color-scheme: dark) {
    .fa-solid {
        color: white;
    }
}
```

Figure 8-17. *The same two icons as earlier, but in a dark mode. Both are now white icons on a dark background, with the pound sign (pictured right) still slightly bigger.*

Decorative vs. Functional Icons

Font Awesome has also done some good work on distinguishing between what are known as **decorative** and **functional** icons (as we discussed earlier regarding static images) and how to ensure good a11y standards for both types using their "auto-accessibility" feature. For each example in the following, I'll show the code that Font Awesome generates automatically so that you can follow the same approach if you're using another library or your own icons.

Decorative Icons

By default, Font Awesome will ensure that icons are hidden from screen readers by applying the aria-hidden="true" attribute **for you**, like the icon shown in Figure 8-18:

```
<i aria-hidden="true" class="fa-solid bacon"></i>
```

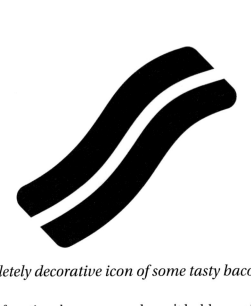

Figure 8-18. *A completely decorative icon of some tasty bacon*

If an icon serves no functional purpose or doesn't hold meaning not covered by text, it's the right move to hide it.

Semantic Icons

For non-decorative, semantic icons, you simply need to set a `title` attribute on the icon and fill that attribute with text in the same way you would add `alt` text to an image:

```
<i class="fa-solid fa-envelope" title="You have 1 unread message"></i>
```

Font Awesome will then hide the icon from screen readers as it does for decorative icons but also add visually hidden text next to the icon, so as to better describe it:

```
<i aria-hidden="true" class="fa-solid fa-envelope"></i>
<span class="sr-only">You have 1 unread message</span>
```

Interactive Icons

A small note on interactive icons that have *focusable* elements (typically links). There are various options to include alternative text or a label to an interactive element, without the need for adding visually hidden code like earlier. For instance, simply adding the `aria-label` attribute to the interactive element (that we learned about in Chapter 2 "Blindness") and adding `aria-hidden` to the icon set up a clear audible action for screen reader users:

```
<a href="/cart" aria-label="View your shopping cart">
    <i class="fa-solid fa-basket-shopping" aria-hidden="true"></i>
</a>
```

If you need to provide a visual tool tip on mouseover/focus, I'd recommend also adding a `title` attribute. This text will appear both visually and audibly when a user interacts with it.

Animations

Font Awesome comes bundled with basic animations, such as bouncing, shaking, and flipping. I know what you're thinking: a popular library offering bouncing icons isn't a good sign for accessibility. Luckily, these animations actually make use of the `prefers-reduced-motion` media rule that we covered earlier to detect if a user has requested that sites minimize the amount of nonessential motion they use. This means that you can safely use animation within Font Awesome, knowing that your icons (and their movement) will be mindful of your user's preferences. The code for this matches the code shown earlier in this chapter.

Building Your Own Icons

It's clear that icon fonts are a step up from the approaches of the past when it comes to adding icons to websites, but there do remain some drawbacks. Much like image sprites, you're *still* loading a whole font set of icons, even if you're only using a couple on the page. They may be much smaller in file size compared to the latter, but many still consider it needless loading. Furthermore, the popularity of fonts like Font Awesome may also be its drawback for many designers – if every site uses the exact same icons, you lose the originality of design. For both reasons, many sites look to build **variations** of common icons themselves and use only the ones they need.

As I mentioned, all of the important accessibility improvements added to Font Awesome's icon library are replicable when you make your own icons. All you need to do is follow the code examples earlier and, importantly, test them with assistive technology to ensure they're making sense.

There's even more you can do to control an icon, and its accessibility, when you make them yourself – the very best of all the options you've read so far. So, how are people making their own? The key is an image format – the SVG.

SVG

The Scalable Vector Graphic (SVG) is a web-friendly image format. Contrary to standard image files you may know like JPEGs that are based on pixels, SVGs are made using mathematical formulas based on points and lines on a grid, which are then *interpreted* by a browser to display an image. You can actually open a .svg file (the SVG file extension) in a code editor and see what's used to make the image. The following code creates a red circle (as shown in Figure 8-19):

```
<svg height="100" width="100">
    <circle cx="50" cy="50" r="40" fill="red" />
</svg>
```

Figure 8-19. *A red circle, created by the preceding SVG code*

Despite its drastic rise in popularity over the last few years, the SVG format itself is quite old. The history of the SVG file goes back to the late 1990s when the World Wide Web Consortium (W3C) invited proposals from developers for a new type of vector graphic format. Six competing proposals were submitted and helped inform what eventually became the W3C's SVG format.[23] However, there was relatively little support for them until 2017 when people began to see the benefits of using SVGs in modern web browsers.

Benefits

We'll go into the various ways you can add SVGs to your site and edit them, but let's first cover the benefits of using the image format as they cover all of the issues we've encountered with previous icon approaches:

- As they're written in code, they can be announced to screen readers and interacted with using assistive technologies.

- Thanks to this, they can also be styled and animated using CSS.

- That same benefit means they can also respond to user preferences around size, color scheme, or even brightness and transparency.

- They offer even more freedom for customization – because they're made using code, they can have **multiple** colors as part of the same icon (instead of just one like icon fonts).

- On sizing, SVGs can be significantly resized without losing *any* of their quality, which makes them ideal for icons and logos.

- An SVG file size is *very* small as it's just text. Some are literally only a couple of bytes.

- When the SVG is in your code, as soon as the browser processes it, it renders it. You don't have to wait for other network requests to complete as you would with an icon font. This makes them incredibly fast to load.

- With the SVG code in your site, search engines like Google can read them for their keywords, which can potentially help a website move up in search rankings.

Figure 8-20. *The same SVG icon displayed four times in four different sizes. Despite increasing in scale from its original size, it shows no change in the sharpness of the icon.*

All of this is great news for both designers and developers, but most of all users. It's a new level of accessibility for imagery as it can now be as flexible to change and user preferences as text can be. They've therefore become particularly popular for creating icons. As an extra seal of approval for SVGs, Font Awesome actually converted their entire font library to SVG in their fifth version.[24]

Still, it's important to consider accessibility when a technology receives a surge in popularity, and SVGs do come with their own set of requirements to achieve a good level of accessibility. Here are the key things you need to consider, based on the various ways that you can add an SVG to your website.

<img> Tag

This is the simplest approach and one you've seen before. You can add an SVG to a page using the <img> tag like you can with any other image format. However, if you are displaying SVGs through the <img> tag, it's important to have the alt attribute describing the asset:

<img src="**apple.svg**" alt="Silhouette of an Apple" />

The main problem with this approach is that it makes customization through code impossible, which is a big part of the appeal of using SVG. If the SVG code isn't *actually* on the page, which it wouldn't be here, you won't be able to style or animate parts of it, so I wouldn't advise it.

CSS Background Image

Much like any other image, you can set an SVG as a background image in CSS. You can scale and position it this way, but as with setting any background image, there is nothing in the code of the page to describe it or the content it might hold. Much like placing them in an `<img>` tag, I'd avoid this route.

Inline SVG

As SVGs are made using code, the most accessible way to use them is by placing them **in** your web page's code (this is what we mean by "inline" – in the code of the page). This way you have full control over altering their appearance and behavior while also making it possible for them to be read out by assistive technologies like screen readers, all without having to recreate different versions of the same icon for different purposes.

You can also change the color of **multiple** parts of an image rather than just one like you can with icon fonts. For example, Figure 8-21 shows the same SVG shown in Figure 8-20 but altered in different ways using CSS:

- Different **sizes** (with rem units so it responds to user font settings)

- Different **positions** (some have been rotated)

- Different **colors** (both colors in the original lightning bolt icon have been changed)

```
<!-- HTML -->
<svg class="bolt">
    <path class="bolt--dark" d="..." fill="orange" />
    <path class="bolt--light" d="..." fill="lightorange" />
</svg>
<svg class="bolt bolt-blue">
    ...
</svg>
<svg class="bolt bolt-pink">
    ...
</svg>
```

```
/* CSS */
.bolt-blue {
    width: 1.5rem;
    transform: rotate(45deg);
}
.bolt-blue .bolt--dark { fill: blue; }
.bolt-blue .bolt--light { fill: lightblue; }

.bolt-pink {
    width: 2rem;
    transform: rotate(-45deg);
}
.bolt-pink .bolt--dark { fill: pink; }
.bolt-pink .bolt--light { fill: lightpink; }
```

Figure 8-21. *The same SVG is shown three times, with each of them being displayed in different sizes, colors, and positions through CSS. This is possible as the SVG code itself is on the web page.*

Again, this is all possible with the **same SVG**. You don't need to understand the code, but the different parts of the SVG have been given class names, so we're able to edit the icon as a whole, as well as those individual parts, in CSS.

This customization is great, but the preceding code is inaccessible. It tells assistive technology nothing about the icon or its purpose. There are, however, a few things we can add to an SVG's code to ensure that they're accessible. Let's go through them.

role Attribute

Firstly, an ARIA `role` attribute of "img" is required to make the asset's purpose clear to screen readers:

```
<svg role="img">
    ...
</svg>
```

This is because we're not using the native `<img>` tag but still want the **clarity** the role brings to users and assistive technology. Next, let's *describe* the SVG.

aria-labelledby

Another way to give your SVGs the same level of accessibility as images is to provide a `<title>` tag. As the name suggests, this provides a title for the image that can be read out, just like an `alt` tag would for an image. We have to do a little more to make sure that this tag can be recognized and read out by all popular screen readers though. Once you've added your `<title>` tag, you then need to add the ARIA attribute `aria-labelledby` to the `<svg>` tag, whose value matches the ID attribute on the `<title>` tag, like so:

```
<svg aria-labelledby="logo-title" role="img">
    <title id="logo-title">Apple logo</title>
    ...
</svg>
```

It's worth noting that you *can* place the `<title>` tag in an SVG without linking it using the preceding attributes; however, not all screen reader software will make the connection between the two, so it's better to be safe and add it.

aria-describedby

With your `<title>` tag added, you can actually provide **more** context to screen readers than a standard `alt` tag using the `<desc>` tag. By adding this to your SVG, you can provide a more detailed description of the image's contents. The corresponding ARIA attribute you need to add is `aria-describedby`:

```
<svg aria-labelledby="logo-title" aria-describedby="logo-desc" role="img">
    <title id="logo-title">Apple logo</title>
    <desc id="logo-desc">A silhouette of an apple with a bite taken out of
    it</desc>
    ...
</svg>
```

There are a couple of extra things to note about adding this tag:

- Never put the **same** content in both the `<title>` and `<desc>` tags as it'll just be repeated by screen readers.

- Don't add the additional `<desc>` tag if there isn't useful additional information to share. Instead, just use the `<title>` tag with the aria-labelledby attribute.

Hiding Icons

In the same way that we covered icons in the previous section, some SVGs may simply be decorative and so don't need to be described by screen readers. In this case, we can add the exact same ARIA attribute to the `<svg>` tag as we did there:

```
<svg class="icon" aria-hidden="true">
    ...
</svg>
```

This is the SVG equivalent of a blank `alt` attribute on an `<img>` tag.

I know this is a number of things to remember to include when using SVGs, but the resulting level of accessibility makes them the most inclusive image format to date. Applying *some* of these things can make things more accessible than the default, but the results can be mixed. If you're interested in what various combinations of the preceding attributes will read out on various screen readers, Smashing Magazine maintains an excellent suite of tests, which I've added to the reading list for this chapter. You can find that at `inclusive.guide/reading/chapter8`.

I've also added these points as "Dos and Don'ts" in this chapter's practical example for easy reference. This can be found in the "Chapter 8" folder of the GitHub repository or by visiting `inclusive.guide/examples/imagery`.

Adaptive SVGs

For all of that work, this is what you get: an icon that scales beautifully to whatever size and can be styled and animated in CSS while being available and accessible in code for accessibility and SEO benefits. It really is the gold standard for illustrative imagery. But, there's even more – they can be adaptive to any user preference. Let's take our earlier circle example (shown in Figure 8-22):

```
<svg height="100" width="100" class="my-svg">
    <circle cx="50" cy="50" r="40" fill="red" stroke-width="3" />
</svg>
```

Figure 8-22.   *The same red circle from our earlier SVG example, but now with a black outline*

I've added a `stroke` (outline) property and given it a class name so we can target it in CSS. Now, you've seen these media rules earlier when we covered displaying different background images based on a user's color scheme preferences. Here's how you can use the same rules, on the same SVG, to achieve the same result – no additional images required! The result is shown in Figure 8-23:

```
@media (prefers-color-scheme: dark) {
    .my-svg circle {
        fill: orange;
        stroke: lightorange;
    }
}
```

```
@media (forced-colors: active) and (prefers-color-scheme: light) {
    .my-svg circle {
        fill: black;
        stroke: grey;
    }
}
```

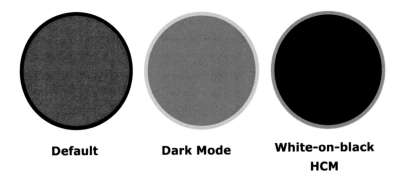

Default   **Dark Mode**   **White-on-black HCM**

Figure 8-23. *The circle SVG displayed three times. The first (pictured left) is its default style – red with a black outline. The second (pictured middle) is in dark mode – orange with a light orange outline. The third (pictured right) is in the "white-on-black" High Contrast Mode – black with a gray outline. All three styles are set in the preceding code, and the SVG changes when the user is using that color scheme.*

Again we're able to target the whole SVG but also **specific** pieces of the SVG – the fill *and* the stroke. If there was a rectangle in the SVG (written in code as <rect>) as well as a circle, for example, we could set entirely different styles on it to the circle without issue:

```
@media (prefers-color-scheme: dark) {
    .my-svg circle {
        fill: orange;
    }
    .my-svg rect {
        fill: green;
    }
}
```

What's more, CSS rules like `fill` and `stroke` can be automatically changed by High Contrast Mode when it changes things like background color and text for a user, so in some circumstances, SVGs will change automatically without you needing these rules. As for the rules themselves, you can do this for `prefers-color-scheme`, `forced-colors`, `prefers-reduced-contrast`, `prefers-reduced-transparency`, and any other setting that appears. This is great but requires specifying a color every time, just like we had to for icon fonts. Can it be smarter?

currentColor

It can! Rather than setting explicit colors for every situation, you can set an SVG's color in CSS using the `currentColor` rule. This rule pays attention to the elements on the page with the SVG (the text next to it, the header it's under, the `<div>` tag it's in, etc.) and the color that's been set on it and follows its lead by using that color too. This means that as a color scheme changes between various themes and contrast modes, the SVG will **automatically** update. In the following code example, the SVG takes the color from the body tag that's been set for when a user prefers dark mode and uses that as its fill color:

```
@media (prefers-color-scheme: dark) {
    body {
        color: white;
    }
    svg {
        fill: currentColor;
    }
}
```

Figure 8-24 shows an example from Octopus Energy, with their SVG logo displaying well on both their standard color scheme and in High Contrast Mode, without explicitly specifying colors for **either**.[25]

Figure 8-24. *The Octopus Energy logo as an SVG, responding to a change in High Contrast Mode, thanks to the* `currentColor` *attribute*

Doing this means that you don't have to worry about whether your SVGs will be accessible between themes, as long as your site's color scheme is. You also won't need to worry about *other* user preferences that might become popular in the future, such as the experimental `prefers-reduced-transparency` setting we mentioned earlier. If a browser alters the color scheme of your background and text colors, your SVGs will simply follow suit.

The latter is brilliant for `a11y` as it means that **all** content on web pages can adapt quickly and seamlessly to avoid situational barriers, without users needing to constantly change their settings. Having imagery that can adapt to these changes on the fly will improve long-term accessibility without requiring additional effort from designers and developers.

Conclusion

In this and the preceding chapters, we've now covered the three main areas of visual media that are commonly present on the Web – images, video, and iconography. Hopefully, you now feel confident in your ability to both add content that you know will be inclusive *and* go back retrospectively to make content like this accessible. To place content on the Web is quick and easy. To go back and make it inclusive is tough but essential.

The fact is, a lot of these issues **can** be solved practically with the inclusion of a couple of attributes, or even automatically moving forward, by using libraries like Font Awesome or SVG attributes like `currentColor`. Small things like this can make a big difference, and hopefully, they'll become more commonplace throughout the Web in the future.

Finally, I hope that this chapter has also acted as an advert for the flexibility and accessibility of SVG as an image format. Being able to add attributes directly to them that make them accessible to screen readers, their ability to adjust automatically to circumstances like a user's color settings, and their potential for animation, scaling, and styling through code means that SVGs are a highly versatile form of online imagery.

So much of our web is made up of imagery. You now have the tools to ensure that **everyone** can enjoy them.

CHAPTER 9

Accessible Email

Websites only form one part of a user's online journey. We've talked about providing multiple ways for customers to access information and complete tasks online, and this concept equally applies to email. Over **345 billion** emails are sent and received daily around the world each day, an increase of over **18%** since the first edition of this book was published just a few years ago.[1] Thanks to their sheer volume, and the fact that they are coded using the same language as websites, they deserve special attention.

In this chapter, we'll look at how to ensure that your email formats, content, and styling are all accessible – even if you rely on a third-party email service to handle yours. After that, we'll look into a feature that makes user actions both quicker to complete and possible without even *opening* the email you send them.

From a feature that's designed to make interacting with email easier than ever, we'll turn our attention to a feature that makes interacting with emails next to impossible: no-reply email addresses. This tactic can affect your accessibility, your delivery rates, and your reputation, so it's worth exploring the benefits of removing them.

Issues with Email

Email is the most common way that sites and brands communicate with their users, and it's far from a dying technology. According to data from Statista, there are roughly 4.3 billion email users worldwide at the time of writing – over half of the world's population.[2]

This popularity certainly isn't lost on brands nor apparently is the importance of making this form of communication accessible. In recent research, **77%** of brands say that email accessibility is a priority for them.[3] This is a comforting statistic, but these responses are *not* supported by data about the emails that are sent. In 2023, the Email Markup Consortium tested hundreds of thousands of emails across multiple industries and languages. They found that **99.97%** of HTML emails tested contained accessibility issues categorized as "serious" or "critical." Only **0.01%** of emails tested passed without issue.[4] This is damning evidence of the current state of email accessibility. In this chapter, we will cover the areas these emails failed on so you can avoid joining them.

It might sound a little counterproductive, but part of me doesn't blame companies *entirely*. While web accessibility is undoubtedly a significant undertaking, in my personal opinion, building an accessible email can be even harder. Back when I wrote the first edition of this book, the single biggest problem with building emails was the *massive* variety of email clients. With the Web, there are a few quirks between the few popular browsers, but their approach to displaying a web page is largely consistent. With email, there are dozens of different clients, including many different ones from the same company, released over the years. All of these require different methods and code to ensure consistency and accessibility, making that effort orders of magnitude larger on email.

Years later though, for this edition, that wide variety has started to coalesce. For reference, here are the ten most popular email clients – first, at the time of publication of the first edition in 2019 and second at the time of publication of this edition at the end of 2023:

2019	2023
1. Gmail (29%)	1. Apple (58%)
2. Apple iPhone (27%)	2. Gmail (28.72%)
3. Outlook (10%)	3. Outlook (4.14%)
4. Apple iPad (8%)	4. Yahoo! Mail (2.55%)
5. Apple Mail (7%)	5. Google Android (1.59%)
6. Yahoo! Mail (6%)	6. Outlook.com (0.66%)
7. Google Android (3%)	7. Thunderbird (0.25%)
8. Outlook.com (2%)	8. Samsung Mail (0.14%)
9. Samsung Mail (1%)	9. Web.de (0.06%)
10. Thunderbird (> 1%)	10. Windows Live Mail (0.05%)

In the last few years, Apple has begun to truly dominate the email space through its suite of devices that all operate the same email client. The next biggest share, Gmail, has less than half of its market share. Another important evolution is the **consolidation** of market share among the top three platforms – in 2019, they held **66%**. In 2023, it moved to over **90%**.

In my opinion, this is good news when it comes to accessibility. The reduction in variety among popular platforms means less potential issues and barriers for users to face, both in design decisions around the interface and in the commitment to accessibility *of* those popular platforms – top email clients are now known for robust, consistent rendering, which wasn't always the case.

However, our job when it comes to accessibility in email is far from solved. With platforms becoming generally more accessible, we need our **emails** to follow suit. This is just as important whether it's 3 popular email platforms or 30. There's the content, the delivery method and presentation of that content, how they work with assistive technologies, and how users can respond to that communication to consider, to name a few.

Then there's the fact that not *everyone* uses those main platforms – 90% is a lot of people, but it's *far* from everyone. Much like with the Web, the smaller percentage of those with access needs can often be overlooked when it comes to building email. The assumptions being made on email can also be similar, which is why you'll see some overlaps between the practical solutions offered in this chapter and previous ones.

But this is important because on the Web, users come to you. With email, you go to **them**. You place something in their inbox, usually requesting their attention or acting on something, and so you have to be respectful of that.

Before we explore some of the issues that emails typically have when trying to be accessible and how to overcome them, let's first look at the trickiness of even getting them to behave consistently across the many email platforms that exist.

Different Approaches to Email Rendering

Prior to the consolidation of market share mentioned earlier, most platforms had their own way of displaying an email to a user (known as a rendering engine), and many still do. They each take the code and contents of an email and use a different method to display the result in an inbox. As you can imagine, this results in the same email looking different depending on the platform a user has chosen, which is far from ideal. It also results in differing levels of support for things like styling through CSS, laying out content, and even displaying text. Internet browsers went through the same difficulties years ago, but email didn't standardize as quickly.

Outlook is a particularly good (or bad) historical example. From 2000 to 2003, Outlook was using their then browser, Internet Explorer, as a rendering engine to display emails. Then in 2007, they switched to using Microsoft Word to render and display emails instead – yes, seriously.[5] In Outlook 2011 (known as Outlook for Mac), they switched again to use the "WebKit" engine, and it provided great support and capabilities, but then they switched **back** to Word again in 2013 and continued to use it for a decade. The result was three completely separate sets of rules and restrictions regarding how an email can be displayed, all under the same brand name.

The good news is that Microsoft now uses a WebKit-based browser (the rendering engine behind Google Chrome and Safari), rather than Microsoft Word, to display emails in its latest version of Outlook. Based on testing with developers in the email community, it is reported to have an almost identical handling of HTML/CSS features to the web version of Outlook.[6] Furthermore, it is ending support for the last version of Outlook that used the Microsoft Word rendering engine, but this won't be until October 2026.[7] Therefore, this good work will take a while to set in – people don't upgrade their email platform very often, and so the faults of previous versions will be something designers and developers will have to consider for years to come.

This situation extends to all email clients though and causes havoc when it comes to creating emails that work consistently for everyone. Here are just a few examples of features that work well on websites but are fundamentally unreliable in emails:

- The ability to make an email responsive using media queries is possible in Outlook 2000–2003 but not in Outlook 2007–2016 and is possible in the Outlook app but not in the Outlook mobile web mail.

- Using a custom font is possible in iOS mail but impossible in older Outlook versions, Gmail, Yahoo!, and Windows mail.

- Adding rounded corners to elements like buttons works everywhere apart from in AOL desktop, even though it's possible in AOL web mail.

- The ability to add CSS animations for emails is impossible in every form of Gmail, Outlook (apart from Outlook for Mac), Windows mail, and Yahoo!.

- Want to change the style of an element when a user hovers over it? You can do this in Gmail's web mail and Android app, but not in the mobile web mail or iOS app.[8]

These inconsistencies might seem small in isolation, but they can lead to broken layouts and features. Some can prevent users from completing actions, and this can be especially distressing for users with impaired **mental health** or **cognitive** function. Other inconsistencies (like animation and responsive design) can lead to confusing and exclusionary layouts and visuals, complicated experiences, and a lack of functionality.

The result is email developers are stuck writing code to work around these various restrictions rather than focusing on making a wonderful, inclusive experience – it's a platform-first approach, not a user-first one.

So what's the solution? I had the following quote from Rebelmail in the first edition of this book. Given the increase of email platforms with marginal market shares, it's worth keeping in:

> People spend a lot of time worrying about email clients with 1% usage; accessibility is a much bigger issue.[9]

A popular way to follow this idea is to focus on the **content** and **layout** of your email in order to make them accessible, then "outsourcing" a lot of the consistency problems to a service. Due to the issues and time required to build and test emails properly, many people have turned to email service providers (ESPs), such as Mailchimp or SendGrid, as they're designed to take the stress away from managing and sending emails for companies and offer a range of templates that can render consistently across different email clients.

This is not to suggest a *complete* detachment from the code behind an email though – as you'll see in the following points, there are things you need to check or change there. An email service can build an accessible template, but this can then be rendered *inaccessible* by the content that's added to it. Therefore, whichever approach you have opted for or have to maintain, whether internal or external, must be reviewed and tested to ensure that it is accessible.

With that in mind, here are some common things to consider in order to ensure that everybody on your send list can readily access your emails. Alongside each point, I have also added whether email service providers typically support this or a similar solution.

Include a Link to View Your Email as a Web Page

First, you should provide users with a way to view your email **outside** of the email platform they typically receive mail in. Internet browsers are *far* more consistent and feature-rich than most email clients, so many of the issues involving emails displaying incorrectly or inconsistently may simply disappear in a browser. This gives users another chance to interact with content they've been sent if it's not displaying correctly in their inbox (a reasonable possibility given the inconsistencies I raised earlier). An example of how this may look is shown in Figure 9-1 below, and is especially important if your email is image-heavy or features interactive content where the likelihood of it rendering incorrectly on an email platform is high.[10]

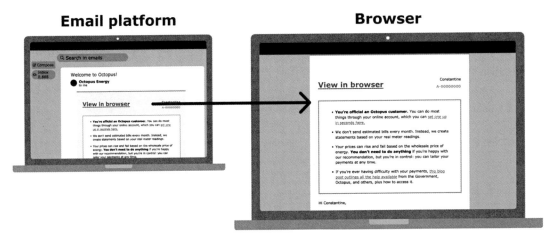

Figure 9-1. *Two illustrations. The first (pictured left) shows an email in a user's email inbox. The second (pictured right) shows that same email being displayed on a web browser after the user clicked a "view in browser" link.*

Now you may be surprised that code for building emails can simply be placed in a web page and work correctly. Well, emails are actually written in HTML just like web pages are (although they use an older approach that largely relies on frequent use of the `<table>` tag). I won't go into the details of how to code an email here, but what this similarity means is that a browser is fully capable of displaying the code for an email on a web page. Therefore, providing this backup is a useful feature that will allow users to take advantage of **any** software or assistive technology they typically use on browsers, such as screen readers, applications that magnify text, or ones that change color scheme or contrast.

Does an Email Service Provider Handle This?

Most templates an email service provider (ESP) offers will come with a "view in browser" link, which will open a copy of the email in their browser of choice. It's also a feature that many services recommend, such as Mailchimp:

> Most Mailchimp templates include a "View this email in your browser" link that goes to a browser-based copy of your campaign. This campaign page link helps contacts who aren't able to view your content in their email client.[11]

This feature requires no extra coding on your part and gives users a second chance to engage with content the way they prefer if they struggled the first time. Make sure you add it.

Provide a Plain-Text Version of Your Email

Much like rendering HTML in a browser, a plain text version of your email is far more likely to display consistently across all email clients. Instead of code in HTML that's used for layout or aesthetics, this version of an email **just** has text. In fact, the very first emails ever sent were only plain text.[12] As a result, many users opt for this level of simplicity, even if they don't have access needs, as opposed to the potential rendering issues and complex layouts that come with stylized HTML emails.

Plain text emails are much easier for **screen readers** to read through correctly (or anyone skimming content for that matter), they guarantee acceptable contrast levels as they're just text (which benefits those with **low vision**), and their layout is always consistent and linear (making them more accessible to users with **cognitive impairments**). To top it off, spam filters are kinder to emails that include a plain text alternative, and plain text emails work better on smaller devices like smartwatches that have really grown in popularity.

Given the high potential impact on users and accessibility and the low amount of effort required to achieve it, providing a plain text alternative to your HTML email is a slam dunk for inclusivity.

Does an Email Service Provider Handle This?

All major ESPs allow you to add or edit a text version of your email. In some services, like SendGrid, they automatically generate a plain text version of the HTML code you provide (it's always worth checking this to ensure it's accurate and complete though). Beyond accessibility, they do this so the plain text version can be displayed as a fallback. The reason they do this is very important:

If you only send HTML emails and a recipient's server or mail client blocks HTML content, they will not see anything in your emails.[13]

If a user opts to receive only plain text emails, an email without a text version to fall back on won't be seen at all. This, plus all the preceding ones, means it's very important to make sure that a plain text version accompanies the emails you send.

Content

It's good to offer multiple ways to access an email, but let's now turn our attention toward some choices you can make to ensure that the email's **content** is as accessible as possible.

`alt` Tags and Images

We've covered `alt` tags quite heavily in Chapter 2 "Blindness" and Chapter 8 "Imagery," but images are also frequently used in emails, and **blind** users need to be able to perceive them here too. They're actually used as more of a crutch in email than the Web due to all of the rendering and layout inconsistencies across email platforms. This has often forced designers and developers to resort to placing important content *inside* images to achieve the layout they want, often at the expense of those with disabilities. As you know from previous chapters, I wouldn't recommend doing this.

If you do though, it means that providing `alt` tags on images is just as, if not more, important in emails as they are on websites. Most importantly, you need to describe **any** text present in the images so it's not accidentally trapped. Seeing as you need to do this when creating a plain text version anyway, this makes it easier to remember to do.

While we're on `alt` text, we should touch on images again. Despite the layout advantages, you should avoid lots of images in email wherever possible – they take longer to load, and some people see HTML emails as a security and privacy risk, and so choose not to load images at all.[14] It's also important to consider that many email clients now block images from displaying **by default** because images became a popular delivery method in spam emails. With many email clients incorporating spam filters to keep suspicious content out of user's inboxes, spammers turned to embedding content in images so it couldn't be picked up as easily as text.[15] Adding `alt` text therefore not only lets users know what's in an image in the event that it's not displayed immediately but also goes a long way to proving that your email isn't spam – thereby identifying you as a "trusted sender."[16]

Finally, a format that tends to be more popular in emails than websites is the GIF (Graphics Interchange Format). This is because it allows for moving imagery on a platform that doesn't have great support for video. The result is that it's used with the intention of catching a user's attention but creates barriers when it appears suddenly and with no way for the user to pause or control it like they can with video on the Web. Overusing animations or moving imagery can be very distracting for anyone, but if they are too intense or severe (like a flash effect or quick cuts between footage), it can be a real problem for people who suffer from **seizures** or conditions like **epilepsy**.[17]

The combination of toning down your use of imagery, providing a plain text version, and a "view in browser" link makes it highly unlikely that your email will end up in a spam folder. Scam emails typically don't take the time to do these things, so you can improve both your accessibility and your sending reputation.

Does an Email Service Provider Handle This?

All major ESPs offer a way to add `alt` text to an image – either through a form field, accessed when specifying details like the source of an image, or through the HTML code itself. However, I've noticed that in many services, these fields are **not** mandatory, meaning that you can easily upload an image without providing `alt` text by mistake. This places the responsibility firmly on the person who creates the email content to make sure it's there.

role="presentation"

As we know, `alt` tags help screen reader users understand what they can't perceive visually. However, it is also just as important to hide superfluous **code** these users might hear read out but don't need to know about.

As I mentioned briefly earlier, emails are typically built using a series of `<table>` tags. This is largely to account for older email clients that don't support new ways of laying out content. In order to accomplish most layouts, a developer has to use quite a few `<table>` tags, nested within one another. Furthermore, inside every table, you will find table rows (`<tr>`), and inside those rows are columns (`<td>`) – all used in emails to separate and lay out content. That's a *lot* of code.

As we learned in Chapter 2 "Blindness," screen readers will read out any tag that it finds and understands in an attempt to provide as much information as possible to the user about the page. However, in this instance, a screen reader could end up reading out several `<table>`, `<tr>`, and `<td>` tags – all of which hold no meaningful information for the user – until it finally reaches a tag with content in it. Hearing it all read out could take so long that a user loses interest before they even reach your actual content. There is, however, a way to avoid this with an attribute that we have used in other situations: `role`.

We've used this attribute before to ensure that SVGs are recognizable as images and that a piece of custom markup can behave like a checkbox. Here, we want to tell screen reader users that certain code is being used purely for **decorative** purposes. The "presentation" value for the `role` attribute does just that:

`<table `**`role="presentation"`**`>`

Adding this means that screen reader software won't read the tag out. Much like the `aria-hidden` attribute that you learned about earlier in the book, we're telling it that this tag is purely for decoration, so ignore it. Ensuring that you add `role="presentation"` on tables that are only used to structure the layout of the email will save a lot of time (and frustration) for those listening to your emails. Of course, if you *are* actually sharing tabular data in your email, don't add this attribute so that the context of what the user is listening to is clear. Figure 9-2 visualizes what listening to an email would be like with and without this attribute.

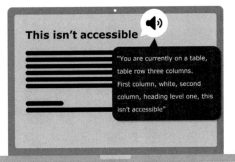
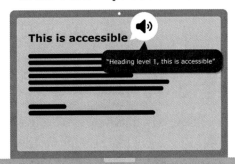

Figure 9-2. *An illustration of two emails. The first (pictured left) is without* `role="presentation"` *and has text that says "This isn't accessible" and a screen reader announcing "You are currently on a table, table row three columns. First column, white, second column, heading level one, this isn't accessible." The second (pictured right) is one with* `role="presentation"` *and has text that says "This is accessible" and just announces the text "Heading level one, this is accessible".*

If you'd like to hear what an email sounds like both with and without this attribute in place, I've placed short videos (created by Email on Acid) in the reading list for this chapter, which you can find at `inclusive.guide/reading/chapter9`.

Does an Email Service Provider Handle This?

This will be handled in *most* templates you select from an ESP, but it's certainly worth double-checking. If you customize a template that uses this attribute but don't continue to add it yourself, you're taking something accessible and making it inaccessible. Adding `role="presentation"` is a big win for very little effort, so it's definitely worth adding.

Set the Language

In Chapter 2 "Blindness," I mentioned the need to set the `lang` attribute in HTML so that assistive technologies could read out content with the correct dialect and pronunciation. This is just as important in email because your send list could include people from multiple countries:

```
<html lang="en">
```

Now unlike websites, a number of email clients will remove the language setting on the `<html>` element when they render the content, so it's worth also including it on the `<body>` tag and any direct children that contain a lot of content.

Does an Email Service Provider Handle This?

Translation in some form is offered by many email services, but its application largely comes down to the level of translation required.

Full localization (adjusting the entire contents of an email based on the location of the recipient) can be done automatically. Mailchimp, for example, can hook up to Google Translate to generate links to translated versions of text for users, as well as tap into the user's preferred language setting.[18]

However, while Google Translate is always getting smarter, it is still less reliable for larger chunks of text. As you have control of the content of an email, both when you build the email and when you use an email service, you can always get the content translated by a professional translator. You could then create multiple campaigns for each language in your send list. I'd recommend assessing the amount of content in your email before deciding and testing anything generated by Google Translate before sending it to your full send list. In the meantime, use the lang attribute.

dir Attribute

Another nice and simple attribute to add. The dir attribute specifies which direction the text on a page should go in. It has three options:

- **ltr** – Ages that are written from the left to the right (like English).

- **rtl** – For languages that are written from the right to the left (like Arabic).

- **auto** – This lets the user agent decide, typically using language settings.

Try to use ltr or rtl rather than auto (although auto is better than adding nothing). Much like the lang attribute, it's worth adding this on children on the <body> tag in case it's stripped out by email clients.

Does an Email Service Provider Handle This?

This is seen less frequently in standard ESP templates and is also related to the content you add (even though it's an attribute added to the code). Therefore, you should consider it your responsibility to make sure it's there.

<title> Tag

The <title> tag is shown when the email is viewed as a web page but is also listed as part of the email description in some email clients, which allows users to quickly see what the email is about, as well as giving screen reader users a quick introduction to the page. Over a third of emails sent typically forget this tag.[19]

Does an Email Service Provider Handle This?

If you've selected a template from an ESP, most will have a title but will need you to populate it. You should create a short, descriptive summary of the email content. Ideally, this would be descriptive of this specific email (like the subject line) rather than something generic like "Email from Joe's Website Emporium."

Use Semantic Elements

This point is aimed more specifically at developers. You can highlight the most important pieces of text using "semantic" elements such as headers and paragraphs (e.g., <h1> and <p>) just as you do on a website, which helps assistive technologies to understand the hierarchy of your content. Placing an <h1> tag in your email means a user can quickly and accurately identify its purpose and also find the main email content.

It sounds obvious (use the right tags for the right content), but developers are sometimes put off because these tags can render slightly differently between email clients. However, they give your subscribers the option to scan through an email more easily. Also, as we know from Chapter 2 "Blindness," headings are the primary way that screen reader users navigate content – that's as true in email as it is on the Web.[20]

Too Long; Didn't Read (TL;DR)s

While we are on the topic of accessible content, it's worth briefly mentioning TL;DRs again. They can help those with **cognitive impairments** understand emails more easily and save time for everybody else. For particularly long emails, a box highlighting and summarizing the main points and identifying any actions required of the user helps get that information across quickly (shown in Figure 9-3), particularly on mobile devices where the smaller screen size means that fewer words can be displayed per line.

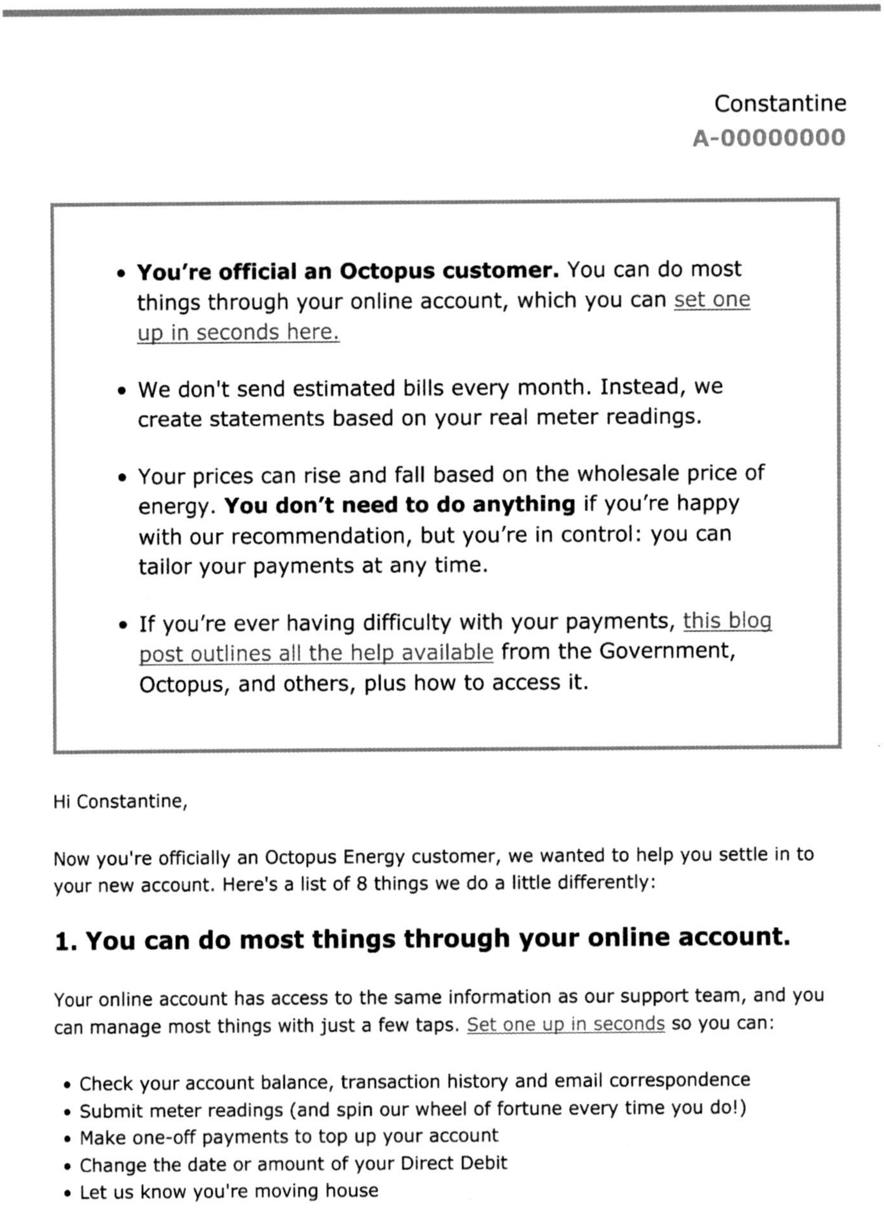

Constantine
A-00000000

- **You're official an Octopus customer.** You can do most things through your online account, which you can <u>set one up in seconds here.</u>

- We don't send estimated bills every month. Instead, we create statements based on your real meter readings.

- Your prices can rise and fall based on the wholesale price of energy. **You don't need to do anything** if you're happy with our recommendation, but you're in control: you can tailor your payments at any time.

- If you're ever having difficulty with your payments, <u>this blog post outlines all the help available</u> from the Government, Octopus, and others, plus how to access it.

Hi Constantine,

Now you're officially an Octopus Energy customer, we wanted to help you settle in to your new account. Here's a list of 8 things we do a little differently:

1. You can do most things through your online account.

Your online account has access to the same information as our support team, and you can manage most things with just a few taps. <u>Set one up in seconds</u> so you can:

- Check your account balance, transaction history and email correspondence
- Submit meter readings (and spin our wheel of fortune every time you do!)
- Make one-off payments to top up your account
- Change the date or amount of your Direct Debit
- Let us know you're moving house

Figure 9-3. *A version of a TL;DR (too long, didn't read) box at the top of a long email. These summaries highlight the main points and actions in the content that will follow it.*

Does an Email Service Provider Handle This?

As this technique concerns the **content** of an email, it is the responsibility of the person adding that content to include a TL;DR. A good general rule is to think about adding one to your email if it's over five paragraphs long and/or has more than one action.

Styling

Now that we've thought about some ways in which an email's **content** can work harder for those with access needs, let's finally turn our attention to how we **style** and present that content.

Don't Center-Align Your Copy

Accessible text is just as important when creating emails as it is online – arguably more so. In Chapter 3 "Low Vision and Color Blindness," we spoke about the importance of letter spacing and how laying out text in a "justified" way (forcing each line to both start and end at the same point, regardless of the text in that line) creates inconsistent gaps between words – thereby making it much harder to read. As a reminder, here it is shown in Figure 9-4.

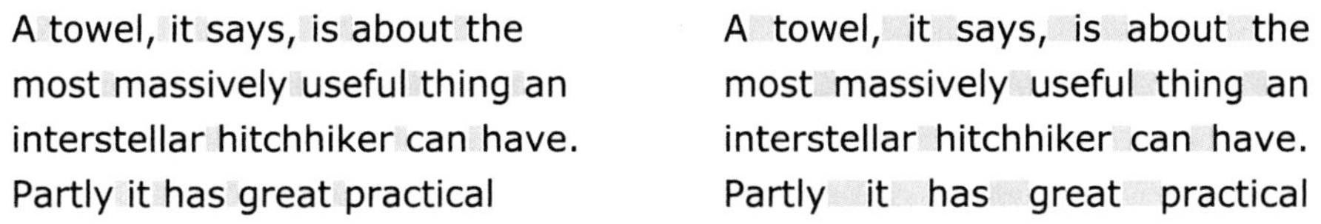

A towel, it says, is about the most massively useful thing an interstellar hitchhiker can have. Partly it has great practical

A towel, it says, is about the most massively useful thing an interstellar hitchhiker can have. Partly it has great practical

Figure 9-4.   Left-aligned (pictured left) and justified text (pictured right) side by side, showing the inconsistent spacing between words that the latter causes. The spaces are highlighted in yellow.

The same can also be true of aligning your text **centrally**. It can often *look* more appealing, but those with **dyslexia** and **cognitive impairments** that affect written comprehension or those with **visual impairments** who rely on tracking or magnification often have to work much harder to read this text. This is because, due to the varied length of content in each line of text, you end up with inconsistent starting points, as shown in Figure 9-5.

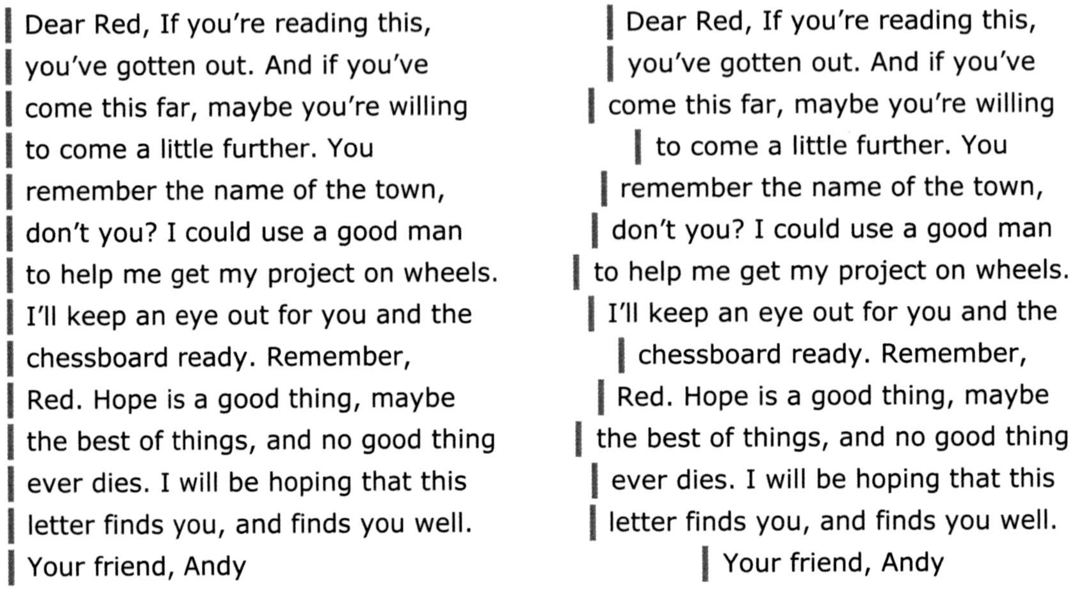

Dear Red, If you're reading this,	Dear Red, If you're reading this,
you've gotten out. And if you've	you've gotten out. And if you've
come this far, maybe you're willing	come this far, maybe you're willing
to come a little further. You	to come a little further. You
remember the name of the town,	remember the name of the town,
don't you? I could use a good man	don't you? I could use a good man
to help me get my project on wheels.	to help me get my project on wheels.
I'll keep an eye out for you and the	I'll keep an eye out for you and the
chessboard ready. Remember,	chessboard ready. Remember,
Red. Hope is a good thing, maybe	Red. Hope is a good thing, maybe
the best of things, and no good thing	the best of things, and no good thing
ever dies. I will be hoping that this	ever dies. I will be hoping that this
letter finds you, and finds you well.	letter finds you, and finds you well.
Your friend, Andy	Your friend, Andy

Figure 9-5. *A visual comparison of the starting points of sentences, in a block of left-aligned text (pictured left) vs. a block of center-aligned text (pictured right). The left-aligned text has the same starting point on every line, whereas the center-aligned text has a different starting point on every line.*

As switching to the next line is the longest break a reader takes when going through a block of text, aligning text in this way increases the chance of readers losing their place and lowers the ease of reading.[21]

Centered text *can* be used sparingly for small pieces of text like headlines that only cover one to two lines without causing problems for users and can even make your page feel more balanced and symmetrical. This is because, at this length, it's easy to scan quickly and doesn't require the repeated line-to-line eye movement that larger pieces of text do. For anything longer though, aligning your text in this way creates a barrier.

Does an Email Service Handle This?

You can handle the alignment of content in most email services, but enforcing it is the job of the person adding the content. It's worth double-checking you've done this – most ESPs display alignment options using icons, like the ones shown in Figure 9-6.

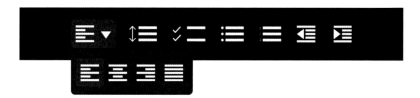

Figure 9-6. *Alignment options are typically displayed to the user as a set of icons. Every icon is made up of five lines, but the length, starting point, and end point of those lines are different depending on the option to reflect what the alignment will do to the text. The options, from left to right, are left-aligned, center-aligned, right-aligned, and justified.*

Line Spacing

We also mentioned in Chapter 3 "Low Vision and Color Blindness" that having a generous spacing between lines of text (also known as line height) can increase the readability of text for all users, but especially for those with **low vision** and impaired **written comprehension**. This is an important point to check for email because the way fonts are displayed may vary between clients much more than they do on the Web (along with the inconsistent support for custom fonts that we mentioned). The W3C guidelines recommend a line height of 1.5–2 times the size of the text you're showing rather than single line spacing.[22]

Although this is best practice, for some text, this amount of spacing may seem like overkill. I'd recommend starting with the lowest of that value range (1.5 times the size of text) and then using your best judgment to see how readable the text is. If you're unsure, ask others to read a few paragraphs in that style and see how comfortable they are with it. Also, remember to use relative units to size both text and line height.

Does an Email Service Provider Handle This?

Most ESP templates have a consistent line height set by default, but that doesn't guarantee that it's an accessible one. You can check and override this setting for an entire email or on a case-by-case basis in every major email service. This is more of a "check and make sure" tip.

Highlight Actions

Most commonly, emails are sent to users in order to convince them to complete an action. This could be making a purchase, providing information, or sharing feedback. Therefore, it's equally important for you and your users to make it clear what the action is. This is especially useful for users with **impaired planning and executive function**, who often have trouble considering and completing multiple tasks, as well as those who suffer from **heightened sensory awareness** or attention-deficit/hyperactivity disorder (**ADHD**).

On a content level, it's important to remember that you shouldn't have more than one or two actions in a single email – ideally, it should just be one. This makes it easier for **anyone** to engage with quickly, access needs or not, as there's less to decipher and it's easier to identify. It has also been proven to drastically increase the chances your users will *complete* that action.[23]

For the actions themselves, you also need to ensure that the text you use, whether in a button or a link, is meaningful and self-contained. We covered this in Chapter 6 "Cognitive Impairments," but as a reminder, if users come across an action that is vague and nondescriptive, this can lead to a confusing and stressful experience. Figure 9-7 shows a comparison between two buttons, with only one of them using text that links directly to the action you want a user to undertake.

Figure 9-7. A comparison of two buttons by themselves, one with text where the result of the action is unclear ("Go!") and one where it's much clearer ("Submit order")

Reducing the ambiguity of links is beneficial for email accessibility but really benefits *all* users – it doesn't require them to read the context surrounding the link, which helps those who scan emails. This practice is arguably *more* important in email than the Web, as the action is typically the **sole** purpose of the communication you've sent. If the action is unclear at a glance, the email has failed its purpose.

Does an Email Service Provider Handle This?

This is a content task, so it's your call on which action you want your users to focus on. Most ESP templates will offer a way to render a button consistently across all email platforms. If you're asked to build an email that has multiple actions in it, use the preceding info to initiate a conversation about why reducing those action options to one helps with conversion **and** accessibility.

Testing

Because of the range of inconsistencies surrounding email, testing is essential to avoiding rendering issues that, unlike the Web, you can't update or take back once your email has been sent. Email testing services like Litmus and Email on Acid offer great platforms to build and test emails. You can see immediately how the email you've built appears in every major email platform and almost every widely used device. They are paid services, but they offer free trials to get you started. Figure 9-8 shows how you can directly compare an email's appearance between two email platforms in Litmus.

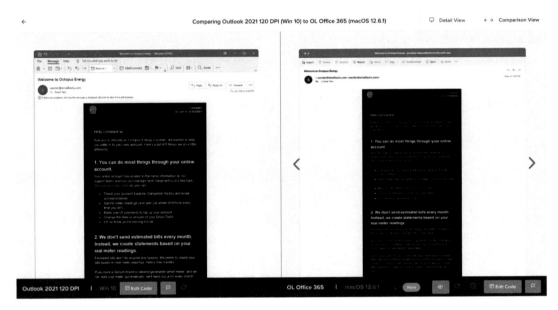

Figure 9-8. *A visual comparison of the same email in Outlook 2021 (pictured left) and Office 365 (pictured right) using the email testing tool Litmus*

Both services also have dedicated tools for testing the accessibility of your email and offering improvements before you send it. I've placed links for both tools in the reading list for this chapter, which you can find at `inclusive.guide/reading/chapter9`.

Understanding Email Support

With so many different email clients in circulation, it's really important to understand the percentage of your send list *using* each email platform. You might be able to cut the time you spend trying to support your email on a platform, as none of your recipients use it, and direct that energy to help all of those who are currently being excluded based on the code or content used instead – especially with there now being so many clients with such a low market share:

> A lot of people think any email they design and build has to be perfect across all clients, when really, the work to do that is kind of wasted effort.[24]

Understanding which clients your recipients use allows you to think about which features are functionally safe to build into emails aimed at your audience. For instance, if you want to add a hover style for your buttons, but you know that the majority of your users use older versions of Outlook, then most of your readers will not benefit from that feature. Equally, it could well be the case that most of your recipients are using newer email clients and devices, in which case you can be more adventurous with your email design. Just remember: you must check and understand the drawbacks of certain email clients and ensure that you implement most, if not all, of the points we've just covered so that nobody is excluded from the communication that you have sent.

Email marketing company Campaign Monitor has a great, free resource they maintain that shows the level of support for various CSS features and approaches in all major email clients. It's something I use when building emails, and I've added this to the reading list for this chapter, which you can find at `inclusive.guide/reading/chapter9`. Pairing this up with whatever analytics service you use to understand your send list and their platform of choice, you can more accurately work out the type of improvements that are actually *worth* adding to your emails and free up time to focus on accessibility.

Overall, my main advice with email is to keep it simple. Focus on the content and build an accessible baseline using the preceding points, and avoid things that add aesthetic value but, in the case of email, could affect someone's ability to even *engage* with the content.

Attachments

In many cases, emails can come with attachments – these could be bills, receipts, or even books. PDFs are one of the most common forms of attachment.

PDFs used to be extremely inaccessible but have made significant progress in recent years. That being said, there are still huge issues with consistency – PDF accessibility varies depending on a user's operating system, browser, and assistive technology. In fact, this process is so complicated that WCAG's guide to creating accessible PDFs is nearly half the size of this entire book.[25] This can create issues for many users, especially those who use screen readers or rely on custom browser settings (which PDFs often ignore).

This topic is far too broad to discuss here, but WebAIM has an excellent introductory guide to PDF accessibility (as hard as it can be) that I've added to the reading list for this chapter. You can find that at `inclusive.guide/reading/chapter9`.

I've raised this topic to say that, where possible, I would recommend putting all information that you *would* send in PDFs into the emails themselves or into web pages with links to those in the email instead. For the same reasons we talked about displaying emails in a browser as an option, publishing content online as opposed to in documents empowers the user to make the most of their custom tools and setups to interact with the content. You do of course have to be mindful of publishing sensitive, user-specific information on web pages, but in many cases, these pages can simply be stored within a user's online dashboard that only they can gain access to.

Google Action Buttons

Earlier we spoke about highlighting actions within your emails so that users can clearly understand what you're asking them to do. There are ways for you to optimize these actions for **all** users, with and without accessibility needs, by exposing them before they've even opened your email.

Google has pioneered "action" buttons, which are a great way to reduce the amount of time that users spend interacting with regular emails from you or emails where the action is clear. With a few lines of code and verification from Google, you can add a button with a link that's visible right from the **inbox** of someone using Google Mail. This allows the user to immediately assess and act on the request rather than forcing the user to open the email, scan (or listen to) the content, and then click the same link. Figure 9-9 shows what these buttons look like.

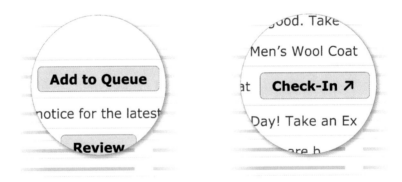

Figure 9-9. *Two examples of how a Google "action" button looks in Google Mail. The first is a "One-Click" button (pictured left) for an action that can be completed without the user leaving their inbox, and the second is a "Go-To" (pictured right), where the action links to an external website.*

Although useful for everyone, action buttons have the potential to make a big difference to those with a range of access needs. Firstly, they can make an email-based journey much quicker and clearer for **motor-impaired** and **assistive technology** users who often take longer to complete actions. The fact that they don't have to open the email, then scan or listen to it in order to find the action, prevents extra unnecessary steps. This also acts as a time-saver for users who are in a rush, especially for communications that you send users regularly that ask for the same action every time (e.g., asking for a meter reading as an energy supplier every month).

They also help many others:

- Those with **heightened sensory awareness**, who are easily overwhelmed by long, busy, pages

- Many different users with **cognitive impairments**, including those who get "lost" in content (e.g., those with **visual-spatial disorders**)

- People who have trouble focusing (like those with **ADHD**) or working out their next step (users with **executive function** and planning disorders)

- Those who experience difficulties remembering what they have to do next (e.g., as a result of **Alzheimer's**)

Because an action button is always visible when the user views their Google Mail inbox, it also acts as a constant signpost to remind users what the purpose of the email is without reopening it. There are two different types of action buttons that Google offers, allowing for a broad range of possible actions you may want a user to perform without ever opening your email. Let's go through the two main parts.

"One-Click" Actions

Figure 9-10. An example of how a Google "One-Click" button looks in Google Mail. This allows an action to be completed without the user leaving their inbox.

There are many scenarios where the expected behavior from the user receiving an email is to just confirm a predefined request. In those instances, a "One-Click" button allows the user to simply click a button next to the subject line to confirm the request, and it'll happen without them having to open the email or even leave Google Mail.[26] A few examples of this behavior might be

- Responding to a calendar invitation

- Confirming registration on a site the user has just signed up to

- Adding a new movie that's been released to their queue to watch later

"Go-To" Actions

Figure 9-11. *An example of how a Google "Go-To" button looks in Google Mail. This allows an action where the button links to an external website to complete an action.*

"Go-To" actions instead highlight the action you want the user to take, but interacting with the button takes the user to your website where the action can be completed. This type of action has more steps but, unlike "One-Click" actions, can be interacted with multiple times.[27] This button offers a lot more potential uses, but a few examples are

- Tracking a package that's being delivered to the user

- Watching a movie that's just been released online

- Reviewing a restaurant they've been to recently

- Checking in to a flight they've booked

Adding an Action Button

The code needed to add a button is fairly simple and is very similar between the different action types. Here is an example of a "Go-To" action, used to encourage users to submit their monthly meter reading for their energy account:

```
<div itemscope itemtype="https://schema.org/EmailMessage">
    <div itemprop="potentialAction" itemscope itemtype="https://schema.
    org/ViewAction">
        <link itemprop="target" href="meter_reading_link_goes_here"/>
        <meta itemprop="name" content="Submit meter reading"/>
    </div>
    <meta itemprop="description" content="Submit your monthly meter
    reading"/>
</div>
```

This simply requires the type of action you want to display, its name, a quick description, and a link that the button will take the user to when it's clicked. This code goes directly into the source code of an email, which is possible for anyone who uses an email service providers (ESPs) like Mailchimp or SendGrid to send their emails, as well as those who build them themselves. They're also *very* useful in terms of metrics – a user interacting with one of these buttons counts as both an open and a click-through for the email.

Unfortunately, there is no equivalent to action buttons that work on all email clients. However, the process of adding these allows you to think about the main purpose of the emails that you send – if you can distill that into one action for these users, you can design your content to be just as direct for users who still have to open the email.

It's worth noting that you will need to register and verify your own button with Google before it will appear. Information on how to register yours, and how to test it, can be found in the reading list for this chapter, which you can find at `inclusive.guide/reading/chapter9`.

No-Reply Email Addresses

It's important to bear in mind that communication generally requires a two-way exchange. If you send an email, text message, or even mail something to your users, they should be able to reply to you with minimal effort.

One of my personal pet peeves is "no-reply" email addresses (emails sent to users from an address that won't allow them to reply). Businesses use them to exercise a degree of control over how they receive customer communications. Instead of accepting queries from multiple places, such as in response to purchase receipts or reminders, no-reply emails ensure that queries **only** come through predetermined channels such as a dedicated email address for customer support.

No-reply emails remove the possibility of an immediate response – they're a one-way street. Even if you provide alternative methods of communication within the email (like a different dedicated support email), you still leave users in a position where, should they wish to contact you, they're forced to leave the email (and the conversation) and try to pick it up elsewhere. This can be infuriating because it's likely that their query will be centered on the particular email you sent them.

As a result, limiting communication affects everyone regardless of disability and access needs. The following sections explore some of the main reasons you should avoid using a "no-reply" email address.

You're Far More Likely to Find a Home in the Junk Folder

When someone receives an email, most email providers will attempt to add the sender's email address to the user's contacts list. This is part of marking you as a trustworthy sender, and emails from someone in a user's contact list typically won't be sent to the "junk" folder. However, this is not possible with a no-reply address.

If the user can't reply to your email address, providers are also likely to mark the communication as spam and send any future messages from that sender directly to the "junk" folder, without the user ever seeing them.[28] Spam filters have also been known to auto-assign "no-reply" emails into junk folders by default.[29] Sifting through mounds of junk mail for your email is tiring and frustrating, and that's if they even bother – those who aren't tech-literate may not even be aware that they can do this.

You're Going to Annoy Your Users

Auto-assign isn't the only way to make it to the "junk" folder. Users have been known to mark emails as spam (rather than going through the process of unsubscribing) in frustration at not being able to respond.[30][31] This categorizes *all* of your future communications, and so any information of value from that address is almost certainly lost.

Moreover, if the user tries to reply and receives an email telling them to get in touch through a different address or channel, they have to decide between going through these extra steps and simply giving up. If they choose the former, any message you receive from them will likely be less positive, thanks to the additional friction in the journey. If it's the latter, then you've lost out on some potentially valuable information or feedback.

What's more, if someone sends an email to a no-reply address and you **don't** have an auto-reply setup, the user may receive a standard "failed to send" email from their email provider. This could convince them that they are doing something wrong or that there's something wrong with **their** email. Anxieties like these can be amplified for users with **panic disorders** or who experience **paranoia**. If they *don't* receive that "failed to send" message, they might assume that you chose to ignore the email – further damaging your relationship with them.

It can be useful from an operational perspective to restrict email responses to just one avenue, which is why no-reply email addresses are appealing, but you have to think about how this affects a user. No-reply emails put extra barriers between you and your users and hinder accessible communication. Alternatively, you could use different email addresses for different *types* of communication (offers, announcements, support, etc.) or send and receive everything from a single inbox and simply manage user expectations by acknowledging their message and letting them know when you'll be able to get back to them.

You Could Be Breaking Laws

Global Data Protection Regulation (GDPR) laws are set forth by the European Union, and they determine how companies are allowed to use the data they collect from users. As a rule, customers **must** be able to request information about the data collected about them.

If you're using a no-reply email for your email marketing campaign or any other purpose, you're not giving customers a way to reply to you. While there's no specific GDPR law that says you can't use a no-reply email address, you may be breaking GDPR compliance if you're using no-reply email addresses for certain purposes.

Good Uses of Email

> We don't often think of email as a social media platform, yet it is. Any communication tool that facilitates two-way communications is, by its very nature, social.[32]

When you choose not to use a "no-reply" email address, you're not just avoiding all of the negative outcomes that we just covered – you're also opening yourself up to a range of **positive** benefits. Let's go through some of the good that can come from sending emails to customers from an address that they can actually respond to.

You Receive More Feedback

Having opened yourself up to replies from an email you send, you might receive more complaints. However, replies could just as easily mention a typo they've spotted, a bug report, or even a healthy dose of praise. Most importantly, from an accessibility perspective, users can quickly and easily let you know if they're having trouble, what they're having trouble with, and whether they need any assistance. This two-way communication promotes honesty and trust and shows that you care what your users have to say, whenever or however they want to say it.

Your Email Reaches More Users

With "no-reply" addresses often marked as spam, doing away with them improves the percentage of your emails that get successfully delivered. As a result, you have a higher possibility of users interacting with the email that you spent so long creating.

It Can Promote Engagement

Because email is used so frequently, opening up this channel for users can drive engagement. Sites like Airbnb and eBay allow you to respond to messages from other users through their platforms by simply replying to the email notification that you receive from them. These sites will then route the message back to the other user. This encourages quicker responses and results in a more active site overall. None of this would be possible with no-reply emails.

Conclusion

We've now looked at the various ways that you can ensure that your emails are more accessible to your users. Despite the inconsistencies between platforms and the trouble that can cause users, applying what you've learned in this chapter will form a strong, accessible foundation upon which to communicate with them without creating unnecessary barriers. You should also be in a better place to decide whether using a third-party service might better suit your circumstances to accomplish this. Our main aim here is to provide ease of use to the greatest number of people, and I believe this can be achieved by focusing on accessibility, instead of trying to support every email client and version that exists.

Now, factors such as content layout, language choice, and even sizing and spacing may seem small in isolation, but together they significantly improve the experience of **all** users who interact with your emails. Accessibility relies on *how* emails are built of course but equally on the **content** you provide within them.

Many emails often require a user to act in some form, so I have encouraged you to reflect upon the clarity of your actions and look at whether implementing features like Google's "One-Click" action buttons could reduce the stress associated with common email-based tasks. Of course, many of these actions rely on the user's ability to communicate with you too, and hopefully, the *many* arguments I've raised against using "no-reply" email addresses will encourage you to examine how easy it is for your users to get in touch with you.

I mentioned earlier the Email Markup Consortium's finding that **99.97%** of emails they tested were failing basic accessibility tests. As designers and developers, we have to do better in order to reduce this number. They did have this to say about their findings though:

When looking at the top 10 issues, the top few most common issues happen in a lot of emails, but when we look at the bottom of the list, the frequency drops dramatically. This means as an industry if we focus on those top few issues, we should be able to reduce the overall results dramatically. A number of these issues should be quick and easy to fix and a lot of them are related so can be fixed at the same time.[33]

This concept is the same one I mentioned at the start of this book about the Web – such a large percentage of the total issues are made up of just a few, easily solved problems. This holds real hope for improving the quality of email, just like the Web, by approaching accessibility improvements in a practical way.

Outsourcing Accessibility

There have been a range of tools and platforms that have risen dramatically in popularity on the Web over the last few years – changing the process of how websites are built and used. Accessibility overlays that you can "bolt on" to your website claim to solve all of your accessibility problems with a line of code and a toolbar, the "build your own website" phenomenon of websites like Wix and Squarespace bringing large numbers of people without accessibility (or coding) knowledge to the Web, and the rise within the development community of pattern libraries, with pre-built accessible components, but a complete disengagement from their maintenance and decision-making process – for each of these, we'll dive into what you're gaining vs. what you're giving up and whether they're helpful or detrimental in the fight to make the Web more accessible.

Overlays

It's fair to say that for many businesses (or at least the senior management of those businesses), their first interaction with accessibility may well be when they're told that their site is not accessible – that they're excluding customers, missing out on revenue, and most seriously, contributing toward ableism. So they search for a solution online, and a tool appears – a tool that describes their issues perfectly and appears to offer to solve all of these problems for them and more, for a fee and with a single line of code. Well, that's a dream come true! A neat, simple solution to a very complex issue. It sounds too good to be true…

And that's because it's too good to be true.

There's been a rapid rise in recent years of overlays – an "accessibility" tool that can be bolted onto a website in order to make it more inclusive and cater to a range of access needs. We'll start by understanding what these tools attempt to do, why they've become popular, and the many drawbacks that not only prevent them from doing what they've claimed they can do but in fact, make the accessibility of a site worse.

© Ashley Firth 2024
A. Firth, *Practical Web Accessibility*, https://doi.org/10.1007/979-8-8688-0152-5_10

What Is an Accessibility Overlay?

An accessibility overlay is a tool, typically written in JavaScript, whose aim is to help users overcome accessibility issues they find on the website or app they're using. This code is added by a company, and changes are applied after the website or web app is rendered by the browser, thereby allowing it to transform its appearance, content, and behavior. You might have seen a pop-up like this on your browser (shown in Figures 10-1 and 10-2).

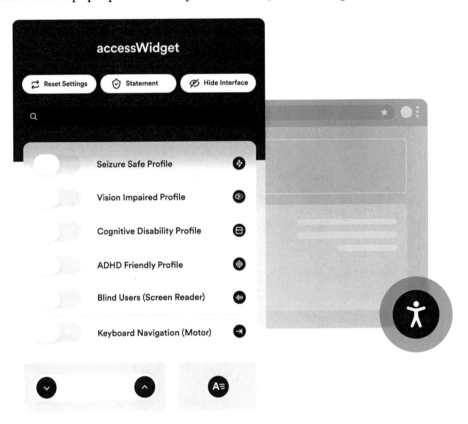

Figure 10-1. *accessiBe's "accessWidget" overlay appears on a website after users interact with the "accessibility" logo, pictured at the far right. It displays a range of modes you can enable to make content on the site more accessible for those with a range of disabilities. This image was taken from accessiBe's marketing website.*

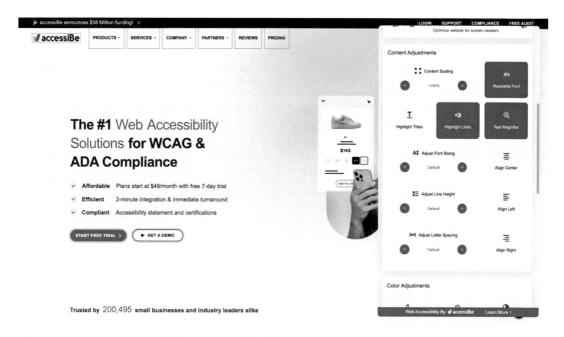

Figure 10-2. *accessiBe's "accessWidget" activated on the accessiBe website. The right-hand pane shows the content adjustment you can make, and the website itself shows visual changes, thanks to the overlay, such as a change in font, and links being highlighted.*

These tools promise to break down accessibility barriers, allow users to engage with your content, and use new technology like AI to dynamically complete certain tasks for you, such as intuitively adding alternative text to your images.[1] More than this though, they claim that you can achieve all of this quickly and with no effort on your part. At the time of writing, here are how some of the major overlay companies market the convenience and protection of their tool:

- **AudioEye** – ADA and WCAG compliance on day one.

- **AccessiBe's "accessWidget"** – Paste a single line of JavaScript code on your website... in up to 48 hours, your website is accessible and compliant.

- **Equalweb** – Just insert one line of code and we will do the rest!

- **UserWay** – Get compliant and avoid lawsuits with only a single line of code. UserWay's solutions provide full WCAG and ADA compliance from day one and every single day thereafter.

Sounds great, right? The problem, however, is that they fail to do just that. We'll get to that later.

Firstly, it's worth noting that sites that have added an overlay are *aware* of the fact that their website has shortcomings when it comes to accessibility. They have contacted an overlay company about their issues and then installed their "widget" to fix the problem.

With that in mind, it raises two questions:

- Why have they added it?

- Does it actually solve the problem?

Why Have They Added It?

This may seem like an obvious question: to solve their accessibility issues! The reason I raise it is that there are a range of reasons why a company may have turned to an overlay, and this reasoning drastically alters the benefit of an overlay and the thinking behind the company using it. It largely comes down to whether the intended use is temporary or not.

Temporary Use

The most common reason someone may temporarily use an overlay is that they've realized that their site is not accessible but want something in place for customers while they **fix it**. Using an overlay in the interim while you solve the underlying problems of a website's accessibility is generally considered a smart move. If you've made the commitment to make your site accessible, and you're in the process of doing so, it's important to ensure that customers still have some way of engaging with your content, even if it's not the ideal long-term solution. For the process of doing the actual fixing, there are a range of auditing and tracking tools that can help with that process, and we'll cover those in the next chapter (Chapter 11 "Tools and Auditing").

In this sense, you can think of an overlay as a bandage on your website. Bandages are, of course, not intended to be left on permanently – they are removed after the injury they cover has healed. In this instance, what would constitute an "injury" would need to be clear to avoid a situation where what started as an imperfect, temporary fix becomes a permanent one that does not serve your users adequately. This could be determined by what's considered as a "critical" accessibility issue by WCAG standards, for example, that would prevent people from accessing your content.

It's worth mentioning that some companies who license overlays also provide the tools to help web teams achieve native accessibility. accessiBe, for example, who license the overlay called accessWidget (pictured earlier), also have a product they call accessFlow – allowing sites to test, monitor, and remediate the accessibility of websites to that end.[2] In this example, it's conceivable that a company would license the overlay, plus the tracking software, to try and put useful measures in place until their site is altered to become inclusive.

If this happens to be a path you choose to go down, it's important that you communicate that to your users either on the widget or on your accessibility statement. Making it clear that the overlay is a temporary solution and that you're in the process of improving your accessibility will give users confidence in you while avoiding deadlines you can't meet.

Permanent Use

To go back to our bandage analogy, imagine using one to cover a stab wound that clearly needs stitches. You can't put your faith in a bandage to heal that wound, no matter how long you leave it. However, we've seen earlier that these overlay companies make bold promises about their tools fixing your accessibility issues for good. So who's right? Let's delve into some of the problems that many within the accessibility community have found with overlays.

Problems

Interference with a User's Tools

The basis of an overlay is that it alters the layout of the content on a web page in an attempt to make it more accessible for those with various disabilities. To achieve this, it makes some assumptions that it shouldn't. The most damaging one is that those with disabilities aren't altering a website themselves.

People with disabilities who use the Web typically have assistive technology to help them. These tools often change a web page to combat barriers they face, and those changes have been dictated by the user to happen all the time – they're always with them and make browsing consistent, whereas these overlays are only on sites that install them. So when a user's preferences *and* assistive technology are personalizing a site for them, as well as an overlay, the result is a clash and an unpleasant experience. Furthermore, the latter is installed on the site and manipulates the content once it's loaded, and many permanent plugins override customization and personalization choices a person relies on.[3]

This forces users with disabilities to use the assistive technology provided by the overlay rather than the assistive technology that is customized for their unique needs. For this reason, many users have said that they actually find it easier to navigate websites when overlays *aren't* present and that their presence has prevented them from completing tasks online.[4]

Compliance Does Not Always Mean Accessibility

The next assumption is one you've been learning throughout this book – that a measurable level of compliance is equivalent to actual accessibility. For example, overlays can check whether an image is missing an "alt" attribute (something we covered in Chapter 2 "Blindness") and choose to hide the image, but what if there's text or useful content in that image that needs describing to a user? If it checks and *does* find an "alt" attribute, it may do nothing, but should it? It can't be certain of the quality of what's *in* that attribute. Is it a poor description of the image itself? Is the attribute there but without content when it should have some? These are all things that a person can check in a second but that a tool cannot simply "fix." As a result, it's impossible for a tool to deliver on the promise of fixing these problems.

Privacy

There is also an issue of privacy here. The entities that build these overlays are private companies, and many do not disclose what they do with the information they collect when someone uses them. Anything from letting clients know how many people use their tools to selling information to third parties could all be happening. As with any form of privacy and tracking online, people rightly do not take kindly to it. Even being identified as an assistive technology user through this tool raises many concerns.[5]

Separation from the Problem

To return to the "temporary" approach we covered earlier, putting an overlay in as a stopgap gives design and development teams time to fix the underlying problems their site has. This involves learning what causes them, *why* they're problems, and how to fix and avoid them – exactly as you've been doing with this book! When you instead set an overlay as a permanent solution, none of this happens – it robs teams of the chance to learn important lessons, as the company has considered the problem solved, and frames the issue as one of covering against risk rather than ensuring inclusivity. The result is the same mistakes being made over and over, and new ones likely being introduced as the site grows.

It's why nearly all lawsuit settlements in this area come with the accused company learning the topic of accessibility to prevent it from happening again. A permanent overlay will never teach you this.

Security

When you add an overlay to your site, you are effectively granting that tool the ability to alter what your site can do and look like. Many are doing this in an attempt to make their site more inclusive, but it can also open them up to security vulnerabilities. As overlays call code that is controlled by someone else, there is also the potential for control over this code to be hijacked, even for experienced and regulated tools. For example, the permanent overlay "BrowseAloud" (now ReachDeck) was hacked to change its code to mine cryptocurrency, affecting thousands of people using their service – from the UK's NHS and ICO to the US government's court system.[6] Luckily, this example only involved an attempt to mine coins rather than anything more malevolent, such as displaying inappropriate adverts, stealing passwords, or tricking people into installing malware, for example. All are possible when an overlay is hacked.

Overlays Themselves Can Be Inaccessible

If you're adding a tool to your site in order to make it accessible, it'd be helpful if the tool itself was accessible. Accessibility consultant and expert Adrian Roselli tested overlay company accessiBe's tool in a number of ways and had this to say:

> Whether you review it with automated tools or manual testing to check for WCAG failures, or you look at it from the perspective of de facto accessibility, both accessiBe and its overlay do not pass muster.[7]

Profit

Above all of this, these companies have a product to sell. We spoke about the constant rise in lawsuits filed against companies on the grounds of insufficient accessibility, and it's this worry that these tools often prey upon. They offer what seems to be an instant remedy to both the legal and digital problems companies are facing. That this is working speaks to the wider issue of accessibility not being a topic that many are familiar with and is also typically why these tools are pitched to those in high-level, decision-making roles rather than people who build sites. It also explains the following practice.

Faking Accessibility Results

This is my gravest concern, and it's by far the most sinister. It's been proven that these tools have ways in which they can fake a sense of progression and accessibility on sites they're installed on. For example, there are a lot of automated a11y testing tools available, but the WAVE extension by WebAIM is a popular one. It can quickly show you a11y-related errors and warnings on the web page you're on.

WebAIM has actually had to build something into their tools to make it clear that overlays may manipulate the content of web pages to suppress the detection of accessibility errors.[8]

One particularly worrying example they posted under their announcement about this was a page that "has 361 detectable errors in its default state. However, when WAVE is activated, UserWay (an overlay) manipulates the page content to make all text black on white, give all images alt="image", etc. resulting in 0 WAVE errors."[9]

This is in no way accessible. It's deeply inaccessible, and a way of lying about the effectiveness of their tools.

So, Does It Actually Solve the Problem?

Clearly not. These tools are not capable of actually making a website accessible or inclusive. They also bring with them a host of *new* concerns to worry about while not solving the initial problem it was brought in to deal with. But at least, given their promise to customers on avoiding legal action, clients using overlays are spared that. Right?...

Lawsuits

> The legal part is easy. If your business wants to avoid getting sued because of an inaccessible website, an accessibility overlay or widget isn't going to help you. I can say this with some certainty because in the last two weeks alone five lawsuits have been filed against businesses that use an accessibility widget or overlay on their websites.[10]

That quote is from a lawyer who defends companies against accessibility lawsuits.

Businesses using accessibility overlays received 575 lawsuits in the United States in 2022, which was a 36% increase from the previous year. Many of these lawsuits cite the features of the overlays themselves as a barrier to equal access, in addition to the accessibility violations and barriers that the tools fail to help users overcome.[11] Here are three brief examples of cases brought against clients using accessiBe's widget, which highlight the range of ways it can get you into legal trouble.

Murphy v. Eyebobs, LLC

On January 7, 2021, a case was brought against Eyebobs – an online reading glass seller. They were using accessiBe as their permanent accessibility tool. Issues were raised that included the following:

- Viewing the accessiBe a11y statement trapped a screen reader user.

- The overlay was not able to make a modal dialog accessible.

- The overlay failed to open a promo pop-up which deprived the user of a discount.

- The overlay failed on a star rating, which prevented the user from understanding the quality of the product.

On October 18 of the same year, they lost the case. A settlement was reached that involved Eyebobs building an accessibility team, writing a policy, and training its staff – all the things accessiBe promises you don't need to do if you use their tool.

Fischler et al v. Dorai Homes

Another lawsuit directly cited accessiBe as of May 12, 2021. In this case, accessiBe's overlay is named as the *reason* for the barrier. It was cited for its failure to provide any alternative text for images – the example I mentioned earlier. This is something accessiBe claims that its use of AI is capable of handling.[12]

Thomas Klaus and Robert Jahoda v. Upright Technologies

The site UprightPose uses accessiBe at the time of writing, and their overlay is cited in this case as inaccessible. The website does not alert screen readers when this pop-up window appears. Instead, a screen reader remains locked on the website's underlying page, making it impossible for users to use the "accessibility widget" independently, thereby defeating its purpose.[13]

Do Users Like Them?

After all of these issues and potential worries, it shouldn't come as a surprise that overlays are not popular with the very people they're designed to "help." In 2021, the largest US Blind Advocacy Group, the National Federation of the Blind, banned accessiBe from its national convention and revoked their sponsorship, accusing the company of engaging in "harmful" practices.[14] They stated that "it is the opinion of the Board that accessiBe peremptorily and scornfully dismisses the concerns blind people have about its products and its approach to accessibility...the nation's blind will not be placated, bullied, or bought off."[15]

A few users have taken to sharing their thoughts online, and the feedback is far from positive. The conclusion from one user, Connor Scott-Gardner, stood out to me in particular:

> In the end, it was far easier to navigate the blog post without accessiBe. Although I'd have liked for better table markup, I could understand the information perfectly well without it, and I could at least navigate the page quickly. With accessiBe enabled, this became impossible.[16]

There's actually an online petition against these very tools called the Overlay Fact Sheet. It has hundreds of signatories from developers and accessibility experts around the world, who all disagree with the use of overlays and the practices those companies engage in to sell them. There is also a declaration, made on behalf of every signatory, that ends with a clear message:

> We hereby advocate for the removal of web accessibility overlay and encourage the site owners who've implemented these products to use more robust, independent, and permanent strategies to making their sites more accessible.[17]

I myself am also a signatory of this.

Public Apology

In 2023, the CEO of accessiBe, Shir Ekerling, issued a public apology to the accessibility community in order to "address our past actions and outline what we are doing and have done to change and improve." It states that he and his co-founders were a "newcomer to the accessibility and disability communities," and "when some community members voiced their concerns, my colleagues and I became defensive and resistant, and we mistakenly treated it with dismissal or, at times, even anger."[18]

The apology doesn't make specific reference to the lawsuits those who've installed it are facing. In fact, on a subsequent episode of the podcast "Living Blindfully," Ekerling stated that

> Those are customers that received lawsuits. That's true. But then, they joined accessiBe to help them with the existing legal situation. Those are not accessiBe customers that were sued because they installed accessiBe, and then it failed and a user sued them, or anything like that.[19]

However, this can't be true as accessiBe is directly cited as part of the complaints in every lawsuit listed earlier. This apology is also not visible on the accessibe site in any place I could find.

Relating to some of my concerns earlier, Ekerling went on to apologize for "emphasizing our marketing on avoiding legal action" rather than on making a site accessible, and in their new "purpose statement" linked to this apology letter, they state that "we don't believe in a single AI-Powered approach to make the internet accessible as we did previously."[20]

It's clear they intend to change their approach, after "seeking guidance and training from disabled leaders, activists, individuals, and disability-led organizations willing to teach us where we fell short," and have altered how they engage with the a11y community. However, they have a long way to go, and they're only one of the *many* overlay companies that exist in the marketplace today. For all of these reasons, I can't recommend using an overlay to improve accessibility on a website.

An Argument Against Overlays

It can be an alluring prospect to have a single integration take away your accessibility issues, especially when you weigh its ease of use against the time and effort required for tasks like rewriting your site or reconsidering your color scheme. However, not only is it clear that an overlay can't provide a lot of what it promises and distances your teams from accessibility, but they often get those that use them into the very trouble that they offer to keep you safe from.

Adrian Roselli has a more direct overview:

> Using [an] overlay widget is a pre-preemptive admission that you know your work is inaccessible and that you took the shortest possible route to find the easiest possible workaround. You are telling users you care more about litigation risk than them.[21]

The best approach is to build for your users – engaging them where you can and creating an organizational process that values accessibility. This takes far more work than adding a couple of lines of JavaScript to your website, but the reward far outweighs the effort – a common trend in this book. Instead of trying to limit risk, work to build loyalty.

It's worth thinking, based on all that's been raised here and the general opinion of overlays from the accessibility community, what users will think of you and your site if they visit and see that you have one active. It's unlikely that they'll view it as you caring about inclusivity. It's more likely that they'll think that you just want the problem to go away. For that reason, overlays are quickly becoming a black mark for sites – a beacon for those mired in legal issues looking for a solution or trying to avoid them with minimal effort.

This is becoming more and more likely to drive away the many customers that could give you their business. Sorting a11y yourself could result in failings. It's true. But think about it this way – every legal case brought against a site by a plaintiff has requested reparations as part of it.

People understand that things go wrong. If you're seen to be engaging with the topic and slipping up, people will let you know. If they see you making improvements and asking for their opinion, your stock with them rises immensely. You perhaps gain a new lifelong customer, an advocate in the community, and a degree of faith that you'll make mistakes, yes, but work hard to fix them.

It makes you a little more vulnerable, but people are human. And the truth is, the alternative of an overlay isn't giving you perfection either far from it.

"DIY Websites"

Another area in sharp incline is the "build your own website" phenomenon, with websites like Wix, Squarespace, and Shopify reaching new lofty heights of popularity. This means users building a site who may have never done so before and platforms building for a mass-market audience while needing their work to be as customizable as those users demand. Let's look into what this trend means for accessibility.

A Web for Everyone

I mentioned at the start of this book that Tim Berners-Lee branded the Internet as "for everyone" and "the great equalizer." This is now very much true when it comes to *adding* content to it. It is now quicker and easier than ever to turn your idea into a beautiful-looking website, with zero coding knowledge and a small amount of money. This change has given rise to some of the most popular sites on the Web and has made the Web more inclusive of those who can bring their ideas to life.

This most recent wave of website creation is being spearheaded by Wix and Squarespace: all-in-one platforms designed to take the fear and confusion out of building websites for beginners. They offer an alternative to learning to code or hiring someone to build a site for you, along with an experience light on technical information that results in a short learning curve. They are attracting an ever-growing audience for a few key reasons:

- They have a more interactive, intuitive interface that people can use to build sites in a design-driven way. Some parts are as simple as dragging and dropping the feature you want onto the page.

- They have hundreds of starter templates that the platform offers to get started.

- They offer an easy way to implement an extensive range of features, such as online shops, mailing lists, and more.

- They're available in dozens of languages and are present in over 190 countries.

Due to this, they've amassed millions of users and paid subscriptions and billions in revenue. At the time of writing, it's estimated that Wix and Squarespace collectively power around 15 million websites – nearly 5% of all of the recorded websites on the Internet.[22, 23]

Now, they are far from the first platforms to allow users to make their own websites without actually coding them. Their predecessors, the likes of WordPress and Drupal, have been around for years and still retain a large market share when it comes to site-builder platforms. However in 2022, for the first time since its creation, the market share of WordPress went down.[24] This was only by a small margin, but coupled with the continued rise of these new platforms, we could be looking at the new big players in the site-builder market in the years to come.

Besides, there has been a *lot* of coverage about WordPress. I'm keen to explore these newer platforms that are rising because they offer something very different and are therefore attracting a different type of audience. According to Forbes, for example, Wix is

> Particularly well suited for small businesses, entrepreneurs and individuals who want to create a website for personal or professional use...without requiring a lot of technical knowledge or design skills.[25]

This poses important questions though: what does allowing so many people to contribute to the Web without training do for, or to, accessibility? And what can (and should) platforms like Wix and Squarespace do to ensure they haven't created the biggest wave of inaccessible websites in history?

Statistics

Firstly, let's look at some recent statistics. At first glance, these platforms seem to be generally more accessible than their predecessors. According to WebAIM's 2023 research, there are far fewer average accessibility issues present on Wix and Squarespace sites than on WordPress and Drupal.[26]

CMS	# of Home Pages	Avg. # of Errors	% Difference
Squarespace	7,671	18.9	−62.3%
Wix	7,501	21.1	−57.7%
Drupal	28,018	39.8	−20.4%
WordPress	333,176	50.9	+1.8%
wpBakery	32,400	61.8	+23.6%

It's worth noting that the sample size here is capable of providing quite skewed results, given that there are over 20 times more WordPress sites in this data set than Squarespace and Wix combined. However, it's still a stark contrast in terms of average errors, and the fact remains that popular sites from these platforms seem to outperform WordPress sites considerably. The next important question is: what are these sites? What are people building?

What Are They Being Used to Build?

A big draw of these platforms is their range. In 2023, Wix shared a list of 27 common website types, along with how you could make *every one of them* on their platform.[27] Squarespace lists significantly less options on their blog, but both lists start with the same thing – online shops.[28]

As of July 2022, eight of the ten most popular Squarespace websites are ecommerce sites.[29] It's also estimated that 2.5 million of the 8.5 million Wix websites that are live are online stores.[30] Shopify, the go-to site builder for selling products, has over 4 million sites that generated over $175 billion in sales between 2022 and 2023.[31]

So, people are building a lot of online stores. This isn't great news from an accessibility standpoint.

What Are the problems?

Legal Concerns

Ecommerce sites rank among the lowest-performing categories of sites for accessibility issues, according to WebAIM. While government, law, and social media sites performed well above the average based on their research, shopping was among the lowest.[32]

Category	# of Home Pages	Avg. # of Errors	% Difference
Government	11,313	28.6	−42.9%
Law, Government, and Politics	27,530	36.3	−27.4%
Social Media	8,033	37.9	−24.3%
…	…	…	…
Shopping	37,459	71.6	43.2%
Real Estate	15,397	72.1	44.2%
Adult Content	16,778	79.7	59.4%

This explains why almost 400 (391) of the Internet Retailer Top 500 list received an ADA-based digital lawsuit in the last five years.[33] However, these lawsuits are far from confined to big companies. In the first half of 2023, *smaller* companies with annual revenue equal to less than $25 million experienced an increase in lawsuits, accounting for 77% of all cases.[34] These are troubling signs for tools that cater primarily to people launching small businesses.

In more positive news, if we look at ecommerce specifically, it seems to indicate that Squarespace and Shopify as platforms outperform other traditional platforms convincingly, with above-average accessibility failings.[35]

Platform	# of Home Pages	Avg. # of Errors	% Difference
Squarespace	7,671	18.9	−62.3%
Shopify	24,647	52.0	+3.9%
WooCommerce	44,586	62.5	+25.0%
Magento	6,246	81.2	+62.5%

Overall though, it's traditionally an area of poor accessibility. Then there's the matter of *where* they're being built. Most of the sites created by users of these platforms are registered in the United States. Of the millions live on each platform, over three-quarters of Squarespace and over two-thirds of Shopify's sites are US-based.[36] In 2022, UsableNet reported that 84% of the thousands of lawsuits brought against websites for being inaccessible were directed specifically at ecommerce sites.[37] Many of the most notable, and landmark, cases surrounding accessibility (such as Amazon and Domino's) were also online stores.

From these statistics, we know that users on the platform are creating sites most commonly known for a11y issues (ecommerce sites), most commonly in the country where most cases are being brought against sites for a11y failings. This is a combination that could spell danger. A cursory search in the forums of these platforms finds people searching for advice after their site has been sued.[38]

Themes

Let's return to the topic of "variety" as it's an important one. After all, if all users were making ecommerce sites, that would at least be a singular accessibility problem to tackle. But we already know that's not the case.

Now typically for those who can't code, they instead fashion their site off of a template, as Wix and Squarespace's blogs encourage you to do – indeed, it's part of the appeal. On Wix, there are more than 900 designer-created templates, covering a very wide array of site types. Away from their own gallery, templates are also available for purchase on external sites, where the platform has little to no control over what's being sold. For example, the popular marketplace site Etsy has thousands of templates for sale for both platforms. I read through the descriptions on the first two pages of both results, and at the time of writing, *none* of them made reference to the fact that the template was accessible.[39] [40]

These templates are not overseen by the platforms and so can't be guaranteed that they meet the same guidelines that they themselves may advocate and aspire to. What's more, a lot of these templates are popular for the very reason some users can't access them. For example, we mentioned in Chapter 8 "Imagery" that moving imagery can often be harmful to users with disabilities such as epilepsy or vertigo. This feature is also very popular on a lot of templates for these platforms, with parallax being the most common. As we covered, parallax scrolling makes a page's background and foreground move at different speeds, creating a 3D effect. Wix boasts that this effect can make your website stand out. The problem is it can cause epilepsy and vertigo in some users too.

There's Only So Much a Platform Can Do

It's important to note that all of the major platforms I've covered have published comprehensive guidelines around accessibility, which is positive in that they're aware of, and engaged with, the topic. Shopify has a very thorough page online detailing things you may wish to consider around accessibility when editing a theme. It's a fair attempt with some good points and visuals, but it finishes with a list of around **20** resources for further reading.[41] I have no statistics on the number of customers that engage with this page or the further reading, but I'm going to go out on a limb and say that the number isn't high. Both Wix and Squarespace also have a checklist for improving a site's accessibility (that is equally as long).

Alongside those checklists, Wix has a good selection of accessibility guides, ranging from how to make videos and documents accessible to focus styles and font choices. Again, they're numerous and lengthy.[42] They also advertise the ability to hire an a11y professional on their marketing site which is wonderful to see.[43] I went through this process myself to see how they approached it, and each of the three professionals it recommended to me had accessibility listed under the "small tasks" category of their services.[44] The guide price for this service was over £300, which is more expensive than a year's subscription to Wix's premium business plan.[45]

And this is an issue. It's a tricky and involved topic, and I don't blame people who are building a site for the first time for feeling overwhelmed by the complexity and cost of the process *before* they reach the nuances of ensuring good accessibility.

My point is this: if you're responsible for putting more websites out into the world than any other platform and your target audience is people who typically haven't built websites before, you have a clear mandate to ensure that what you're helping to put online isn't simply adding to the ocean of inaccessible websites. These platforms have helped birth new businesses that have achieved impressive mainstream popularity and heaps of sales, but many users find themselves locked out of content in the exact same way they have been through traditionally built sites.

Wix mentions that they can't ensure people using their platform that their site will be compliant with accessibility laws and regulations.[46] They also refer to "advanced accessibility features," such as alt text, which aren't included and need to be added by the user.[47] In the FAQs of their accessibility page, Squarespace concedes the same thing as Wix and succinctly summarizes the crux of the issue:

Because Squarespace users have a lot of creative freedom,
they also have the ability to build websites that are not always
accessible by all.[48]

When Platforms Fail, Who Do Users Turn To?

To make matters worse, when you search online for terms such as "Squarespace
accessibility," before you reach Squarespace's own guidelines, you're met with
sponsored adverts from none other than accessiBe, who are offering accessibility
compliance for Squarespace sites with simple installation to save them from having to
engage with "a process that can take months to do manually or cost thousands of dollars
to outsource."[49]

We already know that promise isn't going to be kept…

So we have users who don't know (and can't be expected to know) how to make
a site accessible, platforms that churn out endless websites that can't guarantee
compliance, and overlay companies that are targeting these customers to "help" them –
not a good combination.

What Do Platforms Encourage Users to Do?

We've covered what they encourage people to engage with *outside* of their tools, but
how about within them? I spent some time building sites using the platforms (primarily
Wix and Squarespace) to see what it would flag or encourage me to do for accessibility
purposes. As most users wouldn't be aware of the topic, it's key that people are asked
to consider accessibility when performing actions organically. The following are the
examples I found while performing regular tasks.

Page Titles

Squarespace and Wix both allow you to set page titles that will assist those using screen
readers. Both file it under "SEO" (search engine optimization) settings though and don't
make reference to accessibility (shown in Figure 10-3).

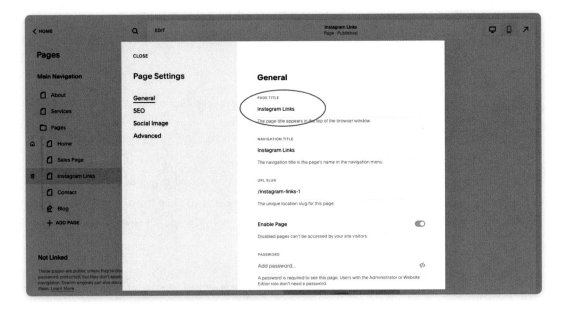

Figure 10-3. *The "General Page Settings" window in Squarespace allows you to specify a page title. It's the first input on the page.*

Colors

There is quick access to the range of colors within a site's theme for consistency on Wix (shown in Figure 10-4), but no checker there that flags if the contrast is insufficient between the foreground and background.

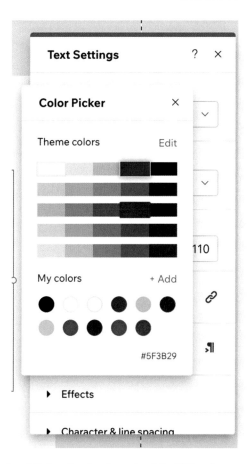

Figure 10-4. *The "Color Picker" window inside Wix shows a panel of theme colors that users can easily access, but there is no contrast level or checker present in the window.*

Headings

Wix offers users the chance to specify a heading tag when styling a piece of text, but it's hidden under the "SEO & accessibility" drop-down menu that's closed by default (shown in Figure 10-5). You'd also need to know what a heading tag is and why heading hierarchy is important (which many wouldn't) in order to use the feature effectively.

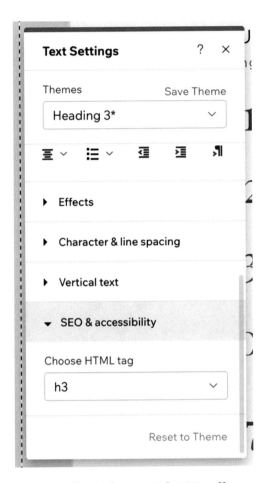

Figure 10-5. *The "Text Settings" window inside Wix allows a user to specify what style of heading that want some text to be, but also what HTML tag it should be, under the "SEO & accessibility" drop-down.*

Text Size

I found a Wix guide *away* from the editor that encouraged users not to set font sizes less than 14px (as many other guides do), but it's possible to set a font as low as 6px through the visual editor.

Videos

When uploading new media to both Wix and Squarespace, I wasn't prompted to add subtitles or a transcript in order to make the content accessible for those not capable of engaging with the audio. A quick search into their guides pointed me to other services you could use to achieve this, but this doesn't seem possible through them directly nor were the guides shown to me when I uploaded the content.

Imagery and Files

Both platforms offer the chance to provide "alt" text for images and files when uploading them (shown in Figure 10-6), but this isn't mandatory and will default to the name of the file when it's first uploaded and so will use that if the user doesn't change it. This, as we know, isn't useful to screen readers. So, like with headings, accessibility is possible but only if the author knows what they're doing.

Figure 10-6. *When the user clicks an image in Squarespace, there is a text field available titled "Image Alt Text"*

This is in no way an exhaustive list, but it deliberately serves that purpose. As you can see, there are some tools in place, but they are far from complete. They're encouraging users to think about certain parts of their content when they're engaging with it, but I wouldn't consider them comprehensive in their coverage or proactive in the education of their users.

Interestingly, Wix had addressed this very concern themselves, when discussing their editor, and the accessibility testing lists they initially published online for users...

Accessibility Wizard

After listening to the feedback of users and accessibility experts (most of whom found the list too heavy and time consuming), we realised this was just a start.[50]

—Wix Accessibility Team

The most impressive tool I've seen from my research is Wix's accessibility wizard. They launched this in 2021 in order to make it easier for their users to find and fix accessibility issues on their sites from directly within the Wix Editor (where they build their site) step by step. The tool is built to comply with WCAG 2.0, with progress being made on 2.1 and 2.2, and will scan a Wix site and display any issues it finds.

What impressed me the most is that the tool displays details of the issue it's found and allows the user to fix it from within the tool itself. Figure 10-7 shows an example of this.

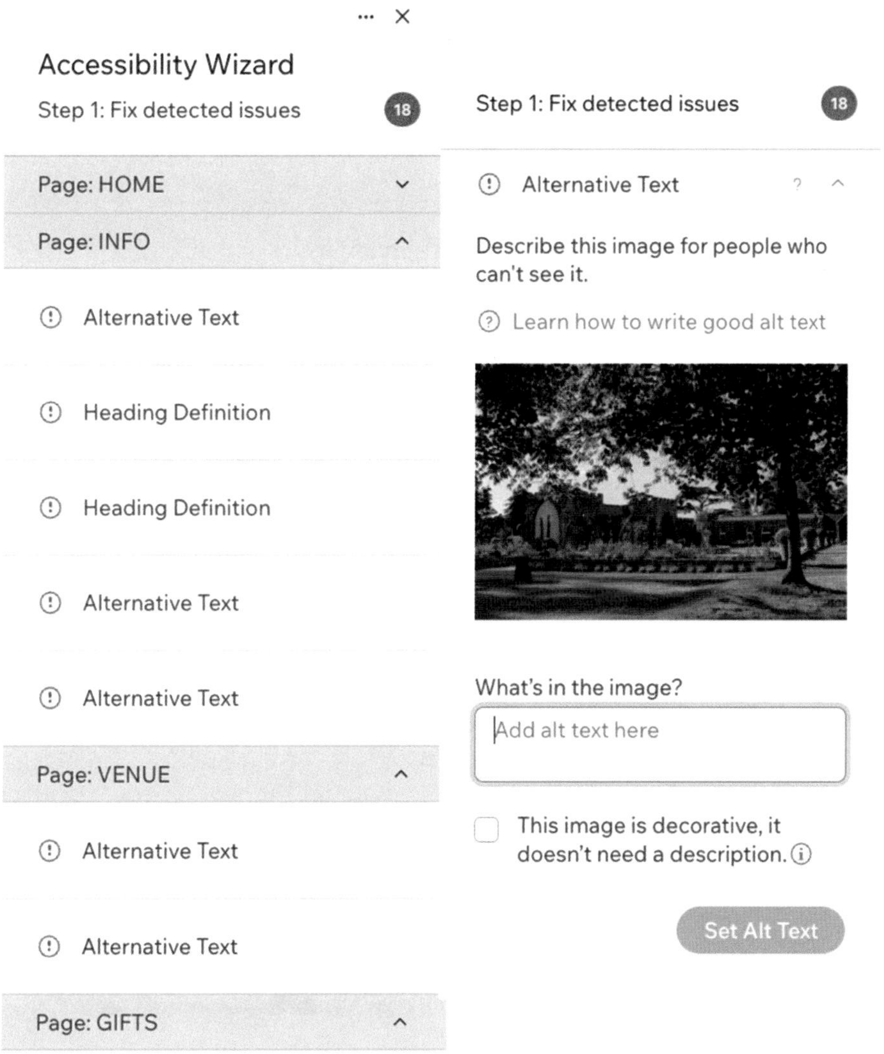

··· ✕

Accessibility Wizard

Step 1: Fix detected issues   (18)   Step 1: Fix detected issues   (18)

| Page: HOME | ⌄ |

| Page: INFO | ⌃ |

⊙   Alternative Text

⊙   Heading Definition

⊙   Heading Definition

⊙   Alternative Text

⊙   Alternative Text

| Page: VENUE | ⌃ |

⊙   Alternative Text

⊙   Alternative Text

| Page: GIFTS | ⌃ |

⊙   Alternative Text   ?   ⌃

Describe this image for people who
can't see it.

⊙   Learn how to write good alt text

What's in the image?

Add alt text here

☐   This image is decorative, it
     doesn't need a description. ⓘ

Set Alt Text

Figure 10-7. *Wix's "accessibility wizard" is pictured, displaying an issue with the lack of "alt" text on the image. It's displaying what the image is for the user and offering them the chance to either describe what's in the image or mark it as a decorative image.*

The tool has found an image without "alt" text. Through this, the tool has taught the user

- What alternative text is and why it's useful.

- That there's a guide they can use moving forward to write useful alternative text.

- Which image is problematic (by displaying it).

- That if the image is decorative, it doesn't require alt text.

Plus it allows you to either submit "alt" text or mark the image as decorative there and then. It does this for each issue it finds. It may not be *every* issue on the site, but it does a tremendous job of teaching about what it finds and solving simple issues with minimal user effort.

The tool is also aware of how each instance fits into the rest of the page. For example, here's a piece of text it's flagged as needing to be a heading of some kind, but it doesn't allow the user to make it a "heading 3" (h3) tag as the text sits within a section headed by a "heading 1" (h1) tag and so wouldn't be semantic (shown in Figure 10-8).

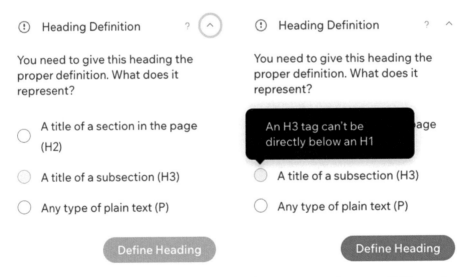

Figure 10-8. *Within a "Heading Definition" issue in Wix's accessibility wizard, the tool prompts the user to decide whether the text is a title of a section on the page or any type of plain text. Conditionally, it will ask if the text is a title of a subsection, but in this example, it's grayed out with a note that says, "An H3 tag can't be directly below an H1".*

What's more, once the user is done with the automated checks that it can test for, it provides a list of recommended checks for the user to carry out *themselves*. These are things we've covered in the previous chapters, like checking whether buttons have vague text like "click here," whether graphs use patterns as well as colors to show differences, and whether content is still readable at 200% zoom (shown in Figure 10-9).

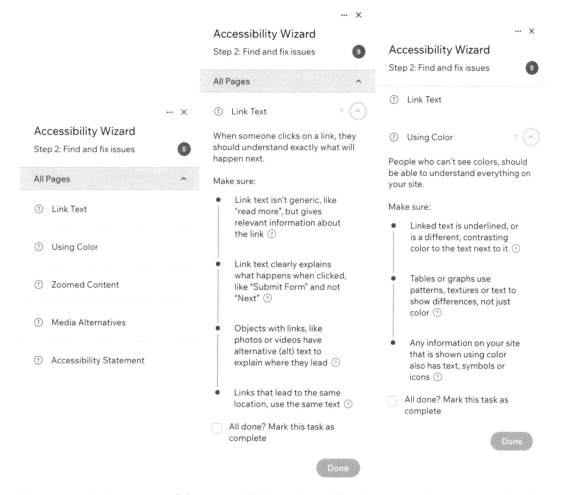

Figure 10-9. *Step two of the accessibility wizard lists five areas for users to check manually for issues on all pages – link text, using color, zoomed content, media alternatives, and accessibility statement. Within each section, there is a list of checks to carry out, along with guides to help the user.*

At this point, the user has already learned a little about the topic and has seen some progress quickly. All of this makes it more likely that they'll carry out these more involved checks and remember what they learn in the process.

Finally, there is a whole feature set within the accessibility wizard that is handled *for* the user (shown in Figure 10-10). The user can control these if they wish, but they're on by default and part of all Wix sites. These features include a "skip to main content" link, added visual indicators on interactive elements for keyboard-only users, and an ordering of page elements to reflect the visual order the user has created through the drag-and-drop interface. It even has a way to allow you to add custom ARIA attributes to different site elements.

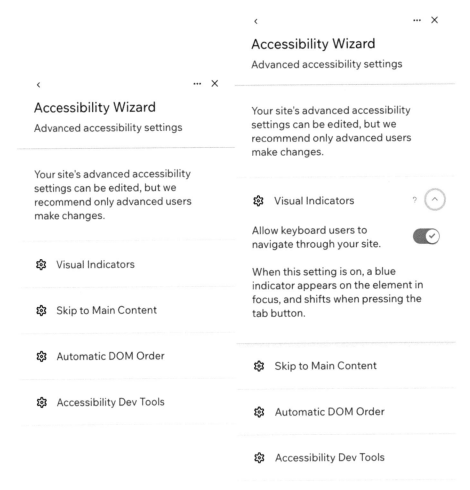

Figure 10-10. *Inside the "Advanced accessibility settings" of Wix's accessibility wizard, there are five tools that are all active by default – Visual Indicators, a 'Skip to Main Content" link, Automatic DOM Order, and Accessibility Dev Tools.*

When using this feature, you see the same message from Wix as you do on their checklists – that they can't guarantee that you'll be compliant with accessibility laws. However, this tool is an excellent example of a platform that is taking responsibility for the sites that it's helping to put on the Web and making good strides toward its users knowing about accessibility, even *without* knowing about coding.

Other Solutions

Tooling

Even with good tooling though, I still see the sheer volume and variety of templates as a large barrier. On the tooling front, Wix is clearly ahead of its competitors. It would be good for the likes of Squarespace and Shopify to mirror their commitment to engaging customers on the topic and making it easy for them to understand issues and fix them. Failing that, it would be good to see their users move onto a platform like Wix that does.

One issue I do have with Wix's implementation is that it's not visible to users by default. You have to head into the settings of your Wix account to view it, which I believe is a barrier to more people finding it organically and learning about how to make their site inclusive. I understand that it can't be an ever-present sidebar on the page, but moving it to a more prominent menu item would help a lot in my opinion.

Accredited Templates

I think it would benefit everyone to see a form of accreditation for templates that have been tested by those with disabilities and have achieved a certain level of compliance. Those templates could, in turn, be advertised by the platform to encourage more new users to start with those as a base. They could still allow all templates to be used as they do now, but it would incentivize those building and maintaining themes to do so with accessibility in mind – more accessibility would equal more publicity, which would then equal more downloads of their theme.

Wix has made a good start on this by having a gallery of "accessible templates" that they advertise from their accessibility page.[51] However, when you visit the home page of the templates gallery, there's no clear way to find this category.[52] With hundreds of templates available, plus the ability to sort by "recommended" and "most popular" that will always receive the most traffic, more needs to be done by platforms to elevate those doing the right thing.

Indeed, the fact that they have an "accessible" templates gallery at all is a clear message – they're aware that other templates *aren't* accessible; otherwise, there'd be no need to have a dedicated section. If the popular list is filled with inaccessible templates, it simply guarantees that more inaccessible websites will make their way onto the Web through their platform.

With constant policing being impossible, this gives the community a chance to police themselves, which would be a good start.

Personal Thoughts

Wix and Squarespace have created something special. They've built the ability to allow anyone to build the site and business of their dreams and have opened up the Web to more people in the last few years than many thought possible.

However, these efforts aren't without danger to the inclusivity of the wider web. With so many templates available, and such wide control over their customization handed over to newcomers to the Web, this is an area that will require constant attention from those maintaining the platforms and education for those using them.

It's admittedly a difficult and unenviable task. Introducing more friction to ensure accessibility is followed in places will undoubtedly create friction and confusion for some users who are unaware of the topic. This is counterproductive to their whole "ease of use" angle that has set them apart from other content management platforms and website builders. However, much like a company has a responsibility to ensure the site they build is accessible, they have a responsibility to teach the importance of it to their users, limit the possibility of them building inaccessible websites without realizing it, and help them fix them quickly and intuitively when they do.

Wix actually said it best themselves on their blog:

> Eventually we realised it's not enough to advance our own product, but that we've got to encourage and support our users to create accessible content, too. While we can't control the way you design your website, we can certainly help our users improve how accessible their site is overall. And in fact, we think **it's our responsibility to do so**.[53]

This is comforting to hear from a platform. Both Squarespace and themselves have written excellent guides, but Wix has also recognized that most wouldn't read them and so built a tool that allows users to fix issues from the same place they're building the site.

Therefore, I'd suggest you choose Wix if you're looking to use a site builder now or in the near future. Ultimately though, whether you're using Wix or any other site builder, it remains your responsibility to make your content accessible.

Component Libraries

The rise within the development community of component libraries has been enormous, with millions of downloads every week for use in building websites. This means teams utilizing pre-built "Lego blocks" others have made for the sake of speed but relinquishing control over how they're built and maintained. We'll dive into what you're gaining vs. what you're giving up.

What Is a Component Library?

A component library is a collection of reusable components. Think of them like Lego blocks that you can put together in any number of ways to build any number of websites, but in the same style and with the same experience for users every time. These components are always self-contained, which allows them to be used again and again. They can be very granular, like a button, or something larger, like a modal. The design of components within a library is often the reflection of a "design system" – a company or group's unique design and approach to visuals, branding, and interactions on the Web.

Often, these components have "parameters" or options that allow for the same component to be used multiple times but in mildly different ways. This helps make them more flexible and, therefore, more reusable. For example, a button component may have a parameter in order to alter its style while allowing developers to use the same core button code (shown in Figure 10-11).

Figure 10-11. *Two buttons, both created using the same component, but with different background colors thanks to a "parameter" that has been given to the second instance*

Open Source

A lot of the Web is built upon "open source" – the concept of people releasing the code they write to allow others the right to use, study, change, and distribute it themselves. Millions of people contribute to open source projects worldwide and do so for a number of reasons including encouraging collaboration and innovation and keeping the Web a free place with healthy competition.

This is also the case with component libraries. Although most libraries are created for internal use, many comprehensive libraries that companies and groups have made are available online for people to use within their own sites for free. It's these free tools, with these pre-built Lego blocks, that people are turning to in order to make their sites. Aside from the major advantage of them being free, they have become very popular for a few reasons:

- They help companies who have multiple websites and want to keep their brand consistent across them.

- They make the building of websites a lot quicker, as designers and developers aren't spending time building simple blocks and functionality that those libraries already have.

- They act as a central source of truth. When changes need to be made, you can make that change and then roll it out to all the websites using the library easily.

All of these points, in my opinion, are also great for building a more accessible web:

- If a company has more than one website, it can split the attention of designers and developers, leading to less attention to detail and more unintentional access failings. With a component library, more of their attention is focused on what's *common* between those sites.

- With the time saved on avoiding repeated efforts on the same components, more time is left to explore the usability of those components, which is extremely useful (especially in the fast-paced worlds of agencies and startups).

- If a component in a library is inaccessible, a change can be made at that single source of truth, and you can be confident that you've made it more usable everywhere.

They clearly hold a lot of power, and their popularity on the Web is still growing. Let's explore some more of the positives around component libraries as they pertain to accessibility.

Positives

They're *Very* Popular

For all of the reasons earlier, people have flocked to use these libraries on their websites. For example, MUI (short for Material UI) is one of the most popular component libraries in the world and is built upon Google's "Material Design" system. It has been used on sites for brands such as Amazon, Spotify, Netflix, and NASA. This high-profile adoption and endorsement of the library naturally makes the library even more popular – at the time of writing, the library receives around four million downloads **a week**.[54]

This large-scale usage holds great power for accessibility on the Web. I mentioned earlier in the book that the Internet's variability in how sites are made is one of the biggest barriers to true accessibility in my opinion. With everyone building sites that look and run differently, it becomes a mountain to climb to keep them all-inclusive.

If more of the Web is using the same library, with the same foundational components and approach to a11y, it's clear that building strong accessibility into that library can have a positive, wide-ranging effect on the Web. I certainly don't want every site to look identical, but I *do* want them all to be usable for everyone.

You Can Learn from a Library

All mature component libraries come with strong documentation and examples. If you're new to the Web, this is an excellent place to read about the considerations that go into designing and building the components in a library and the principles that underpin that process. With accessibility being mentioned in a lot of the popular libraries, this turns even more eyes onto the topic, perhaps for the first time. Furthermore, a new developer using these components gets to see firsthand how components can be adaptive to users, such as their preference on color scheme, font size, and reduced motion.

Support and Growth

The team at MUI currently has over 30 full-time core contributors to the library, as well as 2,700 open source contributors from around the world.[55] For a smaller company or startup, this is basically an outsourced team working on great, accessible components they can leverage quickly. If lack of time to engage with accessibility is a concern, having this much work taken off someone's plate makes it far more feasible.

Moreover, with so many people using them, submitting issues, and feature requests, many of these libraries are always growing healthily, with feedback from an extremely active community.

Negatives

As with anything though, there are considerations and potential pitfalls. Here are some things to think about before making the choice to wholeheartedly adopt a component library through the lens of ensuring that your sites remain accessible.

You Don't Control Those Components

After all, you didn't make them, you're just using them. If they're changed in ways you don't like, or they become inaccessible, you'll have to customize them (which can create issues) or stop using them. Thanks to the nature of open source, you can raise an issue with them or even share a suggestion on how to fix the issue, but it may take time, and it's ultimately up to them whether they do so. This leads us nicely to...

There's No Guarantee of Accessibility

Component libraries may be beautiful, quick, and easy to use when setting up a site, but that doesn't guarantee they'll be easy to use for your users. Most popular open source libraries mention their commitment to accessibility but tend to have a lot of issues raised on the topic as they make new components and features – accessibility is, as we know, a moving target. I raised the example of MUI being used on some of the biggest brand sites on the Web, but this library has had hundreds of accessibility issues raised over the course of its existence.[56]

Then there's the follow-up question: "Those raising the issues know about accessibility, but do those working on the library?" MUI has over 30 people working on its core team as I mentioned but, from my research, no accessibility expert.[57]

At the time of writing, they are actually hiring for one, and the job advert states they'll be ensuring "all products meet or exceed WCAG 2.1 level AA guidelines" and leading "the accessibility training across the company."[58] This is an excellent commitment to a11y, but the library has been running for nearly ten years on millions of sites without one. Plus, leading training across the company insinuates a current lack of knowledge around the topic.

Component Libraries Have Opinions

It's impossible for them not to – they're made by humans, who have inbuilt ways of using sites and accessing content that often don't factor in those with disabilities. Even the biggest companies in the world, who have published their approach to designing components for people to use, have focused from the outset on designing it *for themselves*, not necessarily the wider web. They're also, despite being so big, prone to error. Here's an example:

Google's Text Fields

Google's basic "text field" component, used in Material UI, initially had no borders. This was a deliberate design decision. It was used throughout Google's suite of apps, and thanks to Material UI, many other parts of the Web too. People inevitably struggled to use them, which made them inaccessible. So much so that Google decided to commission some research on why. The research found that it was down to the lack of borders, meaning that they didn't look like text fields, so they changed them.[59] Prior to this research though, a lot more sites than just Google had inaccessible text fields because of the example they set and the components they made available. Figure 10-12 shows how those text fields looked before and after.

Figure 10-12.   *An example of Google's text field before and after research was conducted on why users were struggling to use it. The old field has a single line underneath the placeholder text, making it look like underlined text. The new field has a full border that resembles a native text field.*

Even after this research users continued to struggle with Google's text fields (as shown in Figure 10-13 below), due to the identical styling of its different states (that made it hard to tell whether a field was empty or not), inconsistent labeling (that made the label text small and difficult to read), and the fragility of the label itself (that made it unreadable after a certain length, or if the user had zoomed in).[60]

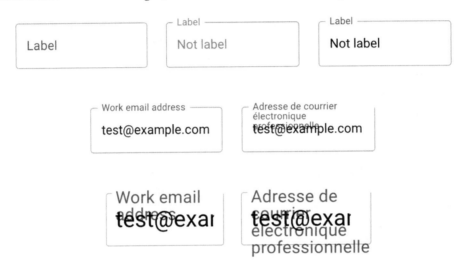

Figure 10-13. *Examples of continued issues with Google's text field component. The color of the fields' various states (pictured top) is so similar that it's difficult to be sure whether the field is empty. The style and positioning of the label text when a field has content makes it difficult to read (pictured middle), and the field becomes completely unreadable when a user has zoomed in (pictured below).*

It's important to reiterate that many of these component libraries (and design systems) are, from the outset, created for the purpose of one company and brand before they're distributed for use by others. They may take input from others and listen to concerns but ultimately retain control over the components. Therefore, a library may reflect how you want your site to look and behave *now*, but this doesn't guarantee that it will be a year from now.

It's a similar concept to the overlays we were discussing previously: You're not in control of parts of your website, so you can't control the accessibility of that part, not truly.

They Could Lose Support at Any Point

Right now, there are a lot of people working full-time on the development and maintenance of Material UI. Tomorrow, they could decide to give up on it, and suddenly it would stop growing. This may be unlikely, but the chance *is* above zero. In this case, you may be faced with the prospect of migrating your site to another library or having to start maintaining components you're using but haven't built, which is a tall order – you don't know what the thinking was when certain decisions were being made or fixes and enhancements that were yet to be made.

Human Error (and Intervention)

Component libraries are created by humans. Humans make mistakes. To be fair, if you or I were building components for ourselves, we'd also make mistakes. However, if you unintentionally released a bug that impacted accessibility, for example, it may come as a shock, but you'd know you changed something and then go back to revert the change or fix the error. On the other hand, if a third party releases a change to the library that you're using, it may change your site the next time you deploy it without you being aware – introducing problems into your site that aren't of your doing. The first you even hear about the issue could be when users are complaining. It could happen when you're away from your computer or away on holiday. This is the nature of having someone else's code as part of the foundation of your site.

The popularity of these libraries is also its curse in many ways. If millions are downloading them every week, that's a potential accessibility bug appearing on millions of sites at the same time. And those are the *unintentional* ones! It can often get worse than that. In the past, we've seen open source developers deleting code and causing site outages and even deploying malicious code as a form of protest.

My favorite open source story is that of "left-pad": a small code package that was only 11 lines long. It had a singular purpose, and most of the Internet had no idea it existed. However, when its author Azer Koçulu deleted the package in protest of NPM giving the name of one of his packages to a corporate company that wanted to use it, developers across the world, including those at companies as big as Facebook, Netflix, and Airbnb, couldn't run their sites. As it turned out, many large packages and sites relied on "left-pad" without realizing it, and its deletion "briefly broke the Internet."[61] For many, it brought into sharp focus how "writing software for the Web has become dependent on a patchwork of code that itself relies on the benevolence of fellow programmers."[62]

Now this isn't an accessibility story, and I don't want to create unnecessary fear here, but the point stands. With so many sites built on open source technology, it holds the potential to cause you problems that you didn't create but **are** responsible for, including accessibility failings.

Note   You can "lock" a component library you're using to a particular version to ensure that changes don't happen automatically, but for developers, this often causes more pain down the line as they fall further and further behind the latest version of a library as it keeps growing, which can result in code conflicts, larger amounts of time invested in migrating to a newer version, and other issues. For this reason, a lot of developers give their apps free rein to upgrade automatically if the version upgrade is minor (i.e., an upgrade from version 1.1.1 to 1.1.2 would be considered minor). This mitigates the problems I've mentioned but doesn't inherently protect you from bugs – indeed, it's often the smaller, innocuous changes that can create them.

You Need to Use Them Correctly

I mentioned earlier that components often come with "parameters" in order to allow those using them to adapt them in various ways for the different scenarios they want to use them in. Components in libraries tend to offer a large array of parameters so that users aren't heavily restricted in what they can do with them, making them more popular. This freedom is a double-edged sword when it comes to accessibility though. If a component is tested and found to be accessible in its default state, it could be completely inaccessible when those parameters are adjusted. Let's return to our button example (shown in Figure 10-14). You have two variants that have been designed for users to choose from:

Figure 10-14. *Two buttons, both created using the same component, but with different background colors thanks to a "parameter" that has been given to the second instance*

If that same component offered the ability to change, say, the text color, it makes it possible for both variants to fail color contrast checks (shown in Figure 10-15).

Figure 10-15. *The same two buttons as earlier, but now altered to have different text colors. This customization means the text now fails contrast checks.*

Material UI buttons allow you to do this through its parameters, along with seven other customizable parameters.[63] They proudly advertise this level of customization on the home page of its documentation.[64] I have no problem whatsoever with them doing this as it allows people building sites to have greater control over what they want to make. It's simply a reminder that you can pick a library to use based on its accessibility but then make it inaccessible through customization if you're not careful.

They Require Full Adoption

This isn't necessarily a bad thing, more of a note. Much like Tim Berners-Lee mentioned the need for "universality" in the world's access to the Web, the power of a component library is in its universal application throughout a website.

For example, if you use an accessible card component in some parts of your site, but in other places, there's a custom implementation, then you can't trust all of the cards on your site. This results in a fractured experience – of the design, user experience, and sometimes accessibility – as you're maintaining more than one source of truth, and inevitably end up with updates (and issues) happening to one area but not the other.

Power to Help

We know that using a component library can help with consistency through having a collection of components and using them throughout a site, but how does that translate into fixing accessibility issues? Let's return to the most common a11y issues within the top million websites by popularity, according to WebAIM, and explore whether using a component library would be able to help our search for accessibility in that area or not:

- Low color contrast (foreground/background)

    - This is technically enforceable through a component library/ design system. If the color scheme you choose for a site passes WCAG contrast checks (for more, see Chapter 3 "Low Vision and Color Blindness") and those components use those colors throughout, you could be confident that your site would be readable. It would require you to be strict with where and how you let people customize components though as changes in color elsewhere could impact it.

- Lack of alternative text for images

    - A component library *could* make "alt" text a compulsory field on anything that includes an image, but that doesn't quite fix the issue as it wouldn't be possible to ensure that the text was useful content or whether it would be better to have an empty "alt" attribute so screen readers ignore it (for more on this, see Chapter 2 "Blindness").

- Empty links

    - This is achievable through a component library by ensuring that every link component has a mandatory "link" parameter.

- Missing form labels

    - This is achievable by ensuring that every input component has a mandatory label parameter. However, like the point on "alt" text, there is no way to guarantee through a component library whether the text added is useful to the user.

- Empty buttons

    - This is achievable through a component library by ensuring that every button component has a mandatory "link" parameter.

- Missing document language on a web page

    - This isn't possible through any one component as the document language is set at the top level of a site (the <html> tag). You could document the need to do this, but a component library can't help enforce it.

- An unsemantic heading hierarchy

  - This is not possible, as a component library focuses on individual components and not on the page as a whole. Because the heading hierarchy of the page is made up of many components that can be placed in any order, you can't guarantee a semantic heading hierarchy (for more on this, see Chapter 2 "Blindness"). Again, you can document the importance of checking the heading order on a page, but it's not enforceable through the library itself.

As you can see, it holds promise, but it's a mixed bag. There are things that it can definitely help with and things it's clearly not responsible for. Let's now look at a couple of the examples in the *gray* area, as I feel it best demonstrates how a component library can move you further in terms of accessibility, but only being able to take you so far.

A Heading Within a "Card" component

Let's say we have a "Card" component that contains a title using a "heading 5" (h5) tag, a small image, and a block of text (shown in Figure 10-16).

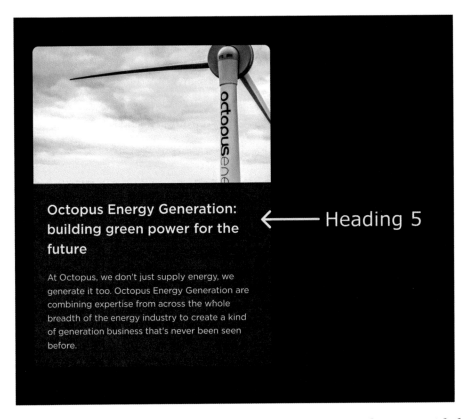

Figure 10-16. *A "Card" component, made up of an image at the top, a title below it, and some text below that. There's an arrow pointing to the heading to show it's a heading 5 tag.*

In isolation, this component is great – it uses the correct markup, has a nice linear layout, and is easy to read. Now consider that this component is a single Lego block, and we want to place it somewhere on our web page. It's entirely possible that this card can be both accessible and inaccessible, depending on where it's placed. Figure 10-17 shows how this is possible.

Figure 10-17. *The "Card" component from earlier, positioned in two different heading hierarchies. In the first (pictured left), its position isn't semantic as the headings drop from h3 to h5. In the second (pictured right), its position is semantic as the heading drops from h4 to h5.*

We covered heading hierarchy in Chapter 2 "Blindness," but as a quick reminder, headings on a page need to drop sequentially by one heading level each time within a section. In the first implementation, the headings on our page will jump from an h3 down to an h5, which is inaccessible, whereas in the second implementation, it will jump down from an h4 to an h5, which is accessible.

Enforcing `alt` Text Within a Component with an Image

In Figure 10-18 below, we have a series of components we'll call "Image with caption." They're each used to display an image showcasing the perks of a service and have corresponding text to describe them underneath.

Figure 10-18. *A series of four illustrations with text underneath each describing a service. There is "alt" text on each image that describes the illustration, which is marked as incorrect as it's not necessary.*

As it contains an image, the component makes it mandatory to provide "alt" text to describe it. In doing this, they're hoping to encourage more people to fill in "alt" text and prevent it from being inaccessible. Except when the component is used in this way, the image is purely illustrative, so there's no value being trapped within it if it hasn't been described. Instead, the better option would be to have an empty "alt" attribute that screen reader software understands to mean that they should skip past it (shown in Figure 10-19).

Figure 10-19. *The same four illustrations as earlier, but now they have an "alt" attribute that is empty. This is good for accessibility as screen readers can ignore them.*

In this example, a well-meaning component that was trying to be accessible by enforcing rules around "alt" text has actually created a situation where screen reader users would need to sit through extra, needless content.

Creating Your Own Component Library

We've covered the sheer amount of work involved in growing and maintaining a large component library, but not all component libraries need to be as feature-rich and customizable as Material UI, nor do they have to be for the public. Having a basic set of accessible, well-tested components that are used commonly throughout your own site can be an excellent start for an internal component library. It's undoubtedly more work than simply installing a third-party one, as you're fully responsible for it, but there are different benefits you unlock when you make your own.

Benefits

Having a library just for your team or company gives you the complete freedom to make changes that make sense for *you* and the control to only change and publish them when you're around to fix potential issues. When there is a competing list of things to improve, you get to decide what is most important, meaning that you can make accessibility the priority when perhaps others wouldn't.

Furthermore, where open source libraries often need to provide a lot of flexibility around customization in order to cater to the greatest number of people, building your own allows you to be more deliberate and strict about what you want to allow people to do to customize components. This minimizes inconsistencies between the sites that use your library, enabling quicker adoption and less rebellion from the brand. It also drastically reduces the number of variations you need to test when ensuring that all of your components are accessible all of the time.

Beyond the components themselves though, how you go about making them, and what you set as a priority when you do, can have a profound effect on how others think about your library and your company. Firstly, you can make it explicit in your documentation how much accessibility matters. Often this point has to be made within companies by a11y advocates – people who will keep asking the question "is this accessible?" Instead, component libraries can be a great way to remind people every time they use it, and before they contribute to it, that accessibility is important – to the company and in general. It can do the work of many accessibility champions and get you closer to the ultimate goal of everyone who works on your site being aware of, and caring about, whether it's inclusive.

For example, in the design system for the Octopus Energy brand, Coral, we've made it abundantly clear that accessibility is thought about in every component, from design to build.

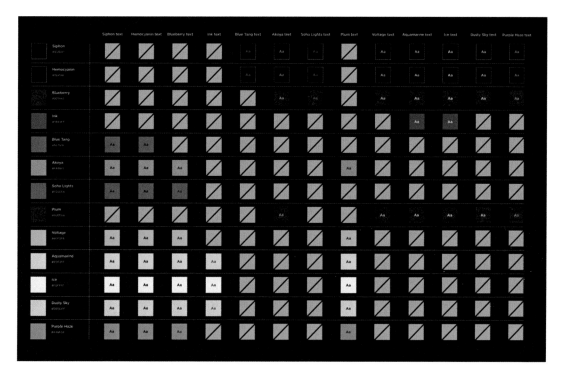

Figure 10-20. *An accessibility chart from Octopus Energy's design system "Coral." It's a grid that shows which color combinations can be used, as they pass contrast checks, and which cannot.*

There is an accessibility chart (shown in Figure 10-20 above) to show which color combinations do and don't work together to pass contrast checks, so it's always clear and easy to know what's possible. We have required parameters for components around things like titles, links, and focus states, which we covered earlier as being particularly useful for catching some of the most common a11y issues on sites. Furthermore, alongside our documentation of individual components, we have a gallery of common *pages*. This allows developers to implement core pages and features quickly in a way that has already been tested and confirmed to be both accessible and enjoyable to use. By doing this, you're giving someone a pre-built car made of Lego blocks rather than simply giving them the blocks each time and hoping that they build a car correctly. It helps with speed, and it helps with accessibility. An example of one of these pages is shown in Figure 10-21 below.

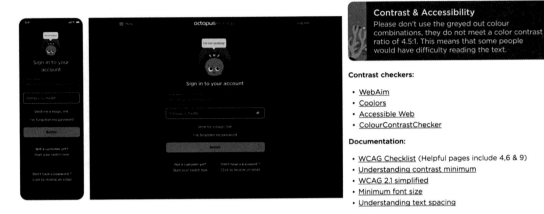

Figure 10-21. *Two sections from Octopus Energy's Coral documentation. On the right, there's a "Contrast & Accessibility" section that provides a reading and tool list, and on the left, there's a visual of a full login page, made up of Coral components, and how it should look when keyboard focus is on the password field.*

Personal Thoughts

I'm in favor of the implementation of component libraries. I think they require some prior thought before using a third-party one though, as well as a healthy skepticism that what they're doing is better or more in tune with your users than you could be.

The spirit of this book is not making a11y someone else's problem, so you shouldn't believe that you've solved this issue for your sites just because you're using a mature component library like Material UI. However, the power of having thoroughly tested, albeit fallible components in your site, created publicly and reviewed by those with a11y experience, has the power to help many websites that are short on time, people, and knowledge in the area of accessibility. For that reason, if you're working in a small team or building quick prototypes, implementing a popular library would put you in good shape to achieve a base level of compliance quickly before setting off on deeper accessibility and usability testing.

When building a component library yourself, you take on more responsibility but can shape it in a way that caters purely to your users. It also has a powerful secondary effect: it teaches every person in your company how important a11y truly is – it's a standard you're maintaining every day, like your test coverage or conversion rate. This sends a great message to everyone. If your company is intending to scale to other sites, or your team is getting bigger and you want to avoid inconsistencies, then I'd consider building an internal component library. There are lots of great libraries online you can look to for initial inspiration, but then create something that is highly usable and uniquely yours. In doing so, it can act as your brand police, but also your accessibility champion.

I don't think it's ever too soon to develop a component library in a team or company; it simply comes down to whether you have the time to invest in one. That said, the earlier you do it, the more time it has to grow as a foundational tool within your company. They take work but scale fantastically, so the trade-off is a decision that is yours to make.

Whichever you choose, having building blocks that can be thoroughly tested, deployed to multiple sites and places, and updated synchronously when an accessibility issue is found has outsized benefits for you and your users.

Conclusion

You've learned about a lot of access needs throughout this book, and now you've learned the fact that there's no tool, platform, or system that will handle accessibility for you.

The overall spirit is this: there are methods and tools that may *aid* your process of achieving accessibility, but none of them can substitute the need to understand the topic and work on it yourself. When it comes to things like overlays, they may actually take you *further* away from the inclusivity you're seeking, without bringing you any closer to understanding what your users need. When it comes to using a website builder, you may start with an accessible template, but you'll need to understand accessibility enough to keep it that way as you add content. When it comes to a pattern library or design system, you can adopt accessible and well-tested components but still use them in an inaccessible way if you don't know how to test the way you've put those building blocks together.

It's this area that we'll now cover to complete our journey: how do you test and audit a website to find what's wrong and, given what you know now, how do you fix it and keep it fixed.

Tools and Auditing

After everything we've covered so far, you must be itching to start testing and improving your sites! Auditing is a vital part of the process of building any website – the more bugs and problems you can find and fix yourself, the lower the chance a user will encounter them instead. Perfecting this process is key to enabling *all* customers to use your site now and in the future.

Testing and auditing take on an added importance when it comes to accessibility. During conventional website use, a bug or design issue can lead to confusion or frustration for users, but for those with disabilities and access needs, these issues can prevent access altogether. Things as simple as missing attributes, a certain use of color, or a missing focus style can inhibit interaction entirely.

Even once you've learned about how to make a website accessible and managed to build it that way, websites tend to change frequently. This means that there is always the danger that new features can accidentally undo your hard work – becoming accessible is great, but staying there is paramount.

Now that you're ready to take the lessons we've covered and put them into action, I'd like to make it even easier! In this chapter, we'll cover a four-stage process that I use to take a website, and the team that made it, on a journey from inaccessible to accessible. This is something I call the **FAIR** framework, and it can make it easier for you to know where to start and how to best approach the challenge.

Within this process, you will also find my checklist called **ACCESS**. This is a series of tests and questions, based on points throughout the book, to quickly assess and improve the current accessibility of a site and its core functions. As starting a new site from scratch simply isn't an option most of the time, the combination of the **FAIR** framework and the **ACCESS** checklist can help you tackle this, ensuring a level of inclusion for all customers on an existing site.

© Ashley Firth 2024
A. Firth, *Practical Web Accessibility*, https://doi.org/10.1007/979-8-8688-0152-5_11

We'll also discuss how automation can make testing easier and is especially useful for convincing groups of developers to embrace accessibility. We'll look at how this makes testing more likely to be adopted consistently moving forward, thereby ensuring that your hard work implementing accessible standards isn't undone over time.

The FAIR Framework

Retrospective accessibility is hard. It shouldn't be a surprise at this point in the book that considering how people with various disabilities can access your content *while* you're designing and building a site goes a long way. On the other hand, arriving at a site that's been designed and built *without* these considerations can seem like a mountain to climb. Knowing what you know now about everything you need to consider, you may be asking yourself: "Where do I even begin?"

The honest answer is that it's tricky but far from impossible.

There's a well-known concept called the **Pareto principle** (better known as the **80/20 rule**). It says that 80% of consequences come from 20% of the causes (known as the "vital few"), and the remaining 20% comes from 80% of the causes.[1] If we think back to the start of the book, we discovered that **96.1%** of all accessibility errors on the home pages of the top one million sites online fall into just *six* categories.[2] These are our "vital few," and a lot of initial progress can be made with relatively little effort.

That being said, our journey through this book has been about catering to *all* and not to *most*. Therefore, it's important to not stop improving after removing a high volume of issues as volume doesn't necessarily relate to severity. However, being able to get the ball rolling quickly builds up confidence in tackling issues, a greater appreciation of why it's important, and a sense of sunk cost (you've gotten this far, so why not go all the way?).

With this in mind, I've developed a short, four-step framework for auditing and tackling the accessibility of an existing site. It's by no means full-proof, but it's a starting point, and sometimes that's most of what you need. These steps are

- **F – Fundamentals**
- **A – Awareness**
- **I – Implementation**
- **R – Reparations**

Together, they make **FAIR** because that's what it is! It's a site that ends up being fair for everyone. This is a four-step process that you can implement yourself or give to others who are at the start of their journey of understanding accessibility.

For each section, there will be some tools that you can use to check off the things on the list and ensure the site you're auditing is in good shape. Many of the tools will help with multiple sections though, so by the time you're done with the list, you'll have a large suite of tools you can refer back to at any time.

To make that reference even easier and to save you the time and effort of typing out website addresses from this book, I have added a link to every resource in this chapter's practical example. You can find the code for this in the "Chapter 11" folder of the GitHub repository or view it live by visiting `inclusive.guide/examples/tools`.

Now, let's go through the framework.

FAIR Framework – Fundamentals

The first step is fundamentals. We need to create a staggered approach that has practical aims and clear benefits from the **beginning**. You do this by handling the biggest, quickest wins to get your content up to a basic level of accessibility. They're the things that appear most frequently in any basic audit you would run and tend to be both the easiest ones to find and fix. If you haven't tested your site's accessibility before, chances are there will be a *lot* of errors. This step brings that initially intimidating number down to something far more manageable.

Our aim in this first step is twofold. Firstly, we want to clear the decks of anything that doesn't need to be judged in real depth by a human. In order to find these quickly, I've created a checklist of things based on the contents of this book, as simply knowing where to start can sometimes be the hardest challenge, particularly when a site is fairly large. These are categorized into six key areas that I have outlined in the following, and together they can be referred to as **ACCESS**:

- **A** – Aesthetics
- **C** – Content
- **C** – Cognition
- **E** – Ease of use
- **S** – Settings
- **S** – Specifics

405

Secondly, given that this may be the first step on many people's journey with auditing and accessibility, we need to ensure that the tools are engaging and, importantly, simple to use. This is why each part of the checklist is coupled with easy-to-use, low-effort tools that I myself take advantage of. The lower the barrier to entry on this step, the more likely it is that someone will maintain their commitment throughout the rest of the process and return to it again and again in the future.

Now, a **big** word of warning here – this list is not designed to be all-encompassing. It's a reflection of the most common and often most noisy errors in terms of volume, but you won't achieve a comprehensive level of accessibility using only this list. Many problematic items aren't included here due to the time it takes to solve them rather than their importance. This is why the **ACCESS** checklist exists *within* the **FAIR** framework: it's the starting point but by no means the end point.

With that being said, let's take a look at the checklist.

ACCESS Checklist – Aesthetics

- Is the base font size of your content big enough (16 pixels as a minimum is ideal)?

- Are the fonts you've chosen easy to read?

- Do you have a sensible line height on your text (1.5 times your font size is sensible)?

- Does the text and content of the site pass a standard WCAG color contrast check?

- Are links clearly underlined rather than only being noticeable through a change of color?

- Does anything on the site rely on color alone to convey meaning (e.g., a status message or graphs with colored segments)?

- Imagery

- Do all images being displayed have an `alt` attribute?

- Do purely decorative images have no `alt` text set so that they are ignored by screen readers?

- Do any images or text rely on each other for contextual meaning?

- Are there any images with text embedded in them (check any content management systems for uploaded images too)?

- Are you providing a text alternative for complex images such as charts, graphs, and maps?

- Do you have any animations on your site? If so, are they potentially excessive, too fast, distracting, and/or potentially harmful to users?

- Do any videos autoplay?

- Do any videos loop unnecessarily?

- Can videos, including background videos, be paused by the user?

- For designers, are there tools within their design process to ensure accessibility is considered from the start?

Tools

Browser Developer Tools

Web browsers are a tool that you work with every day when building and maintaining a website, so it stands to reason that they are among the best places to test accessibility too. Luckily, most modern browsers come complete with tools that help you do just that.

Here are the ways to bring up the developer tools in the major browsers at the time of writing and how to reach the accessibility section:

- **Google Chrome** – `View > Developer > Developer Tools (or by right-clicking and selecting "Inspect Element") > Accessibility`

- **Firefox** – `Tools > Browser Tools > Web Developer Tools > Accessibility`

- **Safari** – `Develop > Show Web Inspector (you may need to go to Safari ➤ Settings > Advanced and turn on "Show features for web developers" first) > Node > Accessibility`

- **Microsoft Edge** – `Pressing F12 > Elements (Accessibility tree will appear on the right)`

I'm going to focus on some quick and useful accessibility tools that exist inside the Google Chrome browser as it's by far the most used browser globally at the time of writing.

Lighthouse

Lighthouse is an open source tool that can audit the accessibility standards of any web page. It can also be run via the command line or as a "module" on your code, but most importantly, it's built into Google Chrome's web browser – you can find it in the "Audit" panel of the Web Inspector – meaning that many of you already have immediate access to it. Figure 11-1 shows you how to find this panel.

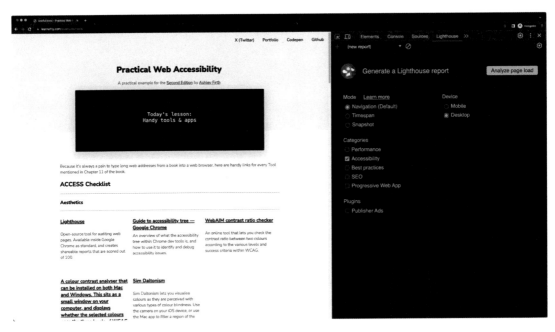

Figure 11-1. *A web page in Google Chrome, with the developer tools open on the "Audit" panel*

This is a brilliant first tool to try as it provides a full report on everything from correct ARIA use, valid HTML, foreground/background contrast ratio, and much more with just a couple of clicks.[3] Figure 11-2 shows the result of an audit like this, along with suggestions for ways that it found to improve the page.

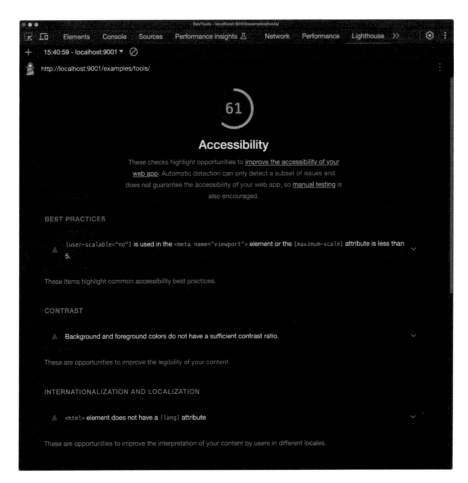

Figure 11-2. *An image of a Lighthouse accessibility audit from within Google Chrome, along with suggestions on improvements for the page it has audited*

Each issue has an explanation, as well as a link to further reading and instructions on how to solve it, so the tool gives you everything you need. Furthermore, Lighthouse tells you about all of the tests you've *passed*, as well as the ones that you've failed. Reports can be saved and shared with others easily, meaning that anyone with Google Chrome installed can perform basic accessibility testing in a matter of seconds, and share them with their colleagues.

Accessibility Tree

We covered in Chapter 2 "Blindness" that, with the web developer tools open, you can click any element within the page to understand and view its properties under the "Accessibility" panel (as shown in Figure 11-3).

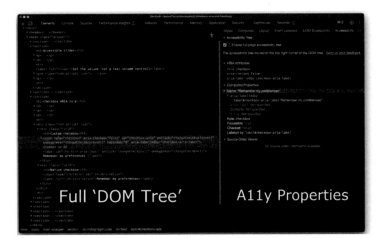

Figure 11-3. *An image of the Accessibility panel inside Google Chrome dev tools*

When an element is selected, it displays the accessibility "tree" that describes where a selected element sits within the context of the page, as well as any ARIA attributes present on the element, and any "computed" properties (ones that the element has applied to by default, such as its role).[4] This provides a visual of how those using screen readers would receive content, so you can ensure that it makes sense, and that content is correctly labeled and described.

Color Contrast

When you click a color from inside the developer tools, you can check the contrast levels between that color and the background color behind it. This is really useful because if your site is failing contrast ratio checks (which a Lighthouse audit would tell you), you might end up trying quite a few different foreground/background color combinations before finding one that passes.

To make this process easier, Google Chrome's dev tools have an interactive color picker (shown in Figure 11-4) that, as you move it, will automatically update to display the new contrast level. It also displays whether it passes AA and/or AAA compliance for contrast levels based on WCAG.

410

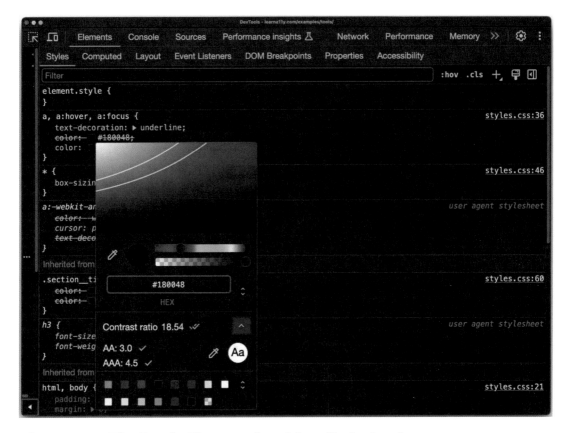

Figure 11-4. *The Google Chrome color picker, displaying the current contrast ratio of the color selected, along with lines for WCAG AA and AAA level contrast compliance*

My favorite part of this feature is the two lines displayed by the color picker – representing the minimum point of compliance for AA and AAA, respectively.[5] This takes a lot of the guesswork out of the process – you simply drag the color picker to below both lines and copy the new color code it provides, and suddenly you're AAA compliant!

This is especially useful as it's another tool that everyone using Google Chrome has access to, even if they're not a developer. Hypothetically a project manager, tester, or anyone else for that matter could run an accessibility audit on a site using their browser, identify a contrast ratio issue, and use the color picker to find a new color that is compliant. Suddenly you've spotted a problem, found a solution, and can give it to a designer or developer, all within a matter of moments.

Contrast Ratio Checkers

WebAIM Contrast Checker

For a more comprehensive and shareable contrast checker, WebAIM has created a site that shows whether your foreground and background colors pass AA and/or AAA WCAG contrast compliance, how the contrast level changes based on different text sizes, and whether the contrast is good enough to be used in "interface" components such as text inputs. On top of this, it gives you the option to use a slider to tweak your noncompliant colors to be lighter or darker until they pass. This is all shown in Figure 11-5.

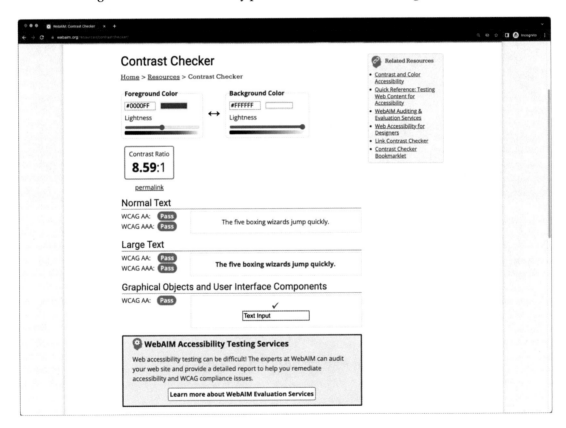

Figure 11-5. *The WebAIM contrast ratio website, showing the contrast level between two colors for normal text, large text, and user interface components*

Once you've found a combination that works, you can share a link with others that shows both of those colors, as well as all of the passing tests. Using this tool means that you can satisfy multiple colors-based WCAG rules and use that color confidently throughout your website. You can find this at webaim.org/resources/contrastchecker. They also have a separate tool dedicated to checking the contrast levels of links on websites as that has its own dedicated WCAG rule.[6]

TPGi Contrast Analyzer

If you prefer a standalone application instead of a website, then accessibility solutions provider TPGi has created a color contrast analyzer that can be installed on both Mac and Windows. This sits as a small window on your computer and displays whether the selected colors pass the three levels of WCAG contrast checks. It also allows you to edit the colors in the application and view a preview of that color scheme and has a swatch tool that allows you to select a color from anything on your screen (shown in Figure 11-6). You can view it at tpgi.com/color-contrast-checker.

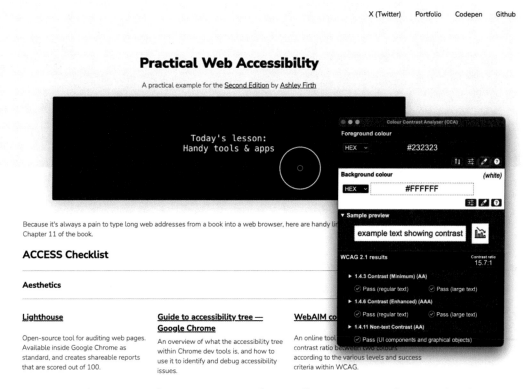

Figure 11-6. *The TPGi color contrast analyzer allows you to select a color from anywhere on the screen and compare its contrast to another color. It displays the contrast ratio and whether it satisfies each of the three WCAG levels.*

Sim Daltonism

For tests involving the dependence on color within a website, this great app by Michael Fortin allows you to overlay a window directly over *anything* you're viewing on a computer (as shown in Figure 11-7) and see a live preview of what it looks like for each form of color blindness. You can resize the window to any size, and it will sit on top of any browser, app, or document on your computer in order to better understand what those with color blindness see – it even offers a quick way to switch between different types. This app also has an iOS version, where you can use the device's camera to achieve the same result with any surroundings. You can find this at michelf.ca/projects/sim-daltonism or in the practical example for this chapter at `inclusive.guide/examples/tools`.

Figure 11-7. *A screenshot of the Sim Daltonism application overlaid on a browser, displaying everything within that window as a person with ritanopia would see it*

Design Tools

Later in the chapter, we'll go through the tools that will help keep accessibility front of mind for developers throughout the process of building a website, but what about design? For many teams, the process of building a site *begins* with a design, and as you

know accessibility is a topic that needs to be considered by *every* discipline in a team —
without it, developers may start building from an inaccessible design and may require
considerable back and forth between teams during the process that could be avoided.

Luckily, there are tools that allow for these things to be considered from the outset,
from *within* the tools designers use. At the time of writing, the popular design tools are
Figma, Sketch, and Adobe XD, and there are plugins available for each of these that
you can install to help you consider various parts of accessibility in your designs. This
includes, to name a few, things like

- Handling `alt` tags

- Checking color contrast

- Viewing a design in various strains of color blindness

- Labeling things using ARIA descriptions

- Designing for various user font size settings

Figma and Sketch also have public plugin libraries that you can bookmark in order
to keep an eye on future tools. I've placed the link for both of these, along with some
popular accessibility plugins for Adobe XD, in the practical example for this chapter. You
can find that at `inclusive.guide/examples/tools`.

ACCESS Checklist – Content

After checking the visuals of a site, it's time to review the state of the content and
underlying code. As you know, many assistive technologies rely on sensibly laid out and
semantic content in order to relay it correctly to users, and many users struggle with
large amounts of content written and displayed in certain ways. Let's make sure the site
you're auditing is doing everything it can to help these people:

- Make sure that your heading structure is logical and linear, starting
  with an `<h1>` and moving down without skipping levels.

- If you look purely at the headings on the page, do they accurately
  reflect **all** content on there?

- Ensure that no text is styled to look like a header without being
  a header.

- Is your HTML semantic, and does it use tags that help assistive technology understand its purpose? (`<nav>`, `<main>`, `<footer>`, etc.)

- Does the page have a unique title using the `<title>` tag?

- Ensure that there are no buttons or links without text in them.

- Does the page have a document language (`lang` attribute) set?

- Check for long bodies of text that can be condensed and moved into other formats.

- Are there large pieces of text that are center-aligned?

- Do any videos contain content that should have captions and/or subtitles?

- Is the content from videos also provided as a transcript separately?

- Check if videos are being served through platforms like YouTube and Vimeo and if so, that they handle closed captioning.

Tools

A quick reminder that you can find links for all of these tools in the practical example for this chapter (`inclusive.guide/examples/tools`).

Headings Map

Another useful tool that's always part of my checklist, the headings map extension generates a "tree" based on the headings on your page (Figure 11-8) and highlights any that are out of place in terms of hierarchy or have been skipped entirely.

Figure 11-8. *An example of the output from the HeadingMap browser extension, showing the heading hierarchy of the page. In this example, there is a jump from an h2 tag to an h4, and so the extension displays the h4 in red as it isn't semantic.*

It's important for both screen reader users and for SEO and so worth one click to check! With this visual, you can also compare it to your page's content to ensure that all sections on the page are reflected in the heading hierarchy.

Remember, if there's a section missing but you feel as though it doesn't need a heading based on the layout, add it and hide it visually. This will have no effect on most users but will greatly aid context and navigation for those using assistive technology.

Validity

This is a nice and simple extension to perform inline HTML validation checks on your pages, with the results being outputted to the browser console (yellow for warning, red for error). This extension is available in most modern browsers. Figure 11-9 shows an example of how page validation errors are displayed.

Figure 11-9. *The output of the Validity browser extension, shown in the browser's console, displaying issues with invalid and non-semantic HTML*

So many accessibility issues are introduced needlessly through the use of incorrect tags and attributes like ARIA, or the incorrect use of tags and markup. As simple as it sounds, having valid code prevents a lot of problems. The test itself is also a nice check-in to ensure that you're using tags that correspond well to the content on the page.

WebVTT Validator

In the chapter "Deafness and Hard of Hearing" (Chapter 5), we spoke a lot about the importance of providing subtitles and captions for your content. This approach was centered around creating your own using WebVTT. Here are two useful tools to ensure that you both create these files correctly and can make use of them in more than one way.

Firstly, you need to ensure that your `.vtt` files have been made correctly. You may encounter unexpected errors when trying to use them on your site or upload them to sites such as YouTube and Vimeo. Despite these errors appearing vague and somewhat ominous, they can often be caused by simple problems with syntax. Checking that they follow valid syntax will make sure that your good work won't go to waste. The W3C has created a simple, free tool where you paste in the contents of your WebVTT file, and it will assess whether it's valid. More importantly though, if there is a problem, it will let you know what you need to do in order to get it in working order. You can find this at `quuz.org/webvtt/` or in the practical example for this chapter at `inclusive.guide/examples/tools`.

Converting a WebVTT File into a Transcript

Now that you have working, valid WebVTT files, it'd be good if you could get them to work even harder for you! There are quite a few sites online that allow you to convert multiple types of caption files into a text file or transcript. This would allow you to provide them as a supplementary download or publish them alongside your audio and video content for those that don't want to interact with it directly.

A company called Happy Scribe offers the ability to convert between a range of caption formats for whichever platform you're using, but also converting a caption file into plain text so that you can also use it as a transcript. This makes it incredibly easy to provide multiple formats, and complete multiple WCAG rules, with little effort. You can find all of their tools at `happyscribe.com/subtitle-tools`.

Reading Time Calculator

As we covered in Chapter 6 "Cognitive Impairments," the "reading time" feature lets people know quickly how long it would normally take someone to get through what's on your page. Everyone reads at different speeds, but the rough agreed-upon average for an adult is **183 words** per minute.[7] Offering an approximate time is useful for setting user expectations and allows those with learning difficulties to decide when and how they interact with your content.

The "read time tool" allows you to paste in any text you've written in order to get an estimate of how long the average reader will take to read it. It's quick and useful for all users, and you can try it yourself at thereadtime.com.

ACCESS Checklist – Cognition

- Is the layout of content clear, linear, and easy to follow?

- Is there good continuity around the site? For example, are key site components like search and menus in the same place on every page?

- Does the site bombard users with too many features or options – things like adverts, overlays, or sign-up requests in a short space of time?

- Does the content use plain language, avoiding jargon or idioms, long sentences, and large words?

- Are there large amounts of content that you could provide a TL;DR (too long, didn't read) box for?

- Is there an overreliance on icons, and are the meanings of those icons clear? Are the icons that are used consistent?

- Does the site provide users with feedback when actions occur or changes are made?

- Is there any accidental coercion in the actions that you offer users – things like framing the option you don't want them to pick negatively or showing messages that encourage unnecessary urgency?

This is an important area to check, filled with important questions to ask, but not all of the items in this list are so clear-cut that a program or tool can tell us whether they're true or not. As a result, we need tools that still give us immediate, useful feedback that we can make a note of so that we ourselves can say whether there's action that needs to be taken. Let's go through a couple of my favorites.

Tools

Web Developer Extension

In Chapter 2 "Blindness," I mentioned that the easiest way for a sighted person to understand what a page's layout would be for those using screen readers would be to simply remove the styles of a page and see how the content was ordered.

For this, and *many* more things, Chris Pederick created the "Web Developer" browser extension, which does a tremendous job of visualizing a lot of the workings of a site *behind* the visuals. It's a free tool available on Google Chrome, Safari, and Firefox and is absolutely loaded with features that'll give you insightful accessibility feedback with a single click.[8] Here are a few common examples:

- **Disable all styles** – Quickly see the order of information as a screen reader would read it out to judge whether it makes sense and is ordered correctly.

- **Populate form fields** – Fills form fields in a journey with dummy information, allowing you to test journeys instantly, but also check the quality of user feedback and any pressure you may apply to them.

- **View form information** – Shows in a separate tab all of the form elements on a page, their type, and their labels. Allows you to quickly check if these are properly labeled and correct.

- **Display `alt` attributes** – Instantly check if `alt` text is present and whether the text itself is actually useful.

- **Outline images with empty `alt` attributes** – So you can ensure that only decorative images have blank alt attributes.

- **View color information** – Brings up a new page with the color code for every image on a page. Ideal for checking color contrasts.

- **Outline headings** – Check with a single click whether any "headings" are actually styled text instead.

Figure 11-10 shows how this looks in Google Chrome.

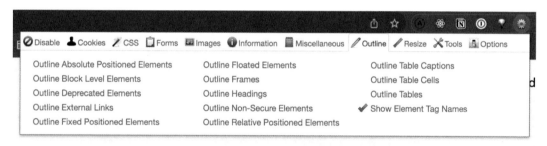

Figure 11-10. *The Web Developer extension offers a wide range of ways to alter a website's appearance or highlight parts of it, and many of these relate to understanding the accessibility of a web page. Once installed, you can activate it on any page with a single click.*

All of these can be turned on and run automatically as you move between pages, so you can test entire journeys under the same constraints quickly. It's also very simple for anyone to install and use, so you can share the more time-consuming tasks with other team members. You can find it at `chrispederick.com/work/web-developer`.

WAVE Evaluation Tool

Along the same lines, the WAVE evaluation tool is a browser extension powered by WebAIM that is handy for taking a more visual and interactive approach to accessibility. You can visit any website, and after activating the extension, WAVE will automatically inject a series of icons and indicators into the page (shown in Figure 11-11) to display not only errors and warnings but also accessibility features that are currently working, like HTML tags and ARIA attributes.[9]

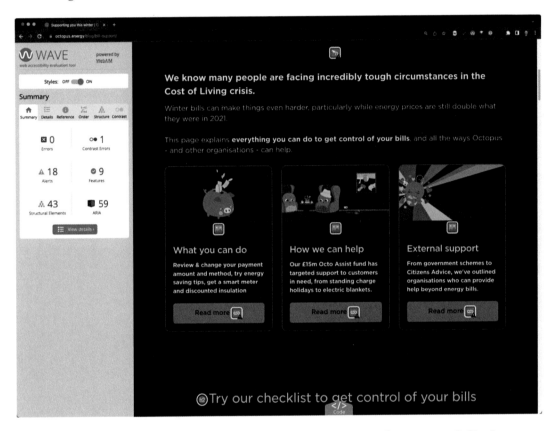

Figure 11-11. *A visual of the way in which the WAVE evaluation tool displays parts of a web page such as HTML5 tags and ARIA attributes*

For every warning and error, there's an explanation on the sidebar as to *why* something is an issue and a link to read in order to understand it further. They also have an "Order" tab that displays the order that a user navigating by keyboard or screen reader would interact with the elements.

This is a nice mixture of displaying what has been optimized alongside what could do with a bit more work – making the testing process a little less negative. It also forms a much tighter connection between an accessibility error and the part of the page it's happening on, which is great for people who are newer to testing.

Flesch-Kincaid Reading Ease Test

When writing copy that is fit for websites and emails, it's always worth making sure that your text is easy to read. One interesting way to test this – the Flesch-Kincaid readability test – was developed under contract for the US Navy in 1975. It was first used by the army for assessing the difficulty of technical manuals in 1978 and afterward became a military standard.[10]

Tech company Readable has created a free online tool using this test, which allows you to paste in text you've written and it will score it from 0 to 100 (with 0 being the most difficult to read and 100 being the easiest). Anything over 60 is considered a good score. This tool will also let you know where your content is letting you down with a scoring system based on factors like sentences with more than 30 syllables, words with more than 4 syllables, and even the amount of adverbs and clichés you include. You also have the opportunity to edit your text within the website, and it will update as soon as you make any changes, so you can instantly see if your score has improved or not. For more granular editing, the online "Hemingway Editor" highlights the specific parts of the text that are causing issues and provides guidance on how to reduce the complexity. You can find both in the practical example for this chapter at `inclusive.guide/examples/tools`.

Dark Patterns "Hall of Shame"

After we covered a range of "dark patterns" in Chapter 7 "Mental Health" that sites use to coerce and manipulate users into certain choices or actions, I mentioned that the man who coined the phrase, Harry Brignull, maintains a "hall of shame" on his website. There, you can see all of the user-submitted examples of dark patterns and the companies responsible for them.

It's used as a deterrent, but I'm placing it here as a tool. This gallery is massively informative for those who don't know what dark patterns are but also for us as website owners to check that nothing on that page rings true with the practices that we ourselves engage in. This is a particularly important tool if you maintain websites in businesses that place an emphasis on metrics like conversion and user drop-off. In these environments, changes made for the purpose of boosting metrics can often be at the expense of user well-being, often without realizing. This is what Amazon was found to have done, and I'm sure you don't want to be guilty of the same thing.

For that reason, head over to `deceptive.design/hall-of-shame` periodically – as awareness of the topic grows, more and more examples will undoubtedly be added.

ACCESS Checklist – Ease of Use

At this point in the checklist, our testing shifts from browser extensions and websites to slightly more involved use of assistive technology. This is required to find common errors that users of tools like screen readers and keyboard-only users encounter. It's also important to have that basic experience with tools that your users actually use as it gives you a deeper connection to the challenges they're facing.

However, these checks are still easy and quick to complete and will only become easier the more you test them. We're testing for common features and identifying basic additions and improvements to increase the ease of use of your site. It's a little more involved, which is why it's later in this checklist, but the effort is certainly worth it:

- Does a user have to wait a long time to hear the unique parts of the page they're on (if they're on a screen reader)?

- Have you added a "skip to main content" link on every page, which allows users to skip common content to what is unique on that page?

- Have you used the correct tags for the features within your page (e.g., a `<button>` tag for a button instead of an `<a>` link tag styled to look like a button)?

- Are buttons a sensible size (minimum 44 x 44px) to make them easier to interact with without the need for precision?

- Does every form element have a label that is associated with it, is that label visible, and is it connected to the form element in code?

- Are there any areas where you could make your journey more error-tolerant for the user (e.g., adding autocomplete on certain form inputs)?

- Do you allow autofill on your common forms like login or registration?

- When navigating using only a keyboard, is it clear where a user's focus is? Is the focus noticeable, and does it have good contrast?

- If a user opens a modal with a keyboard, is their focus moved, and can they close it?

- Do links and actions make sense by themselves, or are there a lot of examples of "Next" and "Click here"?

Tools

Screen Readers

We've spoken a lot about screen readers in this book, but very little about the options available to users and how to use them. Here is a quick overview of some of the main screen readers on the market, along with some complimentary tools that can help you learn how to operate them, and make content easier for those using them.

Apple Devices – VoiceOver

VoiceOver is built into every major Apple operating software (MacOS, iOS, tvOS, watchOS) and provides audible assistance for blind and visually impaired users on everything from personal computers to wearable technology. VoiceOver is also completely free, giving anyone easy access, including yourself for testing.

Google Devices – TalkBack

The Android equivalent to VoiceOver, Google TalkBack, is an accessibility service that handles user interactions with both the Android operating system and the Web. Google has a full overview of TalkBack, its features, and how to enable it in their Android Accessibility section – I've added this link to the practical example for this chapter, which you can find at `inclusive.guide/examples/tools`.

Windows – JAWS

JAWS (Job Access With Speech) is the world's most popular screen reader. It can be installed to read the screen with text to speech but also has a wide array of features (such as refreshable braille display compatibility). It's an application that you pay for on a subscription basis, with the cost depending on your circumstances.[11]

Windows – NVDA

NVDA (Non-Visual Desktop Access) is a free screen reader that was initially developed due to the large cost of other options. It was once considered a "last resort" because it lacked several key features present in screen readers like JAWS, but it has now been fleshed out to include a comparative list of capabilities. It doesn't have a support network that mirrors that of JAWS, but it does represent a free, popular option.

Windows – Narrator

The native Windows screen reader, Narrator, has been part of Windows since Windows 2000 but was only originally designed as a way to help users install a fully featured screen reader. It is available in multiple languages and is also included on all Windows phones. You can learn more about it in Windows' "Complete Guide to Narrator" – you can find this in the practical example for this chapter.

Learning How to Use a Screen Reader

Whichever application you choose to set up, it can take a little time to get used to actually navigating a device using a screen reader. To shorten that learning curve, Deque University published and maintained a series of excellent guides and shortcuts that you can use as a reference until you feel comfortable. They explain the best combinations of screen reader and browser for testing, covering all of the popular options, and many have been condensed to single-page guides that you can print out or have open.

The best starter resource is their "Screen Readers Survival Guide" that shows basic commands and shortcuts for JAWS, NVDA, Narrator, and VoiceOver, so you know how to easily replicate the same behavior on each as you test. The full suite of guides can be found at dequeuniversity.com/screenreaders.

When it comes to assistive technologies, there is no substitute for firsthand experience. Getting comfortable using a screen reader is the easiest way to familiarize yourself with the barriers that those with blindness and significant sight loss face online.

Testing with Screen Readers

You may have spotted an issue earlier that relates to a lot of teams: some of these tools are only available on certain operating systems. This can make testing difficult if you're unfamiliar with a system and expensive if you don't yet have a device that runs that system. For example, the two most popular screen reader programs are JAWS and NVDA, and these are both Windows-only, so on a Mac, you wouldn't be able to test them. Luckily, there is a tool that solves this problem for us.

A company called Assistiv Labs allows you to manually test a range of assistive software directly from your browser by remotely connecting to real assistive technologies. Through this tool, you can conduct manual testing using

- A range of popular Windows and Mac screen readers (VoiceOver, NVDA, JAWS)

- Display modes like Windows High Contrast Mode

- Screen magnifiers

The ability to quickly test a feature on a range of different assistive technologies without setting them up is a huge time-saver that wasn't previously possible. This ease also means that you can conduct testing from any computer and provide the same ease of use for the rest of your team, meaning that a huge barrier that might have prevented them from testing in the first place is gone.

Now this is a paid service, but compared to what it would take financially to replicate what they offer, as well as the effort required to keep it up to date moving forward, the cost is very reasonable. You can find out more at assistivlab.com.

For those who can't afford to do that, or who would like to understand more about the process of setting up screen readers, Sara Soueidan has written a comprehensive guide on how to set up various screen readers on desktop and mobile devices. You can find this at `sarasoueidan.com/blog/testing-environment-setup`.

A Keyboard!

Not all testing requires a dedicated piece of software or a license. I mentioned in Chapter 4 "Motor Impairments" that one of the best tests you can carry out is to simply move your mouse to the side and try navigating the pages and journeys within your site using only a keyboard. It should be possible to do this and clear at all times where your keyboard focus currently sits.

I wanted to raise this again here as not only does it not require any paid license or specialist software to accomplish, but it's such a low barrier of entry for those testing accessibility for the first time. I've found that giving someone this task, using an input device that they often use daily, creates a real fascination around the different ways that people engage with content. This is one of the big challenges: getting people interested in the world of accessibility so that they'll engage with it more and more in the future.

ARIA Authoring Processes Guide

In the top one million websites, WebAIM found a correlation between the use of ARIA and the number of accessibility issues on a page.[12] In Chapter 2 "Blindness," we covered how incredibly important it is to make a site as easy to use as possible, particularly for those using assistive technologies, but more information is clearly needed to ensure that happens – misused ARIA can often be more disruptive than not using it at all.

Because of this, the W3C has created a site to help people understand and implement ARIA correctly. It features patterns, practices, and guides for the correct use of ARIA, including the correct use of landmark roles, accessible names and descriptions, structural roles, and more. I highly suggest looking through it to explore all the possible additions you can make as you assess your site. You can find it at `w3.org/WAI/ARIA/apg`.

ACCESS Checklist – Settings

Here we ensure that users can change or adapt parts of their experience with you to cater to their needs or preferences. A lot of them will require you to edit the settings on your device or browser to simulate these changes. This is an excellent exercise as, like the keyboard exercise above, it requires no specialist software or license to perform and anyone can perform it. Furthermore, given that most settings of this kind are kept in the same place, it's a handy area to keep an eye on for future settings that are offered to the user:

- Does the site work well when using applications like forced colors mode/Windows High Contrast Mode?

- For those without applications like this, do you offer a way to invert or alter color schemes, including automatically by tapping into the `prefers-color-scheme` preference?

- Does the site respond well to changes in a user's font setting? If not, consider using relative units such as `em` or `rem` for your sizing and not pixels (`px`).

- Does the web page allow for zooming content (at least up to 200%)? And does it adapt to prevent the need for horizontal scrolling?

- When a user is zoomed in, are there large gaps between content where a user could get lost?

- Does content use the `lang` attribute so that it can change based on a user's language of choice?

- If you have any animations on your site, could they be removed or reduced based on user preference through `prefers-reduced-motion`?

- Could your site adapt to other user preferences such as `prefer-reduced-contrast` or `prefers-reduced-transparency`?

- Are you relying on a third-party service for your accessibility, such as Recite Me or AccessiBe?

Tools

Persona Profiles

A few years ago, the UK Government Digital Service (GDS) launched their "persona profiles." These "personas" represent hypothetical users with a range of access needs and are designed to encourage people involved in the building of websites to consider how these users would interact with those sites.

Each persona is free to download and comes with a list of devices that they have access to, the goals that they hope to achieve online, and the frustrations that they typically encounter when trying to complete those goals. These profiles encourage people to consciously test with a mindset different from their own by using **only** the tools that a particular persona uses to complete certain actions on their website.

In line with the aim of this book, by considering a user's unique tools and access needs as you design and develop, you're better placed to build an accessible site. At the time of writing, here are the available personas:

- **Ashleigh** – Partially sighted screen reader user

- **Christopher** – User with rheumatoid arthritis

- **Claudia** – Partially sighted screen magnifier user

- **Pawel** – User with Asperger's

- **Ron** – Older user with multiple conditions

- **Saleem** – Profoundly deaf user

- **Simone** – Dyslexic user

Internally, the GDS uses these personas regularly, where they have their designers and developers attempt to complete certain actions within an **hour** using a persona's devices and tools of choice.[13]

The aim is to not only discover bugs in what they've developed (the absence of bugs is, of course, also a win) but also appreciate the effort often required to complete routine tasks and hopefully find ways to reduce that. In my opinion, it's an extremely useful task that everyone should try – it will help you keep access needs in mind, and nothing motivates you to make an experience more accessible than learning more about the struggles people face. The link to these profiles is in the practical example for this chapter, which you can find at inclusive.guide/examples/tools.

Empathy Lab

An empathy lab is a great place to try out a lot of persona profiles. It's a space that contains a range of technologies, from specialist software to devices whose settings mirror those used by people with certain disabilities, so that people involved with website design and development engage with the barriers faced by users with certain access needs more directly.

The GDS set up a lab just like this, and it is open to anyone from the public sector – they also regularly get people to come in and test the technologies for free.[14] Their lab has devices that attempt to mirror access needs themselves, such as goggles that simulate different visual impairments and noise-cancelling headphones to simulate partial hearing loss. The idea behind this is that every time it's used, awareness is raised. Figure 11-12 shows the lab.

Figure 11-12. *An image of GDS's Accessibility Empathy Lab. It features a range of device to test websites on, as well as tools like magnifying glasses, headphones, and specialist glasses in order to simulate a range of disabilities and access needs.*

An empathy lab is a potentially costly investment but provides the opportunity to expose a lot of people to the circumstances that many face every day. If you're part of a large company with lots of people who work on sites, this is something to seriously consider with your leaders – they can provide a space for training, showcase your commitment to accessibility, and make understanding the topic part of your company's DNA. If creating one for your own company (or personal) use is out of the question, the GDS is just one example of an empathy lab that can be booked out, giving you access to some great facilities.[15]

ACCESS Checklist – Specifics

At this point, you've covered the main bases of how your site and content can be accessed by people with a range of disabilities, the ease of use of your core pages and journeys, and how your site can adapt to its users. This means that, if you were to run another series of tests and audits, they would return a significantly lower number of errors. Clearing this noisy, low-hanging fruit means that you've earned yourself enough breathing space to start tackling the topic in more depth – your site might not be perfect, but you've put in the initial effort, got the ball rolling on improving it, and you're ready to go into specific use cases and deeper problems – the 20% requiring the 80% effort. For that, we need to start the next stage of our FAIR framework: awareness.

FAIR Framework – Awareness

After this first stage, your site will be in a much healthier place, which gives those working on it a license to go beyond the basics of accessibility and explore the topic itself. Often I find that after identifying and fixing a lot of these basic issues, the knowledge of those who've done that is still limited – you can fix errors without understanding **why** they were a problem or importantly **how** to prevent them again in the future.

This is expected because the immediate and primary aim of the process is to make life easier for your users. However, to fully achieve that, we also need to *understand* the topic enough to do that in detail moving forward. Without it, a team will end up fixing the same issues again and again.

Therefore, this stage is dedicated to learning and awareness. In order to go beyond what's listed in the **ACCESS** checklist, we need to start thinking about specific access needs or scenarios where there is no automated test you can run. Instead, it relies on you truly understanding the barriers in order to identify and fix them.

Each area on following the list offers a deeper dive and a larger learning curve. They should be tackled one at a time, in no particular order, and the issues you find and what you learn should be documented for yourself and shared with those you work with. Right now we're focused on awareness, so we're not fixing, just finding. This makes it a process of growth for everyone, which builds the collective knowledge of the topic. In certain cases, learning about them may provide an understanding of why certain things you've already fixed were a problem in the first place.

Each item has already been covered in the book, so to make life easier, I've noted which chapter you should head back to for each one when you come to it.

- Try testing core journeys and pages using only a screen reader, listening to the whole page and noting anything confusing, unclear, or missing to fix (**Chapters 2 and 11**).

- Test journeys using only a keyboard, ensuring the journey is possible, the tabbing order is sensible, and it doesn't contain "keyboard traps" where users can't exit content (**Chapter 4**).

- If you are relying on a pattern library or design system for your site's style, review their approach to accessibility and whether it's suitable (**Chapter 10**).

- Testing journeys simulating various strains of color blindness (**Chapter 3**).

- If your site has a light theme, consider implementing your own dark mode that listens to user settings, as well as a theme switcher (**Chapter 3**).

- If you're using animation tied to scrolling like the parallax effect, ensuring that they can be removed through settings like `prefers-reduced-motion` (**Chapter 8**).

- Making sure that form input errors are displayed either inline or above the form after submission, rather than at the top of the page (also use `aria-live` to indicate a change in status) (**Chapter 2**).

- Checking for fixed elements on your site that could obscure focusable elements as you tab between them (**Chapter 4**).

- Ensuring that your site adapts well to a range of screen sizes and device orientations (**Chapter 4**).

- For parts of your journey that rely on gestures like swiping, shaking, or dragging, create an alternate way to achieve those actions (**Chapter 4**).

- Creating BSL-friendly captions for video content or signers overlaid on the video itself (**Chapter 5**).

- For your journeys that impose a time limit on users, add the ability to extend and control those limits (**Chapter 4**).

- Explore the benefits that breadcrumbs could have in your design, either to prime users for the steps in a journey or to help them understand the position of the page they're on within the wider site (**Chapter 6**).

Notice that we're focusing on usability here before thinking about compliance. Completing these tasks is typically harder than ticking the relevant boxes in a particular WCAG level, but the end result is far more impactful to a disabled user's ability to use our site.

This is the part where we also celebrate what you've done throughout this book. Your commitment to accessibility means that you've already completed the learning required for this step and have a strong understanding of the topic and what to consider for a range of access needs. This will make it easier for you to complete the list earlier by putting what you've learned into action and take others through the process of doing the same.

For others, you could recommend they read this book themselves to improve their understanding (which would be lovely) or start them off with some of the items from the reading list from each chapter if you think they learn better piece by piece.

FAIR Framework – Implementation

After improving awareness about the hows and whys of accessibility and completing a series of deeper dives on our site's usability, we now have a better understanding of the topic, as well as a range of deeper, specific issues that we need to solve from the list earlier. With this information, and the easier issues already fixed earlier, it's time to put everything we know into action.

In the implementation step, we start to become more methodical about what we're fixing and aiming for and the process of fixing it but also how to get there and *stay* there. With websites constantly being updated with new content, new branding, and new developers, you could easily find that your site doesn't quite hit the high expectations you set for it six months from now when it comes to accessibility.

This is where levels such as WCAG can actually be useful. We spoke at the start of the book about using WCAG compliance as a baseline for success when aiming for accessibility: you start by conforming to standards that cover well-known barriers and issues that users face and then move forward toward building truly inclusive websites. At this stage in the process though, they can act as important checkpoints to mark progress and clear goals for you and your team to aim for.

You can then extend your WCAG level goal with anything from your awareness stage deep dives **not** featured in that list. They may be part of a higher WCAG level, or not listed at all, but they should still be fixed.

This is another exercise in building momentum, and it's why this is my favorite step – the time you invest here means that all of your hard work up until this point doesn't go to waste. You set yourself a standard that you and your team rise to and put mechanisms in place to ensure that you won't fall below it again.

Here is a checklist for a site hoping to implement a good level of accessibility but also instill some long-term accessibility practices:

- Identify the core journeys and high-traffic pages that you and your team are going to focus on. Try and make this list comprehensive, and if possible, lean on your website analytics to build it – we're aiming to have the most impact possible. If you have a small site, you can apply this process to every page you have live.

- Choose an initial level of accessibility compliance (I would recommend WCAG 2.2 AA, as this is considered a good level of compliance – all government sites have to adhere to this).

- With your level chosen, familiarize yourself with all the criteria at that level and the levels **below** that (e.g., to be WCAG AA compliant, you must *also* satisfy every rule in WCAG A level as well).

- Add to this success criteria list anything from your awareness stage deep dives **not** featured in that list.

- Identify an "accessibility champion" in each team or business function you work in – someone to always be asking "is this accessible" and keeping the topic in the forefront of people's minds. Eventually, the aim is for everyone to be a champion, but this is a handy thing to have at the beginning of the journey.

- Decide on a testing and review practice you and your team can conduct routinely moving forward.

- For the preceding process, work out how to ensure that any new content you're releasing is up to the standard you've set for yourself as it allows you to start as you mean to go on – there's no use publishing inaccessible content as quickly as you can fix the content you already have.

For this stage to be successful, especially with those last two points, you need tools that can hold you and your team accountable at *every* step of the build process of a website – when the code is being written, when you test and review it, and when it's live for users. Let's go through the tools that can help you accomplish that and the benefit of having many of those run automatically.

Automating Your Accessibility Testing

Manual testing is not a bad thing – manually performing actions can help make them routine so that eventually they can be done with relatively little effort, and it can also help you understand needs and barriers. However, considering how many people are sometimes involved in building a website, you can often end up in a situation where not everyone remembers to (or wants to) expend the effort to maintain accessible standards.

This is obviously something that needs to be solved, but you don't want to go to the effort of learning how to test and improve a site's accessibility, and then the *additional* effort of teaching everyone else in your team or company, only for accessibility to gradually fade away over time. As we said in the introduction, many people involved in building websites work under very tight schedules and deadlines – if those running one project decide that they don't have the time to check accessibility, these issues can snowball. To combat this, it can be useful to automate, or at least streamline, as much of the testing and quality assurance process as you can.

Automated accessibility testing is a huge time-saver, it doesn't require special expertise, and it allows teams to focus expert resources on the accessibility issues that really need them. Automation is commonly used to run tests on code and make sure everything is working as expected, and the same concept applies here. You can do the same thing to ensure that any changes that have been made to a website don't create new accessibility issues (or bring back old ones). Here are a few good examples of ways you can automate your accessibility testing:

Axe-core

You can't speak about accessibility testing without axe-core. This is because most tools that check for accessibility issues use it under the hood. It's open source, and so completely free, and is the most popular testing engine in the world, with millions of downloads every week.[16]

With axe, accessibility testing can be performed against any WCAG version or level and as part of any functional testing your team already performs on a day-to-day basis. This means that when a developer writes tests for their code to make sure that it works as expected, they can also write accessibility tests. This association with something that's already part of the development process increases the likelihood that it'll become a practice moving forward. This makes it the best tool if you run a team of developers and want to champion accessibility. It also means that, once these tests are written, they can be run automatically when future code changes are made and will flag if those changes break the tests.

Axe claims that it can find, on average, **57%** of WCAG issues automatically. It will also return elements as "incomplete" where axe-core couldn't be certain and suggest a manual review instead. They also maintain a browser extension you can install to run tests on a live website if you're not a developer (or haven't had a chance to write tests yet), much like Lighthouse that we mentioned earlier (picture in Figure 11-13).

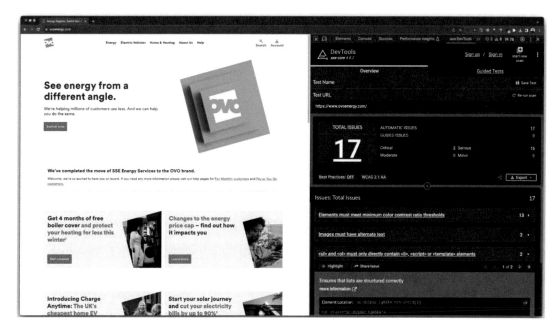

Figure 11-13. *The axe-core browser extension is available in the "axe DevTools" tab of your browser's Web Inspector once it's been installed. It can show you issues with your web page, ordered by severity, and allow you to test against a range of compliance levels.*

Lighthouse actually uses axe-core to run its tests but runs fewer tests than axe, so you can think of this tool as a good step up once you've gotten comfortable with Lighthouse. Axe also maintains extensions for code editors so that it can flag accessibility issues for developers *as* they're writing code.

So Why Would You Use Other Tools?

Well firstly, using axe-core requires you to write tests yourself. This is a great thing to do, as you can run it on things that are specific to your website, but it does take time – both to write the tests and learn how to write them correctly. This is where you want your development teams to get to, but you also want to make accessibility improvements in the meantime.

Secondly, other teams have used axe-core as the foundation to create tools that can exist at different stages of your development process. This means that they can help you in similar ways but in different situations. There are two tools that I think complement the use of axe-core well, and that's AccessLint and Pally.

AccessLint

Use AccessLint to hold on to the hard-earned progress you've made with accessibility, or to inspire your team to start chipping away at issues. That frees you from costly bug-fixes and remediation, and socializes accessibility to your team.[17]

AccessLint (accesslint.com) is an accessibility bot built on axe-core that can be added to a GitHub project (like the one that contains all of the practical examples for this book) and reviews any potential changes to code to ensure that it doesn't contain any accessibility issues.

When someone wants to make a change to a website in GitHub, they open what is known as a "pull request." This request shows the difference between the current site code and what has been added, altered, or deleted. What AccessLint does is automatically cast an eye over any pull request made and, using WCAG guidelines, checks for any problems that could break those rules. For example, in Figure 11-14, a developer has tried to add an image as part of a "pull request," but it doesn't have an `alt` attribute, so AccessLint comments on that line of code to raise the issue.

Figure 11-14. *A screenshot of some advice that AccessLint has left on a GitHub pull request, suggesting that the new* `<img>` *tag that's been added needs an* `alt` *attribute*

It even offers a link for how (and why) you need to solve the issue to help those making changes understand the importance and in this case even offers tips on how to write good `alt` text – neat!

What's also great is that when an issue has been raised, and the person changing the code goes back and *makes* the recommended alterations, AccessLint will check the code again and let them know if the problem is now fixed. In Figure 11-15, a user has fixed an AccessLint suggestion.

Figure 11-15. *A screenshot of AccessLint congratulating someone on fixing an accessibility issue that it had spotted*

AccessLint only adds comments on pull requests rather than stopping new code from being used until the issues it finds are fixed. This is useful because adding something incredibly strict could cause frustration for developers and would likely be removed. However, it still provides consistent advice, visible to all developers, in a way that prevents them from having to search around to discover *how* to solve the problem. Implemented in this unobtrusive way, using AccessLint can quickly become second nature when submitting new code.

AccessLint is free for all open source projects and for projects for educational purposes. They also offer a free trial for any other project so you can try it out.[18]

Pa11y

If AccessLint becomes a developer's friend after they've submitted code, then Pa11y (pa11y.org) is their friend as they write it. With one command, developers can automate a whole range of accessibility tests and receive immediate feedback on any issues that they can then fix before submitting their code. Figure 11-16 shows this command in action.

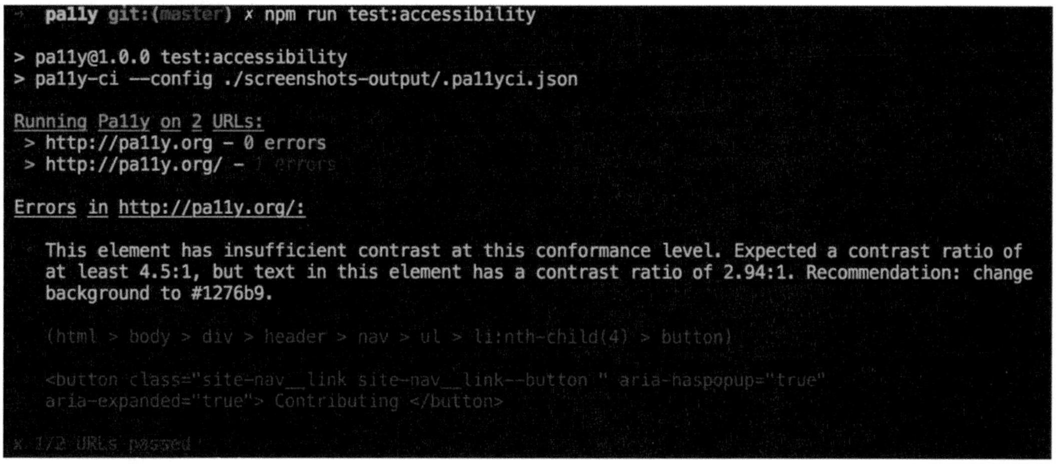

```
→  pa11y git:(master) x npm run test:accessibility

> pa11y@1.0.0 test:accessibility
> pa11y-ci --config ./screenshots-output/.pa11yci.json

Running Pa11y on 2 URLs:
 > http://pa11y.org – 0 errors
 > http://pa11y.org/ – 1 errors

Errors in http://pa11y.org/:

   This element has insufficient contrast at this conformance level. Expected a contrast ratio of
   at least 4.5:1, but text in this element has a contrast ratio of 2.94:1. Recommendation: change
   background to #1276b9.

   (html > body > div > header > nav > ul > li:nth-child(4) > button)

   <button class="site-nav__link site-nav__link--button " aria-haspopup="true"
   aria-expanded="true"> Contributing </button>

 x  1/2 URLs passed
```

Figure 11-16. *A terminal output, showing Pa11y running on two URLs and displaying the accessibility issue for the one that failed*

This is a different style of testing to axe-core, so you will see benefits from running both on your site. To make life easier, these tests can be set up to run every time a developer saves a file they're working on. The main benefit to using Pa11y is how configurable it is – you can specifically choose which rules from the large number available to follow.[19] This is a big win as it allows you to gradually adopt more accessible standards in stages (like moving between the WCAG levels, or even adding one rule at a time) rather than all at once (which can cause a lot of pushback). This sort of consistent exposure and granular control accessibility rules makes it easier than ever to make it a common part of a development process.

One of my favorite parts of Pally is that it comes with a set of available "actions." These mimic the sort of behavior that a user would make on a page, such as clicking a button or inputting form information. This means that rather than just testing the page as it *appears*, Pally can also see if any accessibility issues occur at different stages in a user's journey through your website and can handle password-protected pages too.[20] You can also get Pally to capture a picture of the page that it's tested for so that you can understand the visuals of an issue as well as the text for the rule.

If you set up axe-core, Pally, and AccessLint with the same rules, you can create an environment where developers have immediate, hassle-free access to accessibility rules and solutions as they're writing and testing code, plus a noninvasive reminder of those same rules when they submit it.

Tracking Your Progress

As you've probably noticed, this process is not an immediate one. It's going to take time to cover the four steps, the checklist, and the infrastructure to ensure that you and your team are set up for success moving forward when it comes to accessibility.

As a result, the most successful way I've seen companies tackle this is iteratively and methodically. They set themselves a goal based on the state of their site and work toward it. I mentioned earlier that levels of WCAG compliance can be helpful in that they can act as important checkpoints to mark progress and clear goals for you and your team to aim for.

To keep on top of that progress, and make it a public goal that **everyone** can see, Pally also has a dashboard tool that you can set up for your site (shown in Figure 11-17).

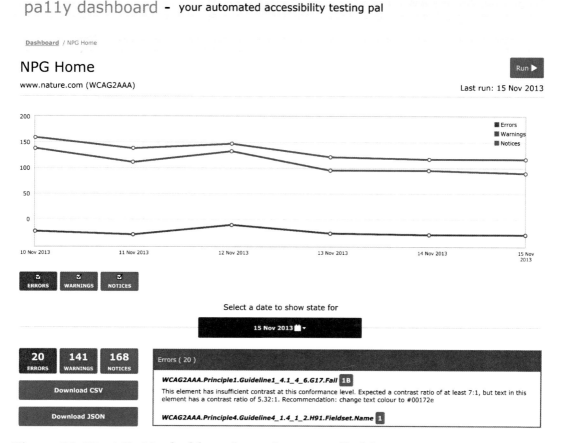

Figure 11-17. *A Pa11y dashboard can show you all of the current errors, warnings, and notices that you currently have on your website. It also shows you how those numbers have changed over time, and you can download that information at any time.*

Based on the compliance level you're currently aiming for, as well as additional rules you've chosen from your awareness stage, it'll detail the errors and warnings left on your site, as well as a graph of how the amount of errors has reduced over time. For those that have more than one site they're working on, the dashboard can accommodate multiple sites with different compliance levels, so you can track your journey in accessibility across the board. To look into how to set it up, head to `github.com/pa11y/pa11y-dashboard` (the link is also in the practical example for this chapter).

443

How to Meet WCAG (Quick Reference)

To help you decide the WCAG compliance level you will aim for and understand what that level entails, the W3C created a handy site – the WCAG quick reference site. It includes all of the guidelines, success criteria, and techniques and failures, organized to make navigating and finding success criteria and their relevant supporting documents easier.

Unsurprisingly, it's still a rather long document with a lot of associated links and descriptions in each section, but it's well laid out, has good examples, and allows you to filter content based on whether you're focused on design, development, or content creation. A lot of the WCAG criteria have been covered in this book, but as I mentioned, it's not an exhaustive list of everything. For the most up-to-date guidance moving forward, head to `w3.org/WAI/WCAG22/quickref`.

Accessibility Statement

When going through this process, it's also important to notify your customers of your progress: what you're aiming for, that you're not where you want to be, and to reach out if they find anything impossible on your site. This is most commonly handled through publishing an accessibility statement, which you can typically find in the footer of most websites. The UK government has a nice sample statement you can adapt for your own use, which I've added to the practical example for this chapter (found at `inclusive.guide/examples/tools`).

Nobody is expecting you to be flawless because it's impossible. With sites growing and expanding all the time, and more and more people contributing toward them, issues will inevitably arise. If you're transparent in that admission and persistent in your progress toward better, that will resonate with people.

FAIR Framework – Reparations

At this point, you have a good, accessible foundation for your site, some deeper knowledge of tools and access needs, and have introduced some good practices into your workflows. Now it's time to cast a wider net for the remaining issues within the site. We take everything we now know and throw it at the remaining content on your site that **wasn't** focused on earlier in the process. This includes pages that aren't in your core journeys or don't receive the highest traffic, but are still used, and may also throw up issues that have still persisted despite your earlier work. This typically includes things like

- Old blogs

- Press releases

- Policy pages

- Older campaigns

- Low-traffic journeys

- Legacy features that are still used

Importantly, it's also a good time to remove anything that *doesn't* need to be on your site. This prevents barriers between your users and your site and improves the general quality of what remains.

For this stage, Experte has created a neat tool where you provide the home page of your website, and it will crawl through all other public pages within that domain to find accessibility issues. It's not all-encompassing in the issues it checks for, but it runs through some of the most common ones and can check up to 500 pages. You can find this at `experte.com/accessibility`.

There's a reason we haven't used this tool before this point in the process. Doing this at the *beginning* of your accessibility journey would likely yield an alarmingly large list of errors. Across a large site, this can be a rude awakening but also something that would actually **prevent** action: where on earth would you start with a list of thousands of issues?

If you like, you could perhaps run one before you begin your improvement process as a benchmark in order to show just how far you've come when you run it again after all of your hard work.

With this done, and everything you've learned applied to *all* pages on your site, you and your team have taken your site as far as you can. However, this isn't the end of the process. With WCAG being useful but not comprehensive, and your team and tools able to identify lots of issues but not *all* of them, it's still likely that there are barriers preventing some people from using your site completely. For that, you need some experts.

Testing with Users

> Who better to test for accessibility than the people who need it most? They have practical life experience using assistive technologies...and they know where their pain points are. They are the real experts in disability access to the web, because they live it.[21]

This is the final part of reparations and the final step in the process. All of your work has been in service of getting your site to a point where users who are experienced in assistive technology can assess how possible it is to use it. I have spoken to a lot of charities, experts, and developers over the years, and all agree that when ensuring accessibility, nothing matches the honest feedback of someone who lives with a disability every day. It's the cornerstone of all accessibility testing we conduct at Octopus Energy.

This final step allows you to understand more about how people who are *familiar* with assistive technology use it, how they navigate, and the things that block them. This is the gold standard for testing, and no tool, automated or manual, can replace it.

Types of User Testing

There are a few ways in which you can engage more with these users. The first, and most obvious one, is to reach out to your own users. They're the ones that will benefit most from your improvements, and whatever changes you make (good or bad) will impact them deeply. Asking for feedback not only yields a group of willing testers but also shows that you care about them and their experiences online. Alternatively, you could run your own testing session, where you bring a group of people together to test a new product or feature at the same time. You could also engage with professional testers or a company who can facilitate a testing session for you.

For running your own testing session, the UK government has created a document that explains how to run a session with users that have disabilities, so this could act as a great starting point.[22] For professional testers, the A11y Project maintains an excellent page filled with people you can contact. The links for both of these are in the practical example for this chapter, available at `inclusive.guide/examples/tools`.

Regardless of which option you choose, it's vitally important to ensure a base level of accessibility **before** bringing in users to test your journeys – it's not a good use of *either* party's time for users to spend their time surfacing errors that are easily identified and fixed through basic testing. More than that though, you want to display a level of respect for the topic ahead of time, which you get by following the earlier steps in this process. This is why this stage is at the end of the four-step process:

> To get the most out of this research, it is best if the participants are not discovering basic accessibility issues that should have been discovered during an accessibility review and/or testing.[23]

This quote is from Peter McNally, Senior Consultant at the User Experience Center at Bentley University. He has run a large number of testing sessions with users who have a range of disabilities. He also echoes another point that we've made throughout the book – being compliant *isn't* the same as ensuring that what you've built is usable. This is why you need **both** to be accessible:

> Typically, in order to ensure that disabled people can use their digital products and services, companies aim for compliance with accessibility guidelines such as the Web Content Accessibility Guidelines (WCAG). While this is critical, it is also important to have users with disabilities try to accomplish real tasks on the site in usability testing. There may be gaps in the overall user experience...[24]

In fact, in the working draft for the new version of WCAG (3.0), there is a proposal to replace the A, AA, and AAA levels with bronze, silver, and gold. In this, it mentions that testing with users could be a part of what's required to achieve gold level.[25] In this way, compliance in the future could well mean conducting user testing.

I mentioned the links earlier for guides on handling this process, but there are some key points for setting up *any* user testing you conduct for success. These include

- Starting with participants who are used to the environment and requirements of user testing

- Having a clear scope for the testing (feature X or journey Y) rather than asking for people to navigate your site generally and see whether they notice anything

- Starting with a small number of participants to ensure you get the most out of your session

- Ensuring that your first testing session consists of people who are highly proficient with their assistive tools of choice so that the focus of the session can be on gathering feedback for your site rather than delving into how they use their tools

It's important to note that every test will find *something* unexpected. This shouldn't be discouraging, even after all of your hard work. Remember that this is the **point** of the process, and so anything they find should be considered a success. After all, without them finding the issue, your site would have remained unusable.

When they find something, use the previous steps in the FAIR framework to sort them, and **try again**. This is the most important thing.

In my experience, this iterative process *always* yields something of value. You always achieve a higher level of accessibility, you always learn something new, and you always engage more with the accessibility community. The more people you can take through this four-step process with you, the more wide-ranging the impact of your efforts will be. That person you teach may go on to teach many others within another team or company. A person you use for testing may tell others about your commitment to accessibility

Conclusion

Having gone through both the **FAIR** framework and **ACCESS** checklist, as well as the preceding chapters in this book, you now know how to introduce anyone to the task of auditing and improving the accessibility of a website, as well as the tools you can use to make meaningful progress on that front right from the beginning. I've found that this really is key to laying the foundation for sustained engagement in the topic as teams move forward.

Of course, we must *understand* before we can hope to fix it in any meaningful, long-term way, and so the process also requires deeper learning. It's a level of commitment to the topic that you have exhibited by reading this book. Advancements from here are iterative and are much easier when tackled as a team. You should make your goals clear and public and ensure everyone contributes in order to maximize the chance that they will all consider accessibility from the **beginning** of a project next time. Finally, it's important to go back and handle **all** pages on a site – either fix them or delete them. There should be no exceptions to your new, accessible approach.

It's equally important to never consider the job fully done. Accessibility remains a moving target as technology changes but also as our own sites and teams change. There will likely always be a page to fix, or a person to teach, but each time you become more inclusive and empower more people online.

While tools (both automated and manual) can pick up a lot of critical issues related to accessibility, there are many other issues that need human analysis. A test can determine whether there is `alt` text on an image, but a human can determine whether the `alt` text makes sense. A test can determine if HTML is valid, but a human can determine whether its order and semantics can be understood by a user. This is why both are required, and while you're using tools to ensure the quality of your sites and engaging with users with disabilities to learn from their expertise, you're constantly improving your ability to spot and solve accessibility issues.

You need an accessible site *and* an accessible process to make this work. As of now, you have everything you need to build both.

CHAPTER 12

Conclusion

Congratulations on making it to the last chapter! I appreciate you sticking with the topic, and I hope that you've enjoyed the book. Web accessibility is a deep well of information, encompassing so many different needs, requirements, and solutions, but I hope that the level of detail we've gone into has shown just how important it is to take this subject seriously.

I also hope that having read this book, regardless of your profession, you now feel as though you've learned enough to think about access needs on your websites and could explain why it's so important to others. This alone will have a massive impact on the awareness and advancement of web accessibility and help take it from being something that *some* people consider to being second nature in every team that puts content online.

I started this book with some alarming statistics about the state of the Web when it came to accessibility. The rise in court cases alongside the distinct lack of reduction in errors didn't paint a positive picture. In the beginning, it's important to truly understand just how much better it needs to get in order to accommodate everyone. Hopefully, it's motivated you to do that.

However, I'd like to end the book with the optimism I have for the future of accessibility. There are so many promising signs that we've turned a corner, and that we'll start to see real progress in the near future. Therefore, I'd like to finish our journey together by covering some of these so that you can start the practical journey toward building more accessible websites knowing that you're part of a wider, positive movement. For a final time, let's get into it.

AI and Its Potential Applications

Artificial intelligence is a topic that's gripped the whole world recently. We're already seeing incredible applications of the technology, and according to many experts, this is just the beginning. For a while, large tech companies like Meta and Google have been training AI to improve accessibility for people online, most notably through automatically generating `alt` text for images and captions for videos.

© Ashley Firth 2024
A. Firth, *Practical Web Accessibility*, https://doi.org/10.1007/979-8-8688-0152-5_12

However, I'd like to highlight two more recent examples that I think demonstrate the **next** step in this amazing journey, both of which are set to drastically improve the lives of those with disabilities.

GitHub Copilot

Copilot is an AI-powered tool that the code management company GitHub launched. It's designed for developers to help them write code faster, and it does this by analyzing the context in the file they're editing, as well as related files, and offers suggestions from within the text editor.

Beyond that though, it can also help you write more **accessible** code. Copilot comes with a chat feature that allows you to provide prompts to it, and those prompts can be about accessibility. For example, you could provide it the following:

> I need to learn about accessibility and need to write code that conforms with the WCAG 2.2 level A and AA success criteria...

> I want you to be my accessibility coach, a subject-matter expert that makes me think and account for all accessibility requirements and usability enhancements. When you answer questions about accessibility please use reputable sources such as w3.org and webaim.org. When possible, please provide links and references for additional learning.

> When you suggest code please use semantic HTML, ensure it is operable using the keyboard, follow WCAG 2.2 sufficient techniques, and follow the ARIA Authoring Practices Guide and related design patterns. Do you understand these instructions?

This prompt can serve as your baseline in your code base and your code, whether you are just starting a website or maintaining one. We spoke about accessibility champions in the last chapter: having that person who asks "is this accessible?" when features and pages are being built. Now, AI can be your accessibility champion![1]

Alongside all of the tools we've mentioned that can flag accessibility issues throughout the various stages of the development process, the prospect of having a code-completion tool that both autocompletes with accessible code by default and suggests improvements, as well as a chat box you can quickly get reliable accessibility answers from, is incredibly exciting. That volume of quick, easy touch points with the subject for everyone would accelerate adoption within the tech community in a big way.

Be My Eyes

AI holds the possibility of creating tools that help people on *and* off the Web. Accessibility company Be My Eyes is working with Open AI to develop "Be My AI" – a dynamic new image-to-text generator for blind and visually impaired users.

The new tool, which is already in beta testing, allows users to take a picture and, within a matter of seconds, get a full description of the image. This is a hugely empowering tool, as it enables users to unlock previously inaccessible content themselves, even when those providing that content haven't done so. Sarah, a beta tester for the app, shared the range of uses she's already found for it:

> I have been using it in several ways: taking my own photos particularly of images in magazines, on Twitter where very few people add descriptions or `alt` text and on WhatsApp where my family send me photos in groups all the time without any context.[2]

Sarah mentioned Twitter, but we know how many images online fail to add appropriate `alt` text, so this could definitely help throughout the Web. For images it can't generate a description for, the user will automatically be passed to a volunteer they can communicate with to get the information they need.

These are just two examples, but more and more are launching quicker than ever. It feels as though we're at the start of something potentially very special for our web *and* our species, and I'm excited to see how that continues. For now though, it's already clear that AI will be a significant ally in the disabled community moving forward.

New Laws

With the latest version of WCAG (2.2) being officially released in late 2023, there are now up-to-date success criteria that reflect many of the barriers that users on the Web face today. Having these is vitally important primarily because they're being used more and more in **laws** that are being passed to demand a level of accessibility online.

In June 2025, the European Accessibility Act (EAA) will be enforced within the European Union. It will establish a firm set of rules and regulations to make a vast range of products and services – including those sold on the Web – accessible to all people. Although each country can decide how it integrates with their local laws, nearly all have chosen to judge the Web part of this law against WCAG.[3]

This means that nearly everything we've covered in this book about WCAG will soon be enforceable in the EU by law. The EAA applies to the following services, all of which can exist online:

- Ecommerce

- Consumer banking

- Video streaming and television

- Telephone services

- Certain elements of air, bus, rail, and water transport services such as websites, mobile services, electronic tickets, and information

- Ebooks[4]

Small businesses are exempt from this (small is defined as less than ten employees and less than €2 million in revenue per year), but this still means that a very large number of websites are going to need to reach a higher level of accessibility by mid-2025. What's more, this law applies to private as well as public companies. It will apply to all countries in the European Union **and** those that do business in the EU.[5]

To top it all off, relevant to what we discussed in Chapter 10 "Outsourcing accessibility," overlay providers like AccessiBe will not be able to make your digital services legally compliant under the EAA. Glorious.[6]

It will need to be followed in the same way the General Data Protection Regulation (GDPR) was when it came into effect in 2018, so **strictly**. There will be penalties for noncompliance depending on its severity. This sets a clear tone for the importance of accessibility and how serious each member state will have to take it. It's a clear demand for a level of inclusivity that all people deserve and something I hope will inspire other countries to pass their own laws that act in a similar way.

WCAG 3

The EAA will be reviewed every five years once it comes into effect, so it's important that the base set of rules that they use to determine compliance *also* evolve and remain relevant. Although WCAG 2.2 was only released in October 2023, work is well underway to create the first **major** version of WCAG since 2008 – WCAG 3. This effort is something that I am actually a part of, as an invited expert in the Accessibility Guidelines Working Group for the W3C.

At the time of writing, WCAG 3 is still very exploratory and will take a number of years to be distilled into something practical that's ready to be used. However, it's a source of hope that the manner of the changes being proposed is **revolutionary** rather than simply **evolutionary**. Even in its draft form, it represents some positive new directions that the area could be heading in – ones that very much align with the aim of this book.

New Levels

WCAG 3 proposes three new levels of conformance: bronze, silver, and gold. While it is easy to replicate the WCAG 2 levels of A, AA, and AAA by renaming them, they're aiming to improve on them by using a more advanced approach.[7]

Bronze would be the minimum conformance level and would feel familiar with the scenario-based rules of WCAG 2. **Silver** level then incentivizes organizations to go further to improve accessibility. One possibility they're examining is that silver level points can accumulate even *prior* to completing bronze but are not usable *until* bronze is achieved. The goal is to develop a model that encourages organizations to go beyond the minimum and continue to improve, especially where organizations want to be *recognized* for their efforts to go beyond it. It would also better reflect the lived experience of people with disabilities, who successfully use sites that have *some* content that doesn't meet a WCAG level or who still encounter barriers with sites that do meet that level.

Finally, **gold** level is earmarked for identifying ways to recognize organizations that achieve silver but also stand out as exemplary, cutting-edge, and role models. There are a number of ideas that will be developed further once more of the structure is solidified, but one concept is to reserve it for those who have actually tested their sites with **users with disabilities**. Given everything I mentioned about the importance and benefits of this in the last chapter, I would certainly welcome a level reserved for the practice that is essential in ensuring a site is accessible.

Overall, the new proposed levels would bring a lot of clarity in my opinion, as the "medal" levels are more commonly known than A, AA, and AAA. This means the level you've achieved is more immediately obvious. It also gamifies the process of obtaining higher levels somewhat – who doesn't want to go for the gold?!

Outcomes

Another notable proposed change for WCAG 3 is changing "success criteria" (like the rules we've covered in this book) to "outcomes." Unlike the simple true or false statements of the current criteria, these outcomes would have **three** different scopes:

- **Items** – A feature or part of the page
- **Views** – A particular page
- **User processes** – An entire journey

This would reflect the **context** of the situation that the rule is being applied in and allow it to be considered at both the micro and macro level – the accessibility of a component in isolation, but also its accessibility within a page or journey, as they're nearly always different. According to the draft, these outcomes can also be tested in two ways:

- **Quantifiable tests** – Tests where there is a high degree of consistency between test results from different testers (these can typically be tested through automated testing)
- **Qualitative tests** – Tests that rely on an evaluation by a tester based on existing criteria (manual testing)[8]

This is admittedly more complex than simple true or false rules but offers a far richer experience for developers, testers, and lawmakers. It also more faithfully reflects the reality of accessibility in a more faithful way.

It would also ensure that people think about accessibility on a larger scale than just self-contained tests. With more and more people referring to WCAG, for it to include a focus on user testing, and testing *entire journeys* as a route to compliance, would be a really positive step in my opinion.

Issue Severity

Finally, under the proposed WCAG 3 rules, they intend to introduce the concept of issue severity. This means that rather than the simple pass or fail approach we're used to, different severity levels would allow rules to be **graded** based on words (fail, pass, great) or numbers (1, 2, 3). This provides a scale that may better match what people with disabilities go through when using a site: something can be *technically* usable, but not perfect. It also opens up the possibility of percentages being used to assess a site and its progress, instead of requiring that accessibility be perfect or you fail. I believe this would drive much greater engagement with the framework, thanks to the ability for teams to make consistent, smaller improvements more often, and think about the user's *experience* while doing so.

In the same way that there's a difference between passing and excelling with a rule, there's *also* a difference between one rule failing and another. One failure results in a color contrast that's *slightly* too low or a button that's *slightly* too small, whereas another may prevent navigation entirely. To that end, they intend to introduce "critical errors" that are the highest level of severity and unquestionable showstoppers when it comes to compliance. For example, a website can have a small number of accessibility errors and still be compliant, but if it has any of what they define as "critical errors," it does not conform to WCAG 3 at **any** level, regardless of how many other outcomes it passes.

At the time of writing, examples of what would be considered a critical issue are a keyboard trap, audio without the ability to pause, and a submit button on a form not being in the tabbing order – all things you're familiar with from this book.[9]

Again, this is the reality of accessibility being reflected in this proposal – if a user was using your beautifully made, highly accessible website using only a keyboard, but suddenly got trapped in a modal they interacted with, or couldn't submit an order they were in the process of completing, this would be a complete showstopper for them.

Now there are no guarantees that *any* of these exact concepts will make it into the ratified version of WCAG 3, but I'm *so* optimistic about the thought process behind them and the sheer volume of talented accessibility experts working on it. I will be doing everything I can to help develop this new major version and, in a few years time, we could be looking at a completely reimagined and robust framework, helping to create beautiful and accessible websites without confusion for those building and testing them.

Legal Precedent

At the end of the first edition of this book, I wrote about a landmark case for accessibility: Robles vs. Domino's Pizza. Since then, the case has developed further *and* reached its definitive conclusion. Alongside talking about the effect that entire governments can have on the direction of accessibility, I wanted to cover the effect that **one man** has had on that same landscape and what we can learn from that.

Robles vs. Domino's Pizza

In 2016, Guillermo Robles, who is blind, filed a lawsuit against Domino's Pizza in the United States. As a screen reader user, Mr. Robles tried on multiple occasions to order food through their website but wasn't able to because the site was inaccessible.[10]

The reaction was mixed. The 9th district court, who oversaw the case, ruled that Domino's had indeed violated the American Disabilities Act by creating a site that was inaccessible to those who are blind or visually impaired. However, the sting here was that, because there were technically no specific guidelines in the United States on *how* to make a site that was compliant, the case was dismissed.[11]

Unlike countries like Australia, America hadn't officially adopted WCAG (or any other set of rules) as their guideline or benchmark test (American courts had been using WCAG to *check* accessibility since a case in 2017, but it has not been enshrined in **law**), so the 9th district court decided there was nothing that could be legally enforced. This was a frustrating decision seeing as the district court actually *sided* with Mr. Robles.

However, in 2019, a federal appeals court reversed the decision of the district court, ruling in favor of Mr. Robles.[12] They argued that the company's website and mobile app are critical avenues for the public to order online and find a nearby Domino's restaurant. More importantly, they made it clear that just because there are no specific rules to legally adhere to in order to be accessible, that doesn't mean that it's fine *not to be*. In his 25-page opinion, Circuit Judge Owens stated that the American Disabilities Act has been clear on equal access for those with disabilities since 1990:

> full and equal enjoyment of the goods, services, facilities, privileges, advantages, or accommodations to people with disabilities.[13]

Furthermore, despite there being no official regulation, the Department of Justice has shown in cases since 1996 that this act applies to websites as well as physical stores:

> While we understand why Domino's wants... specific guidelines for website and app accessibility, the Constitution only requires that Domino's receive fair notice of its legal duties, not a blueprint for compliance with its statutory obligations.[14]

This ruling entrenched WCAG as an even more tenable part of case law – reinforcing a precedent for its use as a guideline and providing a clear (but not exhaustive) set of rules to ensure that websites are inclusive – if sites are not compliant with the lowest level (A), they're now open to penalties under the American Disabilities Act.

Mr. Robles' lawyer, Jacob Manning, summed up the importance of this very neatly:

> We're very happy with this opinion because we think it will
> eliminate many of the common objections to accessibility and
> encourage companies to just start the process of making sites
> accessible instead of quibbling over the precise standard...In the
> case of Domino's, you can't order a pizza. Isn't that the test? We
> aren't arguing over a comma here.[15]

The saga didn't stop there though. Instead of accepting the ruling and making their website accessible, Domino's decided, in what experts called an unprecedented move, to petition the Supreme Court to get the decision reversed.[16]

What makes Domino's actions even more surprising is that, in an affidavit from the original lawsuit, they claimed that it would cost **$38,000** to sort the original issue that Mr. Robles opened the case over.[17] Domino's turnover that same year was **$3.43 billion**.[18] Instead of the minor investment (in the grand scheme of things) to settle the case and make the experience more accessible for blind users, the company decided instead to spend much more than this on legal fees to fight it.

This makes neither moral nor financial sense. Mr. Robles (and I'm sure others) want Domino's to have an accessible website so that they can **buy their products**. Chances are the improvements would also return much more in revenue than the $38,000 required to solve the initial accessibility issue.[19] Christopher Danielson said it best:

> There is a ton of space for innovation in this area. Rather than
> refusing to take the money of those of us with disabilities, why not
> innovate and take our money?[20]

The result of this case, more than any other before it, held immense consequences for the world of web accessibility. If the ruling was upheld, it would send a clear message to all businesses – they must take the needs of people with disabilities online into account – along with clear, approved guidelines, in the form of WCAG, on how to do so.

The alternative was dire. The US government would lose its teeth when it comes to enforcing accessibility – making it easier for companies to avoid their responsibility to these users. Christopher Danielsen of the National Federation of the Blind commented:

> If businesses are allowed to say, "We do not have to make our
> websites accessible to blind people," that would be shutting blind
> people out of the economy in the 21st century.[21]

With charities and disability foundations lining up behind Mr. Robles and business groups like the Chamber of Commerce and the National Retail Federation lining up behind Domino's, the ruling was a big moment for accessibility.

I am pleased to say that in late 2019, the Supreme Court decided to reject Dominos' appeal. This is, without a doubt, a massive win for accessibility, and the ruling was described as "the right call on every level" and "a credit to our society." However, the case wasn't *firmly* closed until June 6, 2022, when after **three more years** of litigation, Dominos conceded defeat and reached a private settlement with Mr. Robles.[22]

The total cost is unknown, but this was six years of court cases across three different courts which, given the nature of the errors that were flagged against Domino's, could have been sorted and settled for a relatively small amount of money and time, back in 2016. Ruling aside, my hope is that it shows just how little sense it makes to fight the idea of providing an accessible experience online

Although this took place in the United States, it impacts *anyone* with a website because websites aren't bound by geographic location. National retailers and other organizations usually have some presence within the Ninth Circuit because their websites are available globally. This means that when a resident of the Ninth Circuit accesses a website, the website falls under the Ninth Circuit's jurisdiction.

The cause for positivity here goes beyond the decision itself. The case has gone on to be cited in well over a **hundred** cases since the ruling, thereby solidifying its importance as a turning point for accessibility thanks to the precedent it set, and cementing the idea that a lack of clear checks or guidance **doesn't** mean that you aren't responsible for ensuring that your site is accessible.[23]

It's clear that despite this victory, a lot more needs to be done to ensure the equal treatment of those with a wide variety of access needs. We spoke at the start of the book about an "onslaught" of accessibility-related lawsuits in the last few years, and the harsh fact is that those who rely most on accessibility and inclusivity online are currently the ones who have to fight for it. If we are to create a more inclusive world, this needs to be a fight we all engage in, not just in courtrooms but in the workplace and whenever we build anything online. If Domino's had won, this fight would have only become more important, but the fact that they lost doesn't mean that we can take a step back. In this corner of the accessibility movement, we still have the ability to ensure that the right things get done on each site we touch, without it ever having to reach the news or a courtroom.

Equal-Opportunity Hiring

In the last chapter, we spoke about the importance of including user testing in the process of auditing a site to make it more accessible. Through this topic, I'm typically asked other questions, such as "how often should I run them?" and "at what stage in a project should I run one?" and these are fair points – accessibility is a never-ending process as a site changes and grows, and even the strictest of testing processes might not catch everything.

Paul Bohman, Director of Training at Deque University, actually suggests an alternative to these constant user testing sessions: hire people with disabilities for quality assurance and testing **full-time**. He describes standalone, ad hoc testing sessions as "piecemeal" because users with disabilities would only be present for the specific things that you've asked them to test and not throughout the entire process. In his mind, the result of this approach "gives the whole company the impression that web accessibility is a checklist item, when it really should be a way of thinking at every stage of development."[24]

It may seem like hiring testers full-time might require more of a financial commitment, but it could actually end up being *more* cost-effective. If they provide feedback throughout the whole process of building a site, it's far less likely that large issues will make it into production, which then require costly redesigns when they're found. Beyond the financial advantage, having testers with disabilities around full-time also highlights the importance of accessibility to the whole company and allows for a constant sharing of awareness and knowledge:

> Working alongside people with disabilities also educates fellow developers and testers, making them more intimately aware of the needs of people with disabilities. You change the company's culture, and that's kind of a big deal.[25]

We're seeing a really promising movement in this area, and for disability employment in general: according to the United States Department of Labor's Bureau of Labor Statistics (BLS), **21.3%** of US adults with disabilities were employed in 2022. Now that's much lower than the **65.4%** rate for persons without a disability, but it represents a *substantial* improvement from 2021 and an all-time high for those with disabilities.[26]

In the United Kingdom, the outlook is even better: in 2017, the Government set a target to get one million more people with disabilities employed by 2027, and they reached that goal five years early, in 2022. At the time of writing, the disability employment rate is **52.6%** (compared to **82.5%** for non-disabled people) and has risen year on year.[27]

These are such positive figures as they show consistent, increased equal-opportunity employment. There is a long way to go of course, but governments are both monitoring the employment levels and putting resources into increasing them.

Now there are many things that are required in order to ensure that a business is an equal opportunity employer, but a major one is the ability to use the tools required for the job. For many companies, these are often their websites and internal tools. So having accessible sites and tools, plus involvement with an accessibility testing expert, makes it possible to have an inclusive workplace as well as an inclusive online presence.

Awards

It's always good to be compliant and accessible, but like any other field, there are those that push the boundaries even further and **champion** accessibility – creating solutions that have never existed before and building interactions that are not simply aimed at providing a *usable* experience and content for those with disabilities but instead create an even *richer* experience. It's important for that work to be recognized in the way other fields do, and these days that is the case!

A great example is the AbilityNet Tech4Good Awards, which have been running for a number of years and get bigger every year. They were set up to celebrate organizations and individuals that use digital technology to improve the lives of others and make the world a better place. They also aim to inspire others to use their skills and resources to deliver social impact and nurture the people, organizations, and networks that are part of the global tech for good movement.[28]

As well as awards that are entirely dedicated to accessibility, existing and high-profile web awards are now creating accessibility award categories in order to celebrate people on a popular and recognized platform. One of the biggest awards of its kind, the "Webby Awards," has now added an "accessible technology" category for the first time this year.[29]

This publicity in popular, established awards ensures that those innovating in the field of accessibility receive the attention and exposure they deserve and naturally encourages others to aspire to do the same.

It's not just the Web where this is happening either. There are now dedicated awards for accessibility in gaming like the Video Game Accessibility Awards but also accessibility categories in major, mainstream gaming awards like the Game Awards and the Golden Joysticks.[30]

The latter also recognized accessibility in their Outstanding Contribution Award, which is only given out on special occasions, when Microsoft's adaptive controller (a controller built to connect with assistive technologies that I covered in the first edition of this book) won the award.[31]

The result of these awards is a massive rise in articles talking about games that are great (and terrible) at accessibility. It's become a common topic of discussion, which makes more and more people aware, which in turn encourages more developers to consider it before they launch a game.

Personal Perspective

On a personal level, to see how many people read and enjoyed the first edition of this book and the government agencies, company leaders, and teams that engaged with it, and the topic, for the very first time was so heartening.

The people I've been fortunate enough to help over the last decade to be more accessible in my capacity as a consultant, who all engaged with the topic with so much enthusiasm and now proudly display their dedication to inclusion online, fill me with a lot of hope. The number who do so rises year on year.

The topic as a whole is now welcomed at some of the biggest conferences in the world, which is a stark contrast from the years prior when the topic was relegated to smaller meetups and audiences.

The kind messages online after the first edition of this book about the knowledge people had gained, and the changes they'd been able to make to both their websites and their teams, were inspiring.

Then there's yourselves, who've taken the time to read this edition. You've read about the topic, perhaps for the first time, and made your way through a rather long book.

All of these things together fill me with more promise about the future of accessibility than I've ever had before.

Final Words

We need to get to a point where **every** site on the Web is accessible. Throughout this book, I've been trying to convince you why you should ensure that your site is accessible, and show you how to accomplish that. Having gotten this far, it's now time for you to take these ideas and move forward with them.

How you move forward now relies not only on understanding these points, but crucially whether you decide to implement them – not just for a few weeks but *every day*. For each day in that journey, this book can be your reference and your companion.

It will always require more work to determine what your unique site needs to do in order to be inclusive, but nobody is in a better position to do that than you. WCAG offers a great baseline as we know, but we *also* know that you can be **compliant** while also being **inaccessible**. This is why no single set of rules will work for all websites and all people, and why we must engage with and understand the **topic** rather than just the regulations. To approach accessibility from the perspective of users, and the challenges and barriers they face. Thank you for doing that.

You've also seen countless examples of how, if you design with accessibility in mind, it will make your websites easier for **everybody** to use. Remember: **access needs are user needs**, regardless of what form they take.

Although this book has introduced you to many needs, barriers, and solutions, it is simply not big enough to cover them all – truthfully, a book could be dedicated to every one of the chapters we've covered. I raise this not to dishearten you but instead to tell you that this topic will continue to offer you challenges, insight, and rewards the more you engage with it. It has been a constant source of fascination for me, giving me far more in joy than it takes in time. It is my sincere hope that it will do the same for you.

I began this book by talking about one of the "fathers of the Internet", Vinton Cerf. On the eve of the twenty-first century, he called on everyone to use that event as a turning point for how they think about the Internet and how they build for it. In a speech at the Computers, Freedom and Privacy Conference, he said that

> As we near the milestone of the third millennium, what better theme could we possibly ask for than making the Internet the medium of the new millennium?[32]

Sadly, that did not come entirely to pass. Exposure to the Internet definitely grew in the years that followed, but the level of accessibility on it remained below where it needed to be. His views on the state of accessibility now are clear: we have the medium (the Internet) and the means (ourselves) to build a truly inclusive web, but until this point, we've fallen short.

His final words in that speech, words he wrote over *20* years ago, ring as true now as they did then:

> The Internet **IS** for everyone – but it won't be unless **WE** make
> it so.[33]

So, let's go and make it so. Let's build a truly inclusive web together for those we care for and those we've never met. It's simply the right thing to do.

Endnotes

Chapter 1

1. World Health Organization, Disability, (07/02/2023), `<www.who.int/news-room/fact-sheets/detail/disability-and-health>` [Accessed 11/06/2023]

2. Vint Cerf, *The Internet Is for Everyone*, Speech to the Computers, Freedom and Privacy Conference, (07/04/1999) `<www.itu.int/ITU-D/ict/papers/witwatersrand/Vint%20Cerf.pdf>` [Accessed 15/06/2023] – Original quote edited slightly. "The Internet is for everyone – but it won't be until it's in every home, in every business, in every school, in every town and every country on the Globe, Internet can be accessed without limitation, at any time and in every language."

3. Brittanica, Vinton Cerf, `<www.britannica.com/biography/Vinton-Cerf>` [Accessed 14/06/2023]

4. Vint Cerf, in *Internet Becomes a Lifeline for the Deaf*, by Tami Luhby, *New York Times*, (12/02/1998), `<https://archive.nytimes.com/www.nytimes.com/library/cyber/week/021398deaf.html>` [Accessed 15/06/2023]

5. ibid.

6. Vint Cerf, in *Internet Inventor: Make Tech Accessibility Better Already*, by Joan Solman, (10/04/2017), `<www.cnet.com/news/internet-inventor-vint-cerf-accessibility-disability-deaf-hearing/>` [Accessed 01/03/2019]

7. W3C, *World Wide Web Consortium Launches International Program Office for Web Accessibility Initiative*, (22/10/1997), `<www.w3.org/Press/IPO-announce>` [Accessed 15/06/2023]

© Ashley Firth 2024
A. Firth, *Practical Web Accessibility*, https://doi.org/10.1007/979-8-8688-0152-5

8. Accessibility Principles, W3C, (10/05/2019), <www.w3.org/WAI/fundamentals/accessibility-principles/> [Accessed 13/06/2023]

9. The WebAIM Million, WebAIM, (29/03/2023), <https://webaim.org/projects/million/> [Accessed 09/06/2023]

10. *Understanding WCAG 2.2*, W3C, (26/02/2019), <www.w3.org/WAI/WCAG22/Understanding/> [Accessed 15/06/2023]

11. *Web Content Accessibility Guidelines (WCAG)*, W3C, (05/06/2018), <www.w3.org/TR/WCAG22/> [Accessed 15/06/2023]

12. James Buller, in an interview by Ashley Firth, (26/02/2019).

13. Sheri Byrne-Haber, *How to Avoid Twitter's Latest Accessibility Mistakes*, (20/08/2021), <https://uxdesign.cc/how-to-avoid-twitters-latest-accessibility-mistakes-e0910f9f0ae7> [Accessed 13/06/2023]

14. What's New in WCAG 2.012, W3C, (2019) <www.w3.org/WAI/standards-guidelines/wcag/new-in-22/> [Accessed 15/06/2023]

15. *Web Content Accessibility Guidelines (WCAG)*, What's New in WCAG 2.1, (13/08/2020), <www.w3.org/WAI/standards-guidelines/wcag/new-in-21/#:~:text=including%20assistive%20technologies.-,4.1.3%20Status%20Messages%20(AA),-In%20content%20implemented> [Accessed 14/06/2023]

16. Vint Cerf, in *Internet Inventor: Make Tech Accessibility Better Already*, by Joan E. Solsman, (10/04/2017), <www.cnet.com/news/internet-inventor-vint-cerf-accessibility-disability-deaf-hearing/> [Accessed 15/06/2023]

17. James Buller, in an interview by Ashley Firth, (26/02/2019).

18. Disabilities, World Health Organization, <www.who.int/topics/disabilities/en/> [Accessed 15/06/2023]

19. Report of the Secretary-General of the United Nations, Our Common Agenda, 2021, <www.un.org/en/content/common-agenda-report/assets/pdf/Common_Agenda_Report_English.pdf> [Accessed 14/06/2023]

20. Gov UK - Legislation, Equality Act 2020, (08/04/2010), < www.
legislation.gov.uk/ukpga/2010/15/contents> [Accessed
27/11/2023]

21. *Beyoncé's Website the Focus of an Accessibility Lawsuit*, Bureau
of Internet Accessibility, (09/01/2019), <www.boia.org/blog/
beyonces-website-the-focus-of-an-accessibility-lawsuit>
[Accessed 15/06/2023]

22. Robles v. Domino's Pizza, LLC - 913 F.3d 898 (9th Cir. 2019),
LexisNexis, <www.lexisnexis.com/community/casebrief/p/
casebrief-robles-v-domino-s-pizza-llc> [Accessed
10/06/2023]

23. Caren Decter, ADA Website Accessibility Lawsuits: What
Advertisers Need to Know, (06/12/2018), <https://
advertisinglaw.fkks.com/post/102f6xu/ada-website-
accessibility-lawsuits-what-advertisers-need-to-know>
[Accessed 15/06/2023]

24. Usablenet, 2022 Year-End Report, (17/11/2022), <https://info.
usablenet.com/2022-year-end-digital-accessibility-
lawsuit-report-download-page> [Accessed 10/06/2023]

25. Bureau of Internet Accessibility, The Robles v. Domino's
Settlement (And Why It Matters), (12/07/2022) <www.boia.
org/blog/the-robles-v.-dominos-settlement-and-why-it-
matters#:~:text=that%20the%20district%20court%20can%20
order%20compliance%20with%20WCAG%202.0%20as%20an%20
equitable%20remedy%20if%2C%20after%20discovery%2C%20
the%20website%20and%20app%20fail%20to%20satisfy%20the%20
ADA.%E2%80%9D> [Accessed 11/06/2023]

26. ibid.

27. Sally Abrahams & Lee Kumutat, *Blind customers locked out by
bank web upgrades*, BBC News, (06/05/2018), <www.bbc.co.uk/
news/business-43968736> [Accessed 15/06/2023]

28. ibid.

29. Purple, The Purple Pound – Infographic, <`https://wearepurple.org.uk/the-purple-pound-infographic/`> [Accessed 11/06/2023]

30. Chris Rourke, *UK Retailers Still Failing to Meet Web Accessibility Standards*, Econsultancy, (14/02/2017), <`https://econsultancy.com/uk-retailers-still-failing-to-meet-web-accessibility-standards/`> [Accessed 15/06/2023] & Gemma-Louise Stevenson, *Shops are "dumb" for ignoring disabled customers*, BBC Newsbeat, (21/12/2016), <`www.bbc.co.uk/newsbeat/article/38370149/shops-are-dumb-for-ignoring-disabled-customers`> [Accessed 15/06/2023]

31. AIR, Policy Panel on the Purchasing Power of People with Disabilities, (22/04/2021), <`www.air.org/event/policy-panel-purchasing-power-people-disabilities`> [Accessed 11/06/2023]

32. Ruth Everett, How & Why Accessibility Matters for SEO, Search Engine Journal, (03/09/2020), <`www.searchenginejournal.com/seo-accessibility/379582/#close`> [Accessed 15/06/2023]

33. WebAIM, The WebAIM Million, (29/03/2023), <`https://webaim.org/projects/million/`> [Accessed 11/06/2023]

34. Stack Overflow, 2022 Developer Survey, (05/2022), <`https://survey.stackoverflow.co/2022`> [Accessed 27/11/2023]

35. WebAIM, The WebAIM Million, (29/03/2023), <`https://webaim.org/projects/million/`> [Accessed 11/06/2023]

36. Accessible Metrics, What are the Levels of WCAG Compliance?, (05/11/2019), <`www.accessiblemetrics.com/blog/what-are-the-levels-of-wcag-compliance/`> [Access 13/06/2023]

37. W3C, Web Content Accessibility Guidelines (WCAG), (05/06/2018), <`www.w3.org/TR/WCAG22/`> [Accessed 15/06/2023]

Chapter 2

1. University of Bath, How blind people see the world, `<www.bath.ac.uk/case-studies/how-blind-people-see-the-world>` [Accessed 08/07/2023]

2. WebAIM, Screen Reader User Survey #9, (30/06/2021), `<https://webaim.org/projects/screenreadersurvey9/>` [Accessed 08/07/2023]

3. Matt Guay, Which Screen Readers and Browsers are best for Accessibility Testing?, Assistiv Labs, (06/01/2023), `https://assistivlabs.com/articles/screen-reader-browser-pairing-stats>` [Accessed 29/11/2023]

4. ibid.

5. WebAim, Screen Reader User Survey #7, (21/12/2017), `<https://webaim.org/projects/screenreadersurvey7/>` [Accessed 08/07/2023]

6. WebAIM, Screen Reader User Survey #9, (30/06/2021), `<https://webaim.org/projects/screenreadersurvey9/>` [Accessed 08/07/2023]

7. W3C, Web Content Accessibility Guidelines (WCAG) 2.1 – Success Criterion 4.1.2 Name, Role, Value, (05/06/2018), `<www.w3.org/TR/WCAG21/#name-role-value>` [Accessed 12/07/2023]

8. W3C, *Validity and Accessibility*, (01/07/2005) `<www.w3.org/WAI/GL/2005/06/validity-accessibility.html>` [Accessed 09/07/2023]

9. W3C, Markup Validation Service, (2013), `<https://validator.w3.org/>` [Accessed 09/07/2023]

10. WebAIM, Screen Reader User Survey #9, (30/06/2021), `<https://webaim.org/projects/screenreadersurvey9/>` [Accessed 08/07/2023]

11. WebAIM, The WebAIM Million, (29/03/2023), <https://webaim.org/projects/million/#CMS:~:text=to%20 that%20technology.-,Content%20Management%20Systems%20 and%20Site%20Builders,-CMS> [Accessed 08/07/2023]

12. ibid.

13. There are actually a few specific situations where leading with a heading tag below an <h1> is acceptable. For example, for three column layouts, it is possible to have a <h2> heading before the main content's <h1> tag if the main content is in the center column.

14. W3C, How to Meet WCAG (Quick Reference) – 1.3.1 Info and Relationships <www.w3.org/WAI/WCAG22/quickref/?showtechniq ues=246#info-and-relationships> [Accessed 14/07/2023]

15. DeafAction, *Guide to Accessible Information*, (08/2014) <www. deafaction.org/wp-content/uploads/2014/08/Guide-to-Accessible-Information.pdf> [Accessed 09/07/2023]

16. WebAIM, Screen Reader User Survey #9, (30/06/2021), <https://webaim.org/projects/screenreadersurvey9/> [Accessed 09/07/2023]

17. Ed Horsford, *Research with blind users on mobile devices*, (09/06/2016), <https://accessibility.blog.gov. uk/2016/06/09/research-with-blind-users-on-mobile-devices/> [Accessed 09/07/2023]

18. WebAIM, Screen Reader User Survey #9, (30/06/2021), <https://webaim.org/projects/screenreadersurvey9/> [Accessed 08/07/2023]

19. Ed Horsford, *Research with blind users on mobile devices*, (09/06/2016), <https://accessibility.blog.gov. uk/2016/06/09/research-with-blind-users-on-mobile-devices/> [Accessed 09/07/2023]

20. ibid.

21. Statcounter, Desktop vs Mobile vs Tablet Market Share Worldwide, <https://gs.statcounter.com/platform-market-share/desktop-mobile-tablet/worldwide/#monthly-201901-202307>, [Accessed 08/07/2023]

22. Whenever they're available 16.8% * Often 14.4% * Sometimes 28.4% * Seldom * 21.6% * Never 14.4% * WebAim, *Screen Reader User Survey #9*, (30/06/2021), <https://webaim.org/projects/screenreadersurvey9/> [Accessed 08/07/2023]

23. W3C, Web Accessibility Initiative, How to Meet WCAG (Quick Reference), <www.w3.org/WAI/WCAG21/quickref/?versions=2.0&showtechniques=241#qr-navigation-mechanisms-skip> [Accessed 08/07/2023]

24. Brandwatch, 99 Amazing Social Media Statistics and Facts, (08/03/2023), <www.brandwatch.com/blog/amazing-social-media-statistics-and-facts/> [Accessed 05/07/2023]

25. WebAIM, The WebAIM Million, (29/03/2023), <https://webaim.org/projects/million/#CMS:~:text=to%20that%20technology.-,Content%20Management%20Systems%20and%20Site%20Builders,-CMS> [Accessed 05/07/2023]

26. WCAG, 1.1.1 Non-text Content (Level A), (07/03/2021), <https://wcag.com/authors/1-1-1-non-text-content/> [Accessed 08/07/2023]

27. WebAIM, The WebAIM Million, (29/03/2023), <https://webaim.org/projects/million/#CMS:~:text=to%20that%20technology.-,Content%20Management%20Systems%20and%20Site%20Builders,-CMS> [Accessed 08/07/2023]

28. Meta, Using AI to Improve Photo Descriptions for People Who Are Blind and Visually Impaired, (19/01/2021), <https://about.fb.com/news/2021/01/using-ai-to-improve-photo-descriptions-for-blind-and-visually-impaired-people/> [Accessed 08/07/2023]

29. W3C, Web Content Accessibility Guidelines (WCAG) 2.1 – Success Criterion 3.1.2 Language of Parts, (05/06/2018), <www.w3.org/TR/WCAG21/#language-of-parts> [Accessed 12/07/2023]

30. Chris Moore, *Accessibility and me: Chris Moore*, (01/07/2016) <https://accessibility.blog.gov.uk/2016/07/01/accessibility-and-me-chris-moore/> [Accessed 08/07/2023]

31. Purple, The Purple Pound – Infographic, <https://wearepurple.org.uk/the-purple-pound-infographic/> [Accessed 11/06/2023]

32. WCAG, Understanding SC 2.5.8: Target Size (Minimum) (Level AA), <www.w3.org/WAI/WCAG22/Understanding/target-size-minimum.html> [Accessed 08/07/2023]

33. WebAIM, The WebAIM Million, (29/03/2023), <https://webaim.org/projects/million/#CMS:~:text=to%20that%20technology.-,Content%20Management%20Systems%20and%20Site%20Builders,-CMS> [Accessed 08/07/2023]

34. ibid.

35. W3C, *Using ARIA*, (27/09/2018), <www.w3.org/TR/using-aria/> [Accessed 09/07/2023]

Chapter 3

1. World Health Organization, Blindness and vision impairment, (13/10/2022), <www.who.int/en/news-room/fact-sheets/detail/blindness-and-visual-impairment> [Accessed 18/07/2023]

2. W3C, *Accessibility Requirements for People with Low Vision*, (17/03/2016), <www.w3.org/TR/low-vision-needs/> [Accessed 24/07/2023]

3. ibid.

4. Wikipedia, *The Dress*, <https://en.wikipedia.org/wiki/The_dress> [Accessed 24/07/2023]

5. María-Carmen Silva-Viguera, Marta C. García-Romera, & María-José Bautista-Llamas. (2023) Contrast sensitivity function under three light conditions in patients with type 1 diabetes mellitus without retinopathy: a cross-sectional, case-control study. *Graefe's Archive for Clinical and Experimental Ophthalmology* 261:9, pages 2497–2505

6. Bert Bos, *EM, PX, PT, CM, IN...*, W3C, (26/09/2018), <www.w3.org/Style/Examples/007/units.en.html> [Accessed 24/07/2023]

7. HTTP Archive Web Almanac, Accessibility, <https://almanac.httparchive.org/en/2022/accessibility#color-contrast:~:text=Figure%2011.5.-,Font%20unit%20usage.,-Another%20thing%20to> [Accessed 17/07/2023]

8. Oliver Reichenstein, *The 100% Easy-2-Read Standard*, iA, (17/11/2006), <https://ia.net/topics/100e2r> [Accessed 25/07/2023]

9. HTTP Archive Web Almanac, Accessibility, <https://almanac.httparchive.org/en/2022/accessibility#color-contrast:~:text=Figure%2011.5.-,Font%20unit%20usage.,-Another%20thing%20to> [Accessed 17/07/2023]

10. W3C, *Accessibility Requirements for People with Low Vision*, (17/03/2016), <www.w3.org/TR/low-vision-needs/> [Accessed 25/07/2023]

11. ibid.

12. Scott Kellum, *A Pixel Identity Crisis*, A List Apart, (17/01/2012), <https://alistapart.com/article/a-pixel-identity-crisis/> [Accessed 25/07/2023]

13. Jakob Nielsen, Guesses vs. Data as Basis for Design Recommendations, (07/06/2009) <www.nngroup.com/articles/guesses-vs-data/> [Accessed 25/07/2023]

14. David Beymer, Daniel Russell, Peter Orton, *An Eye Tracking Study of How Font Size and Type Influence Online Reading*, (2008), <www.bcs.org/upload/pdf/ewic_hc08_v2_paper4.pdf> [Accessed 25/07/2023]

15. Erica McCoy, *Accessible Web Typography for the Visually Impaired*, (05/2018), <https://mdsoar.org/handle/11603/10871> [Accessed 25/07/2023]

16. Tom Clarke, *Best UX practices for line spacing*, JUSTINMIND, (27/11/2018) <www.justinmind.com/blog/best-ux-practices-for-line-spacing/> [Accessed 25/07/2023]

17. W3C, *Understanding Success Criterion 1.4.12*: Text Spacing, <www.w3.org/WAI/WCAG21/Understanding/text-spacing.html> [Accessed 25/07/2023]

18. W3Schools, *CSS letter-spacing Property*, (2023) <www.w3schools.com/cssref/pr_text_letter-spacing.asp> [Accessed 25/07/2023]

19. John Benjamin's e-Platform, The end of the line: A survey of unjustified typography, (01/1995), <www.jbe-platform.com/content/journals/10.1075/idj.8.2.03sti> [Accessed 21/07/2023]

20. W3C, Supplemental Guidance: Text Justification, (06/06/2019), <www.w3.org/WAI/GL/low-vision-a11y-tf/wiki/Supplemental_Guidance:_Text_Justification> [Accessed 21/07/2023]

21. W3C, WCAG 2.2 Understanding Docs – Understanding SC 1.4.8: Visual Presentation (Level AAA), <www.w3.org/WAI/WCAG22/Understanding/visual-presentation.html> [Accessed 21/07/2023]

22. WebAIM, *Fonts*, (2023), <https://webaim.org/techniques/fonts/> [Accessed 25/07/2023]

23. A, Ridder et al., *Impaired contrast sensitivity is associated with more severe cognitive impairment in Parkinson disease*, (07/10/2016), <www.ncbi.nlm.nih.gov/pmc/articles/PMC5222688/> [Accessed 25/07/2023]

24. W3C, WCAG 2.1 Understanding Docs – Understand SC 1.4.3 Contrast (Minimum), <www.w3.org/WAI/WCAG21/Understanding/contrast-minimum.html> [Accessed 21/07/2023]

25. WebAIM, *Contrast Checker*, (2019), <https://webaim.org/resources/contrastchecker/?fcolor=000000&bcolor=FFFFFF> [Accessed 25/07/2023]

26. WebAIM, The WebAIM Million, (29/03/2023), <https://webaim.org/projects/million/#contrast> [Accessed 18/07/2023]

27. HTTP Archive Web Almanac, Accessibility, (26/09/2022), <https://almanac.httparchive.org/en/2022/accessibility#color-contrast> [Accessed 18/07/2023]

28. Erica McCoy, *Accessible Web Typography for the Visually Impaired*, (05/2018), <https://mdsoar.org/handle/11603/10871> [Accessed 25/07/2023]

29. Greg Bullock, *The Ultimate Guide to Photophobia and Light Sensitivity*, (08/11/2018), <www.theraspecs.com/photophobia-ultimate-guide/> [Accessed 25/07/2023]

30. W3C, *Overview of Low Vision*, (09/02/2016), <www.w3.org/WAI/GL/low-vision-a11y-tf/wiki/Overview_of_Low_Vision> [Accessed 25/07/2023]

31. American Academy of Ophthalmology, Digital Devices and Your Eyes, (27/10/2022), <www.aao.org/eye-health/tips-prevention/digital-devices-your-eyes> [Accessed 22/07/2023]

32. Theraspecs, Is Dark Mode Better for Headaches, Eye Strain & Light Sensitivity?, (03/05/2020), <www.theraspecs.com/blog/dark-mode-for-headaches-eye-strain-light-sensitivity/> [Accessed 22/07/2023]

33. CanIUse, Can I Use Filter? <https://caniuse.com/?search=filter> [Accessed 23/07/2023]

ENDNOTES

34. Github – melanierichards / talks, The Tailored Web: Effectively Honoring Visual Preferences, (01/10/2019), <https://github.com/melanierichards/talks/blob/main/2019/color-contrast-view-source/slides/melanie-richards-the-tailored-web--with-notes.pdf> [Accessed 23/07/2023]

35. Microsoft, Styling for Windows high contrast with new standards for forced colors, (17/09/2023), <https://blogs.windows.com/msedgedev/2020/09/17/styling-for-windows-high-contrast-with-new-standards-for-forced-colors/> [Accessed 20/08/2023]

36. Github - W3C / WCAG / Issues, Do issues with Windows high contrast mode fall under WCAG 2.1?, (Comment made 22/06/2021), <https://github.com/w3c/wcag/issues/623#issuecomment-865916948> [Accessed 23/07/2023]

37. Colour Blind Awareness, *Welcome to the Colour Blind Awareness site*, (2023), <www.colourblindawareness.org/> [Accessed 25/07/2023]

38. Colour Blind Awareness, *Causes of Colour Blindness*, (2023), <www.colourblindawareness.org/colour-blindness/causes-of-colour-blindness/> [Accessed 25/07/2023]

39. National Eye Institute, Types of Color Blindness, <www.nei.nih.gov/learn-about-eye-health/eye-conditions-and-diseases/color-blindness/types-color-blindness#:~:text=Red%2Dgreen%20color%20blindness,difference%20between%20red%20and%20green.> [Accessed 25/07/2023]

40. Colour Blind Awareness, *Types of Colour Blindness*, (2023), <www.colourblindawareness.org/colour-blindness/types-of-colour-blindness/> [Accessed 25/07/2023]

41. Hampus Sethfors, *Colorblind Accessibility on the Web – Fail and Success Cases*, Axess lab, (06/09/2017), <https://axesslab.com/colorblind-accessibility-web-fail-success-cases/> [Accessed 25/07/2023]

42. W3C, *Understanding Success Criterion 1.3.3*: Sensory Characteristics, <www.w3.org/WAI/WCAG21/Understanding/sensory-characteristics.html> [Accessed 25/07/2023]

43. Colblindor, *Monochromacy – Complete Color Blindness*, (20/07/2007), <www.color-blindness.com/2007/07/20/monochromacy-complete-color-blindness/> [Accessed 25/07/2023]

44. WebAIM, *Visual Disabilities*: Color-blindness, (2023), <https://webaim.org/articles/visual/colorblind> [Accessed 25/07/2023]

45. ibid.

46. W3C, WCAG 2.1 Techniques – Technique F73: Failure of Success Criterion 1.4.1 due to creating links that are not visually evident without color vision, <www.w3.org/WAI/WCAG21/Techniques/failures/F73> [Accessed 23/07/2023]

47. Michel Fortin, *Sim Daltonism*, (2023) <https://michelf.ca/projects/sim-daltonism/> [Accessed 25/07/2023]

48. W3C, *Understanding Success Criterion 1.4.10*: Reflow (Level AA), <www.w3.org/WAI/WCAG21/Understanding/reflow.html> [Accessed 26/09/2023]

49. Molly Watt, *Accessibility and me: Molly Watt*, Accessibility in government blog, (09/01/2017), <https://accessibility.blog.gov.uk/2017/01/09/accessibility-and-me-molly-watt/> [Accessed 25/07/2023]

50. WCAG, 1.4.4 Resize Text (Level AA), (15/03/2021), <https://wcag.com/designers/1-4-4-resize-text/> [Accessed 22/07/2023]

51. Guy Podjarny, *RWD Ratio in Top 100,000 websites – refined*, (09/01/2014), <www.guypo.com//rwd-ratio-in-top-100000-websites-refined> [Accessed 25/07/2023]

52. Business DIT, *The Importance of Responsive Web Design (With 8 Statistics)*, (07/07/2023), <`www.businessdit.com/responsive-web-design-statistics/`> [Accessed 19/07/2023]

53. Canonicalized, *We Tested 1 Million Websites to See How Mobile-Friendly They Are* [Original Study], (02/04/2018), <`https://canonicalized.com/mobile-friendly-study/`> [Accessed 23/07/2023]

54. ibid.

55. Adrian Roselli, *Don't Disable Zoom*, (06/05/2023), <`http://adrianroselli.com/2015/10/dont-disable-zoom.html`> [Accessed 25/07/2023]

56. HTTP Archive Web Almanac, Accessibility, (26/09/2022), <`https://almanac.httparchive.org/en/2022/accessibility#zooming-and-scaling`> [Accessed 17/07/2023]

57. ibid.

58. Moreno, et al. *Exploring the Web navigation strategies of people with low vision*, (14/09/2018), <`https://dl.acm.org/doi/10.1145/3233824.3233845`> [Accessed 25/07/2023]

Chapter 4

1. International Neuromodulation Society, *Motor Impairment*, (2023) <`www.neuromodulation.com/motor-impairment`> [Accessed 16/10/2023]

2. Microsoft and Forester Research, The Wide Range of Abilities and Its Impact on Computer Technology, (2004), <`www.microsoft.com/en-us/download/details.aspx`> [Accessed 16/10/2023]

3. Similarweb, Mobile vs. Desktop vs. Tablet Traffic Market Share, (10/2023), <`www.similarweb.com/platforms/`> [Accessed 14/10/2023]

4. Parkinson's Foundation, Statistics, (2023), <`www.parkinson.org/understanding-parkinsons/statistics`> [Accessed 11/10/2023]

5. Song P, Zhang Y, Zha M, Yang Q, Ye X, Yi Q, Rudan I. The global prevalence of essential tremor, with emphasis on age and sex: A meta-analysis. J Glob Health. 2021 Apr 10;11:04028. doi: 10.7189/jogh.11.04028. PMID: 33880180; PMCID: PMC8035980.

6. W3C, Understanding Success Criterion 2.1.1: Keyboard (Level A), (2023), <`www.w3.org/WAI/WCAG21/Understanding/keyboard.html`> [Accessed 11/10/2023]

7. W3C – WCAG 2.1 Understanding Docs, Understanding SC 2.4.7: Focus Visible (Level AA), (20/06/2023), <`www.w3.org/WAI/WCAG21/Understanding/focus-visible.html`> [Accessed 09/10/2023]

8. Can I Use, :focus-visible CSS pseudo-class, (10/2023), <`https://caniuse.com/css-focus-visible`> [Accessed 14/10/2023]

9. W3C, Understanding Success Criterion 2.4.11: Focus Not Obscured (Minimum) (Level AA), (2023), <`www.w3.org/WAI/WCAG21/Understanding/target-size.html`> [Accessed 14/10/2023]

10. Western Washington University, Support forced colors modes, <`https://brand.wwu.edu/accessibility/guide/support-forced-colors`> [Accessed 14/10/2023]

11. Microsoft, Accessibility features in Microsoft Edge, <`https://support.microsoft.com/en-us/microsoft-edge/accessibility-features-in-microsoft-edge-4c696192-338e-9465-b2cd-bd9b698ad19a`> [Accessed 14/10/2023]

12. W3C, Keyboard Accessible: Understanding Guideline 2.1, (2023), <`www.w3.org/TR/UNDERSTANDING-WCAG20/keyboard-operation.html`> [Accessed 17/10/2023]

13. W3C, Understanding Success Criterion 2.4.3: Focus Order, (2023), <www.w3.org/WAI/WCAG21/Understanding/focus-order.html> [Accessed 11/10/2023]

14. Léonie Watson, Using the tabindex attribute, TPGi, (04/08/2014), <www.tpgi.com/using-the-tabindex-attribute/> [Accessed 11/10/2023]

15. W3C, Understanding Success Criterion 2.4.11: Focus Not Obscured (Minimum) (Level AA), (2023), <www.w3.org/WAI/WCAG22/Understanding/focus-not-obscured-minimum> [Accessed 14/10/2023]

16. W3C, Understanding Success Criterion 2.4.12: Focus Not Obscured (Enhanced) (Level AAA), (2023), <www.w3.org/WAI/WCAG22/Understanding/focus-not-obscured-enhanced> [Accessed 14/10/2023]

17. Nielsen Norman Group, Sticky Headers: 5 Ways to Make Them Better, (04/04/2021), <www.nngroup.com/articles/sticky-headers/> [Accessed 15/10/2023]

18. W3C, Understanding SC 2.1.2: No Keyboard Trap (Level A), (2023), <www.w3.org/WAI/WCAG21/Understanding/no-keyboard-trap.html> [Accessed 20/10/2023]

19. W3C, Understanding Success Criterion 3.2.1: On Focus (Level A), (2023), </www.w3.org/WAI/WCAG21/Understanding/on-focus.html> [Accessed 11/10/2023]

20. Assistive Technology Guide, *Mouth/Head Stick/Pointers*, <https://at-aust.org/items/2899> [Accessed 11/10/2023] + Cerebral Palsy Alliance, Cerebral Palsy Facts, (2018), <https://cparf.org/what-is-cerebral-palsy/facts-about-cerebral-palsy> [Accessed 11/10/2023]

21. W3C, Understanding Success Criterion 2.5.8: Target Size (Minimum) (Level AA), (2023), <www.w3.org/WAI/WCAG22/Understanding/target-size-minimum.html> [Accessed 01/12/2023]

22. W3C, Understanding Success Criterion 2.5.5: Target Size (Enhanced) (Level AAA), (2023), <www.w3.org/WAI/WCAG22/Understanding/target-size-enhanced.html> [Accessed 18/1001/12/2023]

23. W3C, Understanding Success Criterion 2.5.1: Pointer Gestures (Level A), (2023), <www.w3.org/WAI/WCAG21/Understanding/pointer-gestures.html> [Accessed 13/10/2023]

24. W3C, Understanding Success Criterion 2.5.2: Pointer Cancellation (Level A), (2023), <www.w3.org/WAI/WCAG21/Understanding/pointer-cancellation.html> [Accessed 13/10/2023]

25. W3C, Understanding Success Criterion 2.5.2: Pointer Cancellation, (2023), <www.w3.org/WAI/WCAG21/Understanding/pointer-cancellation.html> [Accessed 13/10/2023]

26. Market US, Global Speech and Voice Recognition Market By Technology Report #100412, (04/2023), <https://market.us/report/speech-and-voice-recognition-market/> [Accessed 15/10/2023]

27. World Health Organization, Rheumatoid arthritis, (28/06/2023), <www.who.int/news-room/fact-sheets/detail/rheumatoid-arthritis> [Accessed 14/10/2023]

28. Rani Nayyar, Accessibility and Me, Accessibility in Government Blog, (19/09/2017), <https://accessibility.blog.gov.uk/2017/09/19/accessibility-and-me-rani-nayyar/> [Accessed 18/10/2023]

29. Nuance, Mousegrid, <www.nuance.com/products/help/dragon/dragon-for-mac6/enx/Content/Navigation/MouseGrid.html> [Accessed 18/10/2023]

30. Nuance, Mouse Commands, <www.nuance.com/products/help/dragon/dragon-for-mac6/enx/Content/Navigation/MouseCommands.html> [Accessed 18/10/2023]

31. W3C, Understanding SC 1.4.2 Audio Control (Level A), (2023) `<www.w3.org/WAI/WCAG21/Understanding/audio-control.html>` [Accessed 18/10/2023]

32. Bureau of Internet Accessibility, Disability Statistics in the United States, (29/11/2018), `<www.boia.org/blog/disability-statistics-in-the-united-states>` [Accessed 11/10/2023]

33. Hampus Sethfors, I Used a Switch Control for a Day, 24 Accessibility, (18/12/2018), `<www.24a11y.com/2018/i-used-a-switch-control-for-a-day/>` [Accessed 20/10/2023]

34. W3C, Understanding SC 2.2.1: Timing Adjustable (Level A), (2023), `<www.w3.org/WAI/WCAG21/Understanding/timing-adjustable.html>` [Accessed 18/10/2023]

35. W3C, Understanding SC 2.2.5: Re-authenticating (Level AAA), (2023), `<www.w3.org/WAI/WCAG21/Understanding/re-authenticating.html>` [Accessed 18/10/2023]

36. W3C, Understanding Success Criterion 2.5.4: Motion Actuation, (2023), `<www.w3.org/WAI/WCAG21/Understanding/motion-actuation.html>` [Accessed 13/10/2023]

37. W3C, Understanding Success Criterion 1.3.4: Orientation (Level AA), (2023), `<www.w3.org/WAI/WCAG22/Understanding/orientation>` [Accessed 15/10/2023]

38. Gov UK – Education Department, Preventing browser auto-fill, (20/01/2022), `<https://becoming-a-teacher.design-history.education.gov.uk/register-trainee-teachers/preventing-browser-auto-fill/>` [Accessed 19/10/2023]

39. Google, Chromium Bugs, Issue 914451: Autofill does not respect autocomplete="off", (12/12/2018), `<https://bugs.chromium.org/p/chromium/issues/detail?id=914451>` [Accessed 19/10/20223]

Chapter 5

1. World Health Organization, World Report on Hearing, (02/03/2021), <www.who.int/publications/i/item/9789240021570> [Accessed 05/08/2023]

2. ibid.

3. Thomas O. Willcox, Gregory J. Artz, Auditory System Disorders (2007), <www.sciencedirect.com/topics/pharmacology-toxicology-and-pharmaceutical-science/central-hearing-loss> [Accessed 06/08/2023]

4. Auditory Disabilities, WebAIM, <https://webaim.org/articles/auditory/culture> [Accessed 05/08/2023]

5. SignSolutions, How many people use BSL in the UK?, (09/02/2023), <www.signsolutions.uk.com/how-many-people-use-bsl-in-the-uk/> [Accessed 05/08/2023]

6. Áine Jackson, (British Deaf Association research and policy coordinator) Interview with author, (16/05/2019).

7. Oberlo, Online Video Consumption Statistics, (2023), <www.oberlo.com/statistics/online-video-consumption-statistics> [Accessed 05/08/2023]

8. W3, WCAG 2.1 Understanding Docs – Understanding SC 1.2: Time-Based Media, <www.w3.org/WAI/WCAG21/Understanding/time-based-media> [Accessed 05/08/2023]

9. Lisa Herrod, Deafness and the User Experience, A List Apart, <http://alistapart.com/article/deafnessandtheuserexperience/> [Accessed 06/08/2023].

10. ibid.

11. Todd Wright, in Deafness and the User Experience, A List Apart, <http://alistapart.com/article/deafnessandtheuserexperience/#comment-14519> [Accessed 06/08/2023]

12. Digiday, 85 percent of Facebook video is watched without sound, (17/05/2016), <https://digiday.com/media/silent-world-facebook-video/> [Accessed 18/08/2023]

13. Kate Cummingam – The Guardian, Mumbling actors, bad speakers or lazy listeners? Why everyone is watching TV with subtitles on, (27/01/2023), <www.theguardian.com/tv-and-radio/2023/jan/28/mumbling-actors-bad-speakers-or-lazy-listeners-why-everyone-is-watching-tv-with-subtitles-on> [Accessed 03/08/2023]

14. REV, Subtitles vs. Captions: What's the Difference?, (26/08/2022), <www.rev.com/blog/subtitles-vs-captions> [Accessed 06/08/2023]

15. Ian Youngs – BBC, Young viewers prefer TV subtitles, research suggests, (15/11/2021), <www.bbc.co.uk/news/entertainment-arts-59259964> [Accessed 03/08/2023]

16. WSC, Video Captions, <www.w3.org/WAI/perspective-videos/captions/> [Accessed 06/08/2023]

17. HTTP Archive – Web Almanac, (26/09/2022), <https://almanac.httparchive.org/en/2022/accessibility#audio-and-video> [Accessed 18/08/2023]

18. Caniuse, WebVTT, (08/2023), <https://caniuse.com/#search=webvtt> [Accessed 05/08/2023]

19. W3C, WebVTT: The Web Video Text Tracks Format, (04/04/2019), <www.w3.org/TR/webvtt1/> [Accessed 06/08/2023]

20. DeafAction, Guide to Accessible Information, (08/2014), <www.deafaction.org/wp-content/uploads/2014/08/Guide-to-Accessible-Information.pdf> [Accessed 06/08/2023]

21. Statcounter Global Stats, Browser Market Share Worldwide – July–August 2023, <https://gs.statcounter.com/browser-market-share> [Accessed 04/08/2023]

22. Lisa Herrod, Deafness and the User Experience, A List Apart, `<http://alistapart.com/article/deafnessandtheuserexperience/>` [Accessed 06/08/2023]

23. Deque University, <audio> elements must have a captions <track>, `<https://dequeuniversity.com/rules/axe/4.2/audio-caption>` [Accessed 05/08/2023]

24. Mozilla - MDN Web Docs, <audio>: The Embed Audio element, `<https://developer.mozilla.org/en-US/docs/Web/HTML/Element/audio>` [Accessed 05/08/2023]

25. HTTP Archive - Web Almanac, (26/09/2022), `<https://almanac.httparchive.org/en/2022/accessibility#audio-and-video>` [Accessed 18/08/2023]

26. Marty McGuire, Native HTML5 captions and titles for audio content with WebVTT, (17/10/2017), `<https://martymcgui.re/2017/10/17/native-html5-captions-and-titles-for-audio-content-with-webvtt/>` [Accessed 06/08/2023].

27. REV, Closed Caption File Format Guide for YouTube, Vimeo, Netflix and More, (21/03/2021), `<www.rev.com/blog/close-caption-file-format-guide-for-youtube-vimeo-netflix-and-more>` [Accessed 05/08/2023]

28. Earthweb, How many videos are on YouTube in 2023?, (16/04/2023), `<https://earthweb.com/how-many-videos-are-on-youtube/>` [Accessed 05/08/2023]

29. Google Support, Use automatic captioning, (2023), `<https://support.google.com/youtube/answer/6373554?hl=en-GB>` [Accessed 05/08/2023]

30. Lisa Herrod, Deafness and the User Experience, A List Apart, `<http://alistapart.com/article/deafnessandtheuserexperience/>` [Accessed 06/08/2023]

ENDNOTES

31. W3C – WCAG 2.1 Understanding Docs, Understanding SC 1.2.6: Sign Language (Prerecorded) (Level AAA), <www.w3.org/WAI/WCAG21/Understanding/sign-language-prerecorded.html> [Accessed 05/08/2023]

32. Áine Jackson, (British Deaf Association research and policy coordinator), Interview with author, (16/05/2019).

33. Lisa Herrod, Deafness and the User Experience, A List Apart, <http://alistapart.com/article/deafnessandtheuserexperience/> [Accessed 06/08/2023]

34. DELTA, Reading and the deaf child, <http://deafeducation.org.uk/home/family-support/reading-and-the-deaf-child/> [Accessed 06/08/2023]

35. Erika Cancio-Bello, The Sources of Deaf Humour, (Swarthmore, Pennsylvania, 2015) <https://scholarship.tricolib.brynmawr.edu/bitstream/handle/10066/16212/Cancio-Bello_thesis_2015.pdf?sequence=1> [Accessed 06/08/2023]

36. Lisa Herrod, Deafness and the User Experience, A List Apart, <http://alistapart.com/article/deafnessandtheuserexperience/> [Accessed 06/08/2023]

37. ibid.

38. Ruth MacMullen, in Sounding out the web: accessibility for deaf and hard of hearing people [Part 1] by David Swallow, (13/02/2017), <https://developer.paciellogroup.com/blog/2017/02/sounding-out-the-web-accessibility-for-deaf-and-hard-of-hearing-people-part-1/> [Accessed 06/08/2023]

39. W3C, Transcripts, <www.w3.org/WAI/media/av/transcripts/>, [Accessed 05/08/2023]

40. Ruth MacMullen, in Sounding out the web: accessibility for deaf and hard of hearing people [Part 1] by David Swallow, (13/02/2017), <https://developer.paciellogroup.com/blog/2017/02/sounding-out-the-web-accessibility-for-deaf-and-hard-of-hearing-people-part-1/> [Accessed 06/08/2023]

41. ibid.

42. James Buller, Interview with the author, (24/02/2019).

43. Áine Jackson, (British Deaf Association research and policy coordinator), Interview with author, (16/05/2019).

44. Qualtrics XM, in Help Scout, 75 Customer Service Facts, Quotes & Statistics, (22/06/2023), <www.helpscout.com/75-customer-service-facts-quotes-statistics/> [Accessed 05/08/2023]

45. HelpScout, 107 Customer Service Statistics and Facts You Shouldn't Ignore, (22/06/2023), <www.helpscout.com/75-customer-service-facts-quotes-statistics/> [Accessed 06/08/2023]

46. PwC, Experience is everything: Here's how to get it right, <www.pwc.com/us/en/advisory-services/publications/consumer-intelligence-series/pwc-consumer-intelligence-series-customer-experience.pdf> [Accessed 05/08/2023]

47. DeafAction, Advisory Services Good Practices Guide, (06/2016), <www.deafaction.org/wp-content/uploads/2014/08/Guide-to-Accessible-Information.pdf> [Accessed 06/08/2023]

48. Áine Jackson, (British Deaf Association research and policy coordinator), Interview with author, [16/05/2019].

Chapter 6

1. Hallam B, Petersen I, Cooper C, Avgerinou C, Walters K. Time Trends in Incidence of Reported Memory Concerns and Cognitive Decline: A Cohort Study in UK Primary Care. Clin Epidemiol. 2022 Mar 24;14:395-408. doi: 10.2147/CLEP.S350396. PMID: 35359800; PMCID: PMC8961006. <https://pubmed.ncbi.nlm.nih.gov/35359800/> [Accessed 28/09/2023]

2. World Health Organization, Dementia, (15/03/2023), <www.who.int/news-room/fact-sheets/detail/dementia>, [Accessed 28/09/2023]

3. American Psychological Association, Optimizing tech for older adults, (01/07/2021), <www.apa.org/monitor/2021/07/tech-older-adults> [Accessed 28/09/2023]

4. Robert McDowell, Neurodiversity and Digital Inclusion, (12/2018), <https://econsultancy.com/reports/neurodiversity-and-digital-inclusion/> [Accessed 05/10/2023]

5. Robert McDowell, Interview with author, (04/04/2019).

6. W3C, Web Content Accessibility Guidelines (WCAG) 2.2, (20/07/2023), <www.w3.org/TR/WCAG22/#:~:text=WCAG%20 2.2%20was%20initiated%20with,with%20disabilities%20on%20 mobile%20devices> [Accessed 28/09/2023]

7. WebAIM, Cognitive, (2023), <https://webaim.org/articles/cognitive/> [Accessed 05/10/2023]

8. Plainlanguage.gov, What is plain language?, <www.plainlanguage.gov/about/definitions/> [Accessed 05/10/2023]

9. European Dyslexia Association, No matter which country – No matter which language – Dyslexia is everywhere, (18/10/2020), <https://eda-info.eu/what-is-dyslexia> [Accessed 29/09/2023]

10. NHS, Aphasia, (23/03/2021), <www.nhs.uk/conditions/aphasia/> [Accessed 05/10/2023]

11. W3C, Cognitive Accessibility User Research, (15/01/2015), <www.w3.org/TR/coga-user-research/> [Accessed 05/10/2023]

12. Steven Zauderer, 55 US Literacy Statistics: Literacy Rate, Average Reading Level, (30/06/2023), <www.crossrivertherapy.com/research/literacy-statistics> [Accessed 30/09/2023]

13. National Literacy Trust, Adult literacy statistics, <https://literacytrust.org.uk/parents-and-families/adult-literacy/>, [Accessed 30/09/2023]

14. Christopher R. Trudeau and Christine Cawthorne, The Public Speaks, Again: An International Study of Legal Communication, 40 U. Ark. Little Rock L. Rev. 249 (2017), `<https://lawrepository.ualr.edu/lawreview/vol40/iss2/3>`

15. Harald Weinreich, Hartmut Obendorf, Eelco Herder, and Matthias Mayer. 2008. Not quite the average: An empirical study of Web use. ACM Trans. Web 2, 1, Article 5 (February 2008), 31 pages, `<https://doi.org/10.1145/1326561.1326566>`

16. Center for Plain Language, About, (2023), `<https://centerforplainlanguage.org/about/>` [Accessed 03/10/2023]

17. Government Digital Service, Content design: planning, writing and managing content, (30/08/2023), `<www.gov.uk/guidance/content-design/writing-for-gov-uk>` [Accessed 05/10/2023]

18. American Press Institute, Readers' Degree of Understanding, (2009)

19. Government Digital Service, Content design: planning, writing and managing content, (30/08/2023), `<www.gov.uk/guidance/content-design/writing-for-gov-uk>` [Accessed 05/10/2023]

20. Harvard University, Use plain language, (2023), `<https://accessibility.huit.harvard.edu/use-plain-language>` [Accessed 05/10/2023]

21. Government Digital Service, Content design: planning, writing and managing content, (30/08/2023), `<www.gov.uk/guidance/content-design/writing-for-gov-uk>` [Accessed 05/10/2023]

22. Dyslexie font, (2023), `<www.dyslexiefont.com/>` [Accessed 05/10/2023]

23. Government Digital Service, Content design: planning, writing and managing content, (30/08/2023), `<www.gov.uk/guidance/content-design/writing-for-gov-uk>` [Accessed 05/10/2023]

24. Kasirer A, Mashal N. Verbal creativity in autism: comprehension and generation of metaphoric language in high-functioning autism spectrum disorder and typical development. Front Hum Neurosci. 2014 Aug 11;8:615. doi: 10.3389/fnhum.2014.00615. PMID: 25157225; PMCID: PMC4128218, <www.ncbi.nlm.nih. gov/pmc/articles/PMC4128218>

25. NHS Inform, NHS inform style guide, (2023), <www.nhsinform. scot/campaigns/nhs-inform-style-guide> [Accessed 05/10/2023]

26. Government Digital Service, Content design: planning, writing and managing content, (30/08/2023), <www.gov.uk/guidance/ content-design/writing-for-gov-uk> [Accessed 05/10/2023]

27. Center for Plain Language, Five Steps to Plain Language, (2023), <https://centerforplainlanguage.org/learning-training/ five-steps-plain-language/> [Accessed 05/10/2023]

28. Wikipedia, Flesch–Kincaid readability tests, <https://en.wikipedia.org/wiki/Flesch-Kincaid_ readability_tests> [Accessed 26/09/2023]

29. Microsoft, Get your document's readability and level statistics, <https://support.microsoft.com/en-gb/office/get-your- document-s-readability-and-level-statistics-85b4969e- e80a-4777-8dd3-f7fc3c8b3fd2> [Accessed 27/09/2023]

30. W3C, Understanding Success Criterion 3.1.3: Unusual Words (Level AAA), <www.w3.org/WAI/WCAG21/Understanding/unusual- words.html> [Accessed 26/09/2023]

31. W3C, Understanding Success Criterion 3.1.4: Abbreviations (Level AAA), <www.w3.org/WAI/WCAG21/Understanding/ abbreviations.html> [Accessed 26/09/2023]

32. Marc Brysbaert, How many words do we read per minute? A review and meta-analysis of reading rate, *Journal of Memory and Language*, Volume 109, 2019, 104047, ISSN 0749-596X, <https://doi.org/10.1016/j.jml.2019.104047>

33. SimpleView, Adding Read Time on Blogs Boosts Engagement by Up to 40%, (07/04/2022), <www.simpleviewinc.com/blog/stories/post/adding-read-time-on-blogs-boosts-engagement-by-up-to-40/> [Accessed 27/09/2023]

34. Hannah Alvarez, Making Your Icons User-Friendly: A Guide to Usability in UI Design, User Testing Blog, (04/08/2015), <www.usertesting.com/blog/user-friendly-ui-icons/> [Accessed 03/10/2023]

35. WebAIM, The WebAIM Million, (2023), <https://webaim.org/projects/million/> [Accessed 27/09/2023]

36. Similarweb, zara.com, (10/2023), <www.similarweb.com/website/zara.com/#overview> [Accessed 01/10/2023]

37. Zara, Home, <www.zara.com/uk/> [Accessed 01/10/2023]

38. Alex J DeWitt, Examining the Order Effect of Website Navigation Menus With Eye Tracking, Journal of User Experience, Volume 6, Issue 1, pp. 39–47, <https://uxpajournal.org/examining-the-order-effect-of-website-navigation-menus-with-eye-tracking/>

39. W3C, Understanding Success Criterion 3.2.3: Consistent Navigation (Level AA), <www.w3.org/WAI/WCAG21/Understanding/consistent-navigation.html> [Accessed 27/09/2023]

40. Claudia Cahalane, How to avoid losing one million customers with inclusive digital design for dementia, ability.net, (05/04/2017), <www.abilitynet.org.uk/news-blogs/how-avoid-losing-one-million-website-customers-inclusive-digital-design-dementia> [Accessed 05/10/2023]

41. National Autistic Society, Sensory differences – a guide for all audiences, (02/09/2020), <www.autism.org.uk/advice-and-guidance/topics/sensory-differences/sensory-differences/all-audiences> [Accessed 05/10/2023]

42. Similarweb, gamesradar.com, (10/2023), <www.similarweb.com/website/gamesradar.com/#overview> [Accessed 03/10/2023]

43. Alex Shellhammer, The need for mobile speed, Google, (08/09/2016), <https://blog.google/products/admanager/the-need-for-mobile-speed/> [Accessed 03/10/2023]

44. W3C, Understanding Success Criterion 2.4.5: Multiple Ways (Level AA), <www.w3.org/WAI/WCAG21/Understanding/multiple-ways.html> [Accessed 01/10/2023]

45. ibid.

46. Sandee LaMotte, Your attention span is shrinking, studies say. Here's how to stay focused, CNN, (30/05/2023), <https://edition.cnn.com/2023/01/11/health/short-attention-span-wellness/index.html> [Accessed 01/10/2023]

47. W3C, Understanding Success Criterion 3.1.5: Reading Level (Level AAA), <www.w3.org/WAI/WCAG21/Understanding/reading-level.html> [Accessed 26/09/2023]

48. Srdjan Stojadinovic, How to write TL;DRs – The Beginners Guide, Text Cortex, (12/04/2023), <https://textcortex.com/post/how-to-write-tldr> [Accessed 01/10/2023]

49. W3C, Understanding Success Criterion 2.4.8: Location (Level AAA), <www.w3.org/WAI/WCAG21/Understanding/location.html> [Accessed 05/10/2023]

50. Jamie Appleseed, Baymard Institute, E-Commerce Sites Need 2 Types of Breadcrumbs (68% Get it Wrong), (07/2014), <https://baymard.com/blog/ecommerce-breadcrumbs> [Accessed 05/10/2023]

51. W3C, Understanding Success Criterion 2.4.5: Multiple Ways (Level AA), <www.w3.org/WAI/WCAG21/Understanding/multiple-ways.html> [Accessed 03/10/2023]

52. Kayle Larkin, Are Breadcrumbs A Google Ranking Factor?, Search Engine Journal, (07/12/2022), <www.searchenginejournal.com/ranking-factors/breadcrumb-navigation/> [Accessed 03/10/2023]

53. Jamie Appleseed, Baymard Institute, E-Commerce Sites Need 2 Types of Breadcrumbs (68% Get it Wrong), (07/2014), <https://baymard.com/blog/ecommerce-breadcrumbs> [Accessed 05/10/2023]

54. Claudia Cahalane, How to avoid losing one million customers with inclusive digital design for dementia, ability.net, (05/04/2017), <www.abilitynet.org.uk/news-blogs/how-avoid-losing-one-million-website-customers-inclusive-digital-design-dementia> [Accessed 05/10/2023]

55. Antonina Dattolo, Flaminia L. Luccio & Elisa Pirone, Webpage accessibility and usability for Autistic Users, a Case Study on a Tourism Website, (2016), <https://core.ac.uk/download/pdf/80136806.pdf> [Accessed 05/10/2023]

56. W3C, Understanding Success Criterion 2.4.4: Link Purpose (In Context) (Level A), <www.w3.org/WAI/WCAG21/Understanding/link-purpose-in-context.html> [Accessed 26/09/2023]

57. WebAIM, The WebAIM Million, (29/03/2023), <https://webaim.org/projects/million/> [Accessed 09/10/2023]

58. Pandu Nayak, The ABCs of spelling in Google Search, Google, (29/03/2021), <https://blog.google/products/search/abcs-spelling-google-search/>, [Accessed 03/10/2023]

59. W3C, Understanding Success Criterion 1.3.5: Link Purpose (In Context) (Level A), <www.w3.org/WAI/WCAG21/Understanding/link-purpose-in-context.html> [Accessed 26/09/2023]

60. W3C, What's new in WCAG 2.1, <www.w3.org/WAI/standards-guidelines/wcag/new-in-21/#:~:text=Understanding%20Orientation-,1.3.5%20Identify%20Input%20Purpose%20(AA),-The%20purpose%20of> [Accessed 05/10/2023]

61. jQuery user interface, Autocomplete, (2023) `<https://jqueryui.com/autocomplete/>` [Accessed 04/10/2023]

62. IBM, Fuzzy searches, (03/03/2021), `<www.ibm.com/docs/en/informix-servers/12.10?topic=modifiers-fuzzy-searches>` [Accessed 05/10/2023]

63. Robert McDowell, Neurodiversity and Digital Inclusion, (12/2018), `<https://econsultancy.com/reports/neurodiversity-and-digital-inclusion/>` [Accessed 05/10/2023]

64. Robert McDowell, Interview with author, (04/04/2019).

Chapter 7

1. Matheson SL, Shepherd AM, Carr VJ. How much do we know about schizophrenia and how well do we know it? Evidence from the Schizophrenia Library. Psychol Med. 2014 Dec;44(16):3387-405. doi: 10.1017/S0033291714000166. Epub 2014 Feb 20. PMID: 25065407.

2. World Health Organization, Mental Health, (2023), `<www.who.int/news-room/facts-in-pictures/detail/mental-health>` [Accessed 14/09/2023]

3. World Health Organization, Mental disorders, (08/06/2022), `<www.who.int/news-room/fact-sheets/detail/mental-disorders>` [Accessed 20/09/2023]

4. Merlyn Holkar and Katie Evans, Levelling the Playing Field, Money and Mental Health, (12/2017), `<www.moneyandmentalhealth.org/wp-content/uploads/2017/12/Levelling-the-playing-field-Regulators-report.pdf>` [Accessed 14/09/2023]

5. Mental Health Foundation, Fundamental Facts about Mental Health, (2016), `<www.mentalhealth.org.uk/sites/default/files/fundamental-facts-about-mental-health-2016.pdf>` [Accessed 17/09/2023]

6. Merlyn Holkar, Senior Research Officer at Money and Mental Health, Interview with author, (14/05/2019).

7. Merlyn Holkar and Katie Evans, Levelling the Playing Field, Money and Mental Health, (12/2017), <www.moneyandmentalhealth.org/wp-content/uploads/2017/12/Levelling-the-playing-field-Regulators-report.pdf> [Accessed 17/09/2023]

8. Forbruker Rådet, Deceived by Design, (27/06/2018), <https://fil.forbrukerradet.no/wp-content/uploads/2018/06/2018-06-27-deceived-by-design-final.pdf> [Accessed 17/09/2023]

9. Chris Fox, Google hit with £44m GDPR fine over ads, BBC, (21/01/2019), <www.bbc.co.uk/news/technology-46944696> [Accessed 17/09/2023]

10. CNIL, Deliberation of the restricted committee No. SAN-2021-023 of 31 December 2021 concerning GOOGLE LLC and GOOGLE IRELAND LIMITED, (12/11/2021), <www.cnil.fr/sites/cnil/files/atoms/files/deliberation_of_the_restricted_committee_no._san-2021-023_of_31_december_2021_concerning_google_llc_and_google_ireland_limited.pdf> [Accessed 15/09/2023]

11. European Commission, Directorate-General for Justice and Consumers, Lupiáñez-Villanueva, F., Boluda, A., Bogliacino, F. et al., Behavioural study on unfair commercial practices in the digital environment – Dark patterns and manipulative personalisation – Final report, Publications Office of the European Union, 2022, <https://data.europa.eu/doi/10.2838/859030> [Accessed 15/09/2023]

12. Forbruker Rådet, Deceived by Design, (2018), <https://fil.forbrukerradet.no/wp-content/uploads/2018/06/2018-06-27-deceived-by-design-final.pdf> [Accessed 17/09/2023]

13. W3C, Diverse Abilities and Barriers, (15/05/2017), <www.w3.org/WAI/people-use-web/abilities-barriers/> [Accessed 17/09/2023]

14. W3C, Cognitive Accessibility Roadmap and Gap Analysis, (11/12/2018), <www.w3.org/TR/coga-gap-analysis/> [Accessed 17/09/2023]

15. Harry Brignull, Deceptive Design, (2023), <www.deceptive.design/> [Accessed 14/09/2023]

16. Deceptive Design, Hard to Cancel, (2023), <www.deceptive.design/types/hard-to-cancel> [Accessed 14/09/2023]

17. YCombinator – Hacker News, Before buying a NYT subscription, here's what it'll take to cancel it, (18/02/2021), <https://news.ycombinator.com/item?id=26174269> [Accessed 15/09/2023]

18. Stylist, Want to leave Instagram? Deleting your account could be harder than you think, (15/09/2021), <www.stylist.co.uk/health/mental-health/instagram-delete-account/574816>, [Accessed 15/09/2023]

19. Rhodri Marsden, The National News, Why is it so hard to delete digital accounts?, (25/10/2021), <www.thenationalnews.com/arts-culture/comment/2021/10/25/why-is-it-so-hard-to-delete-digital-accounts/> [Accessed 15/09/2023]

20. Chris Fox, Google hit with £44m GDPR fine over ads, BBC, (2019), <www.bbc.co.uk/news/technology-46944696> [Accessed 17/09/2023]

21. Lexparency, Article 5 – Confidentiality of the communications, <https://lexparency.org/eu/32002L0058/ART_5/> [Accessed 15/09/2023]

22. CNIL, Deliberation of the restricted committee No. SAN-2021-023 of 31 December 2021 concerning GOOGLE LLC and GOOGLE IRELAND LIMITED, (12/11/2021), <www.cnil.fr/sites/cnil/files/atoms/files/deliberation_of_the_restricted_committee_no._san-2021-023_of_31_december_2021_concerning_google_llc_and_google_ireland_limited.pdf> [Accessed 15/09/2023]

23. Merlyn Holkar and Katie Evans, Levelling the Playing Field, Money and Mental Health, (12/2017), <www.moneyandmentalhealth.org/wp-content/uploads/2017/12/Levelling-the-playing-field-Regulators-report.pdf> [Accessed 17/09/2023]

24. Merlyn Holkar, Senior Research Officer at Money and Mental Health, Interview with author, (14/05/2019).

25. Merlyn Holkar and Katie Evans, Levelling the Playing Field, Money and Mental Health, (12/2017) <www.moneyandmentalhealth.org/wp-content/uploads/2017/12/Levelling-the-playing-field-Regulators-report.pdf> [Accessed 17/09/2023]

26. X, President Biden (@POTUS), (23/03/2023), <https://twitter.com/POTUS/status/1638896377353601028> [Accessed 17/09/2023]

27. Merlyn Holkar and Katie Evans, Levelling the Playing Field, Money and Mental Health, (12/2017), <www.moneyandmentalhealth.org/wp-content/uploads/2017/12/Levelling-the-playing-field-Regulators-report.pdf> [Accessed 17/09/2023]

28. W3C, Diverse Abilities and Barriers, (15/05/2017), <www.w3.org/WAI/people-use-web/abilities-barriers/> [Accessed 17/09/2023]

29. Merlyn Holkar and Katie Evans, Levelling the Playing Field, Money and Mental Health, (12/2017), <www.moneyandmentalhealth.org/wp-content/uploads/2017/12/Levelling-the-playing-field-Regulators-report.pdf> [Accessed 17/09/2023]

30. Merlyn Holkar, Senior Research Officer at Money and Mental Health, Interview with author, (14/05/2019).

31. World Health Organization, Mental disorders, (08/06/2022), <www.who.int/news-room/fact-sheets/detail/mental-disorders> [Accessed 20/09/2023]

32. Mental Health Foundation, Anxiety: Statistics, <www.mentalhealth.org.uk/explore-mental-health/statistics/anxiety-statistics> [Accessed 14/09/2023]

33. Fineberg, N., Haddad, P., Carpenter, L., Gannon, B., Sharpe, R., Young, A., Joyce, E., Rowe, J., Wellsted, D., Nutt, D. and Sahakian, B. (2013). *The size, burden and cost of disorders of the brain in the UK. Journal of Psychopharmacology*, 27 (9), pp.761–770.

34. Merlyn Holkar, Senior Research Officer at Money and Mental Health, Interview with author, (14/05/2019).

35. NHS, Overview – Bipolar disorder, (03/01/2023), <www.nhs.uk/mental-health/conditions/bipolar-disorder/overview/> [Accessed 21/09/2023]

36. BP Magazine, How to Accomplish Tasks When Depressed: Motivation's Mystery, (29/05/2020), <www.bphope.com/getting-things-done-when-youre-depressed-the-mystery-of-motivation/> [Accessed 17/09/2023]

37. Karwai Pun, Dos and don'ts on designing for accessibility, Gov.UK, (02/09/2016), <https://accessibility.blog.gov.uk/2016/09/02/dos-and-donts-on-designing-for-accessibility/> [Accessed 17/09/2023]

38. OCDUK, Occurrences of OCD, (2023), <www.ocduk.org/ocd/how-common-is-ocd/> [Accessed 21/09/2023]

39. Tolin DF, Abramowitz JS, Brigidi BD, Foa EB. Intolerance of uncertainty in obsessive-compulsive disorder. J Anxiety Disord. 2003;17(2):233-42. doi: 10.1016/s0887-6185(02)00182-2. PMID: 12614665.

40. Queue Fair, The Psychology of waiting in line (queuing if you're British), (20/01/2021), <https://queue-fair.com/psychology-of-waiting-in-line-queuing> [Accessed 17/09/2023]

41. Sarah Drummond, Positive Patterns for Designing Mental Health Services, Medium, (05/10/2017), <https://medium.com/@sarahdrummond/positive-patterns-for-designing-mental-health-services-e2d323cdbdf8> [Accessed 17/09/2023]

42. W3C, WCAG 2.1 Understanding Docs, Understanding SC 2.4.8: Location (Level AAA), <www.w3.org/WAI/WCAG21/Understanding/location.html> [Accessed 19/09/2023]

43. Similarweb, booking.com, <`www.similarweb.com/website/booking.com/#overview`> [Accessed 15/09/2023]

44. Roman Cheplyaka, How booking.com uses stress to rush your decisions, The Next Web (21/09/2017), <`https://thenextweb.com/contributors/2017/09/21/booking-com-uses-stress-rush-decisions/`> [Accessed 17/09/2023]

45. Merlyn Holkar and Katie Evans, Levelling the Playing Field, Money and Mental Health, (12/2017), <`www.moneyandmentalhealth.org/wp-content/uploads/2017/12/Levelling-the-playing-field-Regulators-report.pdf`> [Accessed 17/09/2023]

46. Karwai Pun, Dos and don'ts on designing for accessibility, Gov.UK, (02/09/2016), <`https://accessibility.blog.gov.uk/2016/09/02/dos-and-donts-on-designing-for-accessibility/`> [Accessed 17/09/2023]

47. Mind, What is Paranoia?, (2023), <`www.mind.org.uk/information-support/types-of-mental-health-problems/paranoia/about-paranoia/`> [Accessed 17/09/2023]

48. NHS, Borderline Personality Disorder, (04/11/2022), <`www.nhs.uk/conditions/borderline-personality-disorder/`> [Accessed 17/09/2023] + Erin Johnson, Managing Money with Borderline Personality Disorder, Very Well Mind, (26/12/2022), <`www.verywellmind.com/managing-money-issues-425362`> [Accessed 17/09/2023]

49. Roman Cheplyaka, How booking.com uses stress to rush your decisions, The Next Web (21/09/2017), <`https://thenextweb.com/contributors/2017/09/21/booking-com-uses-stress-rush-decisions/`> [Accessed 17/09/2023]

50. Which? Booking.com still misleading holidaymakers with '1 room left' claims, (19/09/2019), <`www.which.co.uk/news/article/booking-com-still-misleading-holidaymakers-with-1-room-left-claims-aSNln2j8gkGl`> [Accessed 20/09/2023]

ENDNOTES

51. Shopify App Store, Hey!Scarcity Low Stock Counter,
    <https://apps.shopify.com/heymerch-sales-stock-counter>
    [Accessed 15/09/2023]

52. W3C, WCAG 2.1 Understanding Docs, Understanding SC
    2.2.1: Timing Adjustable (Level A), <www.w3.org/WAI/WCAG21/
    Understanding/timing-adjustable.html> [Accessed
    19/09/2023]

53. Hacker News, Blog Post by bogomipz, Comment by
    edejong (20/09/2017), <https://news.ycombinator.com/
    item?id=15299001> [Accessed 17/09/2023]

54. Confirm Shaming, Tumblr, <https://confirmshaming.tumblr.
    com/> [Accessed 15/09/2023]

55. ibid.

56. Deceptive Design, Confirmshaming, <www.deceptive.design/
    types/confirmshaming> [Accessed 15/09/2023]

57. NHS, Social Anxiety, (17/05/2023), <www.nhs.uk/conditions/
    social-anxiety/> [Accessed 17/09/2023]

58. NHS, Generalised anxiety disorder in adults, (05/10/2022),
    <www.nhs.uk/conditions/generalised-anxiety-disorder/>
    [Accessed 17/09/2023]

59. Merlyn Holkar and Katie Evans, Levelling the Playing Field, Money
    and Mental Health, (12/2017), <www.moneyandmentalhealth.org/
    wp-content/uploads/2017/12/Levelling-the-playing-field-
    Regulators-report.pdf> [Accessed 17/09/2023]

60. Confirm Shaming, Tumblr, <https://confirmshaming.tumblr.
    com/image/179398684581> [Accessed 17/09/2023]

61. Tom Blake , Sarah Moshary, Kane Sweeney, Steve Tadelis
    (2021) Price Salience and Product Choice. Marketing Science
    40(4):619-636, <https://doi.org/10.1287/mksc.2020.1261>
    [Accessed 15/09/2023]

62. European Commission, Directorate-General for Justice and Consumers, Lupiáñez-Villanueva, F., Boluda, A., Bogliacino, F. et al., Behavioural study on unfair commercial practices in the digital environment – Dark patterns and manipulative personalisation – Final report, Publications Office of the European Union, 2022, <https://data.europa.eu/doi/10.2838/859030> [Accessed 15/09/2023]

63. High Court of Justice, Claim No. FS-2018-000011, Competitions and Markets Authority vs. Viagogo AG, (27/11/2018), <https://assets.publishing.service.gov.uk/media/5bffe2afe5274a0fae2c5397/CMA_v_Viagogo_Order_27.11.pdf> [Accessed 15/09/2023]

64. AirBNB, Airbnb is introducing total price display and updating guest checkout, (07/11/2022), <https://news.airbnb.com/airbnb-is-introducing-total-price-display-and-updating-guest-checkout/> [Accessed 15/09/2023]

65. World Health Organization, Mental disorders, (08/06/2022), <www.who.int/news-room/fact-sheets/detail/mental-disorders> [Accessed 20/09/2023]

66. Zander Brade, Designing a product with mental health issues in mind, Monzo Blog, (27/01/2017), <https://monzo.com/blog/2017/01/27/designing-product-mental-health-mind/> [Accessed 16/09/2023]

67. ibid.

68. Andrei Lanovskii, X, (16/05/2019), <https://twitter.com/gn0me/status/1129133677156458497> [Accessed 17/09/2023]

69. Deepan Ghimiray, Fake Virus Warnings: How to Spot and Avoid Them, AVG (12/09/2022), <www.avg.com/en/signal/spot-fake-virus-warning> [Accessed 17/09/2023]

70. Bogdan Popa, Microsoft Admits It "Went Too Far" with Aggressive Windows Updates, (23/12/2016), <https://news.softpedia.com/news/microsoft-admits-it-went-too-far-with-aggressive-windows-10-updates-511245.shtml> [Accessed 17/09/2023]

71. Mental Health Foundation, Stress, (17/09/2021), <www.mentalhealth.org.uk/a-to-z/s/stress> [Accessed 17/09/2023]

72. W3C, WCAG 2.1 Understanding Docs, Understanding SC 3.2.4: Consistent Identification (Level AA), <www.w3.org/WAI/WCAG21/Understanding/consistent-identification.html> [Accessed 17/09/2023]

73. House of Representatives, Subcommittee on Communications and Technology, joint with Subcommittee on Consumer Protection and Commerce, Committee on Energy and Commerce, Washington, D.C, Disinformation Nation: Social Media's role in promoting extremism and misinformation, (25/03/2021), <https://docs.house.gov/meetings/IF/IF16/20210325/111407/HHRG-117-IF16-Transcript-20210325.pdf> line 5333 [Accessed 15/09/2023]

74. Tim Jones, Electronic Frontier Foundation, Facebook's "Evil Interfaces", (29/04/2010), <www.eff.org/deeplinks/2010/04/facebooks-evil-interfaces> [Accessed 15/09/2023]

75. *New York Times*, Cambridge Analytica and Facebook: The Scandal and the Fallout So Far, (04/04/2018), <www.nytimes.com/2018/04/04/us/politics/cambridge-analytica-scandal-fallout.html> [Accessed 15/09/2023]

76. Midas Nouwens, Ilaria Liccardi, Michael Veale, David Karger, Lalana Kagal, Cornell University, Dark Patterns after the GDPR: Scraping Consent Pop-ups and Demonstrating their Influence, (08/01/2020), <https://arxiv.org/abs/2001.02479> [Accessed 15/09/2023]

77. Bösch, Christoph & Erb, Benjamin & Kargl, Frank & Kopp, Henning & Pfattheicher, Stefan. (2016). Tales from the Dark Side: Privacy Dark Strategies and Privacy Dark Patterns. Proceedings on Privacy Enhancing Technologies. 2016. 237–254. 10.1515/popets-2016-0038.

78. Federal Trade Commission, FTC Imposes $5 Billion Penalty and Sweeping New Privacy Restrictions on Facebook, (24/07/2019), <www.ftc.gov/news-events/news/press-releases/2019/07/ftc-imposes-5-billion-penalty-sweeping-new-privacy-restrictions-facebook> [Accessed 16/09/2023]

79. Federal Trade Commission, FTC Takes Action Against Amazon for Enrolling Consumers in Amazon Prime Without Consent and Sabotaging Their Attempts to Cancel, (21/06/2023), <www.ftc.gov/news-events/news/press-releases/2023/06/ftc-takes-action-against-amazon-enrolling-consumers-amazon-prime-without-consent-sabotaging-their> [Accessed 16/09/2023]

80. Business Insider, Internal documents show Amazon has for years knowingly tricked people into signing up for Prime subscriptions. 'We have been deliberately confusing' former employee says, (14/03/2022), <www.businessinsider.com/amazon-prime-ftc-probe-customer-complaints-sign-ups-internal-documents-2022-3> [Accessed 16/09/2023]

81. ibid.

82. ibid.

83. Business Insider, Internal documents show Amazon has for years knowingly tricked people into signing up for Prime subscriptions. 'We have been deliberately confusing' former employee says, (14/03/2022), <www.businessinsider.com/amazon-prime-ftc-probe-customer-complaints-sign-ups-internal-documents-2022-3> [Accessed 16/09/2023]

84. ibid.

85. Merlyn Holkar, Senior Research Officer at Money and Mental Health, Interview with author, (14/05/2019).

86. W3C, WCAG 2.1 Understanding Docs, Understanding SC 3.3.4: Error Prevention (Legal, Financial, Data) (Level AA), <www.w3.org/WAI/WCAG21/Understanding/error-prevention-legal-financial-data.html> [Accessed 16/09/2023]

87. Business Insider, Internal documents show Amazon has for years knowingly tricked people into signing up for Prime subscriptions. "We have been deliberately confusing' former employee says, (14/03/2022), <www.businessinsider.com/amazon-prime-ftc-probe-customer-complaints-sign-ups-internal-documents-2022-3> [Accessed 16/09/2023]

88. ibid.

89. ForbrukerRådet, You can log out, but you can never leave: How Amazon manipulates consumers to keep them subscribed to Amazon Prime, (14/01/2021), <https://storage02.forbrukerradet.no/media/2021/01/2021-01-14-you-can-log-out-but-you-can-never-leave-final.pdf> [Accessed 16/09/2023]

90. Business Insider, Internal documents show Amazon has for years knowingly tricked people into signing up for Prime subscriptions. "We have been deliberately confusing" former employee says, (14/03/2022), <www.businessinsider.com/amazon-prime-ftc-probe-customer-complaints-sign-ups-internal-documents-2022-3> [Accessed 16/09/2023]

91. ibid.

92. Forbruker Rådet, Amazon makes it easier to cancel Prime following complaints from European consumer organisations, (01/07/2022), <www.forbrukerradet.no/siste-nytt/amazon-makes-it-easier-to-cancel-prime-following-complaints-from-european-consumer-organisations/> [Accessed 16/09/2023]

93. Federal Trade Commission, FTC Action Against Vonage Results in $100 Million to Customers Trapped by Illegal Dark Patterns and Junk Fees When Trying to Cancel Service, (03/11/2022), <www.ftc.gov/news-events/news/press-releases/2022/11/ftc-action-against-vonage-results-100-million-customers-trapped-illegal-dark-patterns-junk-fees-when-trying-cancel-service> [Accessed 16/09/2023]

94. Federal Trade Commission, FTC Finalizes Order Requiring Fortnite maker Epic Games to Pay $245 Million for Tricking Users into Making Unwanted Charges, (14/03/2023), <www.ftc.gov/news-events/news/press-releases/2023/03/ftc-finalizes-order-requiring-fortnite-maker-epic-games-pay-245-million-tricking-users-making> [Accessed 16/09/2023]

95. World Wide Web Foundation, Contract for the Web, (2023) <https://contractfortheweb.org/> [Accessed 21/09/2023]

96. Natasha Lomas, The Web Foundation is taking on deceptive design, TechCrunch, (23/03/2022), <https://techcrunch.com/2022/03/23/deceptive-design-patterns-project/> [Accessed 21/09/2023]

97. Tech Policy Design Lab, Deceptive Design – Strategies for Change, (2023), <https://techlab.webfoundation.org/deceptive-design/strategies-for-change> [Accessed 21/09/2023]

98. ibid.

99. Merlyn Holkar and Katie Evans, Levelling the Playing Field, Money and Mental Health, (12/2017), <www.moneyandmentalhealth.org/wp-content/uploads/2017/12/Levelling-the-playing-field-Regulators-report.pdf> [Accessed 17/09/2023]

100. FlixPatrol, Top Streaming Services by Subscribers, (10/2023), <https://flixpatrol.com/streaming-services/subscribers/> [Accessed 15/09/2023]

101. Forbruker Radet, Deceived by Design, (27/06/2018),
      <https://fil.forbrukerradet.no/wp-content/
      uploads/2018/06/2018-06-27-deceived-by-design-final.pdf>
      [Accessed 15/09/2023]

Chapter 8

1. Photutorial, Number of Photos (2023): Statistics and Trends,
    (27/06/2023), <https://photutorial.com/photos-statistics/>
    [Accessed 18/08/2023]

2. W3Techs, Usage statistics of image file formats for websites,
    (2023), <https://w3techs.com/technologies/overview/image_
    format> [Accessed 18/08/2023]

3. Earthweb, How many videos are on YouTube in 2023?,
    (16/04/2023), <https://earthweb.com/how-many-videos-are-
    on-youtube/> [Accessed 18/08/2023]

4. W3Techs, Market share trends for content management systems
    (08/23), <https://w3techs.com/technologies/history_
    overview/content_management> [Accessed 20/08/2023]

5. W3C, F39: Failure of Success Criterion 1.1.1, (2023) <www.w3.org/
    WAI/GL/2016/WD-WCAG20-TECHS-20160105/F39> [Accessed
    20/08/2023]

6. W3C, WCAG 2.1 Understanding Docs – Understand SC
    1.4.5: Images of Text, (2023), <www.w3.org/WAI/WCAG21/
    Understanding/images-of-text.html> [Accessed 19/08/2023]

7. Molly Watt, Accessibility and Me, Gov.uk, (09/01/2017),
    <https://accessibility.blog.gov.uk/2017/01/09/
    accessibility-and-me-molly-watt/> [Accessed 20/08/2023]

8. VWO, Conversion Rate Optimization Solutions for Revenue
    Growth, (09/08/2023), <https://vwo.com/blog/optimize-
    video-content-for-conversions/> [Accessed 19/08/2023]

9. Unbounce, Video on Landing Pages Means More Conversions, Right? Wrong—Here's Why, (26/08/2021), <https://unbounce. com/landing-pages/video-on-landing-pages-means-more-conversions-right-wrong-heres-why/> [Accessed 19/08/2023]

10. National Library of Medicine, Dora M. Raymaker, Steven K. Kapp, Katherine E. McDonald, Michael Weiner, Elesia Ashkenazy, and Christina Nicolaidis, Development of the AASPIRE Web Accessibility Guidelines for Autistic Web Users, (13/04/2019), <https://pubmed.ncbi.nlm.nih.gov/32292887/> [Accessed 20/08/2023]

11. W3C, WCAG 2.2 Understanding Docs – Understanding Success Criterion 2.2.2: Pause, Stop, Hide, <www.w3.org/TR/ WCAG22/#pause-stop-hide> [Accessed 20/08/2023]

12. W3C, WCAG 2.1 Understanding Docs – Understanding SC 2.3.1: Three Flashes or Below Threshold, (2023), <www.w3.org/WAI/ WCAG21/Understanding/three-flashes-or-below-threshold. html> [Accessed 19/08/2023]

13. W3C, WCAG 2.1 Understanding Docs – Understand SC 1.4.2: Audio Controls, (2023), <www.w3.org/WAI/WCAG21/ Understanding/audio-control.html> [Accessed 19/08/2023]

14. Val Head, *Designing Safer Web Animation For Motion Sensitivity*, in A List Apart, (08/09/2015), <https://alistapart.com/ article/designing-safer-web-animation-for-motion-sensitivity/> [Accessed 20/08/2023]

15. ibid.

16. National Library of Medicine, Acta Otorhinolaryngol Ital: Article PMC4977009 – Point prevalence of vertigo and dizziness in a sample of 2672 subjects and correlation with headaches, (06/2016), <www.ncbi.nlm.nih.gov/pmc/articles/PMC4977009/> [Accessed 19/08/2023]

17. Grey Ghost Visuals, *A primer to vestibular disorders*, in The A11y Project, (15/05/2013), `<https://a11yproject.com/posts/understanding-vestibular-disorders/>` [Accessed 20/08/2023]

18. Mozilla – mdn web docs, color-scheme, (17/07/2023), `<https://developer.mozilla.org/en-US/docs/Web/CSS/color-scheme>` [Accessed 21/08/2023]

19. Can I Use, CSS at-rule: @media: prefers-reduced-transparency media feature, (08/2023), `<https://caniuse.com/?search=prefers-reduced-transparency>` [Accessed 15/08/2023]

20. Val Head, *Designing Safer Web Animation For Motion Sensitivity*, in A List Apart, (08/09/2015), `<https://alistapart.com/article/designing-safer-web-animation-for-motion-sensitivity/>` [Accessed 21/08/2023]

21. W3C, WCAG 2.1 Understanding Docs – Understand SC 2.3.3: Animation from Interactions, (2023), `<www.w3.org/WAI/WCAG21/Understanding/animation-from-interactions.html>` [Accessed 19/08/2023]

22. Gery Teague, Reasons You Shouldn't Use Sprite Sheets, (04/05/2016), `<www.hbdesign.com/sprite-sheets-3-things-know/>` [accessed 21/08/2023]

23. Adobe, SVG Files, `<www.adobe.com/creativecloud/file-types/image/vector/svg-file.html>`, [Accessed 20/08/2023]

24. Font Awesome, Home, `<https://fontawesome.com>` [accessed 21/08/2023]

25. Nick Colley, Supporting users who change colours on GOV.UK, Gov.uk's Accessibility in government blog, (01/08/2018), `<https://accessibility.blog.gov.uk/2018/08/01/supporting-users-who-change-colours-on-gov-uk/>` [Accessed 21/08/2023]

Chapter 9

1. Statista, Number of sent and received e-mails per day worldwide from 2017 to 2026 (in billions), (11/2022), `<www.statista.com/statistics/456500/daily-number-of-e-mails-worldwide/>` [Accessed 29/08/2023]

2. Statista, Number of e-mail users worldwide from 2017 to 2026 (in millions), (11/2022), `<www.statista.com/statistics/255080/number-of-e-mail-users-worldwide/>` [Accessed 29/08/2023]

3. Litmus, The Ultimate Guide to Accessible Emails, Litmus, (02/2020), `<https://litmus.com/blog/ultimate-guide-accessible-emails>` [Accessed 30/08/2023]

4. Email Markup Consortium, Accessibility Report 2023, (18/05/2023), `<https://emailmarkup.org/en/reports/accessibility/2023/>` [Accessed 02/09/2023]

5. Lauren Smith, A Guide to Rendering Differences in Microsoft Outlook Clients, Litmus, (17/03/2023), `<https://litmus.com/blog/a-guide-to-rendering-differences-in-microsoft-outlook-clients>` [Accessed 03/09/2023]

6. DEV, The new Outlook for Windows, (13/03/2023), `<https://dev.to/emailmarkup/the-new-outlook-for-windows-54k7>` [Accessed 30/08/2023]

7. End of Life Date, Microsoft Office, (14/06/2023), `<https://endoflife.date/office>` [Accessed 30/08/2023]

8. Campaign Monitor, The Ultimate Guide to CSS, (03/09/2023), `<www.campaignmonitor.com/css/>` [Accessed 03/09/2023]

9. Campaign Monitor, Accessibility and Email Campaigns, (2023), `<www.campaignmonitor.com/resources/guides/accessibility/>` [Accessed 03/09/2023]

10. Email on Acid, Do You Really Need a "View This Email in Your Browser" Link?, (02/12/2022), <www.emailonacid.com/blog/article/email-development/view-in-browser-link/> [Accessed 03/09/2023]

11. Mailchimp, Add a Campaign Page Link to Your Email Campaign, (2023), <https://mailchimp.com/help/add-a-campaign-page-link-to-your-email-campaign/> [Accessed 03/09/2023]

12. Phrasee, A brief history of email, (10/03/2016), <https://phrasee.co/news/a-brief-history-of-email/> [Accessed 03/09/2023]

13. Sendgrid, HTML Formatting Issues, (2023), <https://sendgrid.com/docs/ui/sending-email/formatting-html/> [Accessed 03/09/2023]

14. Litmus, Why You Shouldn't Dismiss Plain Text Emails (And How to Make Them Engaging), (31/08/2022), <www.litmus.com/blog/best-practices-for-plain-text-emails-a-look-at-why-theyre-important>, [Accessed 03/09/2023]

15. Gary Eckstein, Image spam and how it affects your email campaigns, (25/07/2017), <https://organicweb.com.au/marketing/image-spam/> [Accessed 05/09/2023]

16. Campaign Monitor, Gmail, and Today's Popular Email Clients, (2018), <www.campaignmonitor.com/resources/guides/most-popular-email-clients/> [Accessed 05/09/2023]

17. Email on Acid, Email Accessibility: A Complete Guide for Marketers, Designers, and Developers, (16/02/2023), <www.emailonacid.com/blog/article/email-development/email-accessibilty-in-2017/> [Accessed 03/09/2023]

18. Mailchimp, Translate Content in a Campaign, (2023), <https://mailchimp.com/help/translate-content-in-a-campaign/> [Accessed 05/09/2023]

19. Email Markup Consortium, Accessibility Report 2023, (18/05/2023), <https://emailmarkup.org/en/reports/accessibility/2023/> [Accessed 02/09/2023]

20. WebAIM, Screen Reader User Survey #9, (30/06/2021), <https://webaim.org/projects/screenreadersurvey9/> [Accessed 05/09/2023]

21. W3C, Supplemental Guidance: Text Justification, <www.w3.org/WAI/GL/low-vision-a11y-tf/wiki/Supplemental_Guidance:_Text_Justification> [Accessed 04/09/2023]

22. WCAG, Understanding SC 1.4.12: Text Spacing (Level AA), <www.w3.org/WAI/WCAG21/Understanding/text-spacing.html> [Accessed 05/09/2023]

23. WordStream, 6 Mind-Blowing Digital Marketing Stats from Unbounce's Conversion Road Trip, (22/11/2021), <www.wordstream.com/blog/ws/2015/06/10/digital-marketing-stats> [Accessed 03/09/2023]

24. Emily Ryan, Why Clients Render Email Differently, (30/09/2016), <https://mailchimp.com/resources/why-clients-render-email-differently/> [Accessed 04/09/2023]

25. W3C, PDF Techniques for WCAG 2.0, (2012) <www.w3.org/TR/WCAG20-TECHS/pdf#pdf_notes> [Accessed 05/09/2023]

26. Google, One Click Actions, <https://developers.google.com/gmail/markup/reference/one-click-action> [Accessed 03/09/2023]

27. Google, Go-To Actions, <https://developers.google.com/gmail/markup/reference/go-to-action> [Accessed 03/09/2023]

28. Sendgrid, What Is a No-Reply Email (And Why You Should Never Use Them), (21/01/2023), <https://sendgrid.com/blog/why-you-should-not-use-noreplydomain-com-in-your-emails/> [Accessed 05/09/2023]

29. Mailjet, Noreply email address: Best practices for your email strategy, (03/11/2022), <www.mailjet.com/blog/news/the-noreply-dilemma-going-from-no-to-yes/> [Accessed 05/09/2023]

30. ibid.

31. Raelene Morey, Never Use a "No-Reply" Email Address (and What to Do Instead), MailPoet, (31/01/2019), <www.mailpoet.com/blog/never-use-not-reply-email-address/> [Accessed 05/09/2023]

32. Sendgrid, What Is a No-Reply Email (And Why You Should Never Use Them), (21/01/2023), <https://sendgrid.com/blog/why-you-should-not-use-noreplydomain-com-in-your-emails/> [Accessed 05/09/2023]

33. Email Markup Consortium, Accessibility Report 2023, (18/05/2023), <https://emailmarkup.org/en/reports/accessibility/2023/> [Accessed 05/09/2023]

Chapter 10

1. Accessibe, Everything you need to know to ensure that your website is accessible and compliant with accessiBe, (09/12/2019), <https://accessibe.com/blog/knowledgebase/accessibe-website-onboarding#:~:text=AI%20(computer%20vision)%20engine%20creates%20an%20alt%20text%20from%20the%20objects%20that%20appear%20in%20the%20image%20and%20the%20embedded%20text> [Accessed 19/06/2023]

2. accessiBe, accessFlow, <https://accessibe.com/accessflow> [Accessed 23/06/2023]

3. A11y Project, Should I use an accessibility overlay?, (08/03/2021), <www.a11yproject.com/posts/should-i-use-an-accessibility-overlay/#:~:text=will%20increase%20exponentially.-,Autonomy,-Many%20permanent%20plugins> [Accessed 23/06/2023]

4. NBC News, Blind people, advocates slam company claiming to make websites ADA compliant, (09/03/2021), <www.nbcnews.com/tech/innovation/blind-people-advocates-slam-company-claiming-make-websites-ada-compliant-n1266720> [Accessed 04/07/2023]

5. Léonie Watson, Thoughts on screen reader detection, (27/02/2014), <https://tink.uk/thoughts-on-screen-reader-detection/> [Accessed 23/06/2023]

6. The Register, UK ICO, USCourts.gov... Thousands of websites hijacked by hidden crypto-mining code after popular plugin pwned, (11/02/2018), <www.theregister.com/2018/02/11/browsealoud_compromised_coinhive/> [Accessed 22/06/2023]

7. Adrian Roselli, #accessiBe Will Get You Sued, (09/06/2023), <https://adrianroselli.com/2020/06/accessibe-will-get-you-sued.html#Inaccessible> [Accessed 22/06/2023]

8. WebAIM, Twitter, (02/06/2023), <https://twitter.com/webaim/status/1664660562180194308> [Accessed 19/06/2023]

9. WebAIM, Twitter, (02/06/2023), <https://twitter.com/webaim/status/1664662372504461313> [Accessed 19/06/2023]

10. Accessibility Defense, Is there a silver bullet for ADA website accessibility? Sorry, but the answer is no, (31/03/2020), <https://accessdefense.com/?p=5378> [Accessed 23/06/2023]

11. UsableNet, ADA Digital Accessibility Lawsuit Trends Involving - Websites, Mobile, Apps, Video, (25/01/2023), <https://info.usablenet.com/thank-you-2022-end-of-year-report-on-digital-accessibility-lawsuits?submissionGuid=711cb65a-214e-437d-9ce0-5a03da194d19> [Accessed 19/06/2023]

12. Scribd, Fischler Et al V Dorai Homes, <www.scribd.com/document/509432294/Fischler-et-al-v-Dorai-Homes> [Accessed 22/06/2023]

13. Adrian Roselli, #accessiBe Will Get You Sued, (09/06/2023), <https://adrianroselli.com/2020/06/accessibe-will-get-you-sued.html#Lawsuit:~:text=THOMAS%20KLAUS%20and%20ROBERT%20JAHODA%20v.%20UPRIGHT%20TECHNOLOGIES%2C%20INC.%20complaint> [Accessed 19/06/2023]

14. Forbes, Largest U.S. Blind Advocacy Group Bans Web Accessibility Overlay Giant AccessiBe From Its National Convention, (26/06/2023), <www.forbes.com/sites/gusalexiou/2021/06/26/largest-us-blind-advocacy-group-bans-web-accessibility-overlay-giant-accessibe/?sh=44df73485a15> [Accessed 22/06/2023]

15. National Federation of the Blind, National Convention Sponsorship Statement Regarding accessiBe, (24/06/2021), <https://nfb.org/about-us/press-room/national-convention-sponsorship-statement-regarding-accessibe> [Accessed 22/06/2023]

16. Connor Scott-Gardner, Do Automated Solutions like #AccessiBe Make the Web More Accessible?, (25/02/2021), <https://catchthesewords.com/do-automated-solutions-like-accessibe-make-the-web-more-accessible/> [Accessed 22/06/2023]

17. Overlay Fact Sheet, <https://overlayfactsheet.com/#statement-from-sponsors-and-signatories-to-this-fact-sheet:~:text=we%20hereby%20advocate%20for%20the%20removal%20of%20web%20accessibility%20overlay%20and%20encourage%20the%20site%20owners%20who%27ve%20implemented%20these%20products%20to%20use%20more%20robust%2C%20independent%2C%20and%20permanent%20strategies%20to%20making%20their%20sites%20more%20accessible> [Accessed 22/06/2023]

18. Shir Ekerling on National Federation of the Blind, A Heart-felt Apology and a Chance to Start Again, (03/05/2023). <https://nfb.org/images/nfb/publications/bm/bm23/bm2305/bm230503.htm> [Accessed 19/06/2023]

19. Living Blindfully, Transcript, Living Blindfully episode 232, Apples accessibility bugs, can Bookshare be justified in an era of Apple Books and Kindle, and the CEO of AccessiBe says he's sorry, (07/06/2023), `<www.livingblindfully.com/lb0232transcript/>` [Accessed 19/06/2023]

20. Shir Ekerling on Accessibe, accessiBE Purpose Statement, `<https://accessibe.com/purpose-statement>` [Accessed 19/06/2023]

21. Adrian Roselli, #accessiBe Will Get You Sued, (09/06/2023), `<https://adrianroselli.com/2020/06/accessibe-will-get-you-sued.html#Inaccessible:~:text=1%20at%20YouTube.-,Wrap%2Dup,-%23>` [Accessed 16/06/2023]

22. Colorlib, Squarespace Statistics (How Many Websites Use Squarespace?), (02/04/2023), `<https://colorlib.com/wp/squarespace-statistics/>` [Accessed 22/06/2023]

23. Built With, Wix Usage Statistics, `<https://trends.builtwith.com/cms/Wix>` [Accessed 25/06/2023]

24. ToolTester, WordPress Market Share (2023), (11/01/2023), `<www.tooltester.com/en/blog/wordpress-market-share/>` [Accessed 26/06/2023]

25. Forbes, Wix Vs. WordPress (2023 Comparison), (28/06/2023), `<www.forbes.com/advisor/business/software/wix-vs-wordpress/#:~:text=In%20terms%20of%20user%20experience,invest%20the%20time%20and%20effort>` [Accessed 26/06/2023]

26. WebAIM, The WebAIM Million, (29/03/2023), `<https://webaim.org/projects/million/#CMS:~:text=to%20that%20technology.-,Content%20Management%20Systems%20and%20Site%20Builders,-CMS>` [Accessed 22/06/2023]

27. Wix Blog, 27 common types of websites (with templates to get you started), (09/06/2023), `<www.wix.com/blog/types-of-websites>` [Accessed 26/06/2023]

ENDNOTES

28. Squarespace Blog, Choosing the right template, (10/05/2023), <https://support.squarespace.com/hc/en-us/articles/206545337-Choosing-the-right-template> [Accessed 26/06/2023]

29. Influencer Marketing Hub, The Top 20 Websites Using Squarespace, (14/07/2022), <https://influencermarketinghub.com/squarespace-websites/> [Accessed 22/06/2023]

30. Built With, Wix Stores Usage Statistics, <https://trends.builtwith.com/shop/Wix-Stores> [Accessed 25/06/2023]

31. Colorlib, Shopify Statistics (How Many Websites Use Shopify?), (21/03/2023), <https://colorlib.com/wp/shopify-statistics/> [Accessed 25/06/2023]

32. WebAIM, The WebAIM Million, (29/03/2023), <https://webaim.org/projects/million/#:~:text=to%20that%20technology.-,Content%20Management%20Systems%20and%20Site%20Builders,-CMS> [Accessed 19/06/2023]

33. UsableNet, ADA Digital Accessibility Lawsuit Trends Involving – Websites, Mobile, Apps, Video, <https://info.usablenet.com/thank-you-2022-end-of-year-report-on-digital-accessibility-lawsuits?submissionGuid=711cb65a-214e-437d-9ce0-5a03da194d19> [Accessed 03/07/2023]

34. UsableNet, Web and App ADA Lawsuits: 6 Trends so far in 2023, (28/06/2023), <https://blog.usablenet.com/web-and-app-ada-lawsuits-6-trends-so-far-in-2023> [Accessed 09/07/2023]

35. WebAIM, The WebAIM Million, (29/03/2023), <https://webaim.org/projects/million/#CMS:~:text=Bootstrap%20was%20present.-,Ecommerce%20Platforms,-Platform> [Accessed 26/06/2023]

36. Built With, Squarespace Usage Statistics, <https://trends.builtwith.com/cms/Squarespace> [Accessed 26/06/2023]

37. Usablenet, 2023 midyear report on digital accessibility lawsuits, (29/06/2023), <https://3280432.fs1.hubspotusercontent-na1. net/hubfs/3280432/Remediated%20-%202023%20MidYear%20 UsableNet%20Digital%20Accessibility%20Lawsuit%20Report. pdf> [Accessed 30/06/2023]

38. Shopify Community, Search result for 'sued', <https://community.shopify.com/c/forums/searchpage/tab/ message?advanced=false&allow_punctuation=false&filter=l ocation&location=forum-board:shopify-discussion&q=sued> [Accessed 26/06/2023]

39. Etsy, 'wix template' search results, <www.etsy.com/uk/market/ wix_template> [Accessed 25/06/2023]

40. Etsy, 'squarespace template' search results, <www.etsy.com/uk/ search?q=squarespace%20template&ref=search_bar> [Accessed 25/06/2023]

41. Shopify Help Center, Accessibility for themes, <https://help.shopify.com/en/manual/online-store/themes/ customizing-themes/accessibility> [Accessed 22/06/2023]

42. Wix, Accessibility Guides and Resources, <www.wix.com/ accessibility/guides> [Accessed 25/06/2023]

43. Wix, Accessibility: Checklist for Improving Your Site's Accessibility, <https://support.wix.com/en/article/ accessibility-checklist-for-improving-your-sites- accessibility> [Accessed 22/06/2023]

44. Wix, Wix Marketplace Profile – Small Tasks, <www.wix.com/ marketplace/wix-partner/suman-kumar-phuyal#featured- projects:~:text=Web%20Design%20(5)-,Small%20Tasks,-(9)> [Accessed 25/06/2023]

45. Wix, Choose the Premium plan that's right for your business, <https://manage.wix.com/premium-purchase-plan/dynamo> [Accessed 25/06/2023]

46. ibid.

47. ibid.

48. Squarespace, Accessibility at Squarespace, <`www.squarespace.com/accessibility`> [Accessed 25/06/2023]

49. accessiBe, Web accessibility, WCAG and ADA Compliance for SquareSpace, <`https://accessibe.com/integrations/squarespace#:~:text=a%20process%20that%20can%20take%20months%20to%20do%20manually%20or%20cost%20thousands%20of%20dollars%20to%20outsource`> [Accessed 22/06/2023]

50. Wix Blog, Wix's Accessibility Wizard: Pioneering the Pursuit of Internet for All, (20/05/2022), <`www.wix.com/blog/make-your-wix-website-accessible`> [Accessed 25/06/2023]

51. Wix, Accessible Website Templates, <`www.wix.com/website/templates/html/accessible`> [Accessed 25/06/2023]

52. Wix, Pick the Website Template You Love, <`www.wix.com/website/templates`> [Accessed 25/06/2023]

53. Wix, Wix's Accessibility Wizard: Pioneering the Pursuit of Internet for All, (20/05/2022), <`www.wix.com/blog/make-your-wix-website-accessible`> [Accessed 25/06/2023]

54. MUI, About Us, <`https://mui.com/about`> [Accessed 22/06/2023]

55. MUI, About Us, <`https://mui.com/about`> [Accessed 22/06/2023]

56. Github, Issues - mui/material-ui (issues filtered by their 'Accessibility' label), <`https://github.com/mui/material-ui/issues?q=is%3Aissue+is%3Aopen+label%3Aaccessibility+`> [Accessed 24/06/2023]

57. MUI, About us - Team, <`https://mui.com/about/#:~:text=Followers%20on%20Twitter-,Team,-MUI%20is%20maintained`> [Accessed 24/06/2023] – also checked LinkedIn for past and present Accessibility roles within MUI.

58. MUI, Accessibility Engineer, <`https://mui.com/careers/accessibility-engineer/`> [Accessed 24/06/2023]

59. Susanna Zaraysky, The Evolution of Material Design's Text Fields, (01/11/2019), <https://medium.com/google-design/the-evolution-of-material-designs-text-fields-603688b3fe03> [Accessed 22/06/2023]

60. Matsuko Friedland, Stop using Material Design text fields!, (26/02/2020), <www.matsuko.ca/blog/stop-using-material-design-text-fields/> [Accessed 22/06/2023]

61. Quartz, How one programmer broke the internet by deleting a tiny piece of code, (27/03/2016), <https://qz.com/646467/how-one-programmer-broke-the-internet-by-deleting-a-tiny-piece-of-code> [Accessed 22/06/2023]

62. ibid.

63. Material UI, Button, <https://mui.com/material-ui/react-button/> [Accessed 22/06/2023]

64. Material UI, Material UI - Overview, <https://mui.com/material-ui/getting-started/overview/#:~:text=multiple%20great%20options.-,Customizability,-%3A%20the%20library> [Accessed 22/06/2023]

Chapter 11

1. Wikipedia, Pareto principle, <https://en.wikipedia.org/wiki/Pareto_principle> [Accessed 11/11/2023]

2. WebAIM, The WebAIM Million, (2023), <https://webaim.org/projects/million/> [Accessed 11/11/2023]

3. Google, Tools for Web Developers: Lighthouse, (24/05/2022), <https://developers.google.com/web/tools/lighthouse/> [Accessed 12/11/2023]

4. Kayce Basques & Sofia Emelianova, Accessibility features reference, Google, (19/10/2022), <https://developer.chrome.com/docs/devtools/accessibility/reference/> [Accessed 12/11/2023]

5. Sofia Emelianova, Make your website more readable, Google, (19/10/2022), `<https://developer.chrome.com/docs/devtools/accessibility/contrast/>` [Accessed 12/11/2023]

6. WebAIM, Link Contrast Checker, `<https://webaim.org/resources/linkcontrastchecker/>` [Accessed 12/11/2023]

7. Marc Brysbaert, How many words do we read per minute? A review and meta-analysis of reading rate, Journal of Memory and Language, Volume 109, 2019, 104047, ISSN 0749-596X, `<https://doi.org/10.1016/j.jml.2019.104047>`

8. Chris Pederick, Web Developer, `<https://chrispederick.com/work/web-developer/>` [Accessed 12/11/2023]

9. Webaim, WAVE Evaluation Tool, (2023), `<https://chrome.google.com/webstore/detail/wave-evaluation-tool/jbbplnpkjmmeebjpijfedlgcdilocofh>` [Accessed 12/11/2023]

10. Wikipedia, Flesch–Kincaid readability tests, `<https://en.wikipedia.org/wiki/Flesch-Kincaid_readability_tests>` [Accessed 26/09/2023]

11. Freedom Scientific, Jaws, (2023), `<www.freedomscientific.com/products/software/jaws/>` [Accessed 12/11/2023]

12. WebAIM, The WebAIM Million - ARIA, `<https://webaim.org/projects/million/#aria>` [Accessed 02/11/2023]

13. Anika Henke, Using persona profiles to test accessibility, Accessibility in government blog, (11/02/2019) `<https://accessibility.blog.gov.uk/2019/02/11/using-persona-profiles-to-test-accessibility/>` [Accessed 12/11/2023]

14. Anika Henke, Assistive technology tools you can test with at no cost, Accessibility in government, (27/09/2018), `<https://accessibility.blog.gov.uk/2018/09/27/assistive-technology-tools-you-can-use-at-no-cost/>` [Accessed 12/11/2023]

15. Government Digital Service, Book the GDS user research lab, (20/02/2023), <`www.gov.uk/guidance/book-the-gds-user-research-lab`> [Accessed 12/11/2023]

16. NPM, axe-core, (2023), <`www.npmjs.com/package/axe-core`> [Accessed 08/11/2023]

17. Github, AccessLint, (2023), <`https://github.com/marketplace/accesslint`> [Accessed 12/11/2023]

18. ibid.

19. Github, pa11y, (2023) <`https://github.com/pa11y/pa11y#javascript-interface` [Accessed 12/11/2023]

20. ibid.

21. Paul Bohmon, Hire Real People with Disabilities for QA Testing, Deque University, (2023), <`https://dequeuniversity.com/tips/hire-people-with-disabilities`> [Accessed 04/11/2023]

22. Ariana Mihoc, Conducting remote research with people with access needs, Gov UK, (20/05/2020), <`https://userresearch.blog.gov.uk/2020/05/20/conducting-remote-research-with-people-with-access-needs/`> [Accessed 05/11/2023]

23. Peter McNally, Tips for Conducting Usability Studies with Participants with Disabilities, (12/03/2018), <`www.smashingmagazine.com/2018/03/tips-conducting-usability-studies-participants-disabilities/`> [Accessed 04/11/2023]

24. ibid.

25. W3C, Accessibility Guidelines (WCAG) 3.0 Working Draft, (24/07/2023), <`www.w3.org/TR/wcag-3.0/`> [Accessed 29/10/2023]

Chapter 12

1. Ed Summers & Jesse Dugas, Prompting GitHub Copilot Chat to become your personal AI assistant for accessibility, (09/10/2023), <https://github.blog/2023-10-09-prompting-github-copilot-chat-to-become-your-personal-ai-assistant-for-accessibility/> [Accessed 17/11/2023]

2. Be My Eyes, Announcing 'Be My AI', Soon Available for Hundreds of Thousands of Be My Eyes Users, (2023), <www.bemyeyes.com/blog/announcing-be-my-ai> [Accessed 17/11/2023]

3. Directive (EU) 2019/882 of the European Parliament and of the Council of 17 April 2019 on the accessibility requirements for products and services (Text with EEA relevance) PE/81/2018/REV/1, <https://eur-lex.europa.eu/legal-content/EN/TXT/?uri=CELEX%3A32019L0882> [Accessed 17/11/2023]

4. ibid.

5. Rian Rietveld, The European Accessibility Act 2025: It May Apply to Your Website, (25/07/2023), <https://kinsta.com/blog/european-accessibility-act/> [Accessed 17/11/2023]

6. Dara Golding, Understanding How the European Accessibility Act Will Impact Your Business, (02/03/2023), <www.tpgi.com/understanding-how-the-european-accessibility-act-will-impact-your-business/> [Accessed 21/11/2023]

7. W3C Accessibility Guidelines (WCAG) 3.0 - Working draft, (24/07/2023), <www.w3.org/TR/wcag-3.0/> [Accessed 17/11/2023]

8. W3C Accessibility Guidelines (WCAG) 3.0 - Working draft: Conformance, (24/07/2023), <www.w3.org/TR/wcag-3.0/#conformance> [Accessed 17/11/2023]

9. W3C Accessibility Guidelines (WCAG) 3.0 – Working draft: Critical errors, (24/07/2023), <www.w3.org/TR/wcag-3.0-explainer/#critical-errors> [Accessed 17/11/2023]

10. Tucker Higgins, A blind man couldn't order pizza from Domino's. The company wants the Supreme Court to say websites don't have to be accessible, CNBC, (25/07/2019), <`www.cnbc.com/2019/07/25/dominos-asks-supreme-court-to-say-disability-protections-dont-apply-online.html`> [Accessed 23/11/2023]

11. Courtlistener, Guillermo Robles v. Domino's Pizza LLC, 17-55504 (9th Cir. 2019), (15/01/2019), <`www.courtlistener.com/opinion/4581582/guillermo-robles-v-dominos-pizza-llc/`> [Accessed 23/11/2023]

12. United States Court of Appeals for the Ninth Circuit, Robles v. Domino's Pizza, (15/01/2019), <`http://cdn.ca9.uscourts.gov/datastore/opinions/2019/01/15/17-55504.pdf`> [Accessed 23/11/2023]

13. Liebert Cassidy Whitmore, Website Accessibility Under The ADA: A Tale As Old As 1996, (30/08/2019), <`www.courthousenews.com/wp-content/uploads/2019/01/Dominos-Ruling.pdf`> [Accessed 23/11/2023]

14. ibid.

15. Karina Brown, Court Says Domino's Pizza Website Must Be Accessible to the Blind, (15/01/2019), <`www.courthousenews.com/court-says-dominos-pizza-website-must-be-accessible-to-the-blind/`> [Accessed 23/11/2023]

16. The Supreme Court of the United States, Domino's Pizza v. Guillermo Robles – Petition for a writ of certiorari, (03/06/2019), <`www.supremecourt.gov/DocketPDF/18/18-1539/102950/20190613153319483_DominosPetition.pdf`> [Accessed 23/11/2023]

17. Jared Spool, Twitter, (01/08/2019), <`https://twitter.com/jmspool/status/1157021965020016640`> [Accessed 23/11/2023]

18. S. Lock, Revenue of Domino's Pizza 2006-2018, Statista, <`www.statista.com/statistics/207133/revenue-of-dominos-pizza-2017/`> [Accessed 23/11/2023]

19. These numerous sources have cited this figure from the court documents: Jared Spool, Twitter, (04/09/2019), <https://twitter.com/jmspool/status/1169255821735342080> [Accessed 23/11/2023] + Daniel S. Levine, Domino's Fights Website Accessibility Ruling in Supreme Court, Social Media Weighs In, (02/08/2019), <https://popculture.com/trending/2019/08/02/dominos-fights-accessibility-ruling-supreme-court-social-media-weighs-in/> [Accessed 23/11/2023] + Amanda Rush, Domino's is evil, (02/08/2019), <www.customerservant.com/dominos-is-evil/> [Accessed 23/11/2023]

20. Tucker Higgins, A blind man couldn't order pizza from Domino's. The company wants the Supreme Court to say websites don't have to be accessible, CNBC, (25/07/2019), <www.cnbc.com/2019/07/25/dominos-asks-supreme-court-to-say-disability-protections-dont-apply-online.html> [Accessed 23/11/2023]

21. ibid.

22. Seyfarth Shaw LLP, Robles v. Domino's Settles After Six Years of Litigation, (10/06/2022), <www.adatitleiii.com/2022/06/robles-v-dominos-settles-after-six-years-of-litigation/> [Accessed 23/11/2023]

23. Casetext, Robles v. Domino's Pizza LLC, (2023), <https://casetext.com/case/robles-v-dominos-pizza-llc/how-cited?citingPage=1&sort=relevance> [Accessed 23/11/2023]

24. Paul Bohmon, Hire Real People with Disabilities for QA Testing, Deque University, (2023), <https://dequeuniversity.com/tips/hire-people-with-disabilities> [Accessed 04/11/2023]

25. ibid.

26. Bureau of Internet Accessibility, Employment of People with Disabilities Reaches All-Time High, (07/04/2023), <www.boia.org/blog/employment-of-people-with-disabilities-reaches-all-time-high> [Accessed 23/11/2023]

27. Gov UK - Department of Work & Pensions, Official Statistics: Employment of disabled people 2022, (26/01/2023), <www.gov.uk/government/statistics/the-employment-of-disabled-people-2022/employment-of-disabled-people-2022> [Accessed 23/11/2023]

28. AbilityNet Tech4Good Awards, About, (2023), <www.tech4goodawards.com/about/> [Accessed 21/11/2023]

29. Webby Awards, Accessible Technology - 2023, <https://winners.webbyawards.com/winners/websites-and-mobile-sites?years=0> [Accessed 21/11/2023]

30. The Game Awards, Innovation in Accessibility, (2023), <https://thegameawards.com/nominees/innovation-in-accessibility> [Accessed 21/11/2023]

31. Microsoft News Centre UK, Xbox Adaptive Controller wins major award at Golden Joysticks, Microsoft, (16/11/2018), <https://news.microsoft.com/en-gb/2018/11/16/xbox-adaptive-controller-wins-major-award-at-golden-joysticks/> [Accessed 21/11/2023]

32. Vinton Cerf, The Internet is for Everyone, Speech to the Computers, Freedom and Privacy Conference, (07/04/1999), <www.itu.int/ITU-D/ict/papers/witwatersrand/Vint%20Cerf.pdf> [Accessed 21/11/2023]

33. ibid.

Index

A

Accessibility, 1, 2, 18, 20, 40, 45, 102, 127, 133, 145, 211, 232, 275, 277, 282, 286, 288, 302, 303, 311, 323, 325, 329, 342, 451
   attention, 8–10
   blind users, 57
   competitive advantages, 9, 10
   contrast ratio, 71
   disability-driven, 4, 11, 12
   frequently asked questions, 12–14
   guidance, 184
   guidelines, 2
   opposition to, 10, 11
   and readability, 67
   requirement, 166
   statement, 444
   testing, 436
      AccessLint, 438–440
      automation, 436
      axe-core, 436–438
      Pa11y, 441–443
      tracking, 442, 443
   typography and, 64
   video streaming, 148
   WCAG, 3
Accessibility-specific fonts, 68, 69
Accessibility tree, 17–19, 410
   native HTML elements, 20–22
   screen reader, 19, 20
Accessibility wizard, 376–381
Accessible email

assumptions, 325
   communication, 323
   email clients, 324
   evolution, 324
   language, 323
   plain-text version, 329
   rendering, 325–327
   technology, 323
   web page, 327–329
Accessible Rich Internet Applications (ARIA), 48, 49, 428
   aria-hidden, 49, 50
   aria-label, 49
   aria-labelledby, 52, 53
   aria-live, 50, 51
   attributes, 48
   code usage, 46
   components, 52–54
   HTML tags, 46
   roles, 46, 47
   roles and properties, 45
   support and testing, 54
   tags, 47
   W3C, 46
Accessible text, 151
   code, 61
   measurement, 59
   pixels, 60
   user's preference, 62
AccessLint, 438–440
Accredited templates, 381, 382
Active voice, 192

E

P

Y, Z

Printed in the United States
by Baker & Taylor Publisher Services